WHITE COLLAR
CRIME

CORE CONCEPTS FOR CONSULTANTS
AND EXPERT WITNESSES

12073-359

Editors **Debra K. Thompson**, CPA
and **Randal Wolverton**, CPA

Publisher: Amy M. Plent
Managing Editor: Amy Krasnyanskaya
Acquisition Editor: Andrew Grow
Project Manager: Charlotte Ingles

We dedicate this book to the new generation of white collar crime consultants who join the worthy cause of uncovering and combating fraud on behalf of organizations worldwide.

Acknowledgments

We would like to acknowledge the following people who were instrumental in helping us get this book from concept to reality:

Lynda Hartzell, a tireless and consummate forensic accounting professional who assisted in the final days of editing,

Jennifer Miller, the new generation of forensic professionals who was with us from the beginning, and

Lori Diffendaffer, our internal project champion who helped us find the right resources to bring this project home.

About the Editors

Debra K. Thompson, CPA/CFF, CFE
Director, Litigation & Investigation Services,
McGladrey LLP

Debra leads the forensic accounting and fraud investigation services practice in McGladrey's West and Central Regions. She has more than 30 years of finance and accounting experience, including 15 years specifically in the areas of auditing, forensic accounting and fraud examinations. She uses these skills in investigations, due diligence assignments, bankruptcy matters, and disputes. She has been called to be a testifying expert at deposition and trial in relation to her investigative work.

Healthcare, government and education, and financial services are industry sectors in which Debra has extensive experience. She has led numerous corporate investigations on behalf of audit committees, special committees, and management involving potential accounting irregularities, misappropriation of assets, Foreign Corrupt Practices Act violations, and other regulatory inquiries. As part of her investigative work she has traced cash through numerous banks in several countries in Europe and the Caribbean to determine the disposition of funds.

Debra's recent engagements include investigations related to embezzlement, alleged vendor kickbacks, revenue recognition, related-party transactions, inappropriate capitalization of costs, accounting for reserves and cut-offs, and proper accruals. She has also conducted background investigations for gaming vendors including management companies and their principals, for United States gaming operations. These investigations included the analysis of the applicant's disclosures to determine the authenticity of the information provided, including whether the applicant or its principals are reputable and/or have any dealings with disreputable individuals or are involved in criminal behavior.

A frequent national speaker on numerous topics, Debra has been actively involved in the American Institute of Certified Public Accountants. She has assisted with other AICPA publications, including *AICPA Practice Aid 10-1: Serving as an Expert Witness or Consultant, AICPA Special Report 09-1: Introduction to Civil Litigation Services,* and AICPA *Accountant's Business Manual.*

Prior to joining McGladrey, Debra was a principal and the practice leader of the forensic accounting and fraud investigation practice at Clifton LarsonAllen.

Randal A. Wolverton, CPA/CFF, CFE
Independent Forensic Accountant

Randy, a retired FBI agent, is an independent forensic accountant who works extensively with McGladrey LLP. He brings more than 26 years of experience in White Collar Crime investigations. He holds the AICPA's designation of Certified in Financial Forensics and is also a Certified Public Accountant and Certified Fraud Examiner. Randy has actively provided volunteer service at the AICPA, having served on the AICPA Forensic and Litigation Services Committee, the CFF Credential Committee, and Fraud Task Force (as past chairman).

Randy joined the Federal Bureau of Investigation in 1981 and he received training at the FBI Academy in Quantico, Virginia. After graduating from the FBI Academy, he spent 27 of his 28 years as an FBI agent in the areas of White Collar Crime. Prior to retiring, he worked as Supervisory Special Agent in the Financial Crime section at the FBI headquarters in Washington, D.C., where he provided program management for corporate fraud, securities fraud, insurance fraud and others. Randy was accredited as a Certified Instructor after completing the FBI Instructor Development Course and thereafter provided instruction on White Collar Crime matters to FBI Special Agents at the FBI Academy in Quantico, Virginia.

Randy's financial institution and corporate fraud experience includes investigating employee embezzlements, fraud conducted by officers, fraud against bank regulators, check kiting, check manipulation, loan fraud, mortgage fraud, computer fraud, accounting fraud, and bank failures.

He has also investigated complex Medicare/Medicaid fraud schemes and schemes involving the misuse and misappropriation of U.S. Government funds. These investigations required the review of existing laws, rules, contracts and regulations, and a further analysis of financial transactions to support the prosecution of persons responsible for the fraud schemes.

In connection with numerous types of cases, Randy has traced proceeds of fraudulent schemes in order to identify money laundering violations in criminal cases, as well as identify and locate assets procured from illegal proceeds.

Randy has conducted numerous sensitive background investigations involving positions in the United States Government, including background checks of U.S. District Judges, U.S. Magistrate Judges, United States Attorneys, Special Appointments by the White House, and other Federal employees seeking employment or high level security clearances. He has also has extensive experience interviewing witnesses, victims, suspects, and admitted criminals pursuant to criminal investigations. Randy has developed training guidance for the AICPA regarding interviewing skills and conducts training seminars to assist CPAs and other professionals in developing effective interview techniques.

Contributors

Bruce V. Bush (Chapter 1)

Bruce is a director at McGladrey LLP (McGladrey) and the practice leader for the firm's Valuation and Litigation and Investigation Consulting Services practices in Dallas. He has more than 20 years of diversified experience assisting clients with allegations of financial reporting improprieties, investigating employee fraud and misconduct, resolution of post-acquisition and contract disputes, and minimizing the risk of fraud through the development and implementation of prevention, detection and response controls. Prior to joining the firm, he held a leadership role at a Big Four firm and was a member of their national investigative practice. He has testified at deposition and in arbitration matters. Bruce holds the AICPA designation of Certified in Financial Forensics and is a Certified Public Accountant. He received his Master in Business Administration with a Minor in Economics from Texas A&M University-Commerce.

Patrick Chylinski (Chapter 8)

Patrick is a director at McGladrey and the practice leader for the firm's Valuation and Litigation and Investigation Consulting Services practices in Los Angeles. He has extensive experience managing and directing engagements relating to investigations of fraud and financial misconduct, asset tracing, complex commercial litigation, business disputes, partnership disputes, and business valuations. He has also testified as a damages expert. Patrick is a Certified Fraud Examiner and an Accredited Valuation Analyst. He is a former Adjunct Professor of Economics for the Graziadio School of Business and Management at Pepperdine University, where he received his Master of Business Administration.

Seth Craig (Chapter 3)

Seth is a senior associate with McGladrey's Financial Advisory Services practice. He regularly performs valuations for a variety of purposes. Prior to joining McGladrey, Seth was employed by United Bankers' Bank as a financial analyst, working primarily on valuations of closely-held community banks, for a variety of purposes, including employee stock ownership plans, shareholder agreements, and shareholder disputes. He holds a Bachelor of Business Administration – Investments from the University of North Dakota.

Chad Dolly (Chapter 3)

Chad is a manager with McGladrey's Financial Advisory Services practice. He has more than 11 years of experience valuing private and public companies in a variety of industries Chad's experience includes providing valuations in dissenting shareholder and minority oppression cases. He is an Accredited Senior Appraiser with American Society of Appraisers and holds the General Securities Representative designation under the Financial Industry Regulatory Authority (FINRA). Chad received his Master of Business Administration from the Carlson School of Management at the University of Minnesota.

Sue Evelsizer (Chapter 12)

Sue is a director in McGladrey's Valuation and Litigation and Investigation Consulting Services practices.

She has significant experience in business valuation matters, having performed more than 400 engagements involving closely-held business interests for a variety of purposes. Sue has conducted numerous investigations related to employee embezzlement for financial institutions, governmental entities and school districts. Through these investigations she has presented reports to management, boards of directors, the Federal Bureau of Investigations, and the U.S. Attorney's Office, among other parties. She has also investigated the use of government grant funds. Sue is a Certified Public Accountant and an Accredited Senior Appraiser by the American Society of Appraisers.

Adam J. Falconer (Chapters 4, 5)

Adam is a consultant at FAB Group, Inc. and focuses on providing financial advisory services, including dispute advisory and litigation services. He formerly worked as a manager in McGladrey's litigation and investigation consulting services practice. In addition to his financial advisory experience, he brings extensive legal knowledge and holds a Juris Doctor from Syracuse University College of Law.

Christyn Grommesh (Chapters 13, 14)

Christyn is an associate in McGladrey's Litigation and Investigation Consulting Services practice. She has worked on a wide variety of forensic and litigation support assignments, including the investigations of possible misappropriation of funds by a CEO in a not-for-profit company,

bankruptcy claims by a large transportation manufacturer, and misappropriation of loan payments by a vice president for a public bank. Christyn holds a Bachelor of Science in Accounting, with a minor in Management Information Systems, from North Dakota State University.

Lynda Hartzell (Chapters 8, 9)

Lynda is a manager in McGladrey's Litigation and Investigation Consulting Services practice. She has 30 years of experience conducting investigations, regulatory compliance reviews, quality assurance, and other attest work. She brings extensive knowledge of the gaming industry, having recently joined McGladrey after working in the Audit Division of the Nevada Gaming Control Board, where she oversaw the work of 85-plus accounting professionals and most recently served as the chief of that division. Lynda currently serves on the audit committee of the National Association of State Boards of Accountancy. She is a Certified Public Accountant, a Certified Internal Auditor, and Certified Fraud Examiner.

Al Kohl (Chapter 11)

Al is a manager in McGladrey's Litigation and Investigation Consulting Services practice. He has more than 13 years of experience in litigation and forensic investigative matters. Al specializes in internal fraud investigations for financial institutions, especially involving accusations of embezzlement. His experience also includes managing the Resolution Trust Corporation's (RTC) Kansas City regional damage unit in the early 1990s. In this capacity, he directed the analysis and quantification of damages for more than 50 failed financial institutions resulting from the savings and loan crisis of the late 1980s. Many of these cases focused on civil and criminal fraud claims. Al was awarded a certificate of special achievement by the RTC for his investigative work on the Madison Guaranty Savings and Loan case, which was the subject of a special prosecutor's investigation and included the Whitewater probe. Al has also performed investigations for the FDIC. Prior to his litigation and investigative experience, Al was employed as a banker in lending, accounting management, operations, and investments. He is a Certified Fraud Examiner.

Brad Koranda (Chapter 14)

Brad is a manager in McGladrey's Valuation and Litigation and Investigation Consulting Services practices. He specializes in the areas of business valuations, for a wide variety of purposes, as well as damage calculations for litigation and forensic accounting. He has performed loan investigations for the government and outside counsel in which he gathered evidence of negligence and fraud committed by the former bank directors, officers and senior loan officers of various financial institutions and identified a check kiting scheme perpetrated by management. He has also investigated numerous employee embezzlement cases for individual companies and insurance providers. Brad is a Certified Public Accountant and he holds the AICPA designations of Accredited in Business Valuation and Certified in Financial Forensics. He received a Master of Accountancy from University of Wisconsin – Madison.

Daniel Korsman (Chapter 2)

Dan is a senior associate with McGladrey's Valuation and Litigation and Investigation Consulting Services practices. He has conducted valuations for a variety of purposes. Dan is a Certified Fraud Examiner and Certified Public Accountant. He also holds the AICPA designation of Accredited in Business Valuation. Dan received a Bachelor of Science in Accounting and Finance and a Bachelor of Arts in Business Economics from Saint Cloud State University. He also holds a Juris Doctor with a Business Transaction concentration from the University of Nebraska-Lincoln.

Jennifer G. Miller (Chapter 6)

Jennifer is a manager in McGladrey's Litigation and Investigation Consulting Services practice. Her experience includes forensic accounting matters, fraud investigations, data management, and financial statement reconstruction with specific industry experience involving physician owned clinics, pharmaceutical companies and various clinical operations. Jennifer has assisted with Rule 26 expert reports and expert witness testimony preparation in support of both fraud and negligence cases. She is skilled at using data mining software and working with substantial amounts of data, having reconstructed financial statements over periods as long as 20 years. Jennifer also has experience performing corporate asset tracing through numerous different companies, and personal asset tracing through financial institution records. She is a Certified Public Accountant.

Christopher J. Rice (Chapter 13)

Chris is an associate in McGladrey's Litigation and Investigation Consulting Services practice. He has worked on a variety of forensic and litigation support assignments, including an investigation of possible misappropriation of funds by school officials in a school district and a large solvency analysis of a manufacturing company and its numerous subsidiaries. Chris also has experience using data mining software, IDEA, to compile and analyze client data. He holds a Bachelor of Science in Accounting and a Master of Accountancy from North Dakota State University.

Scott M. Richter (Chapter 10)

Scott Richter is a director in McGladrey's Litigation and Investigation Consulting Services practice. He has more than 20 years of experience in corporate finance, auditing and forensic accounting and litigation consulting. Scott's forensic accounting and litigation consulting experience includes conducting investigations relating to Ponzi schemes, CPA malpractice, restatement of financial statements, fraudulent transactions, defalcations, regulatory actions and breaches of contract. Prior to McGladrey, Scott held positions at LECG, Aon Consulting and Kroll. He has also served as vice president of finance for corporate integration at one of the worlds' largest conglomerates in the advertising/marketing sector. Scott is a Certified Fraud Examiner and holds the AICPA designation of Certified in Financial Forensics. He is also a Certified Public Accountant.

Todd E. Sigler (Chapter 8)

Todd is a manager in McGladrey's Valuation and Litigation and Investigation Consulting Services practice. He has provided clients with litigation consulting and forensic accounting services for ten years and has extensive experience planning and executing engagements relating to fraud investigations, contract disputes, construction claims, partnership disputes, royalty inspections, and asset tracing. Todd previously worked in the advisory services practice at Deloitte, LECG, and Alix Partners. He received a Juris Doctor from Loyola Law School and a Master of Business Administration from University of California, Irvine. Todd is a licensed attorney and Certified Public Accountant. He is also a Certified Fraud Examiner and holds the AICPA designation of Certified in Financial Forensics.

Eric Stephens (Chapter 12)

Eric is an affiliated consultant with McGladrey. With more than 20 years of experience, he specializes in complex international investigations and risk management. Eric has provided FCPA-related expertise to mid-sized and large multinational companies for the purposes of investigating potential violations, implementing controls and improving compliance efforts. He frequently acts as advisor to U.S. and foreign governments and he presented on the topic of FCPA for numerous CEOs in attendance at the 2011 Asia–Pacific Economic Cooperation (APEC) conference. Eric has investigated many other types of matters, including ones related to U.S. Patriot Act compliance, money laundering, fraud and illicit activity funding. He has also testified as an expert witness in relation to his work. In private industry, Eric has held positions of international corporate controller and corporate manager of financial reporting.

Patricia M. Tilton (Chapter 7)

Pat is a retired KPMG LLP partner and continues to work as an independent consultant. She has provided audit, advisory and forensic-related services for more than thirty years. During her career at KPMG, Pat led the U.S. KPMG Forensic Services Insurance Channel and the Insurance and Asset Management

Advisory Services group, and also served as a risk management partner for the Forensic Services Practice. Pat's experience includes investigations and fraud risk management services related to a variety of financial and non-financial matters, including earnings management, reinsurance, claims, brokerage, bid rigging, and market timing/late trading. Her litigation support experience includes contract and purchase price disputes as well as operations and insurance-related matters. Pat has served as an expert and as an arbitrator, and has testified as an expert. She is a Certified Public Accountant.

Scott Vanlandingham (Chapter 14)

Scott is a managing director at McGladrey and leads the firm's Southeast Region Consulting practice. He also leads the firm's IPO Readiness services, focused on helping companies put financial controls in place to comply with public company requirements. Prior to joining McGladrey, he was a founding managing director of Protiviti, where his responsibilities included acting as Country Managing Director for Korea, Technology Managing Director for Japan and leader of Supply Chain Risk Management. Scott brings extensive experience in the areas of operational improvement, business process reengineering, controls assessment design and implement, and IT general controls assessment and design. He is a Certified Internal Auditor and received his Master of Business Administration from Duke University.

David Wharton (Chapter 4)

David is a manager in McGladrey's Litigation and Investigation Consulting Services practice. He has over eight years of experience providing forensic accounting, litigation support and financial consulting services covering a wide array of complex matters. His experience includes fraud investigations, determination of lost profits and other financial damages for commercial litigation matters, insurance claim analysis from fidelity bonds to business interruptions, and residential mortgage lending matters ranging from lender investigations to borrower class actions. David holds the Certified in Financial Forensics designation from the AICPA. He is also a Certified Fraud Examiner and a Certified Public Accountant. David holds a Bachelor of Science in Accounting from the University of Missouri-Kansas City's Bloch School.

Matthew Wolf (Chapter 13)

Matt is a senior associate with McGladrey's Valuation and Litigation and Investigation Consulting Services practices. He has experience preparing lost profit analyses and expert reports for litigation. He regularly conducts valuations for a variety of purposes. Prior to joining McGladrey, Matt worked for The Hartford's Investment Finance group, calculating, analyzing and publishing the net asset values of their mutual funds. He was also involved in the year-end reporting and auditing processes, as well as being the lead analyst for The Hartford's money market fund. Matt holds Bachelor of Science degrees in Finance and Operations Management from the University of Minnesota's Carlson School of Management.

Preface

In examining the state of our global society as we go to print with this book, a looming global recession forecasts a very uncertain economic future. Adding to our economic strife, the world continues to become more complex due to the revolutionary advances of the technology that we use on a daily basis. From smart phones to tablets, these devices have become our instant lifelines to news, financial markets, shopping, entertainment, and various other interests, as well as our friends and family. These same devices are used by fraudsters to engage in malfeasance.

As technology has advanced, the methods of conducting fraudulent activity have become more multifarious and often no longer leave a hard copy (paper) trail. Combined with the increasingly complex and rigid regulatory environment, combating fraud is more in the forefront of people's minds.

Some theories surmise that during an economic downturn, or recessionary period, fraud becomes more prevalent. Whether or not that is true, occurrences of fraud are pervasive and continue to make front page news, even as the regulatory environment dictates more stringent management responsibility to ensure that fraud is not occurring within their organizations. Governmental departments and agencies are no exception.

So why is it that despite increased efforts to prevent fraud, fraudsters seem to be one step ahead? Fraudsters are sophisticated. They stay abreast of the latest and greatest publicly available fraud prevention tools and techniques. With chameleon-like guile, they adjust their techniques to evade fraud prevention measures and readily adapt to the regulatory environment. Moreover, they incorporate new technologies into their schemes and meticulously prepare seemingly logical explanations for their activities. The fraud investigator should never underestimate the intelligence of people who perpetrate fraud.

With this in mind the fraud investigator must be as adaptable and engaged as the fraudster. In order to become successful at unravelling fraud schemes, the investigator must develop keen critical thinking and problem solving skills. Often when investigating a fraud the investigator only knows one fact, such as who is suspected of committing a fraud or which regulation is thought to have been violated. From one such obscure suspicion an investigator must craft a series of steps or procedures to determine if some sort of malfeasance has occurred. Yet, because the creative strategies of fraud schemes vary so greatly, there is no one-size-fits-all check list that an investigator can use. Thus, the investigator must think more conceptually and like a fraudster in order to develop an effective approach.

This book is designed to act as an investigator's reference tool with conceptual frameworks that will help the investigator along the lifecycle of the investigation. The investigator needs to understand the origins and purpose of the investigation as well as the desired outcome. For example, is the reason for the investigation to determine if a regulation has been violated and what, if any, the ramifications and required outcomes of the regulatory violation are? In this case, being aware of the regulatory environment will make it easier to prepare the method for uncovering the fraud, its ramifications and outcomes. In addition, the investigator should understand where to go for guidance when dealing with the plethora of constantly changing regulations.

Because regulatory considerations often play into investigative work, this book examines many nuances of heavily regulated industries. However, this book is not meant to be an exhaustive study of all the regulations that need to be considered when conducting an investigation. Rather, the intent of the book is to help initiate the investigator's critical thinking process. Our desire is that as the investigator reads these chapters he or she will start asking questions such as:

- Could this scheme be pulled off by one person or do the circumstances indicate possible collusion?
- What was the fraudster's motive for perpetrating this fraud?
- What would I need to do in order to prove/disprove that theory?
- How do the company's policies and procedures align with the regulatory environment in which it operates?

By continually asking questions, the investigator will be well on the way to thinking as creatively and strategically as a fraudster.

Happy trails…

—Debra K. Thompson, CPA
—Randal A. Wolverton, CPA/CFF, CFE

Contents

Section I

Introduction

Imperfect World—The Practical Differences Between a "Perfect" Investigation and Real Investigation

Bruce V. Bush, CPA/CFF, MBA

Introduction

Assume, for a moment, how a "perfect" fraud investigation might work. Under ideal conditions, the forensic accountant would employ a standardized investigative approach that follows specific stages, including

- gathering documents,
- reviewing and analyzing case information,
- making preliminary observations,
- forming case theories,
- conducting interviews, and
- preparing reports.

The gathering of documents forms the basic foundation for the investigation when key information is secured to be utilized in later stages. Each stage of this standard investigative approach would be concluded prior to the start of the next stage, thus following a linear approach. This works well because each stage forms a building block in the investigative process. When structuring interviews, the standardized approach would begin with witnesses considered to be neutral, who can confirm procedures and processes. The interviews would then move on to witnesses who can corroborate information obtained in the document review and, finally, to a confrontation of those suspected of fraud. Overall, this standardized investigative approach follows a process that builds evidential matter through the securing and analysis of key documents. This analysis is then used to form preliminary observations and theories that are substantiated by corroborating statements, which allow investigators to effectively question those suspected of fraud. In an ideal world, this will ferret out nonresponsive and untruthful answers and elicit a confession of wrongdoing. In addition to this standardized investigative approach, the "perfect" investigation is not constrained by budget limitations or affected by the available documents.

But, in the harsh realities of the real world, significant practical differences often exist between the standardized approach and actual investigations. In the real world, investigators do not always get to pick the time when those who are to be interviewed will be available or have an unlimited amount of time for purposes of collecting documents, planning the investigation, and scheduling interviews. Investigators often deal with budget issues and scope limitations that impact the investigative process. This chapter will review the following critical investigative issues in practical terms:

- Interviewing at the onset of an investigation
- Handling short time frames with respect to collecting documents
- Gathering background information
- Recognizing budgets limitations
- Dealing with scope limitations
- Working with law enforcement and prosecutors
- Preparing for the unexpected

This chapter will conclude with a discussion on the anatomy of a case, which will set the stage for the more in-depth discussions on the statutes and regulations covering white collar criminal activity, the regulatory complexities in which fraudulent activity exists, the advance concepts of finding and fixing fraud, and the working and resolving cases that follows in the later chapters.

Interviewing at the Onset

Although the standardized investigative approach calls for interviewing well after document gathering, there are a number of reasons that the investigator will be required to conduct interviews at the onset of an investigation or reasons that it makes sense for an investigator to conduct interviews at the onset of an investigation. For example, if interviews are held after documentation has been gathered, reviewed, and analyzed, prospective interviewees who possess relevant information will most likely be aware of the data gathering process. That awareness, in turn, may cause them to be less than enthusiastic about participating in an interview, making those sessions less productive and more time consuming. Additionally, prospective interviewees may have quit, been placed on temporary or administrative leave, or simply refuse to speak with investigators after consulting with a company or personal attorney. Any of these scenarios leave the company in the awkward position of possibly terminating a person who may—or may not—have been involved in perpetrating the alleged fraud under investigation.

Uncovering the Basics

A key benefit of early interviews is to quickly uncover information that will improve the odds of a successful investigation. However, the importance of obtaining as much information as possible relative to the allegations must be balanced with the need to avoid initial (or "snap") judgments about an interviewee's information or truthfulness. Ample opportunities will arise later in the investigation to verify information obtained from each person and correlate it with other witness interviews and documentation. With that in mind, the investigator's questions and language should be inquisitive rather than accusatory. As an overall goal, each interview should focus on gathering basic evidence: who, what, where, when, and how, and is discussed in subsequent sections of this chapter.

Consider an interview scenario in an alleged cash disbursement fraud scheme in which the investigator would want to learn key points about the organization's accounts payable process.

At the outset of the case, the investigator begins his or her work by consulting with the CEO of a property management company. This company manages 46 properties, and there are allegations that an accounts payable clerk, who is responsible for 6 of the properties, is conducting a fraudulent disbursement scheme. The company learned of the possible scheme when one of the vendors noted two instances in which a single bill had been paid twice. Because the property management company has a fiduciary duty to the property owners, it is important company executives move swiftly to put a stop to the potential fraud if it is still occurring and to investigate the extent of any past fraudulent activity.

At the time of the initial interview with the CEO, it is clear that the investigator will have only a brief span in which to speak with the accounts payable clerk to gather basic information about processes. The company intends to put the clerk on administrative leave immediately following the brief interview so that the investigation may commence.

The objective of this brief interview is not to determine the nature of the fraud, nor gain a confession. This interview will be geared toward gathering basic information. However, to the extent that particular practices may be at issue, the interview would include questions targeted toward gaining a better understanding of the activities that contributed to the opportunity for fraud.

For example, it would be customary when interviewing someone about cash disbursements to discuss the following:

- What are the responsibilities of the person being interviewed? By asking this question, the investigator can start identifying issues in the segregation of duties between processing and approving transactions that require follow up.
- Where is the hard and soft copy accounts payable information stored? This question assists the investigator in identifying what records need to be preserved and searched.
- When are payments made? Who can initiate the payments? This inquiry can uncover payments that are outliers, thus establishing a pattern that requires further analysis.
- How are approvals documented? Who is authorized to approve invoices or payments? Understanding the internal control processes helps the investigator validate documentation or identify falsified documentation.

The answers to these initial questions not only provide much needed information at the onset of the investigation, but they may also help identify additional individuals who need to be interviewed. By systematically focusing on who, what, where, when, and how, the investigator obtains crucial pieces of information that can later be verified for truthfulness and accuracy. In this case, because double payments were specifically mentioned by the whistle-blower, the brief interview with accounts payable clerk would include a specific question about any circumstances in which a double payment might inadvertently occur and how such instances would be corrected once noted.

The preceding case involving the accounts payable clerk was initiated when a whistle-blower had provided a strong lead not only about the nature of the fraud but also with respect to the identity of the possible perpetrator. Company executives were prepared to place the suspect on administrative leave. Expedient intervention was important so that the property management company could fulfill its fiduciary responsibility to the property owners. However, there are cases when there are significant considerations to balance when determining whom to interview and when.

Whenever it is suspected that a fraud may be ongoing, there is potentially tremendous value to deferring the interviews. Often, it is not so difficult to determine what happened from a purely practical standpoint because of the document trail left behind. What is more difficult, however, is to show the required element of intent. For that reason, strong consideration should be given to being proactive in attempting to capture conversations that demonstrate a conspiracy or obtain evidence of possible payoffs as they occur. Once overt investigative activities, such as interviews, commence, it may be difficult, if not impossible, to capitalize on the opportunities for performing covert work.

On the other side of this equation is the desire to limit losses if greater harm may come to existing victims or if additional persons may be victimized by the activity. One must carefully balance the desire for evidence of criminal wrongdoing that could lead to a conviction against the needs of the victims to limit losses. Moreover, because information leading to suspicion of fraud is seldom perfect, there is always the risk that an investigator, by asking questions, can cause damage to a perfectly legitimate business by scaring off investors through inquiries or other investigative actions. The following case demonstrates this delicate balancing act.

In the course of investigating ordinary mortgage fraud, investigators traced funds from the activity to an account that had the hallmarks of a Ponzi scheme. Because people were continuing to invest in the account, critical planning considerations came into play. The investigators had to ask themselves questions about whether interviewing current investors might cause unnecessary alarm, causing people to not invest in what might later be shown to be a perfectly legitimate investment opportunity. On the other hand, there was the question about the ramifications of allowing further victimization should the investigators' suspicions about a Ponzi scheme prove correct. In the end, to address those considerations, the investigators did some research with regulators prior to starting the interviews with investors. In this case, that decision paid off. The research showed that state regulators had issued a cease and desist order against the owner of the account in question, and this order had not been heeded. The next step was to interview one of the earlier investors just to get an idea of what the investor was told about how the investment was to work. Again, this proved to be a valuable strategy, as this early investor had statements showing the investment was profitable, yet he had not seen the money he expected.

Armed with this information, the investigators weighed the considerations and made the decision to interview more recent investors. It turns out that a Ponzi scheme was clearly involved. In fact, the investors had recently received correspondence requesting the investors' permission to roll over the funds to new investments. The timing allowed the losses to be halted.

This case demonstrates just a portion of the extensive decisions that often must be made. In this case, the strategy involved not only the timing of the commencement of interviews, but also the critical preparatory steps taken to obtain background information and then the selection of whom to interview first. As demonstrated by the stopping of further losses, a good strategy can lead to a positive outcome.

The Value of Listening

The ability of the interviewer to listen to what is being communicated by the witness is a key skill. In discussing his success in several high profile negotiations and investigations, former U.S. Senator George Mitchell (D–Maine) put it this way:

> It's important in a conflict resolution to create a context in which each side can in fact and in perception make its case and have its point of view heard; in other words, listening is critical. … Genuine listening is hard to do. In social and other casual conversations, many people focus on their own words or thoughts. I try to focus by telling myself that I'll have to write a summary of the discussion once it's over. Frequently, I do write such summaries, even when I don't have to do [it], just to keep up my listening skills.[1]

It helps to be patient, positive, and willing listen to what is being said.

Many books about listening skills are available as a quick Internet search will show. A person who is skilled at listening will pick up clues during the interview for further exploration. For example, if the interviewee makes comments about what is "supposed to happen" in a process, the skilled interviewer will want to direct the inquiry into an explanation of what "typically happens."

The bottom line is that the importance of listening as part of the interview process, particularly when interviews are done at the onset of an investigation, cannot be overstated.

Setting the Mood

An essential ability of any fraud investigator is to make an interviewee comfortable during the interview process. Although the underlying purpose for interviews can make this a difficult goal, questions that are straightforward and nonjudgmental will be more likely to put an interviewee at ease and help establish rapport. To help set a positive tone, an investigator should inform the interviewee of the reason for the interview, adding that it is a fact-finding session—not an accusation of fraud or misconduct on the part of the interviewee. To return

---

[1]   "An Interview With George Mitchell," *Fraud Magazine*, May/June 2008, 38.

to the cash disbursements example, the investigator might open an interview by saying, "We are trying to resolve some questions in how the accounts payable processes are being administered." By taking this step, the investigator can help ease any natural tension that the interviewee may feel.

In addition to the meeting's purpose, several other items should be communicated at the start of the interview. Examples include the following:

- The interviewer is working at the request of the company and therefore represents the company and not the employee.
- The expectation is that the employee will cooperate fully, providing complete and accurate responses to questions.
- The understanding is that the investigation is confidential, and an expectation exists that the employee will not disclose information discussed during the interview.
- Although the company intends to keep information about transactions and individuals obtained in the course of the interview confidential, it may ultimately decide to disclose the information pursuant to regulatory processes.
- The interviewer should also be cognizant of any special circumstances that may apply when conducting the interview, such as providing the interviewee with a Tennessen warning.[2]

In conducting these early interviews, investigators should avoid divulging unnecessary information, including the identity of individuals who surfaced the allegations.

On-the-Books Versus Off-the-Books Schemes

In most fraud and misconduct investigations, investigators are dealing with an on-the-books or off-the-books scheme. Those schemes are distinguished as follows:

- An *on-the-books* fraud and misconduct scheme results in false entries made in an organization's accounting records and the modification or falsification of underlying documentation. The focus of interviews for such on-the-books schemes should be directed toward organizational payment points in which funds can be stolen or misdirected. These areas include check processing (vendor and payroll), petty cash and imprest funds, wire transfers, and debit cards. Investigators should look closely at procedures, processes, and people involved in authorizing and recording transactions at these payment points. More specifically, the investigator should identify who authorizes the payments, what the authorization is based on, when the payment is authorized, and how the payment authorization is documented. Although this is not a complete list of questions that may need to be asked, it is a good illustration of how questions can be effectively used to build comprehensive information about the transactions. Information gathered during the interview process can be used later

---

[2]   Information on Tennessen warnings can be found at www.ipad.state.mn.us/docs/tw.html and Minnesota Statues section 13.04, subdivision 2.

during document review to identify transactions that may require further evaluation to support validity.

- *Off-the-books* fraud and misconduct schemes result in organizations paying increased costs for products and services provided by vendors and other third-parties. These fraud schemes are far more difficult to identify and investigate, because cash and other assets are not recorded in the organization's books and records. The focus of interviews for off-the-books schemes should be directed toward the various points in an organization at which goods or services are negotiated and ordered. The investigator's questions should be directed toward procedures, processes, and people that can enable purchase transactions of goods and services. The investigator should identify employees who are authorized to initiate or manage such activity, review what form an authorization takes, determine when an authorization is made, and verify how an authorization is documented. Once again, this is not intended to be a complete list of questions, but a suggested format to uncover critical information regarding processes, procedures, and people involved in the acquisition of goods and services. Once this knowledge base is established, the investigator can more readily identify transactions that fall outside of established parameters and determine if they require further evaluation.

Handling Short Time Frames: Document Collection

In a perfect world, there would be no restrictions on the amount of time it would take to complete a fraud investigation. In real world investigations, however, important decisions must often be made quickly and document collection in fraud assignments must often be concluded within tight timelines. With this understanding, the investigator must successfully handle a variety of document acquisition and management challenges. Some of the challenges are discussed in the sections that follow.

General Considerations

In a real world investigation, a significant possibility exists that once an allegation comes to light, the person or persons engaged in fraud or misconduct may alter or destroy documents critical to the investigation. To manage this risk, an investigator's initial efforts should focus on the types of critical documents that must be secured and the people who have access to—or possession of—those documents. In addition, it is important for the investigator to realize that an organization's normal business processes may alter or modify documents that are important to the case. For example, electronic records that contain reconciliations of account balances may be updated and saved over existing files, or information in e-mail and voice mail records may be purged at specific intervals to lessen data storage requirements. For those reasons, it is imperative that an investigator understand any specific legal requirements related to the collection or preservation of documents.

When collecting documents, investigators must keep in mind that any evidence collected can be used if a matter under investigation goes to trial. This can be managed by establishing a "chain of custody" protocol. The purpose of a chain of custody is to establish from the time the evidence was collected to the time of its presentation to a court that the evidence has been properly preserved from alteration or damage and thus retains its probative value.[3] Maintaining a chain of custody is crucial as to avoid compromising the prosecution of a crime. However, for a chain of custody to be successful, all original documents must be preserved in the same format in which they were collected. This may include appropriate work papers that validate from whom the information was collected. In this way, the investigator can assert that all evidentiary documents are unaltered, and that all review and analysis was based on copies of documents originally collected. For electronic documents, care must be taken to ensure that copies do not alter any original information gathered.

It is possible for investigators to preserve documents for investigative use without an actual physical collection. This may be done by either instructing the document custodians to preserve all relevant documents in their possession or by requesting that the custodian transfer identified documents to a centralized location within the company. However, the investigator must understand that either approach can deliver subpar results unless stakeholders are provided detailed instructions on what documents are to be self-preserved or transferred. For example, employees who have little appreciation for importance of a preservation requirement may be careless in maintaining key documents, which can be later used to support an investigation. For that reason, the document transfer option may be less risky, because that technique requires little more than moving daily backup information from the normal rotation into a designated electronic storehouse. Because of the risk of destruction or alteration, documents in the possession of custodians who might be implicated in any fraud or misconduct should be gathered immediately at the start of the investigation and should not be left in the possession of the holder for self-preservation.

Privacy Issues

Many countries have enacted laws that define personal information, require an individual's consent to collect such information, and govern the transportation of such data across borders. Many of these laws are based on the principles of the Organization for Economic Cooperation and Development (OECD)[4] Examples of the regulations based on these principles are the Privacy Act of 1974 (5 USC § 552A—Records Maintained on Individuals) and the European Data Protection Directive.[5]

---

[3]   Thomas W. Golden, Steven L. Skalak, and Mona M. Clayton, *A Guide To Forensic Accounting Investigation* (2011), 427.

[4]   www.oecd.org.

[5]   Directive 95/46/EC. On January 25, 2012, the European Commission created a draft European Data Protection Regulation that will potentially supersede the Data Protection Directive.

The principles governing OECD's recommendation for personal data protection include all of the following:

- *Notice.* Individuals should be given notice when their personal data is being collected.
- *Purpose.* Personal data should only be used for the purpose stated and not for any other purposes.
- *Consent.* Personal data should not be disclosed without the individual's consent.
- *Security.* Personal data collected should be kept secure from any potential abuses.
- *Disclosure.* Individuals should be informed about who is collecting their data.
- *Access.* Individuals should be allowed to access their personal data and make corrections to any inaccuracies.
- *Accountability.* Individuals should have a method available to them to hold those who collect data accountable for following the above principles.

Investigators need to be aware of sensitive client information during the document collection process. This may include documents that contain information on specific business procedures, proprietary business practices, or trade secrets. This is an important evaluation, because collected documents may eventually need to be turned over to governmental agencies or prosecutors, which makes the material subject to legal discovery and potentially available to customers, suppliers, and competitors.

Although privacy and proprietary business information issues are legitimate concerns, that should not deter investigators from taking a comprehensive approach to document collection. For example, employees might have documents at home or in personal storage units. When seeking documents from individuals, it is appropriate to remind them of these locations and, if required materials are there, to make arrangements for their retrieval. In addition to locations where documents may be physically stored, investigators should also consider the multitude of electronic devices that may contain relevant information, including home computers, cell phones, tablet computers, voice mail records, personal digital assistants, smart phones, and media storage devices, such as external hard drives, memory sticks, compact discs, and flash memory cards.

Detecting False or Altered Documents

Because a multitude of fraud and misconduct schemes are accomplished through the use of false original or altered documents, it is important for an investigator to consider whether documentation received in support of questioned transactions is the "real thing." For instance, one sure way to identify a scheme is to insist that custodians provide original documents during collection. If the investigator receives copied or facsimile documents, the custodian should be questioned on who has the original documentation.

Fraudsters use a variety of methods used to create false or altered documents, and some common schemes include the following:

- *Copied documents.* In its simplest form, original vendor documents are copied and submitted a second time for payment.
- *Original false documents.* Modern digital publishing tools make original false documents both easier to produce and harder to identify. Some issues that may indicate false original documents include addresses that contain P.O. boxes, documents that are sequentially numbered (100, 101, 102, and so on), generic office supply forms, documents from vendors that are not relative to the business location, and documents that do not clearly identify the products or services or documents that require additional explanation.
- *Miscellaneous receipts.* Vendor receipts that are missing the name and address of the vendor or other pertinent information, such as date and time stamps.
- *Facsimile documents.* Used in connection with another scheme, facsimile documents lend an air of authenticity to the transaction. Always look to see that facsimile transaction data is included on all pages accompanying the fax. Most facsimiles contain date and time stamps. Facsimiles have been used in backdating schemes. A clue could be the removal of the time and date from a document.
- *Altered documents.* Altered documents include those on which key information regarding the vendor or service has been modified through physical or digital methods. An example is the removal of specific transaction details on a purchase receipt or altering dates on airline ticket printouts.

Gathering Background Information

In real world fraud cases, investigators under time constraints can mine commercial databases, social networking websites, and the Internet for a wealth of background information, such as home value details that can be obtained from public property tax rolls or real estate databases. This ready access to information adds significant value to an investigation, because it can be quickly reviewed and form the basis for an initial round of questions.

Although online tools are convenient, investigators must also tap a broader array of information sources to build a solid background profile. If thoughtfully constructed, a background investigation can uncover direct evidence of fraud, help ferret out important information on related-party transactions, identify new investigative leads, and facilitate asset searches.[6] For example, background investigations can uncover a wide range of important lifestyle information, such as the number and types of automobiles owned, where individuals reside, their marital status, and past criminal records (including bankruptcy and drug abuse).

Lifestyle information obtained from background investigations that is inconsistent with employment information should be carefully considered. For example, in one particular investigation,

---

[6] Thomas W. Golden, Steven L. Skalak, and Mona M. Clayton, *A Guide To Forensic Accounting Investigation* (2011), 331.

an interviewee related comments by a co-worker about the cost of a daughter's recent wedding, coupled with knowledge of that person's trip to an overseas location and the purchase of a new (and expensive) automobile. Those key pieces of background detail led to an internal investigation that uncovered several years of fraudulent activity, largely because the employee's lifestyle was inconsistent with the compensation earned by the employee and her husband.

Although a lifestyle out of sync with base pay is a major red flag, another important background research issue involves incentive compensation. In this case, most ethical lapses occur from incentive plans in which employees are tempted to manipulate financial information or engage in unacceptable levels of risk. Consider the following example:

> In a particular organization, employee bonuses were paid in cash if the business reached a threshold of net income as a percentage of sales. If the threshold was not met, the bonuses were paid out in stock. In years when the organization was close to meeting the required threshold, certain accounting employees would meet to identify any potential expense reductions that would trigger the target threshold. As a result, various accounting statements were manipulated to ensure the cash payout—a fraud that was perpetuated as a direct result of the company's incentive compensation structure.

The Interview Process

Interviews are an important part of any background investigation. At a basic level, interviews allow an investigator to develop information on an alleged fraud or misconduct, identify critical documents, and determine who is in possession of those documents. Over time, interviews also allow investigators to evaluate the credibility of individual witnesses. Although the initial section of this chapter discussed interviewing at the onset of the investigation, this section will discuss some important interview steps to implement after documents have been reviewed and analyzed.

First, investigators need to develop an interview plan. This plan should be viewed as a "living document," which is updated throughout an investigation as details about the alleged fraud or misconduct are better developed. During this process, some individuals will be dropped from the interview list, while others are added. Some questions that should be considered when creating an interview plan include the following:

- Who are the individuals that should be interviewed?
- Where are these individuals located?
- Are they current or past employees?
- Are there any immediate known changes in employment status?
- Where does the person fit within the hierarchy of the organization?
- Is there a logical sequence for conducting the interviews?
- Will any documents be collected prior to the interview?
- Is the purpose of the interview to gather background information or facts pertinent to the fraud or misconduct?

By answering each of the questions, the investigator will have a detailed framework for conducting the interviews, even within a limited time frame.

Second, if the investigation uses multiple teams during the interview process, it is important to ensure that witnesses with similar knowledge of key transactions or subjects are interviewed by the same people. By taking this approach, the interview questioning will be more efficient, have fewer gaps, and result in a knowledge base that is more reliable.

Third, investigators should view post-document review interviews as an opportunity to obtain (or reinforce) information that effectively answers important who, what, when, why, and how questions related to the alleged fraud or misconduct. This is an important consideration because if interview memoranda is later reviewed by a governmental entity, prosecutor, or law enforcement within a criminal investigation, the organization's interests will not be served if it appears that the fact-finding sessions were (at best) cursory or (at worst) a blatant attempt to protect company officers and employees.

Fourth, if an internal investigation is done in conjunction with a governmental review, it is important for the internal team to interview witnesses before they meet with government officials. Questions posed in these interviews often help witnesses refresh their recollection of events and transactions, and they prod them to consider what documentation they have— or may need to review—before meeting with government investigators.

A deeper discussion of effective interviewing can be found in chapter 13, "Working the Case."

Final Decision Points

As noted at the beginning of this chapter, a standardized investigative approach would include complete document collection, review, and analysis prior to interviews with key witnesses. If real-world time constraints provide only one opportunity to interview key witnesses, the post-document review option is often the better choice, because having a detailed understanding of background materials allows the investigator to elicit more productive interview results. In a perfect world scenario, when high-level employees are under suspicion, lower-level employees should be interviewed before higher-level employees. That is because lower-level workers can provide the investigator with key information on organizational practices, allowing that person to develop a well-rounded scan of the company and departmental environment. That background helps the investigator prepare for conversations with higher-level employees, who may have greater involvement in the conduct under investigation.

Recognizing That Budgets Are Limited

An organization that has identified a fraud resulting in the theft of cash or other assets will not be anxious to spend a significant sum of money to thoroughly investigate and document the time period the theft occurred, the method or methods used to steal the cash or other assets, and the exact dollar amount stolen. Although the "perfect" investigation is not limited by cost considerations and would have an unlimited budget to identify and fully document the details of the fraudulent activity, real world investigations often face the reality of a limited budget. Even investigations that lead to a monetary recovery, either from the person who committed the fraud or from the availability of insurance, must be cost beneficial.

The costs of investigations can vary widely depending on the schemes employed and the number of individuals involved in the fraud or misconduct. Investigations into simple matters involving on-the-books fraud schemes are generally less expensive to investigate than those that involve off-the-books fraud schemes. Matters involving the manipulation of financial statements or other criminal activity have greater risk to the organization in terms of government imposed penalties and, therefore, require a high degree of precision in the outcome of the investigation in order to restore stakeholder confidence in the organization. This higher degree of precision is achieved through increased efforts in the area of document collection, transaction analysis, and interviews, which results in a more expensive investigation. If it is suspected that a significant amount of money has been taken through fraud or misconduct, it may be important to identify the assets before the person committing the fraud or misconduct is alerted to the investigation. Working behind the scenes creates higher costs associated with the investigation.

The pitfalls and challenges of working with a limited budget are interrelated. A limited document collection effort, quick analysis of the documentation, and limited interviews might not provide the investigators with sufficient information to identify all the issues and arrive at correctly supported conclusions or identify all parties involved in the fraud scheme. Limited investigation results might not be satisfactory to governmental regulators and could result in continued government involvement such as the issuance of subpoenas impairing the organization's reputation and interviewing of employees creating a distraction to the ongoing business operations. The evidence obtained may not be sufficient to prosecute those involved in the fraud activities or support insurance claims. The investigator will need to carefully consider these pitfalls and challenges in accepting an engagement with a limited budget. There are reputational and potential economic risks to the investigator should reliance be placed on a limited investigation that has not uncovered all the issues or individuals involved in the fraud. This risk must be actively managed and minimized through complete communication to the engaging party when working with limited budgets.

Notwithstanding the pitfalls and challenges, investigators often face the task of working with a limited budget. When faced with this reality, critical decisions need to be made to ensure that the investigation stays focused on the most important issues of the investigation. The following can help the investigator maintain the necessary focus:

- The investigator working with a limited budget will need to avoid the tendency to make the document collection process over inclusive and recognize that one does not need to collect all the records at the beginning of the investigation. This can be accomplished by collecting documents from only those individuals involved in the questionable transactions for the most recent time period. If the allegations of fraud and misconduct are supported with the limited documentation, a decision can be made to investigate additional time periods. Once the pattern of activity is known, it is likely that the document request can be tailored to specific documents, thereby minimizing the cost of collecting and analyzing documents that are not pertinent to the issues being investigated.

- The investigator should keep in mind that it may not be necessary to determine with an exact precision the amounts involved but rather determine a reasonable estimate. Estimating the loss rather than calculating the exact loss can reduce the time associated with the investigation and potentially reduce the cost of the investigation. If a decision has been made at the beginning of the investigation not to pursue legal action, the investigator can bypass the extended effort of chain of custody requirements associated with document collection. If that decision has not been made, the investigator needs to take care to ensure that even a limited document collection process preserves the chain of custody.

- In the initial stage of the investigation, the investigator should focus on what is known and not get distracted by other issues brought to their attention. Interviewees will often raise issues outside of those being investigated. The interviewee may raise issues to deflect attention from his or her own culpability, actions, or lack of actions in the matter being investigated. Or, the interviewee may have a number of complaints or issues and use the investigation as a platform for venting these issues. It is important that the investigator not get distracted from the primary purpose of the investigation, that is, to identify and uncover the details surrounding the allegations under review. Other issues brought up by those being interviewed should not be ignored but can be noted for follow-up allowing the investigator focus on the primary issue.

- Fraud investigations can be conducted for a wide variety of purposes, including establishing criminal activity, civil claims to recover stolen assets, recovering damages by filing claims with insurance providers, making corrections and adjustments to published financial statements and other public reported information, termination of employees for violation of internally established policies and procedures, and other regulatory or ad-hoc purposes.

- Each of these purposes carries with it a unique burden of proof. In court cases the purpose of the fraud investigation is to prove or disprove the allegation's legal elements. Each legal element must be proven beyond a reasonable doubt in criminal cases and by a preponderance of the evidence in civil cases.[7] Other types of investigations have different levels of proof based upon regulatory or internally determined requirements. The purpose of the investigation can have a significant impact on the time required (and therefore the budget) to conduct the investigation. Understanding the engaging party's ultimate purpose will provide the investigator the ability to work with a limited budget. For example, if a preliminary conclusion has been reached not to prosecute individuals involved in the fraudulent actions, the purpose of the investigation's purpose may only be to determine if the employee violated company policies and procedures rather than actual fraud. A determination of a violation of an organization's policies and procedures would be less costly and likely provide the necessary basis for the organization to terminate the employee.

---

[7] "Opening the Fraud Examiner's Tool Kit," *Fraud Magazine*, March/April 2008, 56.

- Use people in the organization to research and document identified issues. Once the main person responsible for the fraud or misconduct is removed from the picture (administrative leave or termination), those who had some knowledge but not a full picture will likely respond favorably to a request for assistance in putting together analysis, unless the knowledgeable person is sympathetic with the one who engaged in the fraud or misconduct. The investigator must determine a person's loyalties or opinions in the interview and data collection process.
- Critically review the results with the entire investigative team. The collective knowledge can facilitate probable theories and next steps. Also, involve those at the company who have responsibility for the oversight of the investigation. Their assistance can quickly eliminate false leads and help facilitate the next document request, interviewee selection, or procedures.
- The investigator needs to remember not to get in over his or her head. The acceptance of an investigation assignment that the investigator is not qualified to perform most likely will have a negative impact on the budget. It may be possible that the investigator can obtain assistance in an unfamiliar engagement when needed, but generally the investigator should not accept an engagement when the investigation is outside of his or her area of expertise.
- Finally, the investigator should try to determine the client's expectations of the outcome and costs to ensure reasonableness. Unsophisticated clients often underestimate the costs associated with conducting an investigation and expect the investigator to be the trier of fact.

In the preceding paragraphs, we have outlined some of the pitfalls and challenges the investigator faces in working with a limited budget. Additionally, we have highlighted some specific areas in which a focused and diligent effort can help the investigator focus on the cost of the investigation versus the benefits obtained. In some investigations, recovery can be sought from those who commit the fraudulent activity or insurance covering business fraud. In some instances, the minimization of reputational risks to the organization—of not doing a proper investigation—are the benefits obtained by the organization through a properly conducted investigation.

Although government investigators may have more liberal budgets, investigators working in the private sector must often use strategies that limit costs. Cost saving strategies may affect the way in which interviews are conducted in two key ways:

1. More of the interviews must be conducted by means other than in-person meetings.
2. Fewer unannounced interviews may be conducted.

Ideally, interviews are best conducted in person. When interviews cannot be conducted in person, consideration should be given to videoconference capabilities, as it is possible to at least verify who is involved in the meeting and who is talking at the time. It is important to note that persons asked for interviews may engage counsel to attend the conference, so this raises additional planning considerations. It is harder to detect signs of deception when the interviewee is not in the room. Nevertheless, the rule of thumb is to never turn down an opportunity for an interview, even when the circumstances are less than ideal, because the "perfect" opportunity may never present itself.

When working in less than ideal conditions, the interviewer can maximize the value of the meeting by

- knowing the subject matter. Do your homework and be prepared to ask appropriate and sufficient questions.
- being prepared to conduct additional phone contacts. Always make sure before terminating the first contact that you have a means by which to contact the interviewee for follow-up questions.

Not only does a limited budget decrease the investigator's opportunities to travel to conduct in-person meetings, it also means that fewer unannounced interviews can be performed. Unannounced interviews can be very helpful, especially when the case is quite complex. This is not to state that the investigator does not need to do any planning; on the contrary, a successful investigation involves much planning regarding the timing of the interviews. However, if the interviewee is given advance notice of the interview, the chances increase that information about the investigation will spread rapidly and interviewees will have time to work together to "get their stories straight." It is often beneficial to plan multiple simultaneous interviews and then have the investigators compare information. When interviews have to be arranged with the interviewee in advance, the advantages inherent in the simultaneous interviews may be lost or greatly diminished.

However, the additional burden of limited budgets does force the investigator to plan carefully, and doing so may result in the interviewees remaining cooperative as they perceive that the investigator is well prepared and respectful of their time. Planned interviews can be very effective, especially when dealing with neutral parties or victims. The unannounced interviews will be more important as the focus of the investigations turns to those suspected of involvement in the fraud scheme.

As addressed in the next section, investigator might face the reality of a limitation on the investigation due to the availability of documents.

Dealing With Scope Limitations

Investigators may be able to tell the complete fraud story through the careful review and analysis of documentation that substantiates the information obtained through the interview process. Sometimes the documentary evidence presented by an investigator in an interview is sufficient to obtain a confession of the fraudulent acts the person or persons committed; however, often this is not the case. In the "perfect" investigation, the scope of the investigator's work would not be affected or limited due to available documentation. The investigator would have access to all the documents and witnesses that would be required and necessary to complete the investigation. In an investigation, an investigator wants documents from all sides of the transaction, including not only documents in the possession of the organization but also documents that may be in the possession of their customers, vendors, or other parties to transactions, including associated banking related documents.

In real world investigations, the investigator often does not have all the desired documentation and must put the puzzle together without all the pieces or he or she must tell the story of how the fraud happened with some of the pages missing. Sometimes documentation has been destroyed by the person committing the fraud. In fact, missing documentation that would normally be retained in the ordinary course of the business operations or that has been unexpectedly destroyed, say from fire, is often a red flag that fraud is afoot.[8] Other times the document retention policies of the business may be responsible for the document destruction.

A number of pitfalls and challenges in performing an investigation exist when the scope is limited due to the documentation that is available. Similar to other challenges faced by the investigator, a scope limitation due to documentation may not allow the investigator to arrive at totally supported conclusions or identify all the parties involved in a fraud scheme. The investigator should ensure that the pitfalls and challenges are not self-induced through carelessness on his or her part related to preserving documents at the start of the engagement or handling documents during the investigation. This is particularly acute with respect to computer-imaged or harvested documents when the source of those documents must be preserved through the chain of custody requirements.

In on-the-books and off-the books fraud schemes, the investigator should obtain documents from as many sides of the potentially fraudulent transactions as possible. A particular problem in off-the-books fraud schemes may be that individuals and companies outside of the organization who have been active and willing participants in the fraud schemes will generally not meet with the investigator or provide requested documents. Other participants who may not have been willing, but were nevertheless participants, might consider it in their best interest to participate in and assist the investigator, yet be reticent to do so out of fear of embarrassment or other issues. Willing or unwilling individuals and companies outside of the organization may be reluctant to provide the investigator with requested documents due to fear of self-incrimination in connection with the fraud schemes. Financial institutions have a duty of privacy to their customers and will not provide access to or documents associated with bank accounts of those participating in the fraud schemes without proper authorization from the account holder, subpoenas, or other legal authorization. Because the investigator does not generally have subpoena power, obtaining access to these records can and does pose a problem. Unfortunately, there is no easy way for the nongovernmental investigator to overcome these problems.

Securing documents from third parties will likely be easier if those parties are either a customer or vendor of the organization conducting the investigation. These third parties will likely want to preserve the business relationship with the organization, and this relationship can be leveraged to elicit the customer's or vendor's cooperation with the investigation. The request for documentation should be confined to ordinary course business records (expense receipts, invoices, check copies, and so on) and should not be overly broad with respect to

---

[8]   "Missing Disbursement Documents, Part 1," *Fraud Magazine,* July/August 2009, 10.

the time periods involved. It is unlikely that a request for internal information, such as e-mail correspondence, will be honored by a third party. In some business relationships, the agreement between the parties contains an "audit clause" allowing one party reasonable access to the other parties accounting records for the basis of insuring that self-reporting under the agreement is accurate. It is possible that documents could be requested under this audit clause. Another potential method to obtain assistance from customers and vendors is to agree to share findings regarding the investigation with them. An organization would want to seek the assistance of counsel with respect to any plan to share the findings, as doing so might impair the ability of an organization to proceed against those parties for claims they may have related to their employees' participation in the fraud scheme or recovery from outside entities, such as insurance companies. Finally, an organization might need to rely upon the judicial process to obtain documents through a discovery process.

Ultimately, a decision will need to be made by the investigator on whether there is sufficient available documentation and whether it is sufficient to draw conclusions about a participant's role in any fraudulent activity. For example, a company's internal controls may be so lax or nonexistent that the perpetrator of the fraud cannot be determined. The complete story of the fraud may not be known, and the lack of documentation might preclude the prosecution of criminal or civil charges against the individuals who perpetrated the fraud. Nonetheless, most investigations generate sufficient information to form a conclusion about whether the organization's policies and procedures have been followed. If the policies and procedures have not been followed, an organization can make a determination on the appropriate action that should be taken, whether civil or criminal. This might include a warning or formal reprimand or even the termination of the individuals involved in the fraudulent activity.

Working With Law Enforcement and Prosecutors

The perfect criminal investigation ends with the investigator building a case in which law enforcement and prosecutors are able to convict the individuals involved of the fraud and obtain restitution for their client. In the real world, law enforcement and prosecutors may not be eager to take on a fraud case. Although the prosecution of white collar criminal activity[9] and fraud is becoming more common, law enforcement may not be excited about accepting a case for any number of reasons. Many law enforcement and prosecutors are more knowledgeable of and have greater experience in dealing with other forms of criminal activity and may not be specifically trained in dealing with fraud. In some unique circumstances, law enforcement or prosecutors may view the victim of the fraud as being greedy as the suspect or view the victim as having the ability to have prevented the fraud from happening.

---

[9] The United States Department of Justice describes white collar crime as nonviolent crime for financial gain committed by means of deception by persons whose occupational status is entrepreneurial, professional, or semi-professional and utilizing their special occupational skills and opportunities; also, nonviolent crime for financial gain utilizing deception and committed by anyone having special technical and professional knowledge of business and government, irrespective of the person's occupation.

Law enforcement or prosecutors also may have valid concerns about how and when evidence was gathered. It is important to note the previous comments on ensuring the proper chain of custody in the collection and use of documents and how any confessions were obtained.

An important consideration in accepting and moving forward with the prosecution of fraud will be what civil and criminal laws have been violated. It is important that the investigator have a basic understanding of these laws. Civil and criminal laws are covered in greater detail throughout this book and are mentioned in this section so that their importance is understood. If the investigator has a basic understanding of these laws, can articulate their meaning, and considers them in the conduct of the investigation, it will enhance the receptiveness of the case by law enforcement and prosecutors. Typically, white collar crime and fraud require that the prosecutor prove all of the following common elements associated with fraudulent activity:[10]

- The alleged offender had the intent to knowingly commit a wrongful act or achieve a purpose inconsistent with law or public policy.
- The alleged offender disguised the purpose or employed falsities and misrepresentations to accomplish the scheme.
- The alleged offender relied on the ignorance or carelessness of the victim (individual or company).
- The alleged offender concealed the offense.[11]

Ultimately, the evidence provided to law enforcement and prosecutors should contain specific and sufficient information to support each of the common elements identified in the previous paragraphs. Their accepting and proceeding with a case might be contingent upon how well the evidence is packaged and presented. The information presented to law enforcement and prosecutors should clearly demonstrate the following:

- *Solid paper trail.* The paper trail supporting the fraud should be as complete as possible and contain original[12] financial records supporting the activity. The financial records should be maintained in the state they were found, and investigator comments, notations, and cross references should be made on copies of the financial records. Normally, the financial records will be those that are created in the normal course of the business (vouchers, check registers, canceled checks, bank statements, journal entries, general ledger detail, and so on). Altered records should contain annotations and examples of where and how the financial records were altered.
- *Pattern of behavior or activity.* To the extent possible, if a pattern of behavior, such as fraud, exists, it should be developed. Most individuals who commit fraud will continue in their behavior or activity, and in most cases the dollar amount of the individual

---

[10] "Opening the Fraud Examiner's Tool Kit," *Fraud Magazine*, March/April 2008, 57.

[11] The legal definition of *fraud* the investigation is operating under should be obtained from counsel, if appropriate.

[12] Original documents may be electronic or hard copy, depending upon how the documents have been retained.

fraudulent transactions will increase over time. The pattern might also include variations in how the fraud was committed over time. This pattern of activity provides strong circumstantial evidence of intent to knowingly commit a wrongful act.

- *High dollar loss.* Cases in which a relatively high dollar amount of loss has been incurred are more likely to garner the attention of law enforcement and prosecutors. There is no specific threshold that quantifies a loss as high dollar. This does not necessarily translate into a larger recovery for the victim upon conviction.
- *Real loss.* Law enforcement and prosecutors typically want to deal with cases that involve real loss—cash or stolen assets. These cases do not rely upon accounting or economic theory to quantify lost business value or being deprived of investment profits, which can be the loss related to a fraud, such as the backdating of stock options.
- *True victim.* Does the victim who suffered the loss represent a true victim? Is there any part of his or her actions that could be construed as contributing to the loss? Are there any reasonable actions that could have been taken to avoid the loss? The case must establish the fiduciary capacity between the victim of the fraudulent activity and the perpetrator of the fraud so that the victim is truly believable.
- *Potential defenses.* The investigator should consider the potential defenses of those suspected of committing a fraudulent act. Intent, disguise, and concealment are not easily proven. Most cases will require the testimony of other individuals who were knowledgeable of the transactions. In some cases these individuals may have knowingly or unknowingly participated in the fraudulent activity to some extent and may attempt to minimize their roles or describe themselves as observers rather than participants, which can damage their credibility.[13]
- *Confession.* A goal of a fraud investigation may be to secure the confession of those involved in the fraudulent activity.

Preparing for the Unexpected

As part of any real world investigation, the investigator should count on and plan for the unexpected. There will be unexpected difficulties encountered on every investigation. In the preceding parts of this chapter, we have discussed many of the differences between the perfect investigation and real or imperfect world investigations. A fluid investigation plan is essential to ensure that the unexpected does not derail the investigation. There is no "one-size fits all" investigation plan. Although the investigation plan should be well thought out, it does not need to be a long, all-inclusive and exhaustive document, and it will most likely be modified as the investigation proceeds. The facts and circumstances in each investigation will require a unique set of investigative procedures. Ideally, an investigative work plan will outline the preliminary scope of the investigation, identify details of the investigative team organization and logistics, and set forth the initial work steps.

---

[13]   "Opening the Fraud Examiner's Tool Kit," *Fraud Magazine*, March/April 2008, 66.

The investigative plan should cover the preliminary scope of the investigation. Important considerations regarding the preliminary scope include the nature, source, and impact of the allegations. If the allegations are made anonymously, either directly to the organization or through a governmental agency, the preliminary scope may need to cast a wider net over the review of transactions and the interview of potential witnesses. Anonymous allegations, even if sufficiently detailed to identify the transactions involved, require careful consideration to understand who, what, where, when, why, and how related to the transactions. Another important consideration is the determination if the alleged fraud or misconduct has criminal or inappropriate regulatory behavior implications. Criminal behavior implications can lead to governmental fines and sanctions against the organization and public embarrassment resulting in the loss of customers or donors. These results can cause financial hardship to the organization that is far in excess of the impact of the actual underlying fraud. Because of the potential implications, this will also lead the investigators to cast a wider net to ensure the all available knowledge of the behavior is known and informed and appropriate disciplinary actions can be taken. Other considerations in the preliminary scope document include business units involved, locations, and number of employees.

Once the preliminary scope is defined, the investigative plan should address the investigative team and logistics. Key members of the investigative team include the organizational representatives, internal or external counsel, and forensic accounting as well as other specialists. It is important to identify who the key decision makers are for each group and assemble their contact information. Finally, the logistics potentially include information regarding the discussion of potential legal privileges and the relevant laws.

With the preliminary scope defined and team organization and logistics confirmed, the investigative plan should address the initial investigative plan steps. The initial investigative plan steps will be highly contingent on the nature, source, and potential financial impact of the allegations. The different types of on-the-books and off-the-books fraud and misconduct schemes will be discussed in chapter 3. What is important to consider is that initial steps should be identified for what the investigators will do once the documents are collected.

Anatomy of a Case

If investigators understand the anatomy of a case, they will be better positioned to adjust and allow for the practical considerations faced in real world investigations.

Allegations Received

A variety of methods can be used to report allegations of fraud. Allegations can be received in person, by letter, anonymously, and, sometimes, in the form of official actions. For example, qui tam[14] actions can be filed by law firms to report suspicions of fraud to

---

[14]   *Qui tam lawsuits* are those brought by private citizens (also known as "whistleblowers") against a person or company that violates a government regulation or is in violation of law in the performance of a government contract. *Law.com*, s.v. "Qui tam action," http://dictionary.law.com/Default. aspx?selected=1709 (accessed April 23, 2012).

the United States government. Once allegations are received, investigators will want to determine the nature and extent of the issues involved. Investigators will also want to determine if the information is coming in based on first-hand information as opposed to second- and third-hand reporting. *First-hand knowledge* of potential criminal activity means that the person or persons reporting the fraud have actually witnessed an event, whereas persons reporting *second-hand information* would indicate that other witnesses and documents would need to be gathered and reviewed as investigative decisions are being made. In all cases, the initial allegations should be carefully reviewed and analyzed before further investigative steps are taken.

Initial Interviews of Complainants and Whistleblowers

One of the most important aspects of dealing with allegations is understanding if it is based on first-hand knowledge. The initial interviews of complainants and whistleblowers can be used to secure this information. These interviews are used to secure sufficient information to make a determination if a further, more formal investigation is warranted. A consideration during the process of the initial interviews is to maintain the confidentiality of the information obtained. This includes making a request that individuals interviewed keep the inquiry confidential, structuring the questions such that the identities of the complainants and whistleblowers are not known and that only necessary background information is shared. The section of this chapter that dealt with listening skills is particularly important during the initial interviews of complainants and whistleblowers, as are open-ended questions that seek to obtain information regarding who, what, where, when, and how.

Identify Statutes and Elements

If it appears, based on the initial allegations, that further investigation is warranted, it is recommended that investigators identify which rules and regulations pertaining to the victim may have been violated, as well as potential violations of state and federal statutes. If it appears that state and federal statutes have been violated, it is recommended that investigators become familiar with the elements of those particular statutes. With regard to violations of federal statutes, the effect on interstate commerce will have to be evaluated and documented. Many cases will present opportunities to consider a wide variety of state and federal statutes for further investigation. Investigators may want to consider statutes that carry long statutes of limitation and those that identify specific unlawful activity, such as money laundering. Many federal statutes carry a 10-year statute of limitations, as opposed to 5 years. If given a choice, investigators may want to consider using statutes that carry a longer sentence or a mandatory type of sentencing procedure. Once potential state and federal statutes are identified, investigators should become familiar with the elements of those statutes by reviewing existing public information, such as the United States Code.

Review Jury Instructions

It is recommended that investigators obtain a working knowledge of potential jury instructions that may be used for certain statutes. It is always recommended that investigators approach any case as though it will be going to trial. When considering a case, anticipate that a juror will be reviewing evidence admitted by the judge, as well as written instructions on how to deliberate and reach a proper verdict. Jury instructions will provide guidance about definitions, such as willfulness and criminal intent, which are of paramount importance in any white collar crime investigation. (See chapter 5 for a discussion of these terms.) By having a working knowledge of the elements of particular statutes and proposed jury instructions, investigators can incorporate these concepts into the investigative and interview process from the beginning of a case, as opposed to addressing those issues on the eve of or during a trial.

Financial Analysis and Background Due Diligence

It is highly recommended that financial analysis and due diligence procedures be employed in the early stages of an investigation. A financial analysis is often time consuming; however, the information gleaned from analyzing the financial transactions can provide valuable information to investigators in order to prepare for interviews of victims, witnesses, and suspects. Diligence procedures should include public database checks and subscription database checks, if available. The point is to gather as much information as possible about persons who may be interviewed during an investigation prior to the interview process beginning. If possible, personnel files should be reviewed to further enhance information concerning the person being interviewed.

Investigators will want to gather as much information as possible, as well as make personal observations prior to the interviews. In summary, within the time allotted, investigators will want to carefully analyze the initial allegations, identify statutes and elements that may be affected by this information, initiate a financial analysis, conduct appropriate and thorough background checks, and review potential jury instructions to enhance the interview process.

Conclusion

Throughout this chapter we have considered how a real world investigation is different from the "perfect" investigation. We have considered the timing of the interview process, the document collection process, background investigations, the reality of limited budgets, the impact of scope limitations, seeking the cooperation of law enforcement and prosecutors, and preparing for the unexpected. Investigators are often required to deal with numerous factors that are not within their control. It is important for investigators to understand that in the real world, the "perfect" investigation does not exist and this requires flexibility in approaching the investigation. A myriad of real world factors brought about by those individuals involved in the fraud or misconduct will likely affect the investigative process. An understanding of the common problems and issues in the real world provides investigators with the tools and knowledge that can assist in building a flexible investigative plan that is prepared to respond to investigative realities. Real world investigations present issues that must be constantly recognized, addressed, and overcome by investigators. Investigators should recognize that these issues are present and have an understanding of how to respond.

Section II

Armed With Knowledge

2

Legal Foundations of Fraud Investigations

Daniel Korsman, JD, CPA/ABV, CFE
Debra K. Thompson, CPA/CFF, CFE

- Legal Foundations of Fraud Investigations
- On- and Off-the-Books Fraud Schemes
- Civil Process and Criminal Procedure
- Jury Instructions
- Regulatory Complexities
- Working the Case
- Find It and Fix It

Introduction

All successful investigators need working knowledge of key legal principles, which include key elements of fraud cases, an overview of criminal and civil fraud, and federal statutes and regulations that affect fraud cases. This chapter is designed to provide the building blocks of legal knowledge a fraud investigator needs to successfully open and manage a case.[1] In addition, this chapter also outlines the best evidence rule and fraudster characteristics.

---

[1] There are elements of fraud specific to certain industries, such as healthcare fraud, that are addressed in chapters 6–11 of this book.

Key Elements of Civil and Criminal Fraud

Under common law, three elements typically are necessary for *fraud* to exist:[2]

1. A material false statement made with intent to deceive (scienter)
2. Victim's reliance on the statement
3. Damages as a result of the reliance

Although the elements of civil fraud and criminal fraud are much the same, the main difference is that criminal fraud requires a higher burden of proof. *Black's Law Dictionary*[3] indicates that "the distinction between willful (i.e. criminal) and an intentional (i.e. civil) fraud is not always clear, but civil fraud carries only a monetary, noncriminal penalty." *Criminal fraud* is further defined as "fraud that has been made illegal by statute and that subjects the offender to criminal penalties such as fines and imprisonment."

For criminal fraud to occur, and be successfully prosecuted, a defendant is assumed to be innocent. The burden of proof is on the state to prove a defendant is guilty beyond a reasonable doubt. *Beyond a reasonable doubt* means that the judge or jury has *no* factual basis on which to believe a defendant is innocent, opening the door to a guilty verdict.

In civil fraud, the burden of proof shifts to the plaintiff. A guilty finding must be based on the *preponderance of evidence* or, in layman's terms, a more than 50 percent probability that a defendant committed the fraud. The judge or jury's determination typically rests on whether the plaintiff has met the burden of proof, largely through the presentation of stronger—or more compelling—evidence. Issues concerning civil process and criminal procedure are covered in much greater detail in chapter 4, "Civil Process and Criminal Procedure," of this book.

Scienter

Scienter is a material false statement with intent to deceive. Most CPAs are familiar with the term "materiality," typically in the context of whether a specific disclosure would materially change any decisions made by a user of financial statements. This concept is similar to the common law fraud requirement, under which a material false statement is made with the intent to deceive a person, class of people, corporation, or other entities. A representation is material if the statement in question changed the person's or entity's decision to part with its money or other assets.

As defined by *Black's Law Dictionary*, *intent* is the state of mind accompanying an act, especially a forbidden act. Although motive is an inducement to take an action, intent is the mental resolution to actually do it. That is why it is important for investigators to review any contemporaneous documentation created by a fraudster, which can assist the judge or jury in determining whether or not there was fraudulent intent. This documentation can include e-mails, memos, accounting records, invoices, contracts, and many other types of records.

---

[2]   www.journalofacctountancy.com/Issues/2004/Oct/BasicLegalConcepts.htm.
[3]   Bryan A. Garner, ed., *Black's Law Dictionary*, 9th ed. (Thompson Reuters, 2009).

Bear in mind that a lack of contemporaneously created documents can also provide evidence. For example, in a situation in which an agreement or contract was allegedly created, the lack of a signed and dated document can show that no such contract existed. Legal counsel in such cases will often supplement their claims with sworn statements by the victim, which offer circumstantial evidence that no contract or agreement was ever made.

Victim's Reliance on the Statement

Under certain laws, a victim must have relied on a false statement in order for fraud to have occurred. For instance, a person might invest in a corporate security business because the corporation's representative or marketing materials falsely indicate the investment is yielding a 20 percent return. In fact, returns for the underlying business could be yielding much lower returns or, in some extreme cases, the company itself might not actually exist. If the investor had full knowledge of these underlying facts, it is far less likely that he or she would make an investment.

Damages

Continuing with the previous example, the person who invested in the corporate security business based on false statements most likely suffered a loss for some or all of his or her investment.

From a legal viewpoint, compensation for that loss (damages) can be actual or punitive. *Actual damages* are amounts awarded to repay actual losses.[4] On the other hand, *punitive damages* are awarded in addition to actual damages when it is proven that a defendant acted with "recklessness, malice, or deceit; specifically damages assessed by way of penalizing the wrong-doer or making an example of others."[5] Although the fraud investigator typically assists in determining actual damages, a judge or jury is responsible for any punitive damage awards.

Summary

Although many statutes require some aspect of intent or willfulness in fraud cases, some do not. In fact, some state and federal statutes relax or even eliminate the element of reliance, and some do not even require a showing of causation or injury. Therefore, the investigator should always request the applicable statutes from legal counsel.

Federal Legal Principles

The following section outlines some of the more commonly encountered jurisdictional issues and legal principles encountered by fraud investigators when dealing with white collar criminal activity.

---

[4] *Id.*

[5] *Id.*

State and Federal Jurisdiction

The creation and enforcement of most criminal laws was historically left to state statutes. Gradually, the federal government became more active in this area, and modern-day criminal prosecutions are generally subject to overlapping state and federal laws.

To create a criminal law, the federal government must find authority in the U.S. Constitution. Many federal white collar criminal statutes are based upon the commerce clause, which requires that any illegal activities involve interstate commerce.[6] However, the meaning of interstate commerce has been interpreted broadly, and it can even cover purely intrastate activities.[7] Due to the broad construction of the commerce clause, it is rare for federal white collar criminal prosecutions to be overturned for violating the Constitution.

Under the doctrine of dual sovereignty, a defendant may be prosecuted by both the state and federal government for the same crimes without violating the double jeopardy clause.[8] When a state prosecution is ongoing or has concluded, the choice to prosecute at the federal level is left to the federal prosecutor. However, to do so the prosecutor must satisfy the following three federal criteria as listed in the *United States Attorneys' Manual*:

> [F]irst, the matter must involve a substantial federal interest; second, the prior prosecution must have left that interest demonstrably unindicted; and third, applying the same test that is applicable to all federal prosecution, the government must believe that the defendant's conduct constitutes a federal offense, and that the admissible evidence probably will be sufficient to obtain and sustain a conviction by an unbiased trier of fact.[9]

Parallel Proceedings

Criminal proceedings are only allowed to be brought by the government, and any decision to pursue criminal sanctions is usually at the discretion of the prosecutor. Conversely, civil proceedings can be brought by private individuals, organizations, and certain governmental agencies. Both criminal and civil proceedings can be initiated against a defendant at the same time for the same conduct, often referred to as *parallel proceedings*.

Parallel proceedings have the potential to prejudice a defendant's case, because the rights that an individual enjoys under criminal proceedings may not exist in civil matters. For example, the Fifth Amendment right against self-incrimination allows a criminal defendant to refuse to answer questions or produce certain documents that may lead to self-incrimination.

---

[6] Other constitutional provisions that create federal jurisdiction for white collar criminal statutes include the postal clause and the taxing power.

[7] Activities that are conducted solely intrastate may be subject to the commerce clause if the activity could have a substantial effect on interstate commerce. See *Wickard v. Filburn*, 317 U.S. 111 (1942) (the amount of wheat a farmer can grow for personal consumption may be regulated as the national wheat market could be substantially affected if every farmer were to grow wheat for his or her own personal consumption).

[8] *Rinaldi v. United States*, 434 U.S. 22, 27 (1977); *Petite v. United States*, 361 U.S. 529 (1960).

[9] U.S. Department of Justice, "Dual and Successive Prosecution," in *United States Attorneys' Manual* (2009), sec. 9-2.031(A).

The defendant's choice to remain silent cannot be used against him or her during the criminal trial, and the judge or jury is not allowed to draw inferences from the defendant's silence. However, in most civil cases, a defendant has no privilege against self-incrimination. In that legal setting, remaining silent may actually help implicate the defendant.

In cases when parallel proceedings take place, defendants may ask for the civil case to be stayed until the criminal case is completed. The best opportunity for a defendant to obtain a stay is when he or she can show the civil action is being pursued in bad faith or by malicious government tactics, such as using the civil case for the sole purpose of obtaining evidence for a criminal trial.[10]

Federal Prosecutor's Decision to Prosecute

A federal prosecutor has broad discretion in deciding when, who, and how to prosecute under a federal criminal statute. Under Section 9-27.220 of the *United States Attorney's Manual*, a federal prosecutor should proceed with a criminal prosecution

> if he/she believes the person's conduct constitutes a Federal offense and that the admissible evidence will probably be sufficient to obtain and sustain a conviction, unless, in his/her judgment, prosecution should be declined because: 1) No substantial Federal interest would be served by prosecution; 2) The person is subject to effective prosecution in another jurisdiction; or 3) There exists an adequate non-criminal alternative to prosecution.

For white collar crimes, the decision of whether to pursue federal criminal action is perhaps more discretionary than in any other criminal area for two reasons: (1) many white collar criminal statutes are overly broad, allowing for an easier determination that a conviction could be sustained, and (2) most white collar crimes are pursued at the state level or by noncriminal means, such as civil or administrative penalties, which the prosecutor may deem as sufficient punishment.

Organizational Criminal Liability

Legally created entities, such as corporations, partnerships, and associations, are sometimes referred to as "legal persons," because these entities share many of the same rights, and are subject to many of the same duties, as individuals. Among these are the ability to sue and be sued and the potential to be found guilty of crimes. Under the doctrine of respondeat superior,[11] a corporation may be held criminally liable for the illegal acts of its directors, officers, employees, and agents. To hold a corporation liable for illegal actions, the government must establish that the corporate agent's actions "(i) were within the scope of his duties and (ii) were intended, at least in part, to benefit the corporation."[12]

---

[10] *Securities and Exchange Commission v. Dresser Industries, Inc.* 628 F.2d 1368, 1375-6 (D.C. Cir. 1980).

[11] www.law.cornell.edu/wex/respondeat_superior.

[12] U.S. Department of Justice, Principles *of Federal Prosecution of Business Organizations* (Title 9, Chapter 9-28.200).

To satisfy the "within the scope of his duties" criteria, the government must show that the action taken by the corporate agent was one he or she is authorized to perform.[13] For the "intended to benefit the corporation" element to be satisfied, the government must show some nexus between the agent's conduct and a potential benefit to the corporation ("[W]hether the agent's actions ultimately redounded to the benefit of the corporation is less significant than whether the agent acted with the intent to benefit the corporation.").[14] This factor could be met even when the corporate agent is acting primarily on his or her own behalf, if the court can find that the agent's actions will lead to some indirect benefit to the company.[15]

Normally, when deciding whether criminal actions should be brought against a corporation, a federal prosecutor will analyze a case using the same tools as those employed to evaluate individual fraud. However, because organizations can only take actions through the conduct of an agent, some additional facts are taken into consideration. Box 2-1 lists the additional factors that must be considered by federal prosecutors when deciding whether to bring criminal charges against a corporation (note that these factors are neither exclusive nor conclusive).

Box 2-1: Charging a Corporation: Factors to Be Considered*

1. The nature and seriousness of the offense, including the risk of harm to the public, and applicable policies and priorities, if any, governing the prosecution of corporations for particular categories of crime

2. The pervasiveness of wrongdoing within the corporation, including the complicity in, or condonation of, the wrongdoing by corporate management

3. The corporate history of similar conduct, including prior criminal, civil, and regulatory enforcement actions against it

4. The corporation's timely and voluntary disclosure of wrongdoing and its willingness to cooperate in the investigation of its agents

5. The existence and adequacy of the corporation's pre-existing compliance program

6. The corporation's remedial actions, including any efforts to implement an effective corporate compliance program or to improve an existing one, to replace responsible management, to discipline or terminate wrongdoers, to pay restitution, and to cooperate with the relevant government agencies

7. Collateral consequences, including disproportionate harm to shareholders, pension holders, and employees not proven personally culpable, and the impact on the public arising from the prosecution

8. The adequacy of the prosecution of individuals responsible for the corporation's malfeasance

9. The adequacy of remedies such as civil or regulatory enforcement actions

---

* www.justice.gov/dag/speeches/2006/mcnulty_memo.pdf

---

[13] *United States v. Potter*, 463 F.3d 9, 25 (1st Cir. 2006).

[14] *United States v. Automated Medical Laboratories*, 770 F.2d 407 (4th Cir. 1985).

[15] See *United States v. Automated Medical Laboratories*, 770 F.2d 407 (4th Cir. 1985).

Federal Statutes

The following section outlines important federal criminal statutes that white collar crime investigators commonly encounter. The summaries are intended to introduce the statutes as well as some of the critical fraud elements related to each one. For a complete understanding of the intricacies of these statutes, fraud experts should rely upon attorneys or prosecutors because those individuals determine whether a crime applies to alleged conduct and know what elements need to be proven to sustain a conviction.

Criminal Fraud

Criminal statutes aimed at prohibiting fraud differ at the federal and state levels. In state statutes, common law prohibitions against fraud may exist that require certain elements to be proven, such as intentional misrepresentation, reliance, causation, or damages; the federal code has no criminal statute against common law fraud with the aforementioned elements. Instead, federal law uses fraud, or a concept based on fraud principles, as one of the necessary elements to a crime. For example, the mail fraud statute requires the prosecution to a show that a defendant "devised or intended to devise a scheme or artifice to defraud."[16] Because this alone is not sufficient to sustain a conviction, the prosecution will also have to show that the U.S. mail was used to help execute the fraud. As this example shows, federal criminal statutes combine fraudulent conduct with an additional action or requirement.

Because the concept of fraud takes on different meanings in different statutes, it does not need to meet the same proof standard in criminal cases as it does under common law. Although some federal criminal statutes may only require a showing of an intentional misrepresentation and completely disregard the elements of reliance, causation, and damages, others may require all four common law fraud elements to satisfy the fraud criteria. It is this type of flexibility that makes it easier to bring fraud cases under the federal white collar criminal statutes. For instance, the mail fraud requirement that a defendant "devised or intended to devise a scheme or artifice to defraud"[17] is interpreted very broadly, so that even conduct in which no affirmatively false statements were made can meet the requirement.

Conspiracy to Defraud the United States

Crimes and Criminal Procedure, U.S. Code Title 18, Section 371 simply states:

> If two or more persons conspire either to commit any offense against the United States, or to defraud the United States, or any agency thereof in any manner or for any purpose, and one or more of such persons do any act to effect the object of the conspiracy, each shall be fined under this title or imprisoned not more than five years, or both.

---

[16]   *Crimes and Criminal Procedure, U.S. Code* (USC) Title 18, Section 1341.
[17]   *Id.*

This statute is a favorite of prosecutors and was famously referred to as "that darling of the modern prosecutor's nursery."[18] The reasons for this statute's popularity include the vague concepts of "conspire . . . or to defraud the United States," which provide courts and prosecutors with great discretion. To *conspire* is an "inchoate"[19] crime, meaning that the final objective of an alleged crime never needs to be achieved. An individual can be charged under this statute merely by forming an agreement and partaking in conduct that furthers the crime's potential final objective.

Although the concept of defrauding the United States has been interpreted broadly by the courts, it does have limits. In a summary of rulings in which various courts interpreted the term "defraud the United States," a majority found that this element is satisfied if the prosecution showed that the defendants' actions affected the government in at least one of three ways: "1) They cheat the government out of money or property; 2) They interfere or obstruct legitimate Government activity; or 3) They make wrongful use of government instrumentality."[20]

Other notable conspiracy statutes are found in 18 USC 1349. This statute was enacted after the accounting scandals in the early 2000s, and it adds conspiracy violations to the following fraud offenses found in Chapter 63 of the USC:

- Mail fraud (18 USC 1341)
- Wire fraud (18 USC 1343)
- Bank fraud (18 USC 1344)
- Health care fraud (18 USC 1347)
- Securities fraud (18 USC 1348)
- Failure of corporate officers to certify financial reports (18 USC 1350)

Unlike 18 USC 371, these conspiracy crimes do not require the prosecution to show any act or conduct taken by the defendant toward achieving a crime's final objective. In fact, 18 USC 1349 requires only that prosecutors demonstrate that a defendant agreed to partake in unlawful conduct. The penalties for these offenses are also much greater than in 18 USC 371, ranging from 10–30 years imprisonment.

Mail and Wire Fraud

The mail and wire fraud statutes provide powerful tools for federal prosecutors, and they are often added to more substantial offenses. The power of these statutes is based upon their broad construction, combined with minimal proof requirements. For example, to get a conviction using the mail fraud statute, a prosecutor must prove two elements: (1) the defendant devised or intended to devise a scheme to defraud (or to perform a specified fraudulent act), and (2) the mails were used for the purpose of executing, or attempting to execute, the scheme (or specified fraudulent acts).[21] Another reason these statutes are so powerful is that,

---

[18] *Harrison v. United States,* 7 F.2d 259, 263 (2d Cir. 1925).

[19] criminallaw.uslegal.com/incohate-crimes/

[20] U.S. Department of Justice, *United States Attorneys' Manual* (2009), sec. 9-42.001.

[21] *Schmuck v. United States*, 489 U.S. 705, 721n10 (1989).

like conspiracy, they are also inchoate. Therefore, a conviction can be obtained even though the crime was never completed and no injury was sustained.

The requirement that mails be used for the purpose of executing a fraud scheme does not, in and of itself, mandate actual use of the U.S. mails.[22] A finding that the mailing was "incident to an essential part of the scheme"[23] will suffice. The same test applies to wire fraud statutes, but substitutes "any type of wire communication or transfer" (such as phone, Internet, or electronic communication) or "use of the mails."

The statutes also require the defendant to have devised or intended to devise any "scheme or artifice to defraud."[24] This phrase does not mean a case needs to meet the elements of civil fraud. In mail and wire fraud statutes, the phrase "scheme or artifice to defraud" has been left relatively undefined by the courts, which has allowed juries and judges greater discretion in what type of conduct can be subject to these laws. This vague language has created an unclear line between normal business practices and criminal conduct. In *Lustiger v. United States*, the U.S. Supreme Court had to decide whether a land developer, who had mailed an investor kit containing a 32-page color brochure that contained no express false statements, had violated the mail fraud statute. The court concluded that although no individual statement in the materials was literally false, the overall investor kit was fraudulently misleading and deceptive, thus meeting the "scheme or artifice to defraud" requirement.

Fraud and False Statements

18 USC 1001(a) is often referred to as the false statement statute. It prohibits knowingly and willfully making false statements to agents of the federal government. The penalties for violation of this statute may include fines and up to five years imprisonment.

To violate this statute, a defendant must have made a material statement that the individual knew to be false or misleading. Any volunteered statement (whether written or oral) will suffice, and a false or misleading statement may also be found when defendants conceal material facts or remain silent when they have a duty to speak.[25]

To obtain a conviction under this statute, prosecutors will need to show that a defendant knew the statement was false at the time it was made, and that a defendant intended to deceive by making the statement. These factors can become difficult to prove when dealing with contractual terms and future events, and most courts will find that promises made in contracts are not factual assertions and therefore would not likely apply to 18 USC 1001.[26]

---

[22] 18 USC 1341 criminalizes all mailing, even those placed with private parcel carriers, regardless of whether the mailing crosses state lines. See *United States v. Photogrammetric Data Serv.*, 259 F.3d 229, 248 (4th Cir. 2001).

[23] *Schmuck v. United States,* 489 U.S. 705 (1989).

[24] The definition of *scheme to defraud* has been determined to have identical meanings under both statutes. See *Carpenter v. United States*, 484 U.S. 19, 25n6 (1987) ("The mail and wire fraud statutes share the same language in relevant part, and accordingly we apply the same analysis to both sets of offenses here.").

[25] *United States v. Irwin*, 654 F.2d 671, 678–79 (10th Cir. 1981).

[26] See *United States v. Blankenship* 382 F.3d 1110, 1135 (11th Cir. 2004).

However, if the defendant intends to break a contractual promise at the time it is made, some courts will find the deception criteria satisfied.[27]

The fraud and false statements statute also requires a specific statement to be made "within the jurisdiction of the executive, legislative, or judicial branch of the Government of the United States."[28] Some circuit courts have interpreted this quite broadly to include statements that were indirectly made to the federal government, as well as statements that have the ability to influence federal agencies.[29]

A 1998 Supreme Court ruling in *Brogan v. United States* extended the applicability of this statute to explicit statements that deny wrongdoing. The Court concluded that even a simple "no" in response to the prosecution asking about the defendant's guilt fell under the reach of 18 USC 1001. Although the Court acknowledged the defendant's Fifth Amendment right to decline to answer the government's question, it also ruled that such a response mislead and adversely affected the government's efforts. It should be noted that subsections (b) and (c) of 18 USC 1001 exclude most communications used in judicial and congressional proceedings from applicable criminal conduct cited under subsection (a).

Racketeer Influenced and Corrupt Organizations Act

The Racketeer Influenced and Corrupt Organization Act (RICO) is another powerful criminal statute available to federal prosecutors.[30] Unlike most criminal statutes, RICO does not make any act or conduct specifically illegal. Instead, RICO provides additional criminal and civil remedies if past criminal actions were taken and the structural requirements of RICO have been met.

The requirements necessary to satisfy a RICO claim are (1) the defendant committed 2 or more of the statutes enumerated violations within a 10-year period, (2) the existence of an enterprise engaged in interstate commerce, and (3) one of the substantive requirements in 18 USC 1962(a), (b), or (c) are met.

The enumerated federal violations upon which a RICO claim can be based are listed in 18 USC 1961(1) and include federal crimes such as mail and wire fraud, bribery, money laundering, and securities fraud. The statute also includes "any act or threat involving murder, kidnapping, gambling, arson, robbery, bribery, extortion, dealing in obscene matter, or dealing in a controlled substance . . . which is chargeable under State law and punishable by imprisonment for more than one year." Any two of these violations in a 10-year period will satisfy the first requirement. It is important to keep in mind that actual criminal convictions are not necessary in order to meet the two violation requirement.

---

[27] *United States v. Shah* 44 F.3d 285, 296 (5th Cir. 1995).

[28] 18 USC 1001(a).

[29] *United States v. Lutz* 154 F.3d 581 (6th Cir. 1998).

[30] Due to the broadness of the Racketeer Influenced and Corrupt Organization (RICO) Act and the state's interests in prosecuting criminal conduct, the Department of Justice requires that all criminal prosecutions under RICO be approved by its Criminal Division. (See U.S. Department of Justice, *United States Attorneys' Manual* (2009), sec. 9-110.220.)

For purposes of this statute, *enterprise* is defined as "any individual, partnership, corporation, association, or other legal entity, and any union or group of individuals associated in fact although not a legal entity."[31] Because the courts have broadly construed the interstate commerce requirement, they require only a showing of common purpose, a relationship among those associated with the enterprise, and a long enough period for associates to pursue the enterprise's purpose.[32]

Finally, one of the substantive requirements of 18 USC 1962(a), (b), or (c) must be met. Essentially, one of these subsections is met if the prosecutor can show either (1) "[i]ncome derived from a pattern of racketeering activity being invested in, or used to control an enterprise" [33] or (2) "the defendant, as an agent of the enterprise, participated in the enterprise's racketeering activities."[34] A defendant who did not actually commit one of the offenses listed in the 18 USC 1962(a), (b) or (c), but who conspired to commit one of the offenses, can still be found to have violated RICO under the conspiracy requirements of subsection (d).

Civil remedies are also available under 18 USC 1964(c), which states that "[a]ny person injured in his business or property by reason of a violation of Section 1962 of this chapter may sue therefore in any appropriate United States district court and shall recover threefold the damages he sustains and the costs of the suit, including reasonable attorney's fee…" In recent years, private party (or civil) suits have become the primary focus of the RICO statute, and those legal actions have slight differences from the criminal requirements. For example, actions against a private party only need to show a preponderance of the evidence, rather than the more challenging reasonable doubt burden required in a criminal case. In addition, a private party must prove causation and show that damages were suffered as a result of a defendant's illegal actions. This will often require strong evidence showing a connection between the defendant's improper conduct and the plaintiff's damages. A four-year statute of limitation is applicable to civil RICO claims.[35]

Money Laundering

Money laundering is the "act of transferring illegally obtained money through legitimate people or accounts so that its original source cannot be traced."[36] The two main statutes that cover this type of activity are 18 USC 1956 (laundering of monetary instruments) and 18 USC 1957 (engaging in monetary transaction in property derived from specified unlawful activity). Violation of either of these statutes may result in fines in excess of the value of the property involved, lengthy prison sentences, forfeiture of property used in the crime, or a combination of these.[37]

---

[31] 18 USC 1961(4).

[32] *Boyle v. United States*, 129 S Ct. 2237 (2009).

[33] 18 USC 1962(a) and (b).

[34] 18 USC 1962(c).

[35] *Agency Holding Corp. v. Malley-Duff & Associates, Inc.*, 483 U.S. 143 (1987).

[36] Bryan A. Garner, ed., *Black's Law Dictionary*, 9th ed. (Thompson Reuters, 2009).

[37] See 18 USC 1956(a)(1)(B); 18 USC 1957(b); 18 USC 981.

In money laundering cases, 18 USC 1956 applies to transactions used to hide the original source of illegally obtained funds. Like RICO, a previous crime must have been committed before this statute will apply. The statute outlines specific crimes that can serve as the source for illegal funds, including narcotics violations, murder, extortion, fraud (including tax fraud), and bribery, as well as many crimes covered under the RICO statute.

To sustain a conviction under 18 USC 1956, the prosecution must prove the defendant: (1) attempted to or did conduct a transaction, (2) knew that the transaction involved funds from some illegal activity, and (3) knew the transaction was used to conceal or had the intent of concealing the illegal funds. According to Section 2101 of the *United States Criminal Resource Manual,* each separate financial transaction should be charged separately in an individual count. For example, if an individual deposited $100,000 into an account from the original criminal offense, that person would be committing a second offense under 18 USC 1956 if he or she withdraws $50,000 of the illegal proceeds. He or she then would commit a third 18 USC 1956 offense if he or she purchases a car with the $50,000.[38]

18 USC 1957 is satisfied if the transaction, which must involve a financial institution, is for an amount greater than $10,000, and if the defendant knew the property was derived from illegal activities. This section is not concerned with the concealment of illegally obtained property but rather with the transferring of property the defendant knew was obtained from illegal activities. Because "transaction" and "financial institution" are broadly defined in this section, a money laundering crime's critical element usually centers on a defendant's knowledge of the property source.

18 USC 1956(h) adds a powerful tool for prosecutors by subjecting "[a]ny person who conspires to commit any offense defined in [either] section [1956] or section 1957 . . . to the same penalties as those prescribed for the offense the commission of which was the object of the conspiracy." This provision can be useful when the prosecution is looking to make a deal with one of the parties involved.

Computer Fraud and Abuse

Crimes that rely on the use of a computer have their own federal criminal statute—18 USC 1030. This statute is important for white collar criminal experts to understand, because many white collar crimes are facilitated with the use of computers. The prohibited acts in this statute often overlap state laws, the wire fraud statute, and various other federal criminal provisions.

The Department of Justice's *Computer Fraud and Abuse Manual* (CFAA) breaks the criminal conduct of 18 USC 1030(a) into the nine areas listed in Box 2-2.[39] Each of these areas contains separate penalties, which are based upon incident seriousness and the fraudulent outcome. Prison sentences related to CFAA crimes can range from one year to life in prison.[40] 18 USC 1030(b) also criminalizes attempts to commit or to conspire to commit any of the listed offenses.

---

[38]   U.S. Department of Justice, "Money Laundering" in *United States Criminal Resource Manual,* sec. 2101.

[39]   www.justice.gov/criminal/cybercrime/docs/ccmanual.pdf.

[40]   18 USC 1030(c).

Box 2-2: Summary of *Computer Fraud and Abuse Manual* **Provisions**

Offense	Section
Obtaining National Security Information	(a)(1)
Compromising the Confidentiality of a Computer	(a)(2)
Trespassing in a Government Computer	(a)(3)
Accessing a Computer to Defraud & Obtain Value	(a)(4)
Intentionally Damaging by Knowing Transmission	(a)(5)(A)
Recklessly Damaging by Intentional Access	(a)(5)(B)
Negligently Causing Damage and Loss by Intentional Access	(a)(5)(C)
Trafficking in Passwords	(a)(6)
Extorting Involving Computers	(a)(7)

Source: Department of Justice, *Computer Fraud and Abuse Manual.*

Although each of the nine crimes may cover different types of conduct, some recurring conditions exist that can help fraud investigators determine whether this statute will apply. For example, 18 USC 1030(a)(5)(C) prohibits intentionally accessing a "protected computer without authorization," thereby causing damage and loss. A *protected computer* is defined in 18 USC 1030(e)(2) as a computer "which is used in or affecting interstate or foreign commerce or communication," as well as any computer used by the United States government or a financial institution. "Without authorization" normally refers to an outsider who has no permission to use a computer or device. Other sections require the defendant to be "exceeding authorized access,"[41] which refers to an insider who has permission to use a computer or device, but gains access to areas which he or she was not authorized to view.

Note that the line between "without authorization" and "exceeding authorized access" can be grey, and it often must be evaluated on specific facts and circumstances. Although both types of actions are criminalized under some CFAA offenses, many other violations apply only to one or the other.

18 USC 1030(g) provides private parties with civil causes of action for violations of this statute. These actions must be brought within a two-year period beginning on the date of the prohibited act or the date the damage was discovered. Possible remedies include compensatory damages, injunctions, and other equitable remedies.

---

[41] 18 USC 1030(a)(1), (a)(2), and (a)(4).

Tax Related Crimes

Criminal statutes that apply to tax cases are found within the Internal Revenue Code (IRC) as well as the USC. Some of the more important statutes include the following:

- Felony tax evasion (IRC Section 7201)
- Willful failure to collect or pay taxes (IRC Section 7202)
- Willful failure to file a return or supply information (IRC Section 7203)
- Making or assisting in fraud or false statements (IRC Section 7206)
- Conspiracy to commit offense or defraud the United States (18 USC 371)

It is important to understand that only the Department of Justice has the power to bring these actions and not the IRS.[42] In a typical case, an IRS agent will begin an investigation before seeking the assistance of the Department of Justice to bring a criminal action.

All tax crimes require the government to show that the defendant's act, or failure to act, was done *willfully*. In most criminal statutes, the willful element is satisfied if the government can show that the defendant intended to commit the act. Thus, the willfulness element does not require any showing that the defendant intended to break the law; it simply requires proof that the act was committed.[43] In the case of criminal tax statutes, willfulness takes on two requirements. The first is a showing that the defendant intended to commit the act (similar to normal criminal statutes). The second criteria, which requires the government to prove that defendants knew they were violating the law, was established by the Supreme Court in *Cheek v. United States*. This criteria was justified on the basis that the tax code made it difficult for people to understand their obligations and duties.[44]

Tax Evasion (IRC Section 7201)

Tax evasion is a felony, subject to a $100,000 fine, imprisonment of up to 5 years, or both. Common forms of tax evasion include hiding income or overstating expenses and deductions. To commit tax evasion, the defendant must willfully underpay his or her required tax amount by engaging in an affirmative act of fraud or misrepresentation. This statute can often be used to convict those who obtain income from illegal activities, as most taxpayers do not report their illegal income.

False Returns (IRC Section 7206)

The filing of a false return or other related documents is also a felony punishable by up to $100,000, 3 years in prison, or both. In order to prove this crime, the government must show that a defendant willfully submitted a materially false document and that a defendant signed the document under potential penalty of perjury.[45] (Federal income tax returns are subject to

---

[42]   U.S. Department of Justice, *Criminal Tax Manual* (1994), sec. 6-1.100.

[43]   Courts often refer to this concept by stating that "ignorance of the law is no defense."

[44]   498 U.S. 192, 199–200 (1991).

[45]   Internal Revenue Code (IRC) sec. 7206(2) also creates criminal provisions for those who aid or assist in the preparation of a false tax document and subjects them to the same penalties as violations under IRC sec. 7206(1).

the penalty of perjury and have to be signed.) Proving the tax return contained a false statement does not require any tax deficiency. Instead, the government only needs to show that a false statement was made within the document. Like the tax fraud statute, the false statement will usually be related to unreported income or false expense and deductions.

Failure to File or Pay Taxes (IRC Section 7203)

Failure to file or pay taxes is a misdemeanor and will subject a defendant to a fine of not more than $25,000, imprisonment of not more than 1 year, or both, in addition to the actual taxes due with penalties. This section makes it a crime for a taxpayer to willfully fail to act in a manner required by the tax code. Examples of required acts include filing a return, paying a tax, keeping records, and supplying information. The most common use of this statute is for the failure to file a tax return.

Conspiracy to Defraud the United States (18 USC 371)

It should also be noted that the conspiracy statute related to defrauding the United States can also be used to prosecute attempted tax crimes. Therefore, if the government can show that an agreement exists in which the parties to the agreement intend to frustrate the IRS's efforts to determine or collect taxes, the government will have met the requirements of the conspiracy statute.

Federal Asset Forfeiture Provisions

The federal forfeiture provisions are designed to provide the government with tools to remove financial benefits gained by violating the law. The Department of Justice has stated it intends to use "the asset forfeiture statutes to the fullest extent possible to investigate, identify, seize, and forfeit the assets of criminals and their organizations."[46] The use of this power by the Department of Justice resulted in the seizure of more than $2 billion in assets during 2005 and 2006 alone.[47]

The three types of asset forfeiture actions are

- administrative (*Customs Duties, U.S. Code*, Title 19, Section 1607),
- criminal (18 USC 982), and
- civil (18 USC 981).

The process and rules by which assets can be seized under these three statutes differ significantly in some respects and are highly controversial. The following Department of Justice exhibit in Box 2-3 outlines the basic criteria for each type of forfeiture action. The forfeiture power is widely used in drug and white collar crime cases. For that reason, it should be generally understood by a fraud investigator who may be asked to identify potential forfeitable property.

---

[46] U.S. Department of Justice Asset Forfeiture Program, *National Asset Forfeiture Strategic Plan 2008–2012*, 3.
[47] *Id.*

Box 2-3: What Are the Types of Federal Forfeiture?

Forfeiture is the taking of property derived from a crime, involved in a crime, or that which makes a crime easier to commit or harder to detect.

A. Administrative Forfeiture

Administrative forfeiture is the process by which property may be forfeited to the United States without judicial involvement. Federal seizing agencies perform administrative forfeitures. Seizures must be based on probable cause. The authority for a seizing agency to start an administrative forfeiture action is found in 19 U.S.C. § 1607.

Administrative forfeiture can be used to seize and forfeit the following:
- any amount of currency;
- personal property valued at $500,000 or less, including cars, guns, and boats;
- hauling conveyances of unlimited value.

Real property cannot be forfeited administratively.

If the property owner files a claim, the administrative forfeiture process stops and the Government must bring a forfeiture action in federal court or return the property to the claimant. The seizing agency forwards the claim to the United States Attorney's Office for action.

B. Judicial Forfeiture

Judicial forfeiture, civil and criminal, is the process by which property may be forfeited to the United States by filing a forfeiture action in federal court.

Criminal Forfeiture

Criminal forfeiture is an action brought as part of the criminal prosecution of a defendant that includes the forfeiture of property used or derived from the crime. If the defendant is convicted, the judge or the jury may find that the property is forfeitable. Forfeiture is limited to the property interests of the defendant and only to property involved in the particular counts on which the defendant is convicted. Only the defendant's interest can be forfeited in a criminal case because criminal forfeiture is part of the sentence in the criminal case. For example, if the defendant used someone else's car to commit a crime and the owner of the car was not indicted for the crime in which the car was used, the car cannot be forfeited in the criminal case. Instead, a civil forfeiture case can be filed against the car.

If a third party claims an interest in the property that the Government seeks to forfeit criminally, the issue is determined in an ancillary hearing before the court only after the criminal trial is completed, the defendant convicted, and a preliminary order of forfeiture is entered. Once the interests of third parties are resolved, the court issues a final order of forfeiture. The order of forfeiture might not happen for months or years, even if the forfeiture is uncontested, resulting in a delay in the disposal of the property.

If the property subject to forfeiture is no longer available, the court can enter a money judgment or order the forfeiture of substitute assets.

Civil Forfeiture

Civil forfeiture is a proceeding brought against the property rather than against the person who committed the offense. Civil forfeiture does not require either criminal charges against the owner of the property or a criminal conviction.

To obtain a federal forfeiture, the Government must prove the forfeiture and the connection between the property and the crime by a preponderance of the evidence. Forfeiture may be applicable to property that is traceable as proceeds of the offense, that facilitated the offense, or that was involved in money laundering. All claims of interest or ownership in the property, such as property owned by third parties, are resolved in a single trial.

Source: U.S Department of Justice, Criminal Division, "What Are the Types of Federal Forfeiture?," in *Guide to Equitable Sharing for State and Local Law Enforcement Agencies* (April 2009).

Table 2-1: Summary of White Collar Criminal Statutes

Crime	U.S. Code			Key Elements	Penalty
	Title	Chapter	Section(s)		
Conspiracy to Defraud the United States	18	19	371	Conspire—Requires the forming of an agreement or engaging in actions leading to the crime. Defraud the United States—Involves cheating the government out of money or property, interfering with a government activity, or a wrongful use of government instrumentality.	Fine, imprisonment not more than 5 years, or both.
Mail Fraud	18	63	1341	Scheme or Artifice to Defraud—Refers to a liberally interpreted element that allows great discretion. The scheme must involve a parcel carrier.	Fine, imprisonment not more than 20 years, or both.
Wire Fraud	18	63	1343	Scheme or Artifice to Defraud—Refers to a liberally interpreted element that allows great discretion. The scheme must involve a communication, such as a phone, the Internet, television, signs, and so on.	Fine, imprisonment not more than 20 years, or both.
Fraud and False Statements	18	47	1001	Knowingly and Willfully—Requires the offender to understand that his or her actions will mislead. The fraud must be perpetrated upon the executive, legislative or judicial branch of the federal government.	Fine, imprisonment not more than 5 years, or both.

Crime	U.S. Code			Key Elements	Penalty
	Title	Chapter	Section(s)		
Racketeer Influenced and Corrupt Organizations Act	18	96	1961–1968	Requires the defendant to have committed two other crimes while engaged in an enterprise.	Fine, imprisonment not more than 20 years, or both; possible forfeiture of property involved.
Money Laundering	18	95	1956–1957	Knowledge that transacted property was involved in or obtained from illegal activity.	Fine of $500,000 or twice the value of the property involved, whichever is greater, imprisonment for not more than 20 years, or both.
Computer Fraud and Abuse	18	47	1030	This statute covers various activities conducted with computers and other devices when the user has accessed the device without authorization or by exceeding his or her authorized access. Without Authorization—Refers to someone who does not have permission to use a device. Exceeding Authorized Access—Refers to someone with permission to use a device but not in the manner he or she used it.	Various fines, prison terms, or both, depending on the subsection.
Tax Evasion	26-F	75-A	7201	Willfully—Refers to a voluntary, intentional violation of a known legal duty; requires the defendant knew the rules and chose not to follow them. The violation must result in an underpayment of taxes.	Fine of not more than $100,000, imprisonment not more than 5 years, or both.
Failure to File or Pay Taxes	26-F	75-A	7203	Willfully—Refers to a voluntary, intentional violation of a known legal duty; requires the defendant knew the rules and chose not to follow them. Violations include, not filing a return, paying a tax, or keeping required records.	Fine of $25,000, imprisonment not more than one year, or both.
False Returns	26-F	75-A	7206	Willfully—Refers to a voluntary, intentional violation of a known legal duty; requires the defendant knew the rules and chose not to follow them. The violation must result in a false statement being made on a tax return or statement.	Fine not more than $100,000, imprisonment not more than 3 years, or both.

Best Evidence Rule

Fraud investigators must also be aware of the *best evidence rule*, which *Black's Law Dictionary* defines as

> the evidentiary rule providing that, to prove the contents of a writing (or a recording or photograph) a party must produce the original writing (or a mechanical, electronic, or other familiar duplicate, such as a photocopy) unless it is unavailable, in which case a secondary evidence—the testimony of the drafter or a person who read the document—may be admitted.

This definition offers a good rule of thumb: Fraud investigators should make immediate photocopies of their evidence and lock down any original pieces of evidence so that accidental or intentional destruction of evidence is avoided at all costs.

3

On- and Off-the-Books Fraud Schemes

Seth Craig
Chad Dolly, MBA
Randal A. Wolverton, CPA/CFF, CFE

| Legal Foundations of Fraud Investigations |
| On- and Off-the-Books Fraud Schemes |
| Civil Process and Criminal Procedure |
| Jury Instructions |
| Regulatory Complexities |
| Working the Case |
| Find It and Fix It |

Introduction

Occupational frauds, those perpetrated within the scope of someone's employment, may be either on–the–books or off-the-books frauds. This chapter is devoted to an overview of both types of frauds.

On-the-Books Schemes

An *on-the-books* scheme is characterized by illegal transactions, such as employee embezzlement of funds or corporate financial statement fraud, that are recorded on a company's books. These types of transactions create an audit trail, which can aid in detecting the fraud. As noted in figure 3-1, on-the-book fraud schemes initiated by employees typically involve deliberate misuse of cash receipts, disbursements, or inventory and other assets.

Figure 3-1: On-the-Books Employee Fraud Schemes

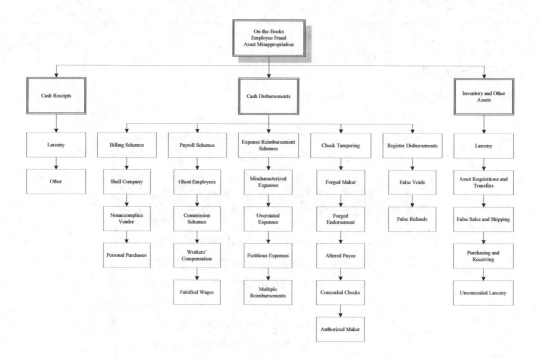

The following sections provide a closer look at the three main on-the-books categories, and the multiple subcategories, involving employee fraud that fraudsters often use to pursue illegal activities.

Larceny Schemes

The primary on-the-books cash receipts fraud is *larceny*, which is any scheme in which cash is stolen after it has been recorded on an organization's books.[1] For example, assume an employee steals $100 in cash or checks from $500 in daily receipts before a bank deposit is made. Under this example, the books will reflect that $500 was deposited into the bank, instead of

---

[1]   Association of Certified Fraud Examiners (ACFE), *Report to the Nations on Occupational Fraud and Abuse: 2010 Global Fraud Study* (2010).

the $400 that was actually deposited. A journal entry or some other type of adjusting entry will be made to the cash account to "reconcile" the general ledger to the bank statement.

A second larceny scheme involves cash on hand misappropriations.[2] An example of this activity is when an employee steals cash from an organization's vault. In order to account for the missing money, some type of false entry is recorded on the books.

Cash Disbursements

Cash disbursement schemes are those in which a payment or other transfer of company funds is made in what appears to be a normal manner. These schemes can be perpetrated by forging a check, submitting a false invoice, or manipulating documentation.[3] Illegal cash disbursement activity can be further broken down into schemes involving billing, payroll, expense reimbursement, check tampering, and cash register operation.

Billing Schemes

Billing schemes occur when a person causes an employer to issue payment based on false or misleading information. An example of a billing scheme is when an employee creates a shell company and then bills the employer for services not actually rendered. Another example is when an employee purchases personal items and then invoices the employer for payment.[4] Billing schemes are popular among fraudsters, because the individual does not have to physically take cash or merchandise from the company.

Example

A man who was a computer expert and worked on a system conversion for his employer was able to set up a shell company thus becoming a payee of his employer. He billed the company many thousands of dollars for airplane parts using four invoices. Two invoices were paid, and the man cashed the checks.

In examining the man's financial records, FBI agents noted trips to Las Vegas and expensive perfume. The man indicated he had taken his wife to Las Vegas because they like to gamble and that he bought her the perfume. Questioning of the wife disclosed she never took trips to Las Vegas with her husband and he never gave her perfume. (The man had his share of problems after that conversation.) Again, the fraud left its trail not only on the books of the company but in the financial records of the fraudster whose spending was outside the norm.

---

[2]   *Id.*

[3]   Joseph T. Wells, *Occupational Fraud and Abuse* (1997).

[4]   ACFE, *Report to the Nations on Occupational Fraud and Abuse: 2010 Global Fraud Study* (2010).

> **Example**
>
> A man sold merchandise to his employer for $600,000 that he purchased for $20,000. There was no disclosure to his employer's company that he owned the company selling the merchandise. Not only was the man lacking in remorse for the failure to act in his employer's best interest, he also had an unusual sense of how significant his actions were. All he would admit to was that he had perhaps "charged the company just a little too much."

Sometimes, the transfer of goods does occur just as the books reflect, but the transaction itself is one that is based on a significant conflict of interest wherein the company pays far more than it should for the goods and someone on the inside of the company profits.

As the previous two case studies (and those elsewhere in this book) demonstrate, fraudsters often expect a day of Armageddon, when their actions come to light, and typically they have a story ready to explain their actions. They also hope that they can repay just a small amount of their theft and that everyone will just move on. Even when legal counsel gets involved, the fraudster holds back on disclosures, often causing the attorney to be taken by surprise by the investigator's findings.

Payroll Schemes

Payroll schemes occur when an employee causes the employer to issue payment by making false claims for compensation. These schemes can take on a number of different forms. For example, a ghost employee ruse happens when an employee "creates" a nonexistent worker, often using his or her personal address as supporting documentation. If successful, payroll checks are generated for the ghost employee and sent directly to the fraudster, who can easily cash them.

Some additional payroll schemes include

- falsifying hours schemes, when an employee claims overtime for hours not worked.
- commission schemes, when a fraudster may either falsify sales figures or increase the rate of commission.
- false workers' compensation schemes, when an employee simply fakes an injury on the job and collects workers' compensation.

Expense Reimbursement Schemes

Expense reimbursement schemes happen when an employee claims reimbursement for fictitious or inflated business expenses.[5] Like payroll fraud, expense schemes can manifest themselves in a variety of ways. A fraudster may mischaracterize expenses by simply submitting

---

[5]   *Id.*

personal expenses for reimbursement, or he or she may overstate expenses by either altering actual business receipts or exceeding "usual and customary" business costs. An example of the latter, taken from Joseph T. Wells's *Occupational Fraud and Abuse*, occurred when a fraudster purchased two tickets for business travel—one expensive and one cheap. He returned the expensive ticket but retained the receipt, and then flew using the cheaper airline ticket. Upon his return, he submitted the more expensive receipt for reimbursement.

Other common fraudulent expense reimbursement activities include fictitious expense schemes in which an employee invents a purchase and submits false documentation or receipts for reimbursement and multiple reimbursement schemes, which occur when an employee submits the same expense multiple times but uses different documentation for each submission.

Check Tampering Schemes

Check tampering is a type of fraudulent disbursement scheme in which an employee either prepares a check for his or her own benefit or intercepts a check intended for a third party and converts the check to his or her own benefit.[6] The most common methods to perpetrate this type of ruse include forged maker, forged endorsement, altered payee, concealed check, and authorized maker schemes.

A forged maker scheme takes place when a fraudster actually signs another person's name on a check. For that reason, a fraudster typically has access to the check(s) before such forgery can take place, although in today's electronic environment similar checks can be created using home computer software. Forged maker frauds typically happen in one of three ways:

1. *Free-hand forgery*—The fraudster physically signs the authorized individual's name.
2. *Rubber-stamped forgery*—The fraudster has a stamp with the authorized individual's name.
3. *Electronic forgery*—The fraudster has access to an electronic version of the authorized individual's signature.

In the third scenario, the fraudster is easily able to print a check with the signature already on it

In the forged maker scheme, fraudsters can use any of the following four methods to cash a check:

1. They can make the check payable to themselves, even though that raises the risk their real names will be associated with a fraudulent check.
2. They can make the check payable to an accomplice, who then cashes it and splits the proceeds with the fraudster. In this instance, no direct documentation exists to identify the fraudster.
3. They can make the check payable to cash.
4. They can make the check payable to a vendor.

---

6   Joseph T. Wells, *Occupational Fraud and Abuse* (1997).

In the fourth option, the fraudsters would receive goods or services paid for by company funds. Other check tampering ruses include

- forged endorsement schemes, which occur when an employee intercepts a company check intended for a third party and then converts the check by signing the third party's name on the endorsement line.[7]
- altered payee schemes, which occur when a fraudster intercepts a third party's check, alters the payee to be either him or herself or an accomplice, and then cashes it.
- concealed check schemes, which occur when a fraudster prepares a fake check and submits it to an authorized individual for a legitimate signature.

In order for the latter scheme to be successful, the authorized individual cannot be paying attention to what he or she is signing.

Finally, an authorized maker scheme occurs when an authorized individual prepares a fraudulent check for his or her own benefit and then signs his or her own name in order to cash it.[8]

Example

A woman admitted that she concocted a check tampering scheme because, in her words, "they (her bosses) were stupid" (Her words, uttered during pre-sentencing discussions, did not serve her well, and the look on her attorney's face was priceless as she uttered them). She stole company checks and wrote them to herself. She always took checks that were later in sequence than the checks being used for legitimate transactions. The bank did not return original checks, but it did supply a copy of each check in sequential order on printouts attached to the statements. Because her checks were last in the sequence, she recopied the last pages with those checks covered up.

The previous example highlights a few things that are important to fraud examiners. First, the woman's co-workers had noticed her spending (a classic red flag), but she told them that she "inherited money." Second, a simple, cost-effective and efficient technique could have led to early detection of this problem. In addition to showing the total dollar amount of the disbursements, the bank statements typically show the total number of disbursements. A quick comparison between the total disbursements and the number of checks visible on the printouts would have yielded the first clue that something was amiss.

Also, the company's owners had been scratching their heads wondering what was happening to the money. The company's revenues were good, but it was moving towards the brink of bankruptcy. The woman perpetrating the fraud was in a position of trust and was able to deflect the owners' questions. This is yet another example of why *trust is not an internal control*, and when something doesn't look right, an independent examiner may be well worth his or her cost.

---

[7] *Id.*

[8] *Id.*

Cash Register Disbursement Schemes

Cash register disbursement schemes involve any circumstance in which an employee makes false entries on a cash register to conceal the fraudulent removal of cash.[9] Typically, cash register disbursement schemes are perpetrated by means of false refunds or false voids. A false refund occurs when an employee processes a refund through the register in a normal way, but with no customer and no inventory returned to the company. In this scam, the cash register indicates that money was appropriately removed as a part of the refund, when in fact the fraudster stole the cash from the register. A key risk for this type of scheme is overstated inventory, unless the fraudster has access to the inventory system and can make appropriate adjustments.

When processing a legitimate void on a cash register, common practice is to request the original cash register receipt and obtain a manager's signature. In order for a fraudster to execute a false void, he or she will usually keep a customer's receipt, process a void on the transaction, and pocket the cash amount authorized through the register. As a next step, the fraudster will present the void to a manager for signature. All too often, the manager will simply sign the void, not knowing a fraud has occurred.

Inventory and Other Assets

Inventory and other asset schemes are those in which an employee steals or improperly uses an organization's noncash assets.[10] Examples of improper use of noncash assets include using company vehicles, technology, or equipment for personal purposes. In cases when noncash assets are stolen, the ruse most often involves larceny, asset requisitions and transfers, purchasing and receiving, and false shipment schemes.

Like cash larceny, noncash asset larceny schemes occur when an employee simply takes inventory from the company after it is recorded on the books. A key characteristic of this scheme is that the fraudster does not attempt to conceal stolen goods by creating fictitious documentation. In an asset requisition and transfer scheme, the fraudster has access to internal systems and documentation, and he or she simply transfers noncash assets from one location to another. In the midst of the transfer, the fraudster will take the merchandise for personal use or sale. In a purchasing and receiving noncash asset larceny scheme, the fraudster will take home a portion of company-ordered goods. This means that the firm not only paid for product it did not receive but also is short that number of goods needed for the intended use. Finally, false shipment noncash asset larceny schemes occur when a fraudster takes assets from the company, and he or she creates false shipping documentation to make it appear like the missing inventory was shipped to a customer. In these instances, the shipping documentation most often will have fake shipping information.

---

[9]   ACFE, *Report to the Nations on Occupational Fraud and Abuse: 2010 Global Fraud Study* (2010).
[10]   *Id.*

On-the-Books: Corporate Fraud

Although many frauds begin on the balance sheet, many educated fraudsters attempt to move that illegal activity to the income statement through a journal entry. This occurs for two reasons: (1) balance sheet accounts are currently subject to more scrutiny by auditors than income statement accounts, and (2) after 12 months, income statement accounts are closed out to one of the largest numbers on the balance sheet—retained earnings—never to be reviewed again.[11] For example, if a fraudster is embezzling receivable payments, a subsequent journal entry would remove the receivable to the income statement by writing off the account.

Improper Asset Valuations[12]

One type of financial statement misstatement is improper asset valuations, as shown in figure 3-2. Two common asset valuations, which are often done improperly, include the overstatement of inventory or receivables. Other improper asset valuations involve manipulating business purchase price allocations in an effort to inflate future earnings, misclassifying fixed assets, or improperly capitalizing inventory or startup costs. In accordance with U.S. generally accepted accounting principles (GAAP), most assets must be recorded at their historical or acquisition cost. However, for some balance sheet items, particularly inventory, the "lower of cost or market" rule requires that when an asset's cost exceeds its current market value, the asset must be written down to market value.

Figure 3-2: On-the-Books Corporate Fraud Schemes

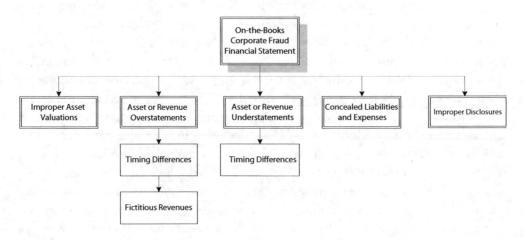

---

[11] Thomas W. Golden, Steven L. Skalak, and Mona M. Clayton, *A Guide To Forensic Accounting Investigation* (2011).

[12] Additional information can be found in Joseph T. Wells' *Corporate Fraud Handbook* Second Edition (2007).

Inventory Valuation Schemes[13]

Inventory is initially recorded at the acquisition cost. Subsequently, if cost is determined to be higher than current market value, inventory should be written down to its current value (or written off altogether if it has no value). When appropriate write-downs do not take place, the result is overstated assets and a mismatch of cost of goods sold with revenue.

Inventory valuations can be manipulated in several ways, such as altering the physical inventory count, creating fictitious (phantom) inventory, inflating unit costs used to price out inventory, and failing to record inventory for cost of goods sold. Inventory valuation schemes may also include creating fake documents such as inventory count sheets and receiving reports. Many of these inventory fraud techniques can be detected through the use of computer-assisted audit review techniques.

Accounts Receivable Schemes[14]

Similar to inventory valuations, accounts receivable can be easily manipulated, and the schemes are often conducted together. Two of the most common accounts receivable frauds are the creation of fictitious accounts receivable and failure to write off accounts receivable as bad debt. Fictitious receivables are often the result of fake revenue, often created by companies experiencing financial problems as a ruse to mask underlying issues. The common scheme is to debit (increase) accounts receivable and credit (increase) sales. The typical time for these illegal acts to occur is around the end of the accounting period, because accounts receivable should be paid in cash within a reasonable time period. The illusion of fictitious receivables can often be extended by providing false account balance confirmations to auditors and by setting up fake customer locations that are typically either a home address or the business address of a co-conspirator. Common methods to detect such fraud include a review of business credit reports, public records, and even on-line telephone books to identify allegedly significant customers with no verifiable physical address.

Under Financial Accounting Standards Board (FASB) *Accounting Standards Codification* (ASC) 450, *Contingencies*, companies are required to book losses on uncollectible receivables (bad debt) when certain conditions are met and to record impairment of goodwill intangibles[15] and long-lived assets.[16] Because booking losses will have a negative impact on earnings, companies struggling to show profitability may be tempted to avoid recognition of such losses in order to avoid the negative impact on earnings.

---

[13] *Id.*

[14] *Id.*

[15] See Financial Accounting Standards Board (FASB) *Accounting Standards Codification* (ASC) 350, *Intangibles—Goodwill and Other.*

[16] See FASB ASC 360, *Property, Plant, and Equipment.*

Business Combination Schemes[17]

Companies that undergo a business combination are required to allocate the purchase price to tangible and intangible assets of the acquired business under FASB ASC 805, *Business Combinations*. As a result, companies must determine the fair value of the acquired tangible and intangible assets, with any excess of the purchase price over the value of acquired assets treated as goodwill. Although goodwill is no longer amortized for book purposes (but is tested for impairment annually), definite-lived intangible assets are amortized over their remaining useful life. As a result, companies have an incentive to reduce the value allocated to amortizing intangibles, while overstating the value of goodwill in order to avoid reducing current earnings. To accomplish this, companies may argue for significant buyer specific synergies or overvalue the assembled workforce—both of which are components of goodwill. Other common tactics include overstating attrition rates on customer relationships or underestimating the remaining useful life on acquired trademarks and trade names.

Fixed Assets Schemes[18]

The final category of improper asset valuations involves the manipulation of fixed assets. Common illegal activities in this category include booking fictitious assets, misrepresenting asset valuations, and improperly capitalizing nonasset costs.

Perhaps the easiest way to misrepresent asset values is to record fictitious assets, which affect account totals on a company's balance sheet. One basic method is to create fictitious documents that contain fake (and often inflated) asset amounts and illegitimate receivables. Another method includes recording expenses for business use that are actually for personal use. To cover the fraud, companies will often raise cash through illegal offerings of securities, which may lead to bankruptcy if the fraud is uncovered.

The second example of fixed asset manipulation is to misrepresent the asset value. In accordance with GAAP, fixed assets should be recorded at cost. Although it is widely recognized that assets may appreciate in value, the increase generally should not be recognized on a company's financial statements. Several financial statement fraud cases involve the reporting of fixed assets at market values instead of the lower acquisition cost. Companies may also overinflate the value of fixed assets by failing to record impairments of long-lived assets under FASB ASC 360, *Property, Plant, and Equipment*, and goodwill under FASB ASC 350, *Intangibles—Goodwill and Other*.

A final way in which asset values are misrepresented is through capitalizing nonasset costs and misclassifying assets. Typically, the price of a purchased asset excludes the interest and finance charges incurred in the purchase. For example, monthly payments associated with a capital equipment purchase include both principal reduction and interest payments. However, on initial purchase, the original cost of the asset alone should be capitalized, with the associated interest payments charged to interest expense. However, many companies will choose to capitalize the interest and finance charges as a way to overinflate asset values. On misclassification, some companies

---

[17]   Additional information can be found in Joseph T Wells' *Corporate Fraud Handbook* Second Edition (2007).

[18]   *Id.*

will place assets into incorrect general ledger accounts in order to meet budget requirements. This can skew financial ratios and allow the company to comply with loan covenants the business might not otherwise meet. These schemes can go undetected for long periods of time, because a detailed fraud examination would be necessary to uncover overvalued and misclassified assets.[19]

Example

Enron was created in 1985 as a merger between Houston Natural Gas and InterNorth, a Nebraska pipeline company. Although Enron originated as a traditional natural gas supplier, it quickly developed into a "gas bank," meaning the company made money by buying gas from a network of suppliers and selling to a network of consumers. It made money by charging a fee for its service of contractually guaranteeing both the supply and the selling price of the gas. Under this business model, Enron was required to borrow substantial sums of money to finance operations. It created special-purpose entities (SPEs) to borrow money, which allowed it to keep the debt off its own balance sheet. The accounting rules in place at the time allowed Enron to contribute up to 97 percent of assets and equity to an SPE, which would allow the SPE to borrow its own money. However, Enron could still claim the profits or losses on its own books.

Enron also took advantage of "mark-to-market accounting" to boost profits. Mark-to-market accounting requires a company to book both realized and unrealized gains and losses on energy-related contracts each quarter. Enron took advantage of the fact that no specific rules existed on how to value such contracts. As a result, Enron consistently valued them to show gains, which would offset the effect of issuing more stock to fund the SPEs. In addition, Enron was allowed to claim the income from unrealized holdings gains, which helped increase its return on assets. More than half of its $1.4 billion pretax net income was generated by unrealized holding gains by 1999. Enron eventually setup thousands of SPEs for various purposes, including hiding losses from derivative contracts when the economic boom of the 1990s started to dwindle. The various SPEs which Enron created to hide its losses should have been disclosed in the footnotes to the financial statements, but management failed to be transparent in its dealings. In October 2001, the Enron scandal began to unfold when it was forced to disclose that it was taking a $1.0 billion charge to earnings to account for the poorly performing business segments. It also had to reverse $1.2 billion in assets and equities booked as a result of the failed SPEs. Enron filed for bankruptcy on December 2, 2001, and Enron's auditor, Arthur Andersen & Co., closed its doors on August 30, 2002.

Key warning signs that improper asset valuation may have occurred include the following:[20]

- Companies reporting earnings and earnings growth, yet displaying recurring negative cash flows from operations
- Increased number of business failures in either the industry or the overall economy
- Atypical increase in gross margin or margin in excess of industry peers
- Atypical growth in the number of days' sales in receivables
- Atypical growth in the number of days' purchases in inventory

---

[19] *Id.*

[20] *Id.*

- Allowances for bad debts, obsolete inventory, or both that are shrinking in percentage terms or out of line with industry peers
- Large and unexplained changes in the relationship between fixed assets and depreciation

Asset or Revenue Overstatement or Understatement Schemes

One of the most difficult and controversial areas of accounting is determining when revenue should be recognized. A fraud investigator must understand the general rules of revenue recognition, as well as any revenue considerations that may pertain to a specific industry (see FASB ASC 605, *Revenue Recognition*, for more detail).

Fictitious Sales of Products Schemes

FASB ASC 605-10-25-1 states that "the recognition of revenue and gains involves the consideration of two factors a) being realized or realizable and b) being earned."[21] Thus, revenue is realized when products (goods or services), merchandise, or other assets are exchanged for cash or claims of cash. Similarly, revenue is realizable when assets received or held are readily convertible to known amounts of cash or claims of cash. For revenue to be earned, an entity must have substantially accomplished its assigned objectives, such as delivering or producing goods or performing services or other activities central to its operations. These general principles are imperative for the fraud investigator to understand when looking for improper revenue recognition schemes.

When investigating the possibility of fictitious product sales, motive is one of the first things a fraud investigator should consider. Typical questions a fraud investigator will ask are as follows:

- Does the potential fraud perpetrator want to under record revenue for tax savings reasons?
- Are there debt covenants that a company would want to manipulate, which would increase retained earnings and accounts receivable or decrease inventory?
- Is there an incentive for a sales representative to increase revenue for a bonus or decrease revenue to shift compensation to another period?
- Are there sales to related companies or the same companies at the end or a period?

Financial statement schemes involving general revenue recognition at the sales representative or management level typically involve simple concepts, including the following:

- Recording fictitious sales in one period, then writing them off to the sale returns and allowances expense account in another period. In this situation, the revenue has neither been realized nor earned. Examples of fictitious or sham sales include swaps

---

[21] For revenue recognition criteria when the right of return exists or when repurchased and subject to an operating lease refer to FASB ASC 650-15-25 for further guidance.

or round-trip trades. A *swap* occurs when two entities, typically related or closely affiliated, exchange goods, making it appear that each sold a product and has an account receivable. The financial statement effect of this product swap is to increase assets and retained earnings at the end of the period. Meanwhile, a *round-trip trade* would culminate with the products being returned to the original company and the transaction being reversed on the company's books in a subsequent period.

- Accelerating product shipments. This is usually an attempt to record the products shipped as a sale, despite the fact that revenue has not been realized because products have not been exchanged for cash or claims of cash at the time of the shipment. According to FASB ASC 605-10-S99-1, persuasive evidence of the timing of an exchange arrangement is typically determined by correspondence and sales documentation.

- Holding the books open for sales made subsequent to the end of the accounting period. This is similar to accelerating product shipments in the sense that the revenue has not been realized because products have not been exchanged for cash or claims of cash during the accounting period. Again, the investigator should look for persuasive evidence about when the sales occurred, because this is necessary to determine the correct accounting period in which to record the sale.

- Recognizing revenue for transactions that do not actually qualify as sales. This may include consignment sales not yet sold to the end user, sales with special conditions, certain bill-and-hold transactions, and products shipped for trial or evaluation purposes. Again, when investigating these types of frauds, understanding general revenue recognition principles is imperative.

Overstating Percentage of Completion Schemes

According to FASB ASC 605-35-25-51, the "percentage-of-completion method recognizes income as work on a contract progresses." There are specific circumstances when this revenue recognition method can be used. The percentage-of-completion method is a preferred accounting policy for entities that can reasonably estimate settlement terms, such as when goods or services will be provided, consideration is exchanged, and buyer and contractor can be expected to perform their contractual duties.

The key to cost-of-completion revenue recognition lies in the ability of a contractor to make "reasonable estimates." The presumption is that contractors who perform work as part of their continuing operations have sufficient knowledge to make such estimates (FASB ASC 605-35-25-58). Because of this reliance on the entity for a reasonable estimate, the opportunity exists for the business to create a false estimate, leading to fraudulent or misleading financial statements. With that in mind, the fraud investigator needs to look at how the estimate was created and determine if, given the contemporaneous facts and circumstances, it was or was not reasonable. An important consideration is documentation created when the estimate was made, including any evidence about possible motivation for creating fraudulent or misleading estimates (such as loan compliance or income tax considerations). The fraud investigator should consider the following key indicators:

- Hours of labor expended compared to the hours of labor bid, which helps to determine the progress of the contract
- Cost of materials compared to the total cost of materials anticipated for the contract
- Similar contract estimates in other periods, such as previous or subsequent quarter or year-end
- Debt covenant restrictions or requirements, such as monthly or quarterly management submissions to financial institutions
- Previous reliability of the contractor's estimates

Other Revenue Recognition Schemes

Inquiries into suspected improper revenue recognition usually begin with confirmation that the company's financials are in alignment with GAAP accounting (unless another type of accounting method is specified), and with the terms of customer contracts. In order to understand improper or illicit revenue recognition, the fraud investigator must understand GAAP policies. The following are overviews of revenue recognition policies, each of which reinforces the underlying concept that revenue must be realized or realizable and earned in order to be recognized.

1. *Multiple-element arrangements*—In this case, revenue recognition is based on the concept that multiple deliverables should be divided into separately identifiable units at the onset of an arrangement. This type of arrangement occurs when

   a. the product can be sold on a standalone basis by the customer;
   b. the fair value of the undelivered items can be determined; and
   c. if the delivered items can be returned, control of such returns is owned by the entity, not the customer (FASB ASC 605-25-55-1).

   The potential for improper or fraudulent revenue recognition in multiple-element arrangements occurs when revenue is recognized for the delivered portion of a contract, but the criteria for the undelivered portion are not met. For example, if a customer takes delivery of the first shipment, but has the ability to reject all remaining shipments because of quality or other concerns in the first shipment, revenue cannot be recognized on any of the shipments.

2. *Grouping of contracts*—In contrast to a multiple-element arrangement, a group of contracts may be combined for accounting purposes if the contracts

   a. are negotiated as a package;
   b. are essentially an agreement to do a single project;
   c. require closely interrelated construction activities with substantial common costs; and

    d. are performed concurrently and are in substance with a single customer. (FASB ASC 605–35–25–8).

Consistency is an important consideration for fraud investigators when assessing this type of revenue recognition policy. With that in mind, it is important to review current and past group contract arrangements, seeking to verify that revenue recognition was handled in the same fashion for all contracts meeting these criteria.

3. *Industry specific revenue recognition policies*—GAAP accounting provides for particular revenue recognition policies based on industry specific criteria and timing. When a fraud investigator is working within a specific industry, it is imperative to have detailed familiarity with the revenue recognition policies of that industry. Table 3–1 provides a list of industry revenue recognition codification topics that a fraud investigator should reference when during a revenue recognition case.

Table 3-1: Industry Revenue Recognition Codification Topics

Codification Topic	Description
605–905	Agriculture
605–908	Airlines
605–910	Contractors—Construction
605–912	Contractors—Federal Government
605–915	Development Stage Entities
605–920	Entertainment—Broadcasters
605–922	Entertainment—Cable Television
605–924	Entertainment—Casinos
605–926	Entertainment—Films
605–928	Entertainment—Music
605–932	Extractive Activities—Oil and Gas
605–940	Financial Services—Brokers and Dealers
605–942	Financial Services—Depository and Lending
605–944	Financial Services—Insurance
605–946	Financial Services—Investment Companies
605–948	Financial Services—Mortgage Banking
605–952	Franchisors
605–954	Health Care Entities
605–958	Not-for-Profit Entities
605–970	Real Estate—General
605–972	Real Estate—Common Interest Realty Associations
605–974	Real Estate—Real Estate Investment Trusts
605–976	Real Estate—Retail Land
605–978	Real Estate—Time Sharing Activities
605–980	Regulated Operations
605–985	Software

Concealed Liabilities and Expenses

Concealed or understated liabilities and expenses are the mirror image of overstated assets. The easiest way to understand how to conceal liabilities is by analyzing the underlying motivations. Executive management's motivation to conceal liabilities is completely different from the impulse that might drive an accounts receivable clerk to commit a fraudulent act. Typically, executive management's motivation would focus on how the recorded liability would affect the balance sheet for external reporting purposes. For example, an on-the-books concealment of a liability would be altering accounts payable to falsify a company's compliance with its lending institution's debt service coverage ratio.[22]

Example

A lending institution that initiated a commercial real estate mortgage may stipulate and monitor a debt service coverage ratio threshold to determine the debt an income producing property can support. If the debt-service coverage ratio is 1.00x, the commercial property is breaking even, whereas a debt-service coverage ratio of less than 1.00x would indicate that the property would not break even.

If the lending institution requires a debt-service coverage ratio of 1.20x, a company having financial troubles might conceal the problem by underreporting its mortgage liabilities. A fraud in which a mortgage is not reported would typically be perpetrated by executive management or owners because they have the authority to make or authorize journal entries, change auditor reports, or take other actions to maintain the company or property.

Understanding liabilities is the first step in comprehending how they could be concealed, manipulated, or not appropriately disclosed in an entity's financial statements. Certain types of liabilities are common to all types of entities, whereas certain liabilities are unique to one type of industry. Thus, it is important for an investigator to understand the types of liabilities that the entity under investigation might potentially have.

Understatement of liabilities and expenses is the mirror image of overstatement of assets, and auditors can use various analytical indicators to search for such schemes, including the following:

- An increasing current ratio (current assets divided by current liabilities) or quick ratio (cash plus marketable securities plus net receivables divided by current liabilities) from one period to the next
- Unexpected improvements in gross margins from one period to the next
- Change in inventory with no simultaneous increase in accounts payable or accrued expenses between periods
- A percentage of change in the accrued expense account that shows revenue to be increasing faster than accrued expenses

---

22 Debt-service coverage ratio equals net operating income divided by total debt service.

— Unrecorded accounts payable
— Improper classification of long-term versus short-term liabilities
— Unrecorded environmental liabilities
— Unauthorized debt extinguishment
— Off balance-sheet financing

Improper Disclosures

Improper disclosures involve inaccurate, incomplete, unintelligible, or fraudulent notes and footnote disclosures in the company's financial statements. This type of fraud is most likely perpetrated by the company's management because it is in the position to write and influence the disclosures.

Off-the-Books Schemes

Off-the-book fraud schemes normally occur outside the accounting environment, where audit trails are unlikely to exist. Examples of off-the-book fraud schemes include asset misappropriation, corporate fraud, corruption, and cyber crimes, as shown in figure 3-3. For fraud investigators, it is important to note that these frauds are often detected in an indirect manner.

Figure 3-3: Off-the-Books Employee Fraud Schemes

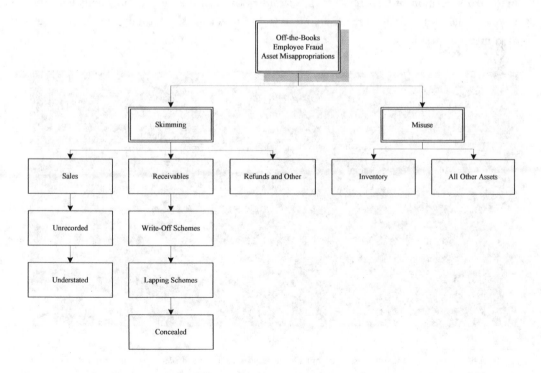

Asset Misappropriations

Fraud examiners can easily spot disbursement fraud by checking for falsified, missing, or destroyed documents.[23] However, when the asset misappropriation occurs off-the-books, it becomes more difficult to identify and investigate the fraudulent activity.

Skimming

Skimming is any scheme in which cash is stolen from an organization before it is recorded on the books. An example would include an employee who accepts a customer payment, but then pockets the money without recording the sale.[24]

Register manipulation can also assist with a skimming scheme. For example, a fraudster may choose to ring a "no sale" or other noncash transaction and again pocket the money received from the customer. While the false transaction is processed as a true sale, the employee is actually stealing the customer's money. Another common occurrence of register manipulation is when the employee rigs the cash register to not record false transactions on the register tape. With no documentation of a sale, there is no audit trail to be investigated.

Nonbusiness hour schemes are also a prevalent way for fraudsters to pursue off-the-book skimming. In this type of scam, employees conduct sales during nonbusiness hours without knowledge of the business owners. The proceeds are then pocketed by the fraudsters. Any documentation, such as register tapes, that result from nonbusiness hours sales are simply destroyed.

Even though asset misappropriations made up nearly 90 percent of reported fraud cases in 2010, Association of Certified Fraud Examiners (ACFE) reports such incidents have the lowest median losses of the three main fraud types (financial statement fraud, corruption, and asset misappropriations).

Example

In the banking world, unique frauds can occur simply because of the large volume of cash that is handled and the number of transactions processed. One scheme involved a woman in a position of authority at a bank. She was stealing money from the vault. To cover the shortage in the bank, she had to find a way to replace the money. To do this, she used the dormant accounts of elderly bank customers. She would process cashier's checks against the accounts and cash those checks elsewhere. To defer detection by the customers, she found a way to withhold the statements and concocted a story for the customers to explain the absence of the statements until she had time to replace the funds and was also able to falsify the statements. This fraud went on for 6 or 7 years. The woman has admitted her role. A comment made by her son demonstrates the kind of cavalier attitude people sometimes have toward fraud. He said to investigators that he did not get what the big deal was because his mother had the loss narrowed down to $79,000.

---

[23] Joseph R. Dervaes, "Missing Disbursement Documents, Part 1," *Fraud Magazine*, July/August 2009.

[24] ACFE, *Report to the Nations on Occupational Fraud and Abuse: 2010 Global Fraud Study* (2010).

Misuse

Misuse of inventory or other assets is simply an employee using an employer's assets for nonsanctioned personal use. For example, a cabinetmaker uses his or her employer's cabinetmaking equipment to construct desks and cabinets for friends and family without the employer's approval.

Off-the-Books: Corporate Fraud

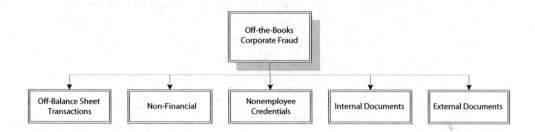

Off-Balance Sheet Transactions

In this type of fraud, a company retains the benefits of assets which do not appear on its financial statements. Substantial liabilities may also be excluded. Thus, the company looks more financially attractive. Historically, off-balance-sheet treatment has been used in the following situations:

- For securitization transactions, in which financial assets such as receivables are sold to an off-balance-sheet vehicle, while the seller retains a subordinated interest in that entity
- For leasing transactions, in which long-lived assets are acquired by an off-balance-sheet entity and the use of the assets is then conveyed to a third party through an operating lease
- In noncontrolling investments, in which assets or businesses are held by an entity that does not convey control back to the investors or unrecorded or inflated related party transactions
- Borrowing or lending either interest free or significantly above or below market rates
- Selling real estate at prices that differ significantly from appraised value
- Exchanging property for similar property in a nonmonetary transaction
- Loans with no scheduled terms for repayment[25]
- Loans with accruing interest that differs significantly from market rates

---

[25] Paragraph 3 of Statement on Auditing Standards No. 45, *Related Parties* (AICPA, *Professional Standards*, AU sec. 334 par. .03).

- Loans to parties lacking the capacity to repay
- Loans advanced for valid business purposes and later written off as uncollectible[26]
- Nonrecourse loans to shareholders
- Agreements requiring one party to pay expenses on the other's behalf
- Business arrangements whereby the entity makes or receives payments of amounts at other than market values
- Failure to adequately disclose the nature and amounts of related-party relationships and transactions as required by GAAP[27]
- Consulting arrangements with directors, officer, or other members of management
- Land sales and other transactions with buyers that have marginal credit worthiness
- Monies transferred to or from the company from or to a related party for goods or services that were never rendered
- Goods purchased or sent to another party at less than cost
- Material receivables or payables to or from related parties such as officers, director, and other employees[28]
- Discovery of a previously undisclosed related party
- Large, unusual transactions with one party or a few other parties at period end

Corruption

Corruption is one of the oldest white-collar crimes known to mankind, with documented cases of bribery that date back to biblical times. History also identifies instances of bribery and corruption into the sixteenth and seventeenth century, specifically around the time of King James I. Francis Bacon had worked his way into King James I good graces to the highest position in the king's court as lord chancellor. It was later discovered that Bacon abused his power and used his influence to sway many cases. In the 1920s, Washington, D.C., was rocked with the Teapot Dome Scandal, an incident surrounding a group of Naval Oil Reserves that were improperly handled by several key members of President Warren G. Harding's staff.[29]

Corruption can be broken down into four main elements, as discussed subsequently and identified in figure 3-4.

---

[26] Paragraph 3 of AICPA Practice Alert No. 95-3, *Auditing Related Parties and Related Party Transactions* (AICPA, *Technical Practice Aids*).

[27] See FASB Statement No. 57, *Related Party Disclosures.*

[28] See AICPA, *Accounting and Auditing for Related Parties and Related Party Transactions, A Toolkit for Accountants and Auditors* (December 2001).

[29] Joseph T. Wells, *Occupational Fraud and Abuse* (1997).

Figure 3-4: Off-the-Books Corruption Fraud Schemes

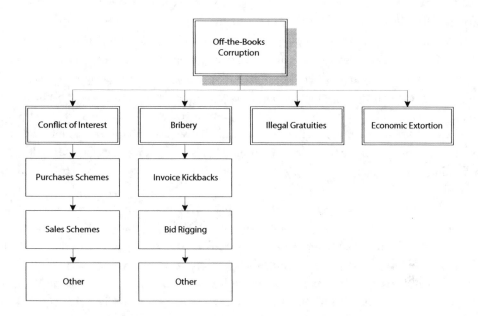

Conflicts of Interest

According to the ACFE's *Fraud Examiner's Manual,* a conflict of interest occurs when an employee, manager, or executive has an undisclosed economic or personal interest in a transaction that adversely affects the company. *Black's Law Dictionary* describes a *conflict of interest* as "a real or seeming incompatibility between one's private interests and one's public or fiduciary duties." A conflict of interest scheme occurs when an individual capitalizes on fiduciary duties and has the ability to gain from the situation. In most cases, when the fraudster takes advantage of his or her employer, the company is completely unaware of its employee's divided interests.

Conflict of interest schemes can be separated into purchases and sales. Purchase schemes occur when an employee has an undisclosed interest in a vendor. Inflated or overbilled invoices from that vendor are sent to the company for payment, appearing to be legitimate bills. For that reason, the invoices are paid, the vendor directly benefits from the inflated or overbilled amounts, and the fraudster indirectly benefits from an undisclosed interest in the vendor.

Sales schemes occur when a company sells its goods or services to another company at a severe discount, often at a loss. In most cases, the fraudster will have an undisclosed interest in the company purchasing the goods or services. For example, Bob, the fraudster, works for ABC Company. He sells discounted inventory to XYZ Company. However, Bob has not disclosed to ABC Company that he is a 50 percent silent partner in XYZ Company. By facilitating this sale, Bob helps XYZ Company benefit by receiving discounted inventory that it will turn around and sell at a higher profit. At the same time, ABC Company suffers a significant loss due to the sale.

Bribery

Black's Law Dictionary defines *bribery* as "the corrupt payment, receipt, or solicitation of a private favor for official action." The ACFE defines *bribery* as the "offering, giving, receiving, or soliciting anything of value to influence an official act." Although common belief is that bribery is associated with government agents or employees, commercial bribery occurs when something of value is offered to influence a business decision or transaction. Keep in mind that merely *offering* a payment can constitute a bribe, even if the payment is not actually made. Bribery can be further broken down into kickback and bid-rigging schemes.

Kickback schemes are undisclosed payments made by vendors to company employees, most often in the purchasing function of the business. Most commonly, the fraudster will accept a fraudulent or inflated invoice, pay it, and then receive some type of kickback from the vendor.

On the other hand, *bid-rigging schemes* take place when an employee fraudulently assists a vendor in winning a contract. For example, Joe of ABC Company is managing a project to build a commercial building. Although Joe asks several companies to submit bids for the project, he has a very good relationship with Contractor M, who recently took Joe on a trip to Las Vegas. Later, five companies submit bid proposals, with Contractor M having the most expensive bid. Rather than choosing the most economically sound proposal for ABC Company, Joe chooses Contractor M due to the "benefits" he receives from that contractor.

Conflict of interest and bribery schemes are closely related, but a key distinction exists. In a bribery case, the fraudster approves the invoice in return for a kickback. In a conflict of interest case, the employee approves the invoice because of his or her own hidden interest in the vendor.[30]

Illegal Gratuities

Although illegal gratuities are similar to bribery schemes, the former does not necessarily involve an intent to influence a particular business decision. An example of an illegal gratuity would be if a city commissioner negotiated a land development deal with a group of private investors. After the completion of the deal, the private investors "rewarded" the city commissioner with an all-expenses paid international trip. Acceptance of this gift would constitute an illegal gratuity, and it would be prohibited by most government and private company codes of ethics.[31]

Economic Extortion

Economic extortion is essentially the opposite of a bribery scheme. With this type of scam, the company demands payment from a vendor in exchange for a decision in the vendor's favor. If the vendor chooses not to make the payment, it would most likely lose business from that company.

---

[30] *Id.*

[31] *Id.*

Cyber Crime

A *cyber crime* is an electronic attack on an information system, whether individual, corporate, or governmental. The Computer Crime and Intellectual Property Section of the Department of Justice is responsible for combating worldwide computer and intellectual property crimes.[32] The categories of cyber crime are shown in figure 3-5.

Figure 3-5: Off-the-Books Cyber Fraud Schemes

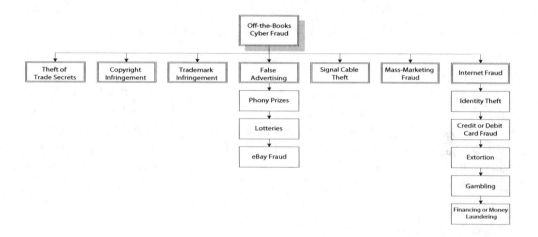

Because of the Internet's ease and global reach, clever and sophisticated fraudsters are increasingly utilizing it to steal money from victims and make the instantaneous trail of transactions difficult to reconstruct. Many online schemes are designed to obtain the personal information, account numbers, and password information, which is then resold by fraudsters to organized domestic and international criminal syndicates for future exploitation. The motives for fraudsters can range from simple vandalism to an elaborate hijacking of entire systems with hidden viruses to hide sophisticated schemes. Theft of government and business trade secrets are also known threats to the safety and security of computer networks.

Some of the most prevalent schemes are described in the following sections.

Mass Marketing Fraud

Mass marketing fraud includes any plan, program, promotion, or campaign that is conducted through solicitation by telephone, the Internet, or other means to induce multiple persons to (1) purchase goods or services; (2) participate in a contest, sweepstakes, or lottery; (3) invest for financial profit; and (4) otherwise pay advance fees or "taxes" for services that are promised but not delivered.

Put simply, mass marketing fraud schemes exploit mass communication techniques such as bulk mail, telemarketing and, more recently, the Internet. Such scams generally try to trick

---

[32]   Department of Justice Computer Crime and Intellectual Property Section, www.cybercrime.gov/.

victims to forward money or personal information for the promise of future prizes, products, or services that never come.[33]

As the name implies, international mass marketing fraud is a crime that uses distance and location as its primary means of success, making it more difficult for law enforcement to track and prosecute the perpetrators. In part, this is due to jurisdictional limits of law enforcement agencies throughout the world.

Auction Fraud

These schemes involve nonexistent products, misrepresentation of advertised products, or the nondelivery of products purchased through an Internet auction site.

Counterfeit Cashier's Checks

The biggest targets in this scam are individuals who respond to online classified advertisements. Typically, an interested party outside the United States agrees to make a purchase and then sends a cashier's check for payment in excess of the requested sales price. The seller is instructed to deposit the cashier's check and wire the difference to another location. Because banks will often release electronic funds before the fake paper check moves through the banking system, the person making the deposit is ultimately held accountable for the loss.

Credit Card Fraud

Stolen credit and debit card numbers are often used in Internet fraud schemes. The stolen numbers can be obtained through unsecured websites, stolen customer information, implanted viruses, or other online forms of identity theft.

Debt Elimination Schemes

Many legal entities use websites to advertise a legal way to dispose of mortgage loans and credit card debt. Many fraudsters will also advertise the same services, but they will require an upfront fee along with specific account details about the debt or granting of power of attorney. This usually leads to unauthorized financial transactions and, in some cases, title transfers of actual property.

Employment or Business Opportunities

Persons seeking home employment opportunities can fall victim to schemes that promise lucrative returns from work at home. Prospective employees are required to provide personal information, such as driver's license numbers, birth certificates, Social Security cards, and bank account information in which "paychecks" will be deposited. However, these bogus paychecks are often in excess of the amount owed, and the employee will be instructed to deposit the check and wire transfer the difference to the alleged employer. This poses similar problems as those noted in debt elimination schemes.

---

[33] Internet Crime Complaint Center, www.ic3.gov/media/massmarketfraud.pdf.

Escrow Services Fraud

Fraudsters will often propose the use of a third-party escrow service to facilitate the exchange of money and merchandise. The victim is unaware the perpetrator has actually compromised a true escrow website and, in actuality, created one that closely resembles it. In such cases, the victim sends money to the phony escrow service and receives nothing in return. Or, the victim sends merchandise to the subject and waits for reimbursement, which is never received.

Internet Extortion

These schemes involve fraudsters who hack into various industry databases, promising to release control to the company if funds are received or the perpetrators are given Internet administrator jobs. In many cases, the fraudsters will threaten to compromise information about consumers in the company's database unless funds are received.

Lotteries

In this scam, people are notified by e-mail that they have won an international lottery. However, an initial fee is requested by the fraudster to pay bribes or taxes to release the money. Clever concealment of the Internet address can lead victims to believe they are dealing with legitimate persons and companies in the United States when, in fact, most perpetrators are located in foreign countries.

Phishing and Spoofing

Phishing and spoofing are somewhat synonymous in that they refer to forged or faked electronic documents. *Spoofing* generally refers to the dissemination of e-mail that is forged to appear as though it was sent by someone other than the actual source. *Phishing*, often utilized in conjunction with a spoofing, is the act of sending an e-mail that falsely claims to be from a legitimate business. The goal of phishing is to dupe the unsuspecting recipient into divulging personal information, such as passwords, credit card numbers, and bank account information after directing the user to visit a specified website. The website, however, exists only as a lure to steal the user's information.

Ponzi or Pyramid Schemes

Ponzi schemes promise high financial returns of dividends to investors. However, instead of investing the funds, the con artist will take money from current investors to pay previous investors to create the appearance of earnings or interest. The scheme generally falls apart when the operator flees with the proceeds or when a sufficient number of new investors cannot be found to pay previous investors.

Pyramid schemes are similar to Ponzi schemes, however, in Pyramid schemes, the victims themselves are induced to recruit further victims through the payment of recruitment commissions. The schemes are mathematically impossible to continue and will eventually collapse leaving the last "investors" to suffer the losses.

Reshipping

Reshipping schemes usually require individuals in the United States, at times co-conspirators and at times unwitting accomplices, to receive packages at their residence. Those shipments are subsequently repackaged and sent to foreign countries. For example, assume a job applicant is hired for a role to forward, or "reship," merchandise purchased in the United States to the company's overseas office. The packages begin to arrive and, as instructed, the employee forwards the packages to their overseas destination. Unbeknownst to the "reshipper," the merchandise was purchased with fraudulent credit cards.

Spam

With improved technology and world-wide Internet access, spam (unsolicited bulk e-mail) is now a widely used medium for committing traditional white collar crimes, such as financial institution fraud, credit card fraud, and identity theft. Spam can also act as a vehicle to access computers without authorization and transmit viruses or botnets[34] to a company's systems. The subjects masterminding this spam often provide hosting services and illegally sell open proxy information, credit card information, and e-mail lists.[35]

Theft of Intellectual Property

The rise of digital technologies and Internet file sharing networks provides opportunities for fraudsters to steal intellectual property. This may include everything from trade secrets and proprietary products to movies and software, causing billions of dollars in economic losses to domestic businesses. Beyond the financial impact, theft of trade secrets and infringements on intellectual property can have a negative effect on consumers' health and safety.

Box 3-1: Quote from United States Department of Justice Acting Deputy Attorney General Gary G. Grindler

Businesses that create and rely upon intellectual property, from large entertainment conglomerates to small biotech firms, make up among the fastest-growing sectors of the U.S. economy. These industries also represent a significant portion of U.S. exports, with intellectual property now comprising a significant – and growing – share of the value of world trade.

The proliferation of worldwide Internet access and advances in traditional distribution methods, such as transportation and shipping, now allow American businesses of all sizes to market their intellectual property throughout the world. Digital content, whether embodied in software, books, games, movies, or music, can be transmitted from one corner of the world to another almost instantly.

---

[34] A *botnet* is a collection of compromised computers connected to the Internet (each compromised computer is known as a 'bot'). "Botnet," last modified April 22, 2012, http://en.wikipedia.org/wiki/Botnet.

[35] Internet Crime Complaint Center, www.ic3.gov/crimeschemes.aspx#item-17.

But these unprecedented opportunities for American businesses and entrepreneurs are put at risk by criminals and criminal organizations that seek unlawfully to profit by stealing from the hard work of American artists, authors and inventors.

For every new technological advancement by American business, there is, unfortunately, a criminal who would seek to misuse it for his own illicit purposes. Criminals are responding to American innovation with their own creative methods of committing intellectual property crimes — from wide-spread online piracy, to well-funded corporate espionage, to increased trade in counterfeit pharmaceuticals and other goods.

When we fail to enforce intellectual property rights aggressively, we fail to protect some of our nation's most important and valuable resources. The theft of even a single trade secret can completely destroy a burgeoning small business.

When criminals sell counterfeit drugs and medical devices to consumers, our nation's public health is compromised. And, when illicit products such as counterfeit airplane parts or pirated electronic components make their way into the marketplace, they place our public safety at risk.

Investment Schemes

Self-Dealing by Corporate Executives

Corporate fraud cases can include self-dealing by inside executives to include insider trading, kickbacks, backdating of executive stock options, misuse of corporate property for personal gain, related party transactions, and individual tax violations related to self-dealing. Fraudulent insider transactions can be deeply hidden without proper related-party disclosures. Back dating options can be used to manipulate the timing of trades to the benefit of the executives.

Conclusion

In this chapter, we have reviewed two major classifications of fraud—on-the-book and off-the-book—and some of the major subcategories in each. The understanding of these basic fraud classifications is imperative for the fraud investigator as this is the knowledge base expected of a practitioner and it is one of the building blocks to investigating frauds.

4

Civil Process and Criminal Procedure

Adam J. Falconer, JD
David Wharton, CPA/CFF, CFE

Legal Foundations of Fraud Investigations

On- and Off-the-Books Fraud Schemes

Civil Process and Criminal Procedure

Jury Instructions

Regulatory Complexities

Working the Case

Find It and Fix It

Introduction

Forensic accountants and fraud investigators[1] ("investigators") are commonly retained by attorneys as expert witnesses or consultants in the context of fraud investigations, civil litigation, and white collar criminal cases. Before undertaking these important tasks, it is vital

---

[1]   Each state may have different meanings for the term "investigator." When used in this book, investigator does not refer to a "private investigator" but rather forensic accountants working on fraud investigations.

that practitioners fully understand key aspects of their role in civil and criminal litigation procedures.

A must-read for all forensic accountants is AICPA Forensic and Valuation Services (FVS) Section Special Report 9-1, *Introduction to Civil Litigation Services.* This report is an excellent educational and reference primer for the practitioner who provides, or is considering, civil litigation services for clients. In addition, practitioners should also review AICPA FVS Section Practice Aid 10-1, *Serving as an Expert Witness or Consultant.*"

As a supplement to the resources noted previously, this chapter will provide the practitioner with a solid overview of five main procedural aspects of civil and criminal cases:

- Law enforcement and prosecutor investigations
- Discovery or disclosure procedures
- Tactics and other considerations
- Overview of rules of civil procedure
- Overview of rules of criminal procedure

Each high-level overview is designed to help practitioners better understand their role in an investigation and maximize their case value to client attorneys, judges, and juries.

Law Enforcement and Prosecutor Investigations

In the most general sense, fraud investigations involving law enforcement follow a pattern. Initially, a law enforcement agent or prosecutor will meet and interview the complainant (the party filing a criminal complaint). The purpose of this step is to establish why the complainant thinks the alleged fraud has been committed and how the complainant can produce facts in support of the claim. In this meeting, the complainant will be asked for documents to substantiate the loss and for the names of any potential suspects who may have had access to missing assets. Additionally, investigators will request any video footage, electronic data, or other evidence to substantiate the fraud. With this information in hand, investigators will perform preliminary research to determine whether the complainant's story has merit. If so, law enforcement typically requests help from the prosecutor's office to subpoena specific records that may uncover fraudulent activity.

Depending on the investigation's complexity, this coordination of effort between law enforcement and prosecutors may involve several rounds of subpoenas and interviews. If the resulting evidence is compelling enough, the case will be handed off to the prosecutor's office. At this stage, the prosecutor may ask law enforcement to gather additional documents or witnesses before deciding to formally charge a defendant.

Once the defendant is charged, a prosecutor may request the services of a forensic accountant or fraud investigator, particularly in complex and high-stakes cases in which evidence in the criminal investigation could be bolstered by an expert witness or consultant. Third-party investigators may also be retained by a business complainant, such as an insurance company, bank, or brokerage firm, to assist law enforcement and build a concurrent civil case against a defendant.

For complainants, law enforcement agents, and prosecutors, fraud cases can be extremely frustrating, especially when lost money or assets are converted to cash. Absent lavish spending by a suspect, it is extremely difficult even for experienced investigators to reconstruct what happened with assets converted to cash or trace where the money was spent or hidden. This is especially true when the fraud perpetrators are experienced criminals.

Another frustrating aspect of a fraud or white collar criminal case is motive—understanding why perpetrators did what they did. But in many cases, there is no obvious rationale for the illicit behavior. That lack of clear motive can make it difficult to secure a conviction (or damages in a civil case), because it runs counter to human nature for a judge or jury to convict when the alleged behavior is not easily explained. Under these circumstances, the investigator can truly add value by using forensic data, documentary support, and objective evidence to uncover the foundation of a fraud scheme. This fact-based, third-party investigative work can help prosecutors prevail in fraud cases when lack of motive might otherwise be a significant barrier.

Another frustration for complainants, law enforcement, and prosecutors occurs in smaller value fraud or white collar criminal cases, when estimated losses are deemed not enough to support the expense of hiring a forensic accountant. In such a case, an investigator may be asked to do a limited scope investigation (or even to provide pro bono assistance). Investigators must evaluate these options on a case-by-case basis, seeking to balance value they can bring to a specific investigation with the real-world needs of remaining financially viable.

Finally, investigators must understand the frustration nonfinancial people have with complex financial, accounting, legal, and business concepts. Although credible forensic accountants can perform a sound, detailed analysis of a fraud case, many use too much technical jargon when communicating their findings in front of a judge or jury. That failure to communicate can result in wasted time and a lost case.

To allay these concerns, investigators need to clearly explain what facts and documents were considered in an investigation, and then translate arcane terminology into understandable language that all parties can grasp. Armed with a thorough and understandable report, counsel can better prepare an effective line of questioning for the investigator. Just as important, a clear, easy-to-understand fraud report may force defense lawyers to decide if they want to go up against well-presented evidence—or try to cut a deal with the prosecutor.

For all of these reasons, investigators must balance the need to be technically accurate with the common sense need to be understood.

Resources for "Following the Money" in Investigations

Virtually all law enforcement agents and prosecutors will advise a novice investigator to "follow the money" in cases of suspected fraud. This is very sound advice, and the procedures and techniques employed in the realm of fraud and white collar criminal investigations give investigators the tools to pursue that objective. In addition to an investigator's own forensic accounting and fraud examination skills, two particular resources are very helpful in white collar criminal investigations.

The first, titled *Financial Investigations Guide* (with its corresponding *Financial Investigations Checklist*),[2] is published by the Asset Forfeiture and Money Laundering Section of the United States Department of Justice. This 72-page pamphlet is designed to acquaint fraud examiners with basic financial techniques that should be considered in every investigation. The guide's central theme is that by "following the money" and other assets, forensic fraud investigators can reveal the complex structure of major criminal organizations and build a case for seizures and forfeitures that will disarm those organizations.

The guide outlines various databases and tools that can aid both law enforcement and investigators, some of which are not available to the private sector. These resources can aid investigators with a variety of tasks, such as developing a work plan or crafting language for a subpoena to seek relevant bank or brokerage firm records.

A specific overview of resource categories contained in the *Financial Investigations Guide* includes the following:[3]

- Databases—Government Law Enforcement (for example, Bureau of Alcohol, Tobacco, and Firearms; Drug Enforcement Administration; INTERPOL; U.S. Customs Service; and so on)
- Databases—Commercial (for example, financial data; financial ratios, averages, and norms; and so on)
- Public records (for example, bankruptcy records, real estate records, state gaming commissions, judgment index, civil and criminal court records, and so on)
- Other records (bank examiner, credit card companies, Securities and Exchange Commission, parole and probation departments, tax files, Immigration and Naturalization Service, and so on)
- Banks and financial institutions (Right to Financial Privacy Act, account records, criminal referral forms, bank and regulator correspondence, loan records, wire transfers, and so on)
- Securities and commodities brokerage firms (account statements, securities position records, payment receipts, and so on)
- Net worth (how to calculate net worth, how to evaluate legitimate and illegitimate sources of income, ownership of assets and liabilities, beneficial ownership, and so on)
- Model subpoena language (provides sample subpoena language for various areas such as financial institution records, corporate records, telephone records, and so on)
- Debriefing informants (addresses topics on how to best use and obtain information from an informant)

---

2   U.S. Department of Justice, Asset Forfeiture and Money Laundering Section, *Financial Investigations Guide* (June 1998), available at www.justice.gov/criminal/afmls/pubs/pdf/fininvguide.pdf.

3   U.S. Department of Justice, Asset Forfeiture and Money Laundering Section, *Financial Investigations Checklist*, available at www.justice.gov/criminal/afmls/pubs/pdf/fininvcheck.pdf.

The guide does not provide an exhaustive list of all resources and information. For areas outside of these categories, it recommends that investigators identify and follow up with information specialists who can best provide any needed case-specific information.

The *Electronic Crime Scene Investigation: A Guide for First Responders (Second Edition)*[4] is another resource that is very helpful in white collar criminal investigations, particularly in the areas of recognizing, collecting, and safeguarding digital evidence at a crime scene. This guide, which is heavily focused on general forensic investigative procedures and best practices, is divided into seven chapters:

- Chapter 1, "Electronic Devices: Types, Description, and Potential Evidence"
- Chapter 2, "Investigative Tools and Equipment"
- Chapter 3, "Securing and Evaluating the Scene"
- Chapter 4, "Documenting the Scene"
- Chapter 5, "Evidence Collection"
- Chapter 6, "Packaging, Transportation, and Storage of Digital Evidence"
- Chapter 7, "Electronic Crime and Digital Evidence Considerations by Crime Category"

A key theme of this guide is covered in the introduction, which points out that there are legal ramifications for improperly accessing stored computer data. In addition, the guide reminds first responders that computer data and other digital media are fragile, and that only properly trained personnel should attempt to examine and analyze digital evidence.

Discovery and Disclosure Procedures

In civil litigation, the process of exchanging relevant information between the parties is called *discovery*. In criminal cases, the process is referred to as *disclosure*. Discovery generally consists of interrogatories, requests for admissions, stipulations, requests for the production of documents, written sworn statements (affidavits) and declarations, expert reports, and depositions. The following list provides a closer look at each of these terms and how investigators may assist legal counsel in these areas:

- *Interrogatories* are written questions prepared and submitted to an opposing party, which require written answers under oath. A practitioner may provide assistance to counsel in drafting actual interrogatory questions and in answering interrogatory questions posed by the opposing side.
- *Requests for admissions* are formal written requests for an opposing party to agree to—or admit the accuracy of—facts that are not in dispute. Again, the practitioner may be able to provide valuable assistance to counsel in crafting these requests.

---

[4]   U.S. Department of Justice, Office of Justice Programs, National Institute of Justice, *Electronic Crime Scene Investigation: A Guide for First Responders, Second Edition* (April 2008), *available at* www.ncjrs.gov/pdffiles1/nij/219941.pdf.

- *Stipulations* are voluntary agreements between opposing parties about any matter relevant to a dispute. Although not a common occurrence, practitioners may be asked to assist counsel with the formation of appropriate stipulations.

- *Requests for production of documents* ask that an opposing party produce—or make available for inspection and duplication—certain materials counsel believes are relevant to the dispute. Because the materials may be in hard copy or digital form, the request should state the desired format for documents to be produced. For investigators, it is usually quite helpful to have relevant documents produced in digital media, as that format allows for more efficient data analysis.

- *Written sworn statements (affidavits) and declarations* are another discovery activity. An *affidavit* is a statement or account given under oath that is written and signed by a defendant or witness. A *declaration* is another form of signed and written statement. The difference between the two is that a notary must be involved with an affidavit, and no such requirement exists for a declaration. Depending upon the specific jurisdiction, investigators retained as expert witnesses may be asked to submit an affidavit or declaration attesting to their analysis or findings. Investigators may also be of assistance to counsel in reviewing and analyzing affidavits or declarations submitted by the opposing side in a fraud case.

- *Preparation of expert reports*, which may include analysis and rebuttal of the opposing side's expert statements, is the discovery phase activity during which investigators are most often employed by counsel. These expert reports are written by investigators (or other experts) based on specific reporting requirements, such as Rule 26, "Duty to Disclose; General Provisions Governing Discovery," in the Federal Rules of Civil Procedure. In both civil and criminal matters, all parties are required to disclose expert reports or any documents they intend to use at trial.

- *Depositions* are out-of-court (no judge present) oral testimony, given under oath by a witness or expert before each side's legal counsel. Although this testimony is captured in writing, usually by a certified court reporter, depositions also may be videotaped and played during trial. It is possible that a witness or expert's deposition may be the only testimony required in cases that go to trial. Depositions serve to elicit witness testimony in advance of trial, so that both sides may fully prepare their legal arguments.

A handful of major differences exist between disclosure procedures of criminal matters and the discovery procedures of civil matters. Three of the most significant include the following:

1. In a criminal case, the prosecution is required to turn over exculpatory evidence (anything tending to prove the defendant is innocent). This is referred to as "Brady material," which is discussed further in the section titled "Tactics and Other Considerations" of this chapter.

2. In certain cases brought by federal prosecutors, statements provided by a government witness (other than the defendant) or reports in the possession of the United States are not subject to subpoena, discovery, or inspection. However, after a witness called by the United States has testified on direct examination, the defendant's counsel can

request that the court compel the government to produce any evidence related to the witness's specific testimony. If the entire contents of such evidence relate to the witnesses' testimony, the court shall order that it be delivered directly to defendant's counsel for examination and use. This is called "Jencks Act material," discussed further in "Tactics and Other Considerations" of this chapter.

3. In a criminal proceeding, when state or federal government officials want to obtain bank, cell phone, or any other records for which the defendant could expect a reasonable degree of privacy, a prosecutor needs to show probable cause as a basis for searching records and potentially arresting suspects. In civil cases, probable cause may be used as a means to search property, but not as a basis for arrest.

Tactics and Other Considerations

Clearly, prosecutors and defense attorneys use a range of tactics to sway opinion in their favor. For example, prosecutors often seek to color the facts as clear cut—right versus wrong. With that in mind, prosecutors typically like to develop a line of argument that shows a jury where the money went after the defendant took it, thus playing into a jury's sense of civic duty and lawfulness. On the other hand, defense attorneys often seek to introduce contradictory facts and evidence, which serve to muddy the waters. To this end, defense attorneys often develop a theme that paints the prosecution's case as messy, sloppy, biased, or confusing. Other common defense themes include demonstrating lack of intent, questioning motive, disputing amounts at issue, and arguing a lack of evidence that links a loss to the defendant.

A sampling of common defense tactics or arguments used in white collar criminal cases includes the following:

- *Duress.* According to *Black's Law Dictionary, duress* is "a threat of harm made to compel a person to do something against his or her will or judgment."[5] This is a common theme that defense counsel will attempt to employ in fraud cases.
- *Absence of intent.* Because intent is an inherent part of most white-collar crimes, if the defendant's attorney can convince prosecutors or a judge that the defendant lacked the intent to commit a crime, a favorable outcome may be more easily realized.
- *Brady material.* Brady material is any evidence known to the prosecution that is favorable to the defense. In the U.S. Supreme Court case *Brady v. Maryland,*[6] the prosecution's failure to hand over such exculpatory evidence was found to be a violation of the defendant's due process rights. However, if the defendant had been found guilty, this error would not have necessarily resulted in a reversal of the conviction.[7] Although the *Brady* issue is not directly applicable to civil cases, there are still some important lessons to learn. First, an expert in a civil matter should maintain

---

[5] Bryan A. Garner, ed., *Black's Law Dictionary*, 9th ed. (Thompson Reuters, 2009).

[6] U.S. Supreme Court; *Brady v. Maryland* – 373 U.S. 83 (1963).

[7] *Wex*, s.v. "Brady Material," http://topics.law.cornell.edu/wex/brady_material (accessed April 24, 2012).

professional skepticism throughout the engagement to sustain credibility as an independent and objective witness. Additionally, all forensic analysis must be fact based, because a subjective mindset might cause the investigator to miss the extent of the fraud or culpability of other employees, which could possibly result in the investigator being less than fair to the accused.

- *Jencks Act.*[8] In part, this act made it federal law that in any criminal prosecution brought by the United States, no statement or report in the possession of the United States which was made by a government witness or prospective government witness (other than the defendant) shall be the subject of subpoena, discovery, or inspection until said witness has testified on direct examination in the trial of the case. Once the government witness has testified, the court upon motion by the defense must order the material to be turned over to the defense team. Failure to comply could result in the defendant walking.

  With this in mind, be thorough when taking any notes related witness statements or interviews as these notes must eventually be turned over to the defense. The defense will look to exploit any inconsistencies between the notes and what has been previously stated or learned through the court proceeding.

- *Repayment or return of property.* In embezzlement cases, repayment or returning the property may aid the defense in getting a lesser sentence—or it may do nothing. It depends on the extent of the embezzlement, the amount of harm caused, and the way in which the property or assets were repaid.

- *State of mind.* If an embezzler took money because he or she thought he or she was entitled to it, that is a potential defense. However, if an embezzler took the funds but did not know that taking the money was illegal, that is not a defense. Bear in mind that, upon being caught, fraudsters will try to explain away their actions to victims as a means to influence the victim's future statements on the matter. This is important to understand, because it is a technique that fraudsters often use in an attempt to minimize the damage—and prospective liability—in their case.

- *Moment in time.* The defense will often use a "moment in time" tactic to attempt convincing the court that a fraudulent act was, in theory, just a normal disagreement over money. To counter this argument, it is important to leverage any emotional circumstances that may exist, while keeping the overall report factual and objective. For example, when interviewing witnesses or defendants, investigators must take a person back to the moment that the fraud occurred, dig out what was going through his or her mind at the time, and specifically note both factual and emotional issues identified in the interview. This approach can help prosecutors potentially counteract this defense tactic ahead of time.

- *Nothing to hide.* Another common defense tactic is that the accused "has nothing to hide." Typically, the defense will claim that because any alleged fraudulent transactions are in the company's books and records, those records were in plain view, subject to audit, and therefore not hidden. If this claim is made, the defense will usually

---

[8]   The Jencks Act, 18 U.S.C. section 3500.

follow up by suggesting if the accused was truly trying to defraud the company, he or she would not have allowed everything to be recorded. This feeds into the "absence of intent" tactic raised earlier in this section.

- *Tunnel vision.* The opposition will try to claim that the practitioner had tunnel vision when performing the engagement. To counteract this potential line of attack, be sure to interview anyone who is possibly involved or connected in the matter— even if the initial connection seems remote. If the defense performs this level of due diligence, but the prosecution does not, it can damage the value of the investigator's overall credibility and testimony.
- *Fees and certifications.* A recurring defense tactic is to look for opportunities to attack an investigator's fee level, professional training, or credentials. Arguments can be made that the investigator's fees were too high or too low, that the investigator was simply a "hired gun" whose testimony was purchased by the prosecution, or that the individual did not follow proper guidelines for fraud examinations. For those reasons, investigators must be vigilant about ensuring their fees are consistent with market and experience level and that their work is in line with generally accepted professional standards. For the latter, holding appropriate certifications or designations can be a valuable tool to help investigators fend off credibility attacks. These credentials may include CPA, Certified in Financial Forensics (CFF), Accredited in Business Valuation (ABV), Certified Fraud Examiner (CFE), Accredited Senior Appraiser (ASA), Certified Valuation Analyst (CVA), and Charted Financial Analyst (CFA).

In addition to these common courtroom tactics, investigators should be aware of a number of other prospective traps when involved with civil or criminal proceedings. The most common pitfalls include the following:

- *Interplay between criminal and civil cases.* In many cases, a civil fraud case eventually leads to a criminal investigation. Typically, a civil case will involve an insurance company or large corporation, both of which generally have the money to engage a damage expert. Under these circumstances, civil defendants will often try to settle that case in order to avoid exposing facts that can be used against them in a criminal prosecution. By recognizing this possibility, investigators can more effectively manage their fraud investigations and reporting.
- *Defense rebuttals regarding investigative scope.* When conducting background work on a company's financial documents, investigators should consider potential ways in which defense counsel can deflect or attack the analysis. For example, assume a company has multiple entities, which have not been examined one-by-one because they share common management. In this scenario, the defense may plausibly argue that had investigators looked specifically at each entity, they could have uncovered a reasonable explanation for questionable activities. Or, if an investigator sampled one year of invoices, the opposing side can do a two-year sample and potentially impeach the conclusions. For those reasons, a seasoned investigator will head off these possibilities by thoroughly considering the case facts and laying out an appropriate

scope and work plan. This approach will help an investigator rebut defense theories regarding appropriate scope and objective analysis.

- *Potential counterattacks.* A favorite defense tactic is to take an investigator's report and tear it apart by looking for contradictions, mistakes, or missed items. To minimize any potential damage to the case, investigators should always engage a qualified third party to analyze their work and provide honest, credible feedback. A best practice is to have all preliminary summaries and follow-up reports reviewed by the same individual and to encourage that person to challenge all facts, assumptions, and information sources. This is a critical step, because the opposing side will look at any and all errors, including calculations, statements, or assumptions that are not clearly supported by the facts. In addition, investigators should allow time for a completed report to be validated against all workpapers and notes completed during the engagement. If a mistake is found after the report has been issued, it is always better to address the error quickly—rather than taking the chance of being called on it in court.

- *Not double-checking sources.* When performing an analysis or investigation, be sure to find the original sources of the information whenever possible. For example, investigators who conduct witness interviews should keep their original written narrative of the session. Without it, opposing counsel can challenge an investigator's memory, thus inciting a "he said, she said" controversy. To prevent this occurrence, take steps to transcribe interview notes as close to the date of the interview as possible. In addition, document the date the notes were transcribed as well as the original interview date. It is also good idea for investigators to perform background checks on important witnesses, which can reveal any personal, professional, or reputational issues the other side may use in a bid to impeach their credibility.

- *Not effectively corroborating whistleblower claims.* Although a credible whistleblower can make a fraud case, a shaky one can cause it to fall apart. For that reason, investigators should not shy away from digging out important details, such as a track record of providing false information or a personal history involving drug abuse, mental, or financial problems. By seeking out any potential whistleblower weaknesses before trial, the investigator can determine if the individual has questionable reasons for bringing an accusation and help legal counsel manage any prospective lines of attack by opponents. In all cases, investigators must stay within a company's policies (and legal limits) when gathering this information. The bottom-line is that just because someone is accused of something does not mean it is true. By maintaining healthy skepticism, investigators can avoid the trap of giving one person too much weight until corroborating facts are in place to support his or her claims.

- *Not being aggressive in getting help when needed.* When investigators have engagements that involve substantial data gathering from electronic media (such as computer hard drives, servers, or smart phones), they should hire qualified specialists with appropriate credentials, equipment, and direct experience in computer forensics. By using an expert, investigators can avoid defense claims of evidence spoliation or any attempts to question the legitimacy of information pulled from electronic media. Additionally, if a computer was used to perpetrate fraud, that fact raises broader legal issues, which reinforces the urgency of having top-notch computer forensic expertise close at hand.

Overview of Rules of Civil Proceedings

Civil litigation is the legal process used to resolve a dispute between private citizens and corporations. Civil disputes generally fall into two categories: tort or contract claims. Tort actions are civil wrongs that result in a remedy of damages to the harmed party (negligence is the most common type of tort claim). Contract claims stem from a disputed contract, ranging from complex business transactions to small disputes between ordinary citizens (breach of contract is the most common type of contract claim).

In addition to litigation, alternative dispute resolution tools, such as mediation and arbitration, are available to resolve civil matters. In general, mediation is voluntary, and the findings of the mediator are nonbinding (an attempt to settle the dispute rather than litigate). On the other hand, arbitration has historically been viewed as binding, and it may be required under certain contractual provisions, court orders, or statutes.

Each party to a civil litigation proceeding is referred to as a *litigant*. The party that initiated the complaint is referred to as the *plaintiff*. The party that is subject to the complaint is referred to as the *defendant*. Both the plaintiff and the defendant may engage their own attorneys who will represent them and assist them with the civil litigation proceeding. The plaintiff and defendant may each engage their own consultants, expert witnesses, or both if it is determined that retention of these professionals would be helpful as they navigate the civil litigation process. During a case, the litigants and third parties involved may change, based on the discovery process, the court granting dismissal motions, or parties that choose to settle the matter.

In general, courts observe special rules of civil procedure, as well as rules of evidence within the civil litigation process.[9] It should be noted that state courts in the United States follow their own rules of civil procedure and evidence, which are based on a model set of rules developed by legal scholars, professionals, judges, and lawmakers. If investigators are retained to assist in a state court matter in an unfamiliar jurisdiction, they should ask attorneys on the specific case for guidance regarding any nuances of that jurisdiction's procedural and evidentiary rules. It is not uncommon for these rules to vary from jurisdiction to jurisdiction and also vary depending on the subject matter of a case.[10]

---

[9] *See* United States Federal Rules of Civil Procedure and United States Federal Rules of Evidence; *see also* state rules of civil procedure (varies from state to state). One easy way to access the Federal Rules of Civil Procedure is via the Cornell University Law School Legal Information Institute website, www.law.cornell.edu/rules/frcp/, and the Federal Rules of Evidence website, www.law.cornell.edu/rules/fre/.

[10] A good starting point for researching state statutes can also be found on the Cornell University Law School Legal Information Institute website, which compiles an index by state statute category.

As investigators prepare for an engagement, they should understand that the majority of suits are settled before trial through negotiated settlements, mediation, or arbitration. For that reason, it is important to remember that the rules of civil procedure apply only to litigation, and not to matters that do not go to trial. In either litigation or nonlitigation assignments, investigators should keep best practices in mind to guide their conduct.[11]

There are generally eight phases[12] to the civil litigation process:

1. Dispute
2. Precomplaint
3. Complaint
4. Answer or response
5. Discovery
6. Pretrial
7. Trial
8. Post-trial

During and between these phases, various litigation activities may occur. These include motions, rulings and orders, interrogatories, requests for admissions, stipulations, requests for production of documents, written sworn statements (affidavits) and declarations, expert reports, depositions, pretrial conference, settlement, direct examination, cross examination, and the calculation and distributions of judgments and awards (many of these activities were explained in more detail in "Discovery and Disclosure Procedures" in this chapter). A detailed chart laying out the typical steps in a civil proceeding is found at the end of this chapter.[13] The chart also shows potential services that a forensic accountant may provide, when applicable.

In some civil cases, the defendant may believe that a complaint fails to meet the legal standard for claim relief. This often leads to a *motion to dismiss*, which is an attempt to exclude claims without legal merit, regardless of the alleged facts. In other situations, the defendant will answer the plaintiff's complaint and also assert his or her own claim (called a counterclaim or a cross-complaint). Hence, the plaintiff becomes a cross-defendant, who must answer and defend against the counterclaim or cross-complaint at trial.

Excluding certain specialized courts, such as the federal tax court, the disputing parties have the right to request a jury or a bench trial (in a bench trial, the judge serves as the finder of fact). In either situation, the judge is responsible for interpreting and applying all laws during the trial. A panel of judges hears any appeal of a trial court decision.

Figure 4-1 shows the general progression of trial activities.[14]

This state statute listing can be found at http://topics.law.cornell.edu/wex/state_statutes, and the various states' rules of civil procedure can be found at http://topics.law.cornell.edu/wex/table_civil_procedure.

[11] For the remainder of this section, reference is made to various aspects of the AICPA Forensic and Valuation Services (FVS) Section Special Report 09-1, *Introduction to Civil Litigation Services.*

[12] AICPA FVS Section Special Report 09-1, 7.

[13] AICPA FVS Section Practice Aid 10-1, *Serving as an Expert Witness or Consultant,* 38–41.

[14] AICPA FVS Section Special Report 09-1, 10.

Figure 4-1: Trial Activity Progression

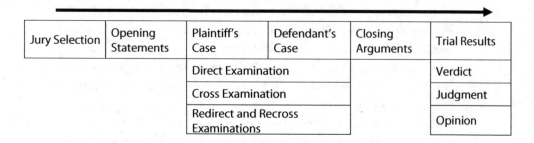

Jury Selection	Opening Statements	Plaintiff's Case	Defendant's Case	Closing Arguments	Trial Results
		Direct Examination			Verdict
		Cross Examination			Judgment
		Redirect and Recross Examinations			Opinion

Trial activities can be broken down as follows:

- *Jury selection.* For a jury trial, attorneys may analyze and challenge the suitability of potential jurors through a process called *voir dire* ("to speak the truth"). After final jury candidates are accepted by the attorneys, the judge approves the selections and empanels the jury for trial.[15] The selection of jury members is vital to both the plaintiff and defense, as each will look for certain types of individuals who they believe may be more sympathetic to the facts and circumstances of their case.

- *Opening statements.* One of the first activities in a trial is opening statements by the attorneys representing the plaintiff and defense. The defendant usually has the option of deferring an opening statement until the time comes to present his or her case later in the trial proceedings. Opening statements allow the attorneys to present an overview of their case by describing key issues and presenting evidence, decisions, and remedies they believe the jury must hear to understand their side of the case.[16]

- *Plaintiff's case.* In most cases, the plaintiff has the burden of proof and must present competent and relevant evidence supporting the essential facts, claims, and allegations contained in the complaint. *Direct examination* is the initial questioning of a witness at trial, and it consists of a series of questions designed to solicit admissible evidence in the form of responsive testimony. Legal issues about questions, the admissibility of evidence, and witness answers may result in objections from opposing attorneys, which are typically handled in subsequent rulings by the judge.

  — Direct examination is the first opportunity for expert witnesses to testify at trial. Prior to hearing expert testimony, an opposing attorney may seek to question the qualifications and suitability of these witnesses in an effort to either disqualify them or limit the scope of their testimony. This is often accomplished when an opposing attorney asks the court to rule for disqualification or exclusion,

---

15 AICPA FVS Section Special Report 09-1, 10–11.
16 AICPA FVS Section Special Report 09-1, 11.

sometimes called a "Daubert motion."[17] Voir dire is also used to challenge an expert witness.[18,19]

— Cross-examination is the initial examination of a witness by the opposing attorney. During cross-examinations, an attorney is given broad latitude to impeach the witness, often by using leading questions that are prohibited in direct examination. Frequently, deposition testimony is used to impeach the witness. For these reasons, cross-examination is often the most challenging part of civil litigation for expert witnesses.[20]

— Redirect examination follows cross-examination, giving the attorney responsible for direct examination another opportunity to question the witness. Redirect examination is limited to facts and issues raised during cross-examination. This may include asking witnesses to clarify the credibility of specific answers that may have been attacked or questioned during cross-examination. After the redirect examination, the opposing attorney is allowed a recross examination of the witness. This is restricted to matters raised in redirect examination. Therefore, this examination tends to be brief and narrow in scope.[21]

- *Defendant's case.* Once the plaintiff rests its case, the defendant is allowed to proceed. An examination of the defendant's testimony and evidence is similar in process to the presentation of the plaintiff's case. When the defendant's case has been presented, the judge may allow the plaintiff to present a responsive rebuttal case. Likewise, the defendant may be provided the opportunity for a surrebuttal response.[22]

- *Closing arguments.* After both sides have presented their cases and rested, each side makes a closing argument. A closing argument summarizes the case and evidence, seeking to convince the judge or jury that their side should receive a favorable decision. When closing arguments have been completed, the judge provides jury instructions in a written statement, which informs the jury of all laws and deliberation rules applicable to the case.[23]

- *Trial results.* Although a judge must consider any post-trial motions or legal briefs, a civil trial usually ends in the following manner:[24]

---

[17] Sometimes referred to as the "Daubert trilogy," the term actually refers to three United States Supreme Court cases which dealt with the issue of the admissibility of expert testimony and the qualification of those witnesses as experts.

[18] The term *voir dire* refers to the practice of removing the jury from the courtroom and then having the party that wants to offer the witness as an expert asks direct questions to show his or her qualifications. The opposing party may then cross-examine the purported expert in an effort to impeach his or her credibility as an expert. When they attorneys are finished with their questioning, the judge makes a decision about whether or not (*a*) expert testimony is necessary and (*b*) whether the person is such an expert.

[19] AICPA FVS Section Special Report 09-1, 11.

[20] AICPA FVS Section Special Report 09-1, 12.

[21] *Id.*

[22] *Id.*

[23] *Id.*

[24] AICPA FVS Section Special Report 09-1, 12–13.

— *Verdict* is the final decision rendered by a jury to the court in a jury trial or by a judge in a bench trial. Verdicts are either general or special in form. A general verdict decides all issues in favor of one party. A special verdict decides only the facts at issue in the case, with the judge deciding how the law applies to each issue. For a special verdict, the jury is asked to make a number of decisions about issues in the case.

— *Judgment* is the judge's formal decision about the case. For example, if a judge accepts a jury's verdict, that becomes the official judgment for that specific case. In relatively rare instances, the judge may set aside a jury verdict and make an independent ruling, referred to as a "judgment as a matter of law."

— *Opinion* is an official summary of the court ruling, typically disclosed in a prepared written opinion statement that describes the reasons and interpretations of the law.

After the trial, the judge may ask opposing attorneys to file briefs (or formal memoranda) that describe the merits of each case, including proven issues, findings of fact, and applicable law. The judge may use these briefs, in part, to write a case opinion for federal courts. Generally, in state courts, there are no written opinions.[25]

After a civil trial, the losing party has the right to appeal the trial court's decision to an appeals court, if it believes the judge made a reversible legal error. In these cases, the appeals court reviews the lower court's original record as the basis for a ruling. If the appeal court determines a reversal is warranted, it can prescribe specific actions to address the issue, such as an order for a new trial.[26]

In cases in which a judgment on damages is required, it is sometimes necessary to prepare a final calculation, including applicable pre- and post-judgment interest, penalties, and attorney fees. A damages calculation may also need to include exemplary, punitive, or other damages awarded by the court. In cases with large numbers of beneficiaries (such as class action lawsuits), practitioners may assist legal counsel with quantifying damage awards and determining the amount allocated to each individual party.[27]

The following figure provides a phase-by-phase description of general litigation procedures and associated forensic services, which may be a valuable resource for both investigators and counsel as they navigate fraud-related matters. Figure 4–2 was originally published in the AICPA FVS Section Practice Aid 10-1.

---

[25] AICPA FVS Section Special Report 09-1, 13.

[26] *Id.*

[27] *Id.*

Figure 4-2: Phase-by-Phase Description of General Litigation Procedures and Associated Forensic Services That Could Be Offered by Practitioners*

Phase	Activity	Description	Forensic Services
Dispute		A dispute is the subject of the potential or pending litigation or a disputed fact, claim, or allegation from one side (the plaintiff) met by the contrary fact, claim, or allegation by the opposing side (the defendant).	• Dispute development and preparation • Early dispute resolution • Fact finding • Investigations
Precomplaint		Prior to filing a formal complaint, the potential plaintiff and defendant gather information related to the dispute.	• Complaint preparation • Case assessment • Case budgeting • Fact finding • Third party corroboration
Complaint		Initiated by the plaintiff, the original or initial complaint is the first pleading in a formal civil litigated proceeding. The complaint names the defendant, identifies the court having jurisdiction, and describes the legal complaints and remedies or relief requested. The plaintiff files the complaint with the court. The official notification of the complaint to the defendant requires official service, or delivery, by a court appointed server.	• Case management • Case strategy (consulting only) • Class action certification • Motion support
	Rulings and Orders	Rulings are the decisions made by the court or judge on disputed legal issues or case matters. These represent the opinions and judgment of the court or judge. Orders are the commands, directions, and instructions of the court or judge.	• Reviews of rulings and orders for insight into court proceedings (that is, timing, discovery, procedures, and so on)
Answer or Response		In response to the complaint, the defendant prepares a pleading, called an answer or response, which denies or admits each of the allegations made by the plaintiff.	• Preparation of materials or verbiage for answer or response • Response preparation • Counterclaim preparation
Discovery		Discovery is the exchange of information and knowledge between the parties after the case has been filed in order to assemble evidence for the trial	• Case strategy (consulting only)
	Interrogatories	Written questions prepared and submitted to an opposing party, which require written answers under oath.	• Assistance with questions for interrogatories • Assistance with responses to interrogatories

Phase	Activity	Description	Forensic Services
	Requests for Admissions	These are formal written requests for an opposing party to agree to, or admit the accuracy of, undisputed facts.	• Settlement assistance
	Stipulations	These are voluntary agreements between opposing parties about any matter relevant to the dispute.	• Settlement assistance
	Requests for Production of Documents	These are requests to have an opposing party produce, or make available for inspection and duplication, certain specifically identified materials believed to be potentially relevant to the dispute. The materials may be hard copy or electronically stored information.	• Drafting production requests and responses • Document, data, and evidence identification, recovery, analysis, and management
	Written Sworn Statements (Affidavits) and Declarations	A sworn statement, or affidavit, is a written and signed out of court statement or account given under oath. A declaration is a signed and written out of court statement.	• Expert witness affidavit • Rebuttal of opposing expert affidavit • Analysis of case documents • Damages quantification
	Expert Reports	Written reports prepared by the practitioner, or other experts, based on the report requirements, such as under Rule 26, "Duty to Disclose; General Provisions Governing Discovery," of the Federal Rules of Civil Procedure for a federal case.	• Expert report • Analysis and rebuttal of opposing expert report
	Depositions	Out-of-court oral testimony given by a witness or expert under oath and reduced to writing, usually by a certified court reporter.	• Deposition assistance • Expert witness deposition testimony • Rebuttal of opposing expert testimony • Witness preparation
Pretrial		Prior to the trial, the disputes may be narrowed by using information obtained during discovery, through court hearings, and by rulings made and orders issued by the judge as a result of numerous pleadings, motions, and objections registered over the course of litigation.	• Trial preparations • Trial demonstratives • Settlement and resolution support

Phase	Activity	Description	Forensic Services
	Pretrial Conference	In most federal cases, a conference is ordered prior to the commencement of the trial to encourage the parties to settle their disputes. In lieu of settlement, the purpose of the pretrial conference is much more oriented to the potential trial. Witness lists are generally exchanged, as are exhibits (if not already identified and exchanged between the parties). The conference also seeks to narrow the issues that are actually in dispute. What the court is interested in is streamlining matters for trial, and addressing disputes between the attorneys without wasting precious court time to do it later during trial.	• Settlement and resolution support
	Settlement	Settlement of all or a portion of the litigated dispute may take place at any time during the litigation process. Settlement occurs when the disputing parties agree on the outcome and resolution of the claims in the complaint.	• Settlement and resolution support • Settlement assistance
Trial		The trial can either be a jury or bench trial (a judge serves as the trier of fact).	• Jury selection assistance
	Direct Examination	Direct examination is the initial questioning of a witness at the trial by the attorney who calls the witness for examination. Direct examination consists of a series of questions designed to solicit admissible evidence from the witness in the form of responsive testimony and other materials.	• Expert witness testimony • Witness preparation • Analysis of opposing expert testimony
	Cross Examination	The initial examination of a witness by the opposing legal counsel, cross-examination follows the direct examination. The opposing attorney can use leading questions that are prohibited in direct examination, and frequently, deposition testimony is used to impugn the witness.	• Opposing expert cross examination assistance • Trial preparation • Witness preparation
Posttrial		After the trial is concluded, a number of activities may occur, including appealing adverse decisions or calculating and distributing monetary damages.	• Calculation of beneficiary allocations • Distribution of judgments and awards
	Calculation and Distribution of Judgments and Awards	Prepare a final calculation of the amount of damages, including applicable pre- and post-judgment interest, and any penalties; attorney fees; or exemplary, punitive, or other damages awarded by the court.	• Calculation of amounts awarded

*   AICPA Forensic and Valuation Services Section Practice Aid 10-1, Serving as an Expert Witness or Consultant, 38–41.

Overview of Rules of Criminal Procedure[28]

Forensic accountants may also serve as an expert witness or a consultant in criminal litigation. In some cases, civil claims and criminal charges may be filed together, requiring consideration of both the unique aspects of criminal litigation and specific consulting services to be provided.

In criminal litigation, the government attempts to identify illegal criminal activity and successfully convict and punish violators, as provided under the law. The key conceptual difference between criminal and civil litigation is that in a criminal matter, the alleged crime is viewed as harm against the safety, security, common morality, or overall well being of society. In a civil case, the dispute is between two private parties. As such, the main risk to those charged in criminal matters in imprisonment, while the risk to those charged in a civil matter is possible financial loss.

Because of the potential loss of liberty in a criminal case, the U.S. Constitution provides increased protection to defendants in such matters as follows:

- The Fourth Amendment prohibits unreasonable search and seizure.
- The Fifth Amendment protects the defendant from unwanted self-incrimination, requires a grand jury indictment for specified crimes, prohibits double jeopardy, and provides the right to due process.
- The Sixth Amendment guarantees the right for a trial by a jury of peers and the right to be represented by legal counsel.

Most of the time, the investigator's involvement in criminal litigation cases will be limited to white collar crimes, such as fraud, financial statement misrepresentation, or insider trading. The focus of work, most commonly, is on financial forensic investigative procedures designed to detect and identify any improper—or potentially illegal—monetary flows.

The criminal litigation process consists of several phases and activities. Typically, a substantial part of the practitioner's work is performed and completed at the front end of the engagement before trial. Because of this timeline, investigators can create deliver value through expert witness and consultant services, which can provide substantial help to prosecutors seeking a criminal indictment from a grand jury.

Conclusion

In this chapter, we have presented more building blocks of the essential knowledge required for fraud investigators. Understanding civil and criminal procedure helps an investigator effectively and efficiently construct the investigation and determine ahead of time how likely it is that a fraud examination will provide the client what he or she is looking for. For example, a client may have the sole objective of putting someone in prison. However, the fraud investigator's review of the documentation during the initial meeting may reveal that the client has a significant misunderstanding regarding what he or she is viewing on the

---

[28] AICPA FVS Section Practice Aid 10-1, 41–42.

documentation. At best, the matter may involve civil action, but no criminal action. By having this foundational knowledge, the investigator is better able to serve the client by identifying the relevant issues. It is important to remember that fraud investigators are independent. It is not the place of the investigator to construct facts to fit the client's objective.

5

Jury Instructions

Adam J. Falconer, JD

Legal Foundations of Fraud Investigations
On- and Off-the-Books Fraud Schemes
Civil Process and Criminal Procedure
Jury Instructions
Regulatory Complexities
Working the Case
Find It and Fix It

Jury Instructions

In chapters 2 through 4, we emphasized the importance for investigators to have a good working knowledge of fraud-related statutes and regulations, common fraud schemes, and the distinctions between civil process and criminal proceedings.[1]

However, even with the most diligent preparation on what fraud is and how fraudsters accomplish their schemes, it can be difficult for investigators to focus on the particulars. When starting an investigation, investigators should consider the following questions:

- What specific documents should I request?
- Which legal issues are pertinent?

---

[1] FBI, *2009 Financial Crimes Report*, available at www.fbi.gov/stats-services/publications/financial-crimes-report-2009.

- How should I organize my factual findings?
- What evidence will likely be presented in the case?
- How do I analyze the findings and the issues?
- How do I apply my analysis to make relevant and accurate investigative conclusions?

The following section in this chapter provides a case study for a discussion of how to apply these questions in a real world scenario.

Jury instructions are a great resource for investigators to tackle the questions introduced in the previous list. In both state and federal courts, jury instructions are used to explain applicable law in a case, helping guide the jury as it reviews facts en route to reaching a verdict. In most cases, attorneys for each side (plaintiff and defendant) will write jury instructions, which are then reviewed by the presiding judge. The judge then decides what final instructions will be presented to the jury immediately before the panel retires to deliberate the case.

Sample jury instructions (sometimes referred to as "pattern" jury instructions) have been developed through years of case law, trials, opinions, and appeals. Criminal and civil cases will almost always have different jury instructions, primarily due to the different burdens of proof ("beyond a reasonable doubt" for criminal cases versus "preponderance of the evidence" for civil cases). State courts, federal courts, and special courts (such as bankruptcy, tax, or international trade court) each have different sample jury instructions. There are even jury instructions specific to causes of action (such as breach of contract, fraud, products liability, or negligence).[2] In all of these situations, the jury instructions frame the elements for each "claim" in a civil case or each "charge" (or "count") in a criminal case.

To illustrate the point, consider the following hypothetical discussion and analysis of a wire fraud case, which is presented to show how jury instructions can be used by a fraud investigator to address key issues in a real-world case.

Analysis of Jury Instructions — Wire Fraud Case

A fraud investigator has been engaged to assist prosecutors on a case of criminal wire fraud, which will be brought in federal court in Chicago (Northern District of Illinois). Because this particular federal court is in the Seventh Circuit, a starting point for applicable jury instructions would be those outlined by the Committee on Federal Criminal Jury Instructions for the Seventh Circuit.[3] The pertinent jury instructions that pertain to wire fraud read in part (*emphasis added*):

> To sustain the charge of [mail] [wire] [carrier] fraud, the government must prove
> the following propositions:

---

[2]   See the box titled "Jury Instructions Resources" in this chapter.

[3]   United States Court of Appeals for the Seventh Circuit, *Pattern Criminal Federal Jury Instructions for the Seventh Circuit*, www.ca7.uscourts.gov/Pattern_Jury_Instr/pjury.pdf. Please note new draft instructions are in the comment phase of approval, including an expanded set of pattern jury instructions for use in criminal trials in the district courts of the Seventh Circuit.

First, that the defendant *knowingly* [*devised*] [or] [*participated in*] the *scheme* [*to defraud*] [or] [*to obtain money or property by means of false pretenses, representations or promises*], as described in Count[s] _____ of the indictment;

Second, that the defendant did so *knowingly and with the intent to defraud*; and

Third, that for the purpose of carrying out the scheme or attempting to do so, the defendant [*used* [or *caused the use of*]] [the United States Mails] [a private or commercial interstate carrier]] [*caused interstate wire communications to take place*] in the manner charged in the particular count.

If you find from your consideration of all the evidence that each of these propositions has been proved beyond a reasonable doubt, then you should find the defendant guilty.

If, on the other hand, you find from your consideration of all the evidence that any one of these propositions has not been proved beyond a reasonable doubt, then you should find the defendant not guilty.[4]

What does this particular instruction tell an examiner about wire fraud? The answer is that the charge of wire fraud generally has three elements:

1. The defendant knowingly devised or participated in a scheme to defraud.
2. The defendant did so knowingly and with the intent to defraud.
3. The defendant used or caused the use of interstate wire communications (to carry out the scheme or attempt to carry out the scheme).

Although the legalese of such pattern instructions may at first be a bit intimidating, fraud investigators will quickly get a feel for how the instructions undergird the elements of a claim or charge. Although it is proper, and quite common, for an investigator to make assumptions about the legal elements of a case (upon consultation with the client, counsel, or both in a particular engagement), it is best for the investigator to ask good questions to ensure a detailed understanding of the elements of each claim and how each element can be supported through a credible investigation.

The wording in jury instructions can help reveal the meaning of each specific element. For example, although anyone can express his or her own understanding of what "scheme to defraud" means, in the legal world, these words have a meaning all of their own. In the Seventh Circuit pattern jury instructions, "scheme to defraud," is defined as follows (*emphasis added*):

A scheme is a *plan or course of action formed with the intent to accomplish some purpose.*

In considering whether the government has proven a scheme to [defraud] [obtain money or property by means of false pretenses, representations or promises,] it is essential that *one or more of the* [false pretenses, representations, promises and] *acts charged* in the portion of the indictment describing the scheme *be proved establishing*

---

[4]   www.ca7.uscourts.gov/Pattern_Jury_Instr/pjury.pdf, 214.

the existence of the scheme beyond a reasonable doubt. However, the government is not required prove all of them.

[A scheme to defraud is a scheme that *is intended to deceive or cheat another and* [*to obtain money or property or cause the* [potential] *loss of money* or *property to another*] [*or*] [*to deprive another of* [description of honest services, including source text of rule or statute]].[5]

What does this particular instruction tell an investigator about the meaning of the words "scheme to defraud" contained in the first element of wire fraud (*the defendant knowingly devised or participated in a scheme to defraud*)?

First, the instruction points out certain factual and proof components, which may include

- a plan or course of action formed with the intent to accomplish some purpose;
- one or more of the acts charged are proved beyond a reasonable doubt to show the existence of a scheme; and
- that a scheme to defraud is
  — intended to deceive or cheat another and
    o to obtain money or property or cause the [*potential*] loss of money or property to another or
    o to deprive another of [*description of honest services, including source text of rule or statute*].

In addition, the instruction shows that the presence of facts—or lack of facts—surrounding a plan intended to deceive another is a central issue a wire fraud case. More specifically, it is important for the investigator to understand whether the plan was created to obtain money or property from another or to deprive another of some service (or other act defined in the applicable criminal statute).

What specific documents to request?

- Look at the wire fraud suspects.
  — The investigator will want to understand who these people are, how they interact, and whether communications among the alleged participants either support or do not support some sort of plan or scheme.
- Consider key documents, including e-mail and phone records; internal investigation reports; surveillance transcripts (if any); key financial instruments and documents; accounting records and related policies; third-party reports prepared by auditors, consultants, or other service providers; and many others.
  — The investigator will want to organize the documents in a logical and orderly fashion, such as by key issue, Bates number,* or some other logical indexing system.
  — This will help the investigator during the document review phase of the engagement, as well as assist in preparation of work papers and reports.

---

[5]   *Id.* at 215.

Which legal issues are pertinent?

- In the wire fraud example, consider whether the alleged fraudsters "knowingly" devised or participated in a scheme.
  - The investigator may be tasked with analyzing volumes of e-mails and other electronic and paper documentation to organize facts that support intent to defraud, or otherwise fail to support intent to defraud.
- Question what the alleged fraudster knew—or did not know.
- Examine the timing of events, date of documents and correspondence, and the omission of information.
  - This can be difficult for an investigator absent a clear understanding of the timing of events and a commanding knowledge of the facts.
  - It may be difficult to reconstruct the thoughts and mental state of another. Be patient to understand the timeline and how the interactions of the people progress and change over time.
- Take advantage of commercially available software to assist in analyzing documents and electronic communications to uncover such fine distinctions, tone, circumstances, and disguised language meaning.
  - Often persons acting together to devise a fraudulent scheme will use code words and nuanced language to communicate; the fine distinctions of language and the tone and surrounding circumstances may need to be further investigated.

How should I organize my factual findings?

- Line up the factual findings with the key legal elements to assist in developing the case.
  - Usually investigations can produce large bodies of documentation that needs to be reviewed.
- Devise a clean, logical document organization system.
  - For example, documentation and records are often organized by some sort of unique identifier (such as Bates numbers or unique numbers for each page of documentation involved in litigation).
  - Additionally, consider indexing or keying each piece of information by a particular person, legal entity, document date, document type, or key search terms.
  - Note that there may be depositions, document requests and other case activity that will utilize the fraud investigator's work product.
- Stick to facts until the analysis phase of a case concludes even though it may be tempting at this phase to draw conclusions.

What evidence will likely be presented in the case?

- Absent in-depth working experience in a particular field, work with counsel, the client representative, or both to establish the scope of the investigator's role in building the overall case.
  - Bear in mind that the client or counsel may have already performed some investigative work or background interviews or they may have been working alongside law enforcement professionals prior to involvement by the fraud investigator.
- Prepare demonstrative exhibits that might be used at trial or otherwise by the legal team (before a regulatory body, board of directors, and so on).
- Understand and master the factual findings of others, in addition to his or her own findings.
  - By having factual findings organized by key issues, legal elements, and the like, preparing exhibits or other work product should be a fairly straight forward process.

How do I analyze the findings and the issues?

- Remember that each case will have unique fact patterns, and no two cases will be the same from a legal, investigative, document review, or management perspective.
- In a case of wire fraud, gather and analyze data in a spreadsheet, database, or summary report.
  - This file would include the factual findings on key issues, such as the alleged plan or fraud scheme, what the alleged fraudsters knew (and did not appear to know) about the plan and alleged victims, and the use of interstate wire communications.
  - The database or spreadsheet tool could include a matrix of facts and source documents presented alongside each legal issue or element.
- Understand how the facts of the case appear to drive certain conclusions by analyzing each piece of factual evidence and assessing how each piece of evidence may fit together with other pieces of evidence.
  - At this analysis phase of the case, the investigator may be asked to express preliminary opinions and help the client, counsel, or both clarify important issues and questions surrounding the fraud case.

How do I apply my analysis to make relevant and accurate investigative conclusions?

- When asked by counsel. the client, or both to express opinions or reach conclusions, ensure any opinion or conclusion is supported by clear and organized work papers and that the investigation was performed in accordance with best practices (AICPA practice guides, Financial Industry Regulatory Authority guides, regulatory agency rules, case law, and so on).
  - In a perfect world, an investigator would be an all-knowing oracle with no limitations. Yet, there are quite often time and budget limitations that restrict the resources available for a particular assignment.
- Most important, make sure the conclusions or opinions rendered are within the assignment's scope and in keeping with policies of the investigator's employer.
- Present opinions and conclusions that are consistent with a case's legal issues and elements, based upon factual findings (based on his or her prior experience in similar matters) and on best practices.
  - Any case presentation may be affected by limitations, reservations or footnotes developed during the fraud investigation.
  - No matter how robust the factual support, it is wise for an investigator to remember that any conclusion or opinion rendered on highly technical or industry-specific data can have minimal effectiveness unless it is communicated in a clear, concise manner.
  - Again, it is important to remember that the investigator is not the trier of fact.

---

* *Black's Law Dictionary* defines Bate-stamp numbers or Bates number as the identifying number that is affixed to a document or to the individual pages of a document. The purpose of Bates numbering is to provide identification, protection and automatic consecutive numbering during the discovery stage of preparations for trial. Bates numbers are stamped on all pieces of information obtained including but not limited to documents, spreadsheets, images or electronic media.

Case Study Conclusions

This wire fraud example examined only a small part of one particular sample jury instruction. As discussed in this chapter, there are different sample jury instructions for various courts and even specific causes of action. In each circumstance, these jury instructions can serve as an accurate roadmap to navigate issues in a complex investigation. Additionally, the instructions are a valuable resource to help an investigator frame the factual inquiry, guide collection of data and information, analyze information as it pertains to key issues, and present findings, conclusions, and opinions. However, it is important to remember that the investigator is not the trier of fact.

There are a number of books, practice guides, and electronic resources for sample jury instructions. The following boxes contain examples and research resources for sample jury instructions, which may be useful to both fraud investigators and other financial or accounting professionals. However, the investigator should ensure he or she is using the right jury instructions by requesting it from the appropriate counsel.

Jury Instructions Resources

United States Attorneys' Manual, *Title 4: Civil Resource Manual*

www.justice.gov/usao/eousa/foia_reading_room/usam/title4/civ00000.htm

United States Attorneys' Manual, *Title 9: Criminal Resource Manual*

www.justice.gov/usao/eousa/foia_reading_room/usam/title9/crm00000.htm

Marquette University Law School, Law Library, *Model Jury Instructions Research Guide*

http://law.marquette.edu/law-library/model-jury-instructions-basic-practice-guide-0

University of Kentucky College of Law, *Jury Instructions & Jury Verdicts*

www.law.uky.edu/files/docs/library/guides/jury%20instructions.pdf

Federal Evidence Review (federal), *Federal Jury Instructions Resource Page*

http://federalevidence.com/evidence-resources/federal-jury-instructions

LLRX.com (state), *Reference from Coast to Coast: Jury Instructions Update*

www.llrx.com/columns/reference53.htm

Section III

Regulatory Complexities

6

Healthcare Fraud

Jennifer G. Miller, CPA

- Legal Foundations of Fraud Investigations
- On- and Off-the-Books Fraud Schemes
- Civil Process and Criminal Procedure
- Jury Instructions
- Regulatory Complexities
- Working the Case
- Find It and Fix It

Healthcare Fraud Defined

Fraud is making false statements or representations of material facts to obtain some benefit or payment for which no entitlements would otherwise exist.[1] Specifically, within federal regulations, *healthcare fraud* is defined as follows:

> Whoever knowingly and willfully executes, or attempts to execute, a scheme or artifice –
>
> 1. To defraud an health care benefit program; or
> 2. To obtain, by means of false or fraudulent pretenses, representations, or promises, any of the money or property owned by, or under the custody or control of, any health care benefit program,

---

[1] www.cms.gov/Outreach-and-Education/Medicare-Learning-Network-MLN/MLNProducts/downloads// Fraud_and_Abuse.pdf.

In connection with the delivery of or payment for health care benefits, items, or services, shall be fined under this title or imprisoned not more than 10 years, or both. If the violation results in serious bodily injury (as defined in section 1365 of this title), such person shall be fined under this title or imprisoned not more than 20 years, or both; and if the violation results in death, such person shall be fined under this title, or imprisoned for any term of years for life, or both.[2]

An important takeaway from both of these definitions is that some type of benefit must be received or attempts to receive, by an individual, for fraud to exist. This may include any type of financial benefit (such as kickbacks or increased revenues) or nonfinancial benefit (such as career enhancement or promotions). Another key takeaway from these definitions is that the fraud may be classified as a criminal act if *intent* is involved. In the absence of intent, the offender may be sued under civil law.

Industry Overview

Healthcare costs have increased exponentially in the past decade. According to the *2009 U.S. Master Employee Benefits Guide*, inflation, technology, escalating malpractice premiums, longer life spans, lack of established controls, cost shifting, and the rising incidence of new and catastrophic diseases have all contributed to this explosive growth. With the considerable rise in these costs, and the growing media spotlight on the healthcare system, there has been a corresponding increase in the amount of industry fraud identified and investigated. In fact, recent industry studies discovered that drug traffickers were debating a switch from drug dealing to healthcare fraud because it was safer, more lucrative, and less likely to be detected.[3]

Without question, healthcare is a vast business in the United States, with significant connections to both private industry and government. For example, in 2011, the Centers for Medicare and Medicaid reported to serve almost 102 million in Medicare, Medicaid, and Children's Health Insurance Program beneficiaries.[4] These numbers, of course, do not include the millions of people who receive healthcare through employer-sponsored or other private market plans. Because of the sheer size of this marketplace, it is easy to understand why healthcare is such a big target for fraudulent activity.

While Medicare and Medicaid are often terms that are used interchangeably, they are very different programs. *Medicaid* is a jointly funded, federal–state health insurance program for low-income and needy people.[5] It provides benefits to

- pregnant women,
- children under the age of 19,

---

[2]   *Crimes and Criminal Procedure, U.S. Code* (USC) 18, Section 1347.

[3]   David A. Hyman, "HIPAA and Health Care Fraud: An Empirical Perspective," *Cato Journal* 22 (Spring/Summer 2002).

[4]   Centers for Medicare and Medicaid Services, Department of Health and Human Services, *FY 2011 Online Performance Appendix.*

[5]   "Social Security," accessed February 13, 2012, www.socialsecurity.gov.

- people age 65 and over,
- people who are blind,
- people who are disabled, and
- people who need nursing home care.

In order to qualify for Medicaid, individuals must apply to the Medicaid agency in their state of residence.

Medicare, on the other hand, is a federally governed program which provides specific medical benefits to individuals

- age 65 or over,
- people under the age of 65 with certain disabilities, or
- people of any age with end-stage renal disease (permanent kidney failure requiring dialysis or a kidney transplant).

Because Medicare is a federally governed program, application for enrollment is made through an individual's Social Security office.[6]

There are four different parts of Medicare that help to cover specific services:

1. *Medicare Part A (hospital insurance).* This will cover the inpatient care that is required within a hospital. It will also assist in covering skilled nursing facilities, hospice, and any necessary home health care.
2. *Medicare Part B (medical insurance).* This portion of Medicare will assist in covering doctors' and other healthcare provider's services, any outpatient care, durable medical equipment (DME), or home healthcare.
3. *Medicare Part C (Medicare Advantage).* This portion of Medicare offers health plan options run by Medicare-approved private insurance companies, and is a way to get benefits covered under both Part A and Part B. Most Medicare Advantage plans will also cover Part D (prescription drug coverage).
4. *Medicare Part D (Medicare prescription drug coverage).* This portion of Medicare will help to cover the cost of prescription drugs by assisting in lowering the current prescription drug costs and attempting to protect against higher drug costs in the future. This portion of Medicare is run by Medicare-approved private insurance companies.[7]

There are five main players in the healthcare provider industry:

1. Patient
2. Provider
3. Payer
4. Plan sponsor
5. Vendor[8]

---

[6]   "Medicare.gov," accessed February 20, 2011, www.medicare.gov.

[7]   *Id.*

[8]   Rebecca S. Busch, *Healthcare Fraud: Auditing and Detection Guide,* (John Wiley & Sons, Inc., 2008).

The following sections provide more detailed definitions of these five players and how they work together.

Patient. The patient is the individual who actually receives healthcare services. Examples of healthcare fraud that may be perpetrated by a patient include the following:

- Submission of a false claim
- Over-exaggeration or complete falsification of workers' compensation claims
- Participation in an extensive healthcare fraud scheme or crime ring[9]

Provider. The provider is the entity *or* individual that performs a healthcare service. The range of these services includes, but is not limited to, the following:

- Doctors of medicine or osteopathy
- Doctors of dental surgery or medicine
- Podiatrists
- Optometrists
- Chiropractors
- Psychologists
- Physical therapists
- Speech language pathologists
- Occupational therapists

Examples of healthcare fraud perpetrated by a provider include the following:

- Submitting a false claim
- Duplicating legitimate claims by submitting the same claim multiple times
- Exaggerating legitimate claims prior to submission[10]

Payer. The payer in a healthcare service is the individual or entity that processes a financial transaction. According to Rebecca S. Busch's *Health Care Fraud: Auditing and Detection Guide*, payer schemes most often attempt to defraud government plan sponsors in the following ways:

- Misrepresenting performance guarantees
- Not answering beneficiary questions on claim status
- Making financial transactions that are not contractually based[11]

Plan Sponsor. The plan sponsor is the individual or entity that funds a transaction. It may include any combination of privately sponsored, employer-sponsored, or government-sponsored entities. Examples of plan sponsored healthcare fraud schemes include the following:

- Failure to pay premiums resulting in no coverage to the patient
- Management activities that discourage employees from seeking medical attention

---

9   *Id.*
10   *Id.*
11   *Id.*

- Encouraging employees to utilize medical facilities that provide the employer with a kickback or other incentive payment[12]

Vendor. The vendor is the entity that provides either the materials or services necessary to provide a patient with necessary healthcare services. Examples of vendor involved healthcare fraud schemes include the following:

- Submission of false claims
- Counterfeit medications
- Use of unlicensed professionals[13]

Note that a recurring fraud scheme perpetrated by all of these healthcare players—either individually or in collusion—is submission of false claims. This type of scheme will be described in greater detail later in this chapter.

Healthcare Regulations and Statutes

In order to gain a better grasp on how healthcare fraud can be prosecuted, it is important to understand key industry regulations and statutes. One of the most sweeping regulations is the Health Insurance Portability and Accountability Act of 1996 (HIPAA). According to *Black's Law Dictionary*, HIPAA provides additional health insurance protections by

- limiting the impact preexisting conditions can have on an individual's ability to obtain insurance;
- permitting an employee to enroll a new dependent acquired by birth, adoption, or marriage;
- making it easier for people to maintain insurance coverage while changing jobs, and
- helping businesses with fewer than 50 workers to purchase group insurance plans.

Under HIPAA, it is illegal for anyone to knowingly and willfully[14]

- defraud any healthcare benefit program or to obtain by means of false representations any money or property of a healthcare benefit program.
- make false statements in any matter involving a healthcare benefit program.
- embezzle, convert, or steal any funds, property, or assets of a healthcare benefit program.
- obstruct, delay, prevent, or mislead the investigation of federal healthcare offenses.

The main purpose of HIPAA is to prevent inappropriate use or disclosure of an individual's health information. In addition, the law requires organizations that use such information to protect the systems that store, transmit, and process sensitive health data. This act applies to both private and public health plans.

---

[12] *Id.*

[13] *Id.*

[14] Health Insurance Portability and Accountability Act of 1996., www.hhs.gov/ocr/privacy/.

Prior to HIPAA, healthcare fraud was typically prosecuted as mail fraud or making false statements and subject to a substantial fine and sentence of up to 5 years' imprisonment for each count. Today, however, crimes that violate HIPAA provisions can result in a penalty of 10 years' imprisonment and a substantial fine, unless the violation results in serious bodily injury. Under those circumstances, the imprisonment term is 20 years (in cases of death, the HIPAA penalty imposes a life sentence).[15]

There are terms found in HIPAA that are important for investigators to understand. Such terms are explained at the end of this chapter.

Although HIPAA is a significant part of modern healthcare law, it is not the only regulation utilized when prosecuting healthcare fraud. For that reason, it is very important for fraud investigators to understand other statutes and regulations that affect healthcare fraud and be knowledgeable about state and federal agencies that have responsibility for enforcing these regulations. For additional research into HIPAA and the specific regulation surrounding HIPAA, see the U.S. Department of Health and Human Services website at www.hhs.gov. Specific information relating to the HIPAA Privacy Rule is located at http://privacyrule-andresearch.nih.gov/.

Criminal Prosecution of Fraud Cases

The Department of Justice has primary responsibility for enforcing federal criminal laws regarding healthcare fraud. This includes all U.S. District Attorney's offices, with assistance from the Federal Bureau of Investigation (FBI). In addition, the federal Office of Inspector General is responsible for investigating fraud cases and bringing enforcement actions.

Meanwhile, individual states have their own statutes relating to fraud control. This typically involves each state's Medicaid fraud control unit, with assistance from local prosecutors.

In criminal fraud cases, whether they are federal or state, charges can involve general statutes or more explicit laws related to healthcare. Penalties imposed for these types of criminal charges may lead to life in prison, depending on the severity of a case.

Title II, "Preventing Health Care Fraud and Abuse; Administrative Simplifications; Medical Liability Reform" of HIPAA specifically relates to healthcare fraud. This section was instrumental in creating the offense of healthcare fraud and clarified how the crimes of theft, embezzlement, false statements, obstruction of a criminal investigation, and money laundering can be incorporated into private health plans and contracts that involve healthcare fraud. Along with strengthening legal sanctions against fraud, HIPAA also introduced key programs that are significant in fraud control, such as the Health Care Fraud and Abuse Control Program and the Medicare Integrity Program.

---

[15] David A. Hyman, "HIPAA and Health Care Fraud: An Empirical Perspective," *Cato Journal* 22 (Spring/Summer 2002).

Health Care Fraud and Abuse Control Program

The Health Care Fraud and Abuse Control (HCFAC) Program is jointly administered by the U.S. Attorney General and the Secretary of Health and Human Services. The program is designed to coordinate federal, state, and local law enforcement activities with respect to healthcare fraud and abuse.[16]

The HCFAC Program's goals are to[17]

- coordinate federal, state, and local law enforcement efforts relating to healthcare fraud and abuse with respect to health plans;
- conduct investigations, audits, inspections, and evaluations relating to the delivery of and payment for healthcare in the United States
- facilitate enforcement of all applicable remedies for such fraud
- provide guidance to the healthcare industry regarding fraudulent practices
- establish a national data bank to receive and report final adverse actions against healthcare providers and suppliers

A special component of HIPAA is its dedicated funding, via the HCFAC account (located within the Medicare Part A trust fund). During fiscal 2010, the Medicare trust fund received transfers of approximately $2.86 billion from healthcare fraud judgments or settlements obtained by the government. This included more than $683 million in federal Medicaid funds transferred separately to the U.S. Treasury as a result of these same efforts.[18] In addition, the FBI was allocated more than $130 million in funding from HIPAA and from the discretionary HCFAC account for healthcare fraud enforcement. As noted previously, all fines, penalties, or other recoveries made as a result of the government's HIPAA-related fraud control efforts are transferred to the Medicare Part A trust fund.[19] This helps ensure the fraud enforcement program will be self-sustaining.

Criminal Statutes Related to Healthcare Fraud

In addition to HIPAA regulations, fraud investigators must understand a number of other very important criminal statutes, as discussed in this section.

Healthcare Fraud

Crimes and Criminal Procedure, U.S. Code (USC) Title 18, Section 1347, provides the following definition of healthcare fraud:

> In connection with the delivery of or payment for health care benefits, items or services, any individual who knowingly or willfully: defrauds a health care benefit

---

[16] Department of Health and Human Services and Department of Justice, *Health Care Fraud and Abuse Control Program Annual Report for Fiscal Year 2010* (January 2011).

[17] *Id.*

[18] *Id.*

[19] David A. Hyman, "HIPAA and Health Care Fraud: An Empirical Perspective," *Cato Journal* 22 (Spring/Summer 2002).

> program or obtains by false or fraudulent pretenses, any money or property owned by a health care benefit program.

This statute is modeled after the federal bank, mail, or wire fraud statute, largely because its application centers on demonstrating a scheme to defraud. With that in mind, fraud investigators must show

- a beginning point,
- an ending point, and
- the participants.

If the scheme to defraud and the involvement of a healthcare entity are both clearly shown, this statute can be used to prosecute the case.

Theft or Embezzlement in Connection With Healthcare

18 USC 669 provides the following definition:

> Whoever knowingly and willfully embezzles, steals, or otherwise without authority converts to the use of any person other than the rightful owner, or intentionally misapplies any of the moneys, funds, securities, premiums, credits, property, or other assets of a health care benefit program, shall be fined under this title or imprisoned not more than 10 years, or both; but if the value of such property does not exceed the sum of $100 the defendant shall be fined under this title or imprisoned not more than one year, or both.

This statute is often used in prosecuting medical practices that are defrauded from the inside due to a dishonest employee(s). This may include employees who have stolen money, drugs, blank prescription pads, or even identities of customers or patients. A key takeaway from cases involving this theft or embezzlement statute is that the healthcare provider may or may not be engaged in the fraud. In fact, it may just be a rogue employee who is responsible for the crime.

False Statements Relating to Health Care Matters 18 USC 1035 provides the following definition:

> Whoever, in any matter involving a health care benefit program, knowingly and willfully—
>
> 1. falsifies, conceals, or covers up by any trick, scheme, or device a material fact; or
> 2. makes any materially false, fictitious, or fraudulent statements or representations, or makes or uses any materially false writing or document knowing the same to contain any materially false, fictitious, or fraudulent statement or entry, in connection with the delivery of or payment for health care benefits, items, or services, shall be fined under this title or imprisoned not more than 5 years, or both.

Other Criminal Statutes to Consider

In addition to these statutes that relate specifically to healthcare, a number of statutes are relevant to fraud investigations in general, and it is important for an investigator evaluating a healthcare fraud case to be aware of them. These statutes are covered in chapter 2, "Legal Foundations of Fraud Investigations."

Mail and wire fraud statutes, covered in chapter 2, are particularly important, because many healthcare fraud schemes use mail or electronic forms of communication. For mail fraud, the investigator does not need to show that a scam actually traveled from one point to another, only that the fraudster was intending to use some type of mail system, such as the U.S. Postal Service, UPS, or FedEx. On the other hand, wire fraud requires the investigator to show that a scheme used or caused to be used some type of wire (electronic) transfer, and that the transfer actually traveled using fax or email within or outside of United States. This is an important distinction, because many healthcare fraud documents are either sent by fax or e-mail, both of which would satisfy the wire fraud statute.

When deciding how to investigate and prosecute a case of healthcare fraud, it is wise to consider what statutes are easiest for jurors or a judge, lacking detailed financial acumen, to understand. A good approach to address that question is to look for ways to combine multiple statutes that possess common specified unlawful activities. For example, a key point in scrutinizing the fraud scheme is to figure out where the money went. By doing this, an investigator determines not only what scheme occurred, but which entity or individual ultimately benefited from the fraud scheme. Through this process, if money laundering violations are found, the doors are thrown wide open for the use of money laundering statutes and criminal and civil forfeiture. In these situations, the government is able to go in and siege funds when the forfeitures standards are present.

The preceding discussion by no means provides an exhaustive summary of statutes that may be utilized for prosecuting healthcare fraud. However, these statutes were chosen because they are often the easiest for fraud investigators to use, and they have the longest statutes of limitations, which provide the most potential exposure for fraudsters to face to criminal jail time and fines. Even though fraud investigators are not the ones to decide what statutes are used to prosecute a fraud scheme, they need to be well versed in these regulations to better assist the prosecution in making its case.

Civil Remedies

Although private parties, under certain circumstances, have the option of addressing healthcare fraud through a civil lawsuit, government agencies always have the option of taking on a case. When fraud cases are filed in civil courts, the False Claims Act (FCA) is often one of the most useful avenues of pursuit.

False Claims Act

Money and Finance, USC Title 31, Section 3729–3733 allows action against any individual who knowingly presents, or causes to be presented, a false or fraudulent claim for payment or approval, or knowingly makes, uses, or causes to be made or used, a false record or statement material to a false or fraudulent claim.

The penalties specifically outlined within the civil FCA statute indicate the following:

> "…[accused] is liable to the United States Government for a civil penalty of not less than $5,000 and not more than $10,000 as adjusted by the Federal Civil Penalties Inflation Adjustment Act of 1990, plus 3 times the amount of damages which the Government sustains because of the act of that person."

At first glance, the stated fines within the FCA seem to be minimal. However, the inclusion of "three times the amount" of damages added to penalties can bring fines to a staggering level. A good example of this multiplier effect can be found in *United States v. Krizek*, a case in which the government filed suit against a psychiatrist for submitting and conspiring to submit false claims to Medicare and Medicaid. The alleged illicit billing practice took place over a 6-year period and totaled more than 8,000 claims. Due to that lengthy time period and high claims total, the potential liability was in excess of $80 million. Ultimately, the Supreme Court found that the alleged damages were unreasonable and submitted the case to a master for calculation of damages.[20]

In addition to the potential for treble damages, the FCA is also highly useful in civil actions because it contains a *qui tam* (or "whistleblower") provision. *Black's Law Dictionary* defines whistleblower as "an employee who reports employer wrongdoing to a governmental or law enforcement agency."

With this provision, citizens who have evidence of fraud against the government or private agencies may sue on behalf of the government in order to recover stolen funds. If the government is successful in this type of action, the whistleblower is awarded at least 15 percent—but not more than 25 percent—of the proceeds from the action or settlement of the claim. The percentage depends on the extent to which the whistleblower "substantially contributed" to prosecuting the action.[21] Because tips and complaints are the most common means through which fraud schemes are uncovered, a monetary award for whistleblowers provides substantial incentive for private citizens to assist with healthcare fraud prevention.[22]

The FCA is not the only useful statute for civil prosecution of healthcare fraud. Other civil statutes that are extensively used include *The Public Health and Welfare*, USC Title 42, Section 1001, which pertains to Medicare and state healthcare programs. The statute provides that "every individual who is a qualified individual under section 1002 of this title shall, in accordance with and subject to the provisions of this subchapter, be entitled to a monthly benefit paid by the Commissioner of Social Security."

42 USC 1001 deals with payments that have been authorized by Social Security and are funneled through federal and military healthcare programs and state Medicaid systems. Investigators benefit from knowledge of this statute because in larger schemes it is common to find that Social Security fraud has occurred.

---

[20] Mark L. Bennett, Jr., "Criminal Prosecutions for Medicare and Medicaid Fraud," available at www.aapsonline.org/fraud/fraud.htm.

[21] *Money and Finance*, 31 USC 3729 (False Claims Act).

[22] *Id.*

Case Studies

There are five basic components to a healthcare fraud investigation:

1. Misrepresentation of a material fact
2. Knowledge of the falsity of the misrepresentation or ignorance of its truth
3. Intent
4. A victim action on the misrepresentation
5. Damage to the victim

The following four healthcare fraud cases are presented to help investigators fully understand how these components work in the real world. Each of these studies reviews the key facts of each case and explains how the five basic fraud components were met.

Whistleblower: *U.S. v. Richard M. Scrushy*

Key Facts

Richard Marin Scrushy was the founder of HealthSouth Corporation, a global healthcare company based in Birmingham, Alabama. At one time, HealthSouth was the largest U.S. provider of inpatient rehabilitation services.[23] During his tenure as CEO of the firm, Scrushy perpetrated a fraud scheme over a 16-year period, creating an overall loss of $2.6 billion to investors during that time. The case included a variety of illicit activities, including on-the-books fraudulent statements, financial statement fraud, asset or revenue overstatement, and creation of fictitious revenue schemes, as shown in the following figure.

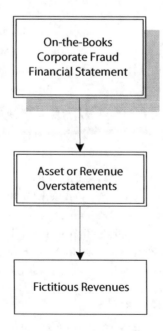

---

[23] Laurence Viele Davidson and David Beasley, "HealthSouth's Scrushy Liable in $2.88 Billion Fraud (Update 3)," *Bloomberg*, June 18, 2009.

In this case, fraud components were met in the following ways:

- *Misrepresentation of a material fact*. Scrushy conspired with many HealthSouth officers and accounting staff to make false entries in the company's accounting system. This fraudulently inflated the results, operations, and financial condition reported by the business, including $2.7 billion in fictitious income reported from 1996–2002.
- *Knowledge of the falsity of the misrepresentation or ignorance of its truth*. Scrushy knew the information provided for financial statements was false, but he still coerced corporate accounting staff to make incorrect entries.
- *Intent*. Because Scrushy instructed the accounting staff to make the incorrect entries, the component of intent was satisfied.
- *A victim action on the misrepresentation*. Because HealthSouth was a publicly traded company, individuals or entities purchased HealthSouth stock. Thus, those stockholders relied upon the firm's false or misleading financial statements, which resulted from fraudulent accounting entries.
- *Damage to the victim*. After the fraud was exposed, the share value of HealthSouth dropped significantly, causing billions of dollars in losses to investors.

Case Results

Scrushy was the first CEO charged with violating the Sarbanes-Oxley Act of 2002.[24] The original indictment in 2003 contained 85 counts of conspiracy, money laundering, securities fraud, and mail fraud. The number of counts was subsequently dropped to 36, and Scrushy was ultimately acquitted on all counts.[25] However, a second criminal trial indicted Scrushy on 30 counts of money laundering, extortion, obstruction of justice, racketeering, and bribery. This time, Scrushy was found guilty and sentenced to 6 years and 10 months in a federal prison. He was also ordered to pay $267,000 in restitution, serve 3 years' probation, and pay a fine of $150,000.[26] In a subsequent civil trial, HealthSouth investors sought damages for money lost due to the scheme. Scrushy was again found guilty and ordered to pay $2.87 billion in damages.

DME Fraud: *District of Kansas v. Ben Carroll*

Key Facts

Ben Carroll was the owner of Bulldog Medical of Kissimmee, Inc. (Florida) and MLC-Geriatric Health Services. These companies supplied DME to many healthcare agencies, including a number of nursing homes. Over time, the nursing homes were eventually persuaded to turn over their medical supply billing to Carroll's companies in exchange for a supply of free adult diapers for each nursing home. With the expanded billing opportunity in place, Carroll then opened offices in each state and invoiced Medicare not for adult diapers, but for reimbursement under Healthcare Common Procedure Coding System Code A4328,

---

[24] Greg Farrell, "Scrushy acquitted of all 36 charges," *USA Today*, June 28, 2005.

[25] *Id.*

[26] Bob Sims, "Siegelman, Scrushy taken into custody," *The Birmingham News*, June 28, 2007.

the code for a female eternal urinary collection prosthetic device. The plan was simple: Carroll had done his research and knew Medicare would reimburse providers for prosthetic devices, but not for adult diapers or convenience supplies used by incontinent patients.[27]

Carroll started in Kansas and identified a carrier of these A4328 prosthetic devices and learned that it was paying $8.54 for each device, whereas the adult diapers were only $0.50 each. Carroll then proceeded to supply the $0.50 diapers, but bill Medicare for reimbursement on the A4328 prosthetic device. Because of surge of billing for device A4328 in Kansas, the carrier began investigating Carroll and his billings. In December 1993, the Kansas carrier advised Carroll that he improperly billed Medicare for the diapers and that all future payments to Carroll's companies for the A4328 were suspended. In addition, Carroll was also advised that the Kansas carrier was off-setting $1.6 million in future payments due to improper billing for ostomy [artificial opening for elimination of bodily wastes] products.[28]

This did not deter Carroll however. He continued to do his research and found a different carrier in Florida. Still using the same coding for A4328, Carroll billed Medicare more than $23 million and was paid more than $16 million. In addition to the A4328 scheme perpetrated by Carroll, he also began to bill for incontinence kits that were not medically necessary. The Florida scheme was uncovered after more than 245 complaints of false and fraudulent billing were reported to the Medicare Fraud Branch of Blue Cross/Blue Shield of Florida[29] due to the explanation of medical benefits; while billing legitimate DME, they are also billing for these extras and waving the co-pay. In order to discover this scheme, the money had to be traced. The legitimate expenses had to be separated from the fraudulent billings, and the fraudulent billings were then traced to the fraudsters involved.

This case study is a clear example of illegal payer activities, which include on-the-books employee fraud, asset misappropriation, cash disbursement fraud, and a billing scheme by a nonaccomplice vendor, as shown in the following figure.

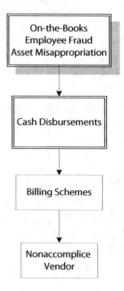

---

[27] "Health Care Fraud Issues," *U.S. Attorneys' (USA) Bulletin*, 45 (April 1997).

[28] *Id.*

[29] *Id.*

In this case, fraud components were met in the following ways:

- *Misrepresentation of a material fact.* When Carroll's companies provided one type of DME but billed for a completely separate DME item, the companies misrepresented a material fact.
- *Knowledge of the falsity of the misrepresentation or ignorance of its truth.* Even after being told by healthcare clients in Kansas that his companies were incorrectly billing for the A4328 devices, Carroll continued to perpetrate the scheme in Florida.
- *Intent.* The government was able to identify agents and doctors who refused to work with Carroll because they were aware of his illegal activities. In addition, interviews during the fraud investigation uncovered that Carroll's companies attempted to package the diapers as "female urinary collection pouches." The firms even created a mock-up of new (and deceptive) packaging for clients and prospects.
- *A victim action on the misrepresentation.* The victim in this scheme was Medicare, because it relied upon billing submitted by Carroll's firms and reimbursed based on these submissions.
- *Damage to the victim.* There was substantial damage, because Medicare reimbursed Carroll's companies more than $27 million—funds that should never have been billed in the first place.

Case Results

Carroll pleaded guilty one week before his trial began. His plea consisted of one count of mail fraud charged in the District of Kansas indictment. Additionally, he agreed to plead guilty to one count of conspiracy that was subsequently filed in the Middle District of Florida. He was sentenced to 10 years in prison and ordered to pay $5 million in restitution to the District of Kansas, and he signed a consent judgment in which he forfeited $32 million to the Middle District of Florida.[30]

Fraudulent Ambulance Claims: *UW v. Muhammed Nasiru Usman*

Key Facts

Muhammed Nasiru Usman (Usman) was the owner/operator of Royal Ambulance Service, Inc. (Royal) and First Choice EMS, Inc. (First Choice). Royal and First Choice were primarily in the business of transferring nonemergency patients to and from dialysis treatments three times per week. Usman, along with co-defendants Shaun (Outen) and David (McNac), conspired to defraud Medicare and Medicaid by submitting false claims related to the transfer of their dialysis patients. The co-defendants instructed employees to omit vital pieces of information from reimbursement claims, such as whether the patients walked to the

---

30 *Id.*

ambulance or whether they required the use of a stretcher in the ambulance. These essential pieces of information are critical to establish reimbursement from Medicare and Medicaid. Ultimately, evidence showed that Usman, Outen, and McNac were responsible for submitting more than $3.5 million in fraudulent claims through Royal and First Choice, receiving payments of more than $1.3 million.[31] This was a clear case of illegal vendor activity, using on-the-books employee fraud, asset misappropriation, cash disbursement schemes, and billing schemes, as shown in the following figure.

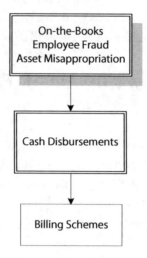

In this case, fraud components were met in the following ways:

- *Misrepresentation of a material fact.* Usman, Outen, and McNac misrepresented the material fact about whether their patients were able to walk to the ambulance or required the use of the stretcher in the ambulance.
- *Knowledge of the falsity of the misrepresentation or ignorance of its truth* Usman, Outen, and McNac knew the information was false when filing for reimbursement from Medicare and Medicaid.
- *Intent.* Usman, Outen, and McNac demonstrated intent when instructing employees of Royal and First Choice to omit these vital pieces of information in reimbursement filings.
- *A victim action on the misrepresentation.* The victims in this scheme are Medicaid and Medicare.
- *Damage to the victim.* Medicaid and Medicare paid out more than $1.3 million in fraudulent reimbursement claims endorsed by Usman, Outen, and McNac.

---

[31] US Department of Justice, Northern District of Texas, "Local Ambulance Company Owner Sentenced to 15 Years in Federal Prison and Ordered to Pay $1.3 Million in Restitution for Running Health Care Fraud Scheme," news release, October 13, 2010.

Case Results

Usman was convicted on 14 counts, including one count of conspiracy to commit health-care fraud, 12 counts of healthcare fraud, and one count of engaging in monetary transactions from specified unlawful activity. He was then sentenced to 15 years in federal prison and ordered to pay $1.3 million in restitution.[32] Outen, who pleaded guilty to one count of conspiracy to commit healthcare fraud, was sentenced to 41 months in federal prison and ordered to pay approximately $360,000 in restitution for his role in the healthcare fraud scheme. McNac, who also pleaded guilty to the same count of conspiracy to commit health-care fraud, was sentenced to 41 months in prison. The $1.3 million in restitution ordered to be paid by Usman is jointly and severally ordered of McNac also.[33]

False Claims: *U.S. v. Charles M. Parrot, M.D.*

Key Facts

Charles M. Parrot, M.D. was a well-known family practice physician in southeastern Connecticut. He was charged with a scheme to defraud insurers and his own patients by billing for services and procedures he did not perform, services that he fraudulently "upcoded," and services and procedures that were not medically necessary. He perpetrated this scheme by altering claims to add false diagnoses, falsifying patients' medical records, and fabricating symptoms, test results, and entire office visits.[34]

Parrot's scheme was reported by patients, employees, and co-workers to both Medicare and the Civilian Health and Medical Program of the Uniformed Services (CHAMPUS). Those agencies, in turn, reported the allegations to federal law enforcement. During the subsequent investigation, the U.S. Attorney's office was able to determine that Parrot was

- altering stacks of healthcare claims late at night or on weekends without review or consultation with other doctors or medical assistants.
- altering claim forms through his computer and modem at his home address.
- creating "draft" claim forms with hand-written notations of upcodes and added procedures and diagnoses.
- altering electronic claim forms for dozens of patients a day, who were identified through data mining of the billing software. For example, evidence showed Parrot added more than $16,000 in fraudulent charges in a single day.[35]
- utilizing a "burn box" at his home to destroy "draft" claim forms.

This case study is a clear example of illegal provider activities, such as on-the-books employee fraud, asset misappropriation, cash disbursement, and expense reimbursement fraud. It also demonstrates mischaracterized, overstated, or fictitious expenses, as shown in the following figure.

---

[32] *Id.*

[33] US Department of Justice, Northern District of Texas, "Defendants Who Worked at Local Ambulance Company Sentenced for Their Role in Health Care Fraud Scheme," news release, January 5, 2011.

[34] "Health Care Fraud Issues," *USA Bulletin*, 45 (June 1997).

[35] *Id.*

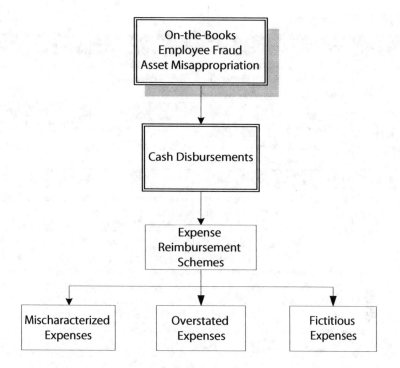

In this case, fraud components were met in the following ways:

- *Misrepresentation of a material fact.* The material facts include every instance in which Parrot falsified procedures, upcoded procedures, or billed for procedures that were not medically necessary.
- *Knowledge of the falsity of the misrepresentation or ignorance of its truth.* Parrot knew this information was false when he created "draft" claim forms with hand-written up-codings and when he altered the claim forms late at night and on weekends.
- *Intent.* Intent is shown by the "burn box," evidence that Parrot was burning "draft" claim forms at his home residence.
- *A victim action on the misrepresentation.* The victims are Medicare and CHAMPUS, both of which relied on false payment information submitted by Parrot.
- *Damage to the victim.* Damage occurred when Medicare and CHAMPUS reimbursed Parrot for procedures and services that were not actually performed.

Case Results

The day before the trial began, Parrot entered guilty pleas on false claims charges. He was sentenced to 15 months in prison, a term of supervised release, and a restitution order covering all counts in the superseding indictment (not merely the counts of conviction). His medical license is suspended indefinitely.[36]

---

[36]   *Id.*

Selected HIPAA Terminology[*]

Term	Explanation
Covered entity	This would include (1) a health plan, (2) a healthcare clearinghouse, or (3) a health-care provider who transmits any health information in electronic form in connection with a covered transaction.
CMS	Centers for Medicare and Medicaid Services within the Department of Health and Human Services.
Disclosure	The release, transfer, provision of, access to, or divulging of any information outside the entity holding the information.
EIN	An employer identification number assigned by the IRS.
Electronic media	Includes (1) electronic storage media, including memory devices in computers (hard drives) and any removable or transportable digital memory medium, such as magnetic tape or disc, optical disc, or digital memory card, or (2) transmission media used to exchange information already in electronic storage media. Transmission media include, for example, the Internet (wide-open), extranet (using internet technology to link a business with information accessible only to collaborating parties), leased lines, dial-up lines, private networks, and the physical movement of removable or transportable electronic storage media. Certain transmissions, including paper, via facsimile, and of voice, via telephone, are not considered to be transmissions via electronic media, because the information being exchanged did not exist in electronic form before the transmission.
HHS	Department of Health and Human Services
Healthcare	Encompasses care, services, or supplies related to the health of an individual. Health-care includes, but is not limited to the following: (1) Preventive, diagnostic, therapeutic, rehabilitative, maintenance, or palliative care and counseling, service, assessment, or procedure with respect to the physical or mental condition, or functional status, of an individual or that affects the structure or function of the body and (2) sale of a drug, device, equipment, or other item in accordance with a prescription.
Healthcare clearinghouse	A public or private entity, including a billing service, repricing company, community health management information system, or community health information system and "value-added" networks and switches that (1) process or facilitate the processing of health information received from another entity in a nonstandard format or containing nonstandard data content into standard data elements or a standard transactions or (2) receive a standard transaction from another entity and process or facilitate the processing of nonstandard data content for the receiving entity.
Healthcare provider	A provider of services, a provider of medical or health services, and any other person or organization that furnishes bills or is paid for healthcare in the normal course of business.
Health information	Any information, whether oral or recorded, in any form or medium that is created or received by a healthcare provider, health plan, public health authority, employer, life insurer, school or university, or healthcare clearinghouse that relates to the past, present, or future physical or mental health or condition of an individual, the provision of healthcare to an individual, or the past, present, or future payment for the provision of healthcare to an individual.
Health insurance issuer	An insurance company, insurance service, or insurance organization (including a health maintenance organization [HMO]) that is licensed to engage in the business of insurance in a state and is subject to any state law that regulates insurance. This term does not include group health plans.
Health maintenance organization	A federally qualified HMO, an organization recognized as an HMO under state law, or a similar organization regulated for solvency under state law in the same manner and to the same extent as an HMO.

Term	Explanation

Health Plan	An individual or group plan that provides or pays the cost of medical care.
	1. A health plan includes the following, singly or in combination:
	  i. A group health plan
	  ii. A health insurance issuer, as defined in this section
	  iii. An HMO, as defined in this section
	  iv. Part A or Part B of the Medicare program under title XVIII of the Act
	  v. The Medicare program under title XIX of the act
	  vi. An issuer of a Medicare supplemental policy
	  vii. An issuer of a long-term care policy, excluding a nursing home fixed-indemnity policy
	  viii. An employee welfare benefit plan or any other arrangement that is established or maintained for the purpose of offering or providing health benefits to the employees of two or more employers
	  ix. The healthcare program for active military personnel under *Armed Forces,* USC Title 10
	  x. The veterans healthcare program under *Veteran's Benefits,* USC Title 38, Chapter 17
	  xi. The Civilian Health and Medical Program of the Uniformed Services
	  xii. The Indian Health Service program under the Indian Health Care Improvement Act, *Indians,* USC Title 25, Section 1601, *et seq*
	  xiii. The Federal Employee Health Benefits Program under *Appendix,* USC Title 5, Section 8902
	  xiv. An approved state child health plan under Title XXI of the act, providing benefits for child health assistance that meet the requirements of Section 2103 of the act, *The Public Health and Welfare,* USC Title 42, Section 1397, *et seq*
	  xv. The Medicare+Choice program under Part C of the Title XVIII of the act, 42 USC 1395w-21–1395w-28
	  xvi. A high risk pool that is a mechanism established under state law to provide health insurance coverage or comparable coverage to eligible individuals
	  xvii. Any other individual or group plan, or combination of individual or group plans, that provides or pays for the cost of medical care
	2. A health plan excludes the following:
	  i. Any policy, plan, or program to the extent that it provides, or pays for the cost of, excepted benefits that are listed in Section 2791 (c)(1) of the Public Health Service Act, 42 USC 300gg-91(c)(1) and
	  ii. A government-funded program (other than the one listed in paragraph (1) (i)–(xvi) of this definition)
	    A. whose principal purpose is other than providing, or paying the cost of, healthcare or
	    B. whose principal activity is
	      1. the direct provision of healthcare to persons or
	      2. the making of grants to fund the direct provision of healthcare to persons.

Individual	A person who is the subject of protected health information.

Term	Explanation

Individually identifiable health information	A subset of health information, including demographic information collected from an individual, that
	1. is created or received by a healthcare provider, health plan, employer, or healthcare clearinghouse and
	2. relates to the past, present, or future physical or mental health or condition of an individual; the provision of healthcare to an individual; or the past, present, or future payment for the provision of healthcare to an individual and
	  i. that identifies the individual or
	  ii. with respect to which there is a reasonable basis to believe the information can be used to identify the individual.

Organized healthcare arrangement	1. A clinically integrated care setting in which individuals typically receive healthcare from more than one healthcare provider
	2. An organized system of healthcare in which more than one covered entity participates and in which the participating covered entities
	  i. hold themselves out to the public as participating in a joint arrangement and
	  ii. participate in joint activities that include at least one of the following:
	    A. Utilization review, in which healthcare decisions by participating covered entities are reviewed by other participating covered entities or by a third party on their behalf
	    B. Quality assessment and improvement activities, in which treatment provided by participating covered entities is assessed by other participating covered entities or by a third party on their behalf
	    C. Payment activities, if the financial risk for delivery healthcare is shared, in part or in whole, by participating covered entities through the joint arrangement and if protected health information created or received by a covered entity is reviewed by other participating covered entities or by a third party on their behalf for the purpose of administering the sharing of financial risk
	3. A group health plan and a health insurance issuer or HMO with respect to such group health plan, but only with respect to protected health information created or received by such health insurance issuer or HMO that relates to individuals who are or who have been participants or beneficiaries in such group health plan
	4. A group health plan and one or more other group health plans each of which are maintained by the same plan sponsor
	5. The group health plans described in paragraph (4) of this definition and health insurance issuers or HMOs with respect to such group health plans, but only with respect to protected health information created or received by such health insurance issuers or HMOs that relate to individuals who are or have been participants or beneficiaries in any of such group health plans

Person	A natural person, trust or estate, partnership, corporation, professional association or corporation, or other entity, public or private.

Protected health information	Individually identifiable health information
	1. except as provided in paragraph (2) of this definition, that is
	  i. transmitted by electronic media,
	  ii. maintained in electronic media, or
	  iii. transmitted or maintained in any other form or medium.
	2. Protected health information excludes individually identifiable health information in
	  i. education records covered by the Family Education Rights and Privacy Act, as amended, *Education,* USC Title 20, Section 1232g;
	  ii. records described at 20 U.S.C. 1232g(a)(4)(B)(iv); and
	  iii. employment records held by a covered entity in its role as employer.

Term	Explanation
Transaction	The transmission of information between two parties to carry out financial or administrative activities related to healthcare. It includes the following types of information transmissions: 1. Healthcare claims or equivalent encounter information 2. Healthcare payment and remittance advice 3. Coordination of benefits 4. Healthcare claim status 5. Enrollment and disenrollment in a health plan 6. Eligibility for a health plan 7. Health plan premium payments 8. Referral certification and authorization 9. First report of injury 10. Health claims attachments 11. Other transactions that the secretary may prescribe by regulation
Use	With respect to individually identifiable health information, the sharing, employment, application, utilization, examination, or analysis of such information within an entity that maintains such information.
Workforce	Employees, volunteers, trainees, and other persons whose conduct, in the performance of work for a covered entity, is under the direct control of such entity, whether or not they are paid by the covered entity.

[*] www.hhs.gov/ocr/privacy/hipaa/administrative/securityrule/nist80066.pdf.

Insurance Fraud

Patricia M. Tilton, CPA

Introduction

The insurance industry is exposed to each of the broad categories of fraud. But, additional nuances exist that are unique to the insurance industry, including factors related to its regulatory environment, particularly with regard to reporting and operational regulations, and the overall complexity of the industry's products, structures, and other operational considerations.

Insurance fraud, for purposes of this chapter, is defined as fraud involving insurance policyholders, claimants, brokers, agents, insurance company employees or management, third-party administrators, and other third parties involved in acts of fraud and misconduct affecting the insurance industry. This chapter emphasizes fraud and misconduct affecting the insurance industry, but excludes specific events of fraud or misconduct at an insured entity, for example, a manufacturing company, that is covered by an insurance policy[1] issued to that entity (for example, directors and officers insurance, fiduciary insurance, errors and omissions insurance).

Insurance policy and claim-related fraud is generally considered to be second only to tax evasion, at least in the United States. Insurance fraud is costly to the insurance industry, and, in turn, to consumers and investors. Numerous efforts are being made by insurance companies, state and federal agencies, and other public and private enterprises to identify, track, and prosecute insurance fraud; monitor insurance fraud schemes and trends; and educate consumers, regulators, law enforcement, and other insurance industry participants about insurance-related fraud. Those efforts often, and increasingly, also include a variety of anti-fraud organizations in other countries.

Among the largest, non-law enforcement, insurance fraud organizations based in the United States are the

- Coalition Against Insurance Fraud,
- National Health Care Anti-Fraud Association (NHCAA),
- Insurance Information Institute (III), and
- National Insurance Crime Bureau.

---

[1] Insurance policies issued by insurance companies generally exclude coverage if fraud or misconduct involving the insured is the causation unless specific contract language provides for such coverage.

In addition to the previously named organizations, numerous other organizations exist that are focused on insurance fraud-related matters, including those that are broker-, agent-, provider-, or consumer-based. In fact, a simple Internet search using "insurance fraud" will produce numerous websites that discuss insurance fraud, including fraud hotlines, schemes, prosecutions, and more.

This chapter will focus on the insurance industry using the following broad areas:

- An overview of the fraud categories and the insurance industry
- The basics of the insurance industry
- Insurance regulatory environment
- Insurance company structures, products, and operations
- Insurance fraud schemes
- Considerations in identifying insurance fraud schemes

Commonalities exist among industries about how frauds are executed. The motivation for insurance-related fraud is the same as for other industries, and it includes the three elements in the fraud triangle:

- *Opportunity*—It is possible for fraud to take place (for example, weak controls, collusion, and so on).
- *Pressure or incentive*—Pressure or incentive outweigh or overcome the incentive to act honestly (for example, financial pressures, sales targets, and so on).
- *Rationalization*—An ability to justify a fraudulent action achieved through a variety of means or reasons (for example, insurance company can afford it, victim will not suffer because he or she is insured, and so on).

This chapter highlights some of the factors to consider with respect to insurance fraud that are carried out through external means, internal means, or a combination of both that can affect an insurance, or insurance-related, enterprise.

An Overview of the Fraud Categories and the Insurance Industry

Insurance fraud and misconduct events can occur related to all types of insurance policies or coverages and involve individuals (including employees, policyholders, and other injured parties), brokers, agents, and other third parties. Further, insurance fraud is committed for a variety of reasons across the three categories of fraud.

Asset Misappropriation

AU section 316, *Consideration of Fraud in a Financial Statement Audit*, (AICPA, *Professional Standards*),[2] defines *misstatements due to misappropriation of assets* as follows:

---

[2] AICPA *Professional Standards* codify the U.S. Auditing Standards to be followed by CPAs in public practice. The "AU" designation is for audit-related matters.

Misstatements arising from misappropriation of assets (sometimes referred to as theft or defalcation) involve the theft of an entity's assets where the effect of the theft causes the financial statements not to be presented, in all material respects, in conformity with GAAP.[3] Misappropriation of assets can be accomplished in various ways, including embezzling receipts, stealing assets, or causing an entity to pay for goods or services that have not been received. Misappropriation of assets may be accompanied by false or misleading records or documents, possibly created by circumventing controls.[4]

Asset misappropriation may be committed by an insured, an employee, or another party through direct theft (for example, cash embezzlement or theft of an asset) or through an intentional misrepresentation, or deceit, to obtain an asset (for example, insurance coverage, claim payments, premiums, commissions, and so on).

Financial Statement Fraud

AU section 316 defines *fraudulent financial reporting* and further states, in part, the following:

Fraudulent financial reporting may be accomplished by the following–

- Manipulation, falsification, or alteration of accounting records or supporting documents from which financial statements are prepared.
- Misrepresentation in or intentional omission from the financial statements of events, transactions, or other significant information.
- Intentional misapplication of accounting principles relating to amounts, classification, manner of presentation, or disclosure.[5]

Financial statement fraud within the insurance industry is an exposure both with respect to financial statements prepared in accordance with GAAP, International Accounting Standards, and, for insurance regulatory reporting purposes, as applicable, statutory accounting principles (SAP) and the respective underlying financial transactions and data. Insurance company financial statement fraud can occur in, among other areas, financial estimations, related party transactions, valuations, intentional erroneous application of accounting principles, and inadequate or erroneous disclosures. Financial statement fraud can also be facilitated by complex corporate structures, transactions, and inadequate controls and processes.

Representations (or misrepresentations) or misstatements may also facilitate fraud and may expose a company to financial or reputational loss. Such representations or statements may include, for example, fraudulent information on a resume that results in employment and payments to an employee who otherwise might not have been hired. Fraudulent statements by an agent may also result in an insurance company contracting with an agent who may not be the person represented and result in commissions being paid by the insurance company.

---

[3] AICPA *Professional Standards* also apply to other comprehensive basis of accounting (OCBOA), which includes statutory accounting principles (SAP) used by insurance companies for regulatory purposes.

[4] AU section 316, *Consideration of Fraud in a Financial Statement Audit* (AICPA, *Professional Standards*).

[5] *Id.*

Fraudulent misrepresentation or statements can also occur to facilitate obtaining licenses or regulatory (or another party's) authorizations to execute business transactions.

Corruption and Prohibited Practice Schemes

Corruption or prohibited practice schemes in the insurance industry are not unlike those of other industries. Anti-corruption and prohibited practices are set forth in, among other guidance areas, certain federal and state laws and regulations. For example, all industries are subject to the Foreign Corrupt Practices Act and Racketeer Influenced and Corrupt Organizations Act, among others, but there are also specific regulations unique to insurance, particularly at the state level.

Corruption and prohibited practices schemes within the insurance industry can include entering into side agreements with another party that are not committed to in written agreements, bid rigging schemes, and unlicensed sales.

The Basics of the Insurance Industry

The insurance industry is a highly regulated industry. A variety of enterprises work in the insurance industry that provide numerous insurance products. Insurance enterprises include the following:

- *Insurance company.* An organization that underwrites insurance coverage.
- *Life (viatical) settlement company.* A company that will purchase from policyowners unwanted or underperforming life insurance.
- *Reinsurance company.* An organization that underwrites insurance coverage for an insurance company.
- *Captive insurance company.* An insurance company that insures the risks of its parent company organization, often commercial enterprises or other financial enterprises.
- *Risk retention group.* A form of organization that allows the pooling of premiums for purposes of insuring a designated group (for example, truckers, or farmers)
- *Insurance exchange.* A market mechanism, such as Lloyd's of London or the New York Insurance Exchange, for obtaining insurance for unique or hard-to-place risks, and, more recently, health insurance exchanges.
- *Insurance holding company.* An organizational structure in which one company is a sole or majority owner of an insurance company. A noninsurance company parent company may be deemed to be an insurance holding company.
- *Insurance broker.* A representative of an insurance buyer, generally a business, enterprise, or government.
- *Insurance agent.* An individual who sells insurance as an insurance company representative.
- *Third-party administrator.* An organization that provides policy or claim-related services to an insurance company.

Repair shops	Restoration companies	Construction companies
Hospitals	Doctors	Nurses
Chiropractors	Therapists	Pharmacies
Nursing homes	Engineers	Federal agencies*

* Examples of federal agencies involved in "insurance" include the Federal National Flood Insurance Program, Medicaid, and Medicare.

A variety of other parties and businesses are also involved in the business of insurance. Those parties and businesses may be involved in assisting in the underwriting process (for example, doctor's exams to facilitate obtaining insurance) or the claim or benefit process (for example, providing home repair, or medical services).

To understand and investigate potential or alleged insurance fraud, it is important to understand the variety of parties that may be involved, directly or indirectly, in an insurance transaction, at any point in the transaction life cycle. Those parties can include any of the parties identified previously but can also include other real or phony company representatives or parties and collusion among two or more participants, including policyowners or beneficiaries.

Insurance Regulatory Environment

Historically, in the United States, the insurance industry regulatory framework has primarily been a state-based regulatory system.[6] However, over time, U.S.-based insurance companies have increasingly been subject to various federal regulations. Most recently, as a result of the Dodd-Frank Wall Street Reform and Consumer Protection Act of 2010,[7] the federal government is becoming more directly involved in the business and regulation of insurance. That involvement includes the establishment of a new federal insurance "oversight" agency, the Federal Insurance Office within the U.S. Department of the Treasury. As of 2012, that office does not have direct rule-making authority over insurance regulation, but it is studying options related to state-based and federal-based levels of regulation for, or related to, the insurance industry.

In addition to the U.S.-based environment, other country-specific regulations also exist, and they must be considered by insurance enterprises that operate globally.[8] Despite

---

[6]   Insurance enterprises, like other enterprises, are, and have historically been, required to follow various federal laws and regulations such as equal opportunity employment laws, fair wage laws, racketeering laws, and so on.

[7]   The Dodd-Frank Wall Street Reform and Consumer Protection Act of 2010 (Pub. L. 111–203, H.R. 4173) contains several provisions affecting insurance companies, including, among numerous other provisions, the establishment of a Federal Insurance Office within the U.S. Treasury Department. The office is authorized to collect data on the insurance industry and make recommendations about regulation at the state and federal level. Refer to the text of the act for more specific details.

[8]   Country-specific regulations should be obtained and reviewed based on both the domiciliary country of the subject insurance company and those countries in which it is authorized or licensed to conduct business. Those regulations may apply to the general operations of the insurance company or financial reporting requirements.

efforts toward standardization, particularly with regard to, among others, anti-corruption, money-laundering, solvency, and financial accounting, local country, or state laws and regulations generally take precedence. As such, particularly with respect to U.S.-based insurance enterprises, it is important for management, employees, regulators, investigators, and others to be aware of an entity's regulatory environment, in totality, in assessing the risk of fraud and in investigating allegations of fraud.

Cultural consideration is also important to understanding and investigating fraud and misconduct. U.S.-based insurance companies are assumed to have a U.S.-centered business culture, particularly with respect to expected ethical behaviors. Foreign insurance companies that operate within the United States may embrace the business culture, mores, and ethical behaviors of its domicile, country, or embody a combination of its domicile country and foreign countries, including the U.S., business cultures and expected behaviors. Business cultural biases can also affect decisions that may affect how instances of fraud or misconduct are viewed or addressed. Fraud risk analysis and investigations of alleged misconduct can be affected not only by laws and regulations, but also by business cultures, mores, and behaviors, all of which need to be considered.

State Regulation

The primary regulator for a U.S.-based insurance company is the insurance commissioner (or superintendent) in the company's domiciliary state. However, an insurance company is also subject to the laws and regulations of each state in which it is licensed to conduct business or does business. In the United States, an insurance company is considered to be a domestic company only in the state in which it is domiciled; that same company is referred to as a "foreign" company in those other states in which it is licensed to transact business or transacts business. (For example, a company domiciled in Michigan that is licensed to transact business in Indiana is a foreign company in Indiana.) Non-U.S.-based insurance companies, that is, insurance companies domiciled in other countries but doing business in the United States, are generally referred to as "alien" companies. (For example, a Germany domiciled insurance company that is licensed [or authorized] to conduct business in New Jersey is an "alien" company.)

State-based regulation literally means that individual states, as well as the District of Columbia and Puerto Rico, have their own laws and regulations related to enterprises operating in the insurance industry. Those regulations affect a variety of areas, including corporate organization, books and records, products, pricing, financial management, benefits or claim management, contracting, licensing, fraud, governance, distribution, marketing, and regulatory reporting. Specific state laws and regulations also exist related to agents, brokers, managing general agents, third-party administrators, providers, reinsurers, life settlement companies, and insurance holding companies.

State insurance regulatory agencies often have published information about insurance fraud, including information about reporting alleged fraud, consumer information (and education) about fraud, common fraud schemes, and so on. That information can generally be accessed through the respective state's website or agency office.

In an effort to bring some level of standardization to the insurance state-based regulatory environment, the various state insurance commissioners created the National Association of Insurance Commissioners (NAIC). The NAIC is a membership organization that provides a national forum that focuses on addressing major insurance issues and developing policies for the regulation of insurance. A variety of committees within the NAIC focus on all aspects of insurance regulation, and some of the NAIC's work is accomplished through public–private committees that may include insurance company representatives, consumers, accountants, lawyers, and other third parties.

The NAIC has undertaken a number of efforts to facilitate the coordination of laws and regulations affecting the insurance industry in several areas, including financial reporting, licensure, regulatory monitoring and oversight, consumer education, and federal government interaction. The NAIC also has an Antifraud Task Force whose mission "is to serve the public interest by assisting the state insurance supervisory officials, individually and collectively, to promote the public interest through the detection, monitoring, and appropriate referral for investigation of insurance crime, both by and against consumers."[9] The Antifraud Task Force has certain working groups that are focused on various topics. It also works with other NAIC committees on matters related to fraud risk and other state and federal regulatory agencies with respect to matters involving such topics as anti-money laundering and the USA PATRIOT Act. The Antifraud Task Force has also developed a draft antifraud plan guideline. Additional information about the NAIC and the NAIC Antifraud Task Force is available at www.naic.org.

The NAIC's efforts have resulted in various "model acts," proposed regulations endorsed by the NAIC, that have been adopted by the various states. Certain of those model acts are adopted as proposed by the NAIC, or they may be deemed effectively, although not factually, adopted if a state's existing laws and regulations are "substantially similar" to the NAIC's proposed model act. Some states elect not to adopt certain of the NAIC's model acts, in whole or in part, for a variety of reasons, although those occurrences have become less common.

The following NAIC model acts[10] are directed toward fraud risk:

- Information and Privacy Protection Model Act (designed to, among other things, protect the use of information obtained from insurance applications; also forbids an insurer or agent from impersonating another party to obtain information about an insurance applicant, unless there is reasonable cause to suspect criminal activity)
- Model Life Insurance Solicitation Regulation (designed to, among other things, govern the selling of life insurance to prevent fraud or misrepresentation by insurers and agents)
- Insurance Fraud Prevention Model Act
- Automobile Insurance Fraud Guideline

---

[9]   National Association of Insurance Commissioners (NAIC) Antifraud Task Force, www.naic.org/committees_d_antifraud.htm.

[10]   See the NAIC website, www.naic.org.

State regulation of the insurance industry extends beyond the state insurance regulatory agencies as other state agencies and departments have also gotten involved in the insurance industry, including federal and state attorney generals and health and human services agencies, both in oversight and enforcement. Other nonspecific state laws and regulations may also affect the insurance industry.

Federal Insurance Regulation

The McCarran-Ferguson Act, federal legislation enacted by Congress in 1945, declared that the states would regulate the insurance industry. However, beyond existing generally applicable business federal laws and regulations described previously, the federal government has enacted legislation and other initiatives that affect, or will affect, the regulation of the insurance industry. Those federal efforts further add to the complexity of regulations facing the insurance industry. In addition to the Dodd-Frank Act previously described in this chapter, some of the other federal laws and regulations affecting the insurance industry include the following:

- Patient Protection and Affordable Care Act
- Employee Retirement Income Security Act of 1974 (ERISA)
- Gramm-Leach-Bliley Act
- Title XIX of the Social Security Act—Medicaid Program
- Title XVII of the Social Security Act—Medicare Program
- Medicare Catastrophic Coverage Act
- Terrorism Risk Insurance Act

The Dodd-Frank Act and the Patient Protection and Affordable Care Act, both of which were passed by Congress in 2010, are two significant federal laws that are still in transition with respect to the clarity and application of their respective provisions. In addition, various regulatory agencies responsible for the oversight and enforcement of those laws are involved in the development of specific rules and regulations related to required compliance by affected organizations. As a result, the impact of those two federal laws on the insurance industry is not yet fully known.

The federal government has also established various insurance programs that also involve the insurance industry directly and indirectly, including the following:

- Federal crop insurance program
- National Flood Insurance Program
- Medicare

Various insurance companies may also provide supplemental coverage related to the previously listed federal programs.

Insurance Company Structures, Products, and Operations

Company Structures

There are various organization structures for an insurance entity, all of which are subject to state rules, regulations, and laws. Those organization structures include the following:

- Stock companies (owned by shareholders)
- Mutual companies (owned by the policyholders)
- Fraternal companies (owned by members)
- Captive companies (parent-owned company)
- Risk Retention Groups (member-owned groups [for example, credit unions] and purchasing groups [for example, truckers] organized to acquire insurance for the homogeneous risks)

Certain of the foregoing structures are restricted to the parties that may be insured and the type of insurance coverage available.

Regardless of how an insurance enterprise is structured, it is subject to the laws and regulations of its domiciliary state and those states in which it is licensed to transact, or transacts, business. Those laws and regulations include provisions related to company structure, products, and business operations. Additional laws and regulations apply to overall corporate holding companies, also referred to as insurance holding companies, which may or may not operate specifically as an insurance company but own at least one insurance company (for example, a bank that owns an insurance company is an insurance holding company, an insurance company with insurance company and noninsurance company subsidiaries is an insurance holding company).

Insurance Company Products

Insurance enterprises may issue a variety of products, depending on the type of company authorization, its product authorizations, and licensure. There are more than 100 types of insurance available to commercial[11] and individual consumers. Although there are multiple categories, or types, of insurance coverage, generally insurance companies may be authorized to provide the following broad categories of insurance:

- *Property or casualty.* Commercial or business or personal coverage (for example auto, homeowners, art, buildings, or machinery)
- *Liability.* Commercial or business or personal coverage (for example, malpractice)
- *Workers' compensation.* Commercial or business employee accident-related coverage
- *Title insurance.* Land-related coverage, including defect or lien related coverage
- *Life.* Group or individual coverage

---

[11] As used in this section, the term "commercial" also includes government agencies and not-for-profit organizations.

- *Health.* Employer or group or individual coverage
- *Financial guarantee.* Coverage for protection against financial loss as a result of default; change in interest rate levels; differentials in interest levels between markets or products; fluctuations in exchange rates; inability to withdraw funds held in a foreign country due to government imposed restrictions; or changes in values of specific assets or commodities, financial or commodity indices, or price levels in general (for example structured investment bond insurance)
- *Surety bond.* A type of coverage for debt default or other default (for example, judicial court bond or construction bond)
- *Mortgage guarantee.* A form of life insurance coverage that pays the balance of a mortgage if the mortgagor dies
- *Credit insurance.* A form of insurance that provides for payment to the lender if the debtor dies (credit life) or is disabled (credit health) prior to repayment of the debt
- *Health maintenance organizations.* Member-based group health plan provided by employers

It is not uncommon for a company to be authorized to provide more than one type of insurance, for example, a property or casualty company may also provide liability or workers' compensation insurance; a life insurance company may also provide health insurance.

There are also reinsurance companies that are involved in the business of insurance for insurance companies (for example, life reinsurance companies, property, or casualty reinsurance). Reinsurance companies have operations similar to insurance companies but issue policies (reinsurance agreements) solely to other insurance companies. Reinsurance companies may be involved in both assuming risks and ceding risks to another insurance company. It is important that each reinsurance contract be in writing and set forth the specific contractual arrangements between the parties.

Based on the respective state's laws and regulations, insurance companies are required to submit, among other submissions, policy forms, material (or significant) reinsurance contracts or agreements, and rates to state insurance departments for approval.

Insurance Company Operations

Although a number of underlying processes and procedures exist, including the original development of the company's insurance policies, an insurance company's core operations include the following:

- Sales or distribution
- Underwriting
- Policy management
- Claims or benefits
- Financial

Underlying all of these operations are a number of processes and procedures and other supporting operations, including general management, human resources, legal, actuarial, and information technology and document management systems.[12,13]

Box 7-1 provides an overview of an insurance company's operational transaction cycles.

Box 7-1: Overview of an Insurance Transaction Cycle		
Underwriting Process	Policy underwriting is performed by underwriting employees of the insurance company (for example, the Underwriting Department) or authorized underwriting agents (that is, managing general underwriter or managing general agent).	Information obtained in the policy application is assessed for purposes of, among other reasons, underwriting risk and premium rating (pricing). If a policy is accepted, it is "underwritten" by the insurance company and an insurance policy can be issued.
Policy Acceptance	Policy acceptance occurs upon the mutual acceptance by the insured and the related insurance company of the policy terms.	Policy acceptance by the parties triggers the issuance of the insurance policy and the obligation of the insured to pay premiums.
Premium Processing	Premium payments are due in accordance with the underlying policy terms. Insurance companies maintain policyholder databases that are, generally, inclusive of premium payment status.	Agents generally do not collect premium due for most polices. Generally, premiums are remitted directly to the insurance company (or a lockbox). Policyholder data is then updated (by the Premium Processing or Policy Services Department) to memorialize, among other items, policy type, premium due, premium payments, and agent code.
Policy Sales Distribution	Policies may be sold through an insurance company's licensed agent or directly by a company.	Policy application is prepared by the policy applicant that provides information requested by the insurance company.
Policy Acceptance	Policy acceptance occurs upon the mutual acceptance by the insured and the related insurance company of the policy terms.	Policy acceptance by the parties triggers the issuance of the insurance policy and the obligation of the insured to pay premiums.

---

[12] A *document management system* is the process used to produce, accumulate, file, store, and retrieve hard copy and electronic documents related to the operations and transactions of a business. Document destruction policies are part of a document management system to allow for management of document destruction in the normal course of operations and preservation of documents for specific purposes (such as, litigation, investigation, or regulation)

[13] An insurance company's document management system and information technology system is often complex and may not be fully integrated across the company.

Commissions	Commissions are payable on policies sold, or renewed, by a licensed agent.	Commissions are paid based on contracts with the agents (an agent or agency contract).
Premium Processing	Premium payments are due in accordance with the underlying policy terms. Insurance companies maintain policyholder databases that are, generally, inclusive of premium payment status.	Agents generally do not collect premium due for most polices. Generally, premiums are remitted directly to the insurance company (or a lockbox). Policyholder data is then updated (by the Premium Processing or Policy Services Department) to memorialize, among other items, policy type, premium due, premium payments, and agent code.
Claim Processing	Claims may be reported by an insured person or a third party. Claims are reported to an insurance company directly or another designated party. Claims for losses are subject to an adjudication process, performed by an insurance company's Claims or Benefit Department or another authorized representative (that is, third-party administrator, managing general agents, and so on).	The claim process is focused on determining that a submitted claim represents a loss payable pursuant to the subject policy coverage and the loss amount, if any. Loss adjustment expenses may be incurred to investigate the claim including information to support or dispute the claimed loss. Claim status is maintained to track whether a claim is opened or closed and whether payment, if any, was made on the claim. Loss related claim payments may be remitted to various parties based on the particular claim. Insurance companies maintain claim information that includes, among other things, the subject loss, parties involved, type of loss, reserves, claim loss payments, claim expense payments, reinsurance, and claim status.

Reinsurance	Reinsurance is a form of insurance between insurance companies. Generally, reinsurance exists in two forms, ceded reinsurance and assumption reinsurance. Simply stated, the insurance company passing on the insurance risk is the ceding company and the insurance company accepting the risk is the assuming company. All reinsurance transactions are based on written contracts between the parties. Reinsurance contracts may be policy or loss specific or cover certain classes of policy coverage or types or loss.	Reinsurance contracts set forth the agreement between the subject companies and information related to the underlying reinsurance. Insurance companies may enter into a variety of types of reinsurance that cover underwriting risks or loss-related risks. A company's policy or claim information related to such reinsurance should identify, either by contract type or otherwise, if reinsurance is applicable and related financial transactions.
Loss and Benefit Reserving	Insurance companies estimate their underlying loss exposure on the policies issued by the company. Loss reserving involves estimating reserves for known unpaid claims and losses for claims that have been incurred by not reported (IBNR) on policy exposures. Unpaid losses and IBNR losses generally involve judgment—either by a claim adjuster or, generally, through actuarial modeling. Reserving for life insurance or annuity companies also involves estimations of future benefits due under issued policies or contracts. Those reserve estimates are often based on actuarial models.	Loss, policy, or contract reserves generally represent the largest liabilities of an insurance company. Although models may be used in the development of those reserves, significant judgments and assumptions are embedded in those models and related decisions with respect to the recorded reserve amounts. A third-party administrator that provides policy, contract, claim, or benefit processing services to an insured person may maintain its own related data systems. That data information is, in turn, provided to the insurance company, in hardcopy or electronically, to be considered in, input to, the overall policy or contract and loss or benefit information used by the insurer in its reserving process.

Financial Reporting	Financial reporting is the process whereby the various transactions supporting the insurance company's business are summarized into a readable format. Insurance companies may maintain financial records on a statutory accounting principles (SAP) basis, U.S. generally accepted accounting principles (GAAP) basis, International Financial Reporting Standards (IFRS) basis, or tax basis of accounting.* Those records must support the underlying business of the company. In addition to the insurance policy specific transactions, financial reporting also covers the investing processes and general business operations of the subject insurance company.	Financial reporting may be performed for a variety of purposes: State insurance regulation—SAP basis of accounting. Securities and Exchange Commission regulatory purposes—GAAP basis of accounting. Global regulatory reporting—IFRS basis of accounting. Federal tax regulatory reporting—tax basis of accounting. Financial reporting also may require a company to make certain financial disclosures as required for each of the aforementioned purposes.

* The various basis of accounting refer to the state regulatory statutory accounting principles, U.S. generally accepted accounting principles, International Financial Reporting Standards, and tax regulatory accounting ("tax") that are applicable based on the respective accounting standard for the related reporting of such financial information by the subject company.

Fraud risk exists in each of the foregoing processes, and it is therefore important to have a general understanding of each of the processes, including the related systems and documents required or produced as a result of those processes. Advances in technology have significantly affected the insurance industry, but they have also opened doorways to fraud, including misappropriation of data and information and identity theft. Technology advances are ever-changing, but advances such as electronic funds transfer, online sales, billing, application processes, electronic bill payment, e-mail, and website form creation are just a few of the areas that have opened doors to fraud and misconduct. As quickly as technology changes, fraudsters are developing ways to leverage those changes.

Insurance Company Operations: Sales or Distribution

Sales, or distribution, of a company's insurance product(s) may be accomplished through a variety of sales methods. The most common sales or distribution means are the following:

- *Direct.* An insurance company sells its products directly to the consumer.
- *Agents.* Individuals or groups of insurance agents sell directly to consumers and are paid commissions for such sales. Agents are required to be licensed and obtain

licenses from the state insurance department for the particular company for whom the agent sells products. Agents are subject to, and required to comply with, the licensing state's rules and regulations. An agent may sell exclusively for a particular company (commonly referred to as direct agent or captive agent) or act as an independent agent selling for multiple companies. Agents are representatives of the insurance company, not the policyholder.

- *Managing general agent.* Often, this is the individual who oversees a group of agents. A managing general agent is licensed and may also sell insurance, but he or she is also responsible for the oversight and management of the agency operations.
- *Brokers.* Individuals or groups who represent insurance buyers, that is, the policyholder, not the insurance company (although for reinsurance brokers, the subject policyholder is another insurance company). Brokers work with individuals or companies to secure insurance coverage required by their clients.

Insurance agents typically are paid on a commission basis, and they may represent one or more insurance companies. Insurance brokers may be compensated on a fee or a commission basis. Insurance agents and brokers may also have performance-based compensation, production recognition programs, contingent commission agreements, or other revenue-sharing structures (that is, for agents in particular, joint venture relationships with an insurance company). Managing general agents may be paid by commissions, fees, or a combination thereof.

Agents and brokers have significant interaction with policyholders. They may not only be instrumental in the policy sale, but also involved in completing the required insurance application, and, in some instances, the insurance agent or broker may also have responsibility for collecting premiums, filing claims, or making or receiving claim payments on behalf of an insurance company.

Sales-related fraud can occur through a variety of means, including sales of fake policies, hiding information, misrepresentation, theft of funds, fee churning, or collusion. Various examples of sales-related fraud are addressed later in this chapter.

Insurance Company Operations: Underwriting

Prior to issuing a policy, an application for coverage is submitted by, or on behalf of, a prospective insured. In some cases, insurance companies may present bids to a potential insured, typically a commercial business, based on information provided by the potential insured (those bids are, effectively, the basis for an application).

The submitted application is reviewed concerning risk, coverage, and pricing in the underwriting process. The veracity of the submitted application is critical to proper underwriting and risk acceptance by the insurance company. As a result of the underwriting process, a policy application will be either accepted or denied. If accepted, a policy will be issued by the insurance company to the insured, which represents the contractual relationship between the two parties—that being the insurance company and the policyholder or policy owner. Statements made by insurance applicants are the basis for acceptance or denial of coverage, including policy type, risk classification, and premium rate.

Fraud can occur at the initial application stage through misrepresentation, hiding or altering facts, identity theft, forgery, or collusion. Fraudulent misrepresentations or lying, hiding, or concealing facts may be grounds for rescission of a policy for nonlife insurance at any time. However, fraudulent misrepresentations in life insurance policies generally provide a two-year contestable period, after which the policy incontestable clause applies. Insurance policy contracts generally include language regarding events that can result in policy rescissions, including intentional or unintentional errors.

Underwriting processes may be performed or completed by insurance company employees, the underwriting department, or third parties (outsourced through a contract), for example, a managing general underwriter, third party administrator, or another insurance company. Insurance companies, including those that effectively outsource some of or all of their underwriting processes, need to have processes in place to assess potential risks of fraud related to the acceptance of an insurance application.

Insurance Company Operations: Claims

A claim is a request by an insured or other claimant for indemnification related to an insured peril. When an insured event occurs, a claim is submitted to the insurance company for adjudication. If the loss is supported in accordance with the policy terms, a payment will be made pursuant to the terms of the subject policy. Insurance companies all have claim or benefit departments that are responsible for reviewing and assessing documented support related to loss or benefit submissions by an insured or by third parties. In addition to in-house, employee-based, claim or benefit departments, insurance companies also may employ third parties to process or investigate claim and benefit submissions by an insured or other third parties, for example, an outside independent claims adjustor or adjusting organization.

Claim fraud is a significant risk to the insurance industry, and the types of claim frauds include, filing false claims, false billings, staged events, arson, collusion, misrepresentation, and identity theft. Insurance companies generally have special investigation units (SIU) within, or in support of, their claims or benefits departments[14] that focus on conducting investigations of suspect claim submissions, generally referred to the SIU by a claim adjuster. SIUs may also have special oversight and monitoring mechanisms in place to evaluate claim activity for indicators of fraud and may investigate suspect claims or claim trends not specifically referred. SIUs and claims departments often work with law enforcement agencies in cases when claim fraud is suspected. Insurance companies may also work with other outside parties to investigate suspect claims or claim schemes. Examples of claim–related fraud appear later in this chapter.

Insurance Company Operations: Financial Reporting

Insurance companies are required to file financial statements and other related information with state insurance regulatory agencies at least quarterly and to submit audited financial statements on an annual basis as of December 31. State insurance regulations may also

---

[14]   Insurance companies that contract with third-party contractors (for example, third-party administrators, managing general agents, or pharmacy benefit administrators) generally expect those parties to also have special investigation units.

require additional financial information be submitted on a product or periodic basis for, among other reasons, rate monitoring, premium taxes, loss experience, or surplus monitoring. Generally, all financial information submitted to state insurance regulatory agencies is presented based on a statutory basis of accounting.

Insurance companies may also be required to comply with the Securities and Exchange Commission's (SEC's) reporting requirements, because the company or its parent is a registered stock company, issues public debt, or sells products that are required to be registered as security products (for example, variable life products, or variable annuity products). Companies that are required to comply with requirements of the SEC are subject to the applicable federal SEC rules and regulations in addition to state insurance laws and regulations.

Insurance companies may also serve in a fiduciary capacity holding funds for individuals and groups, particularly in the area of retirement and health programs and with respect to certain variable life and annuity products. As such, there are also reporting requirements related to those roles under various state and federal regulations (for example, ERISA).

Frauds involving financial reporting include false or misleading accounting and reporting, including matters related to disclosures, nondisclosures, and misrepresentations. Examples of financial reporting frauds are addressed later in this chapter.

Insurance Fraud Schemes

More than 100 types of insurance coverage are available to commercial and individual consumers.[15] Fraud risk exists in each type of insurance coverage and insurance enterprise. Insurance enterprises, through a variety of internal and external means, attempt to stay on top of, and address, those risks. Those efforts also include educating employees, service providers, state regulators, and law enforcement about fraud risks and real or potential fraud schemes.

Disasters can bring out the best in people, but, unfortunately, they can also bring out the worst in those people who "work the system." Flood, storm, and wildfire disasters can be devastating to communities, but they often also result in rampant insurance fraud. Accidents, health-related issues, loss of employment, gambling, financial difficulty, and death are also just a snapshot of potential initiators of fraud schemes.

A recent example of disaster-related fraud is related to Hurricane Katrina, which occurred in 2005. Frauds related to Hurricane Katrina included submission of false property and liability, health, medical, and death-related claims, and several of those frauds are still being prosecuted at both the federal and state level. Frauds identified with Hurricane Katrina ranged from individuals falsely claiming federal assistance dollars from the Federal Emergency Management Agency to both businesses and individuals filing false claims with insurance companies.[16]

---

[15]   Insurance is available for a variety of business and personal purposes. More detailed lists of available insurance can be researched through various websites regarding insurance, including, among others, insurance company, broker, agent, and industry associations. General website searches will also provide information on available coverage types. Only the general classes of insurance have been presented in this chapter.

[16]   See the U.S. Department of Justice website, www.justice.gov, for hurricane-related fraud information.

Economic changes can also affect insurance fraud. Identifying whether an up or down economy affects insurance fraud can be difficult, but economic hardship can affect different types of insurance-related actions or claims. In particular, disability and workers' compensation claims[17] have been noted to increase in times of economic downturn, particularly when layoffs occur or general unemployment levels increase. Changes in the economy can also cause companies to reassess their financial management practices, reporting systems, and disclosure to facilitate market perception or employees to act differently due to a myriad of reasons, such as fear of job loss, loss of bonuses, desire for a bonus or incentive compensation, or other personal financial pressures.

As described previously, insurance fraud is rampant and costly. Further, the various fraud schemes may involve a combination of asset misappropriation, corruption, or fraudulent financial statements and records or corruption or prohibited practices. Fraud schemes vary dramatically and, ironically, seem to evolve with changing markets, products, trends, needs, tragedies, and economic changes. What is old is often new again, and what happens in one state or country can be, and often is, replicated elsewhere. Insurance fraud schemes include, among others, the items listed in the following table.

Arson	Bid rigging	Billing inflation
Billing scams	Clean sheeting	Earnings manipulation
Fake insurance sales	False claims	False representations
Fee churning	Identity theft	Kickbacks
Misappropriation	Misrepresentation	Money laundering
Nonexistent assets	Premium diversions	Premium diversions
Stated events	Surplus management	Undisclosed claims

The schemes provided in the previous table become somewhat endless as a result of the numerous policy types, insurance coverages, and variety of fraudsters focused on the insurance industry. Those fraudsters include unscrupulous policy owners, contract owners, beneficiaries, employees, agents, brokers, service providers, medical providers, associations, crime rings, and insurance company management that participate in or perpetrate fraud and misconduct for a variety of reasons. It is especially tragic when a legitimate event, or tragedy, is used as a backdrop to perpetrate a fraud.

Some well-known "mega" insurance frauds that made national and international headlines are worthy of study. One such mega insurance fraud was perpetrated by Martin Frankel, a con artist operating during the 1992–99 timeframe. Frankel swindled more than $200 million from the insurance industry and investors. His con involved the fraudulent diversion of insurance company assets (for example, premium diversions and money laundering) from companies he had "acquired" through fraudulent misrepresentations.[18] Frankel was convict-

---

[17] See the Coalition Against Insurance Fraud website, www.insurancefraud.org, for more information about workers' compensation related fraud.

[18] Con Artist Hall of Infamy, www.thehallofinfamy.org; and Ellen Joan Pollock, "The Pretender: How Martin Frankel Fooled the Financial World and Led the Feds on one of the Most Publicized Manhunts in History" (Simon & Schuster, 2002).

ed of fraud, and he began serving a federal sentence in 2004. Certain of his associates also have served or are serving time in various penitentiaries.

The Equity Funding Corporation of America case is another well-known mega fraud case that was perpetrated with the aid of data technology in the late 1960s to early 1970s. Effectively, management of Equity Funding Corporation of America was involved in manufacturing fake life insurance policies by manipulating its data processing systems for purposes of inflating its financial results as reported to the public markets through falsely reporting increased premium revenue related to those false policy sales.[19]

Box 7-2 illustrates some of the types of insurance related frauds that may occur, generally classified by fraud category.[20] Other general business related schemes common to other industries may also be perpetrated in the insurance industry, but some of those have been presented elsewhere in this book and are not repeated herein.

Box 7-2: Insurance Related Frauds by Category

Asset Misappropriation

Cash	Noncash
False claim or claim expense payments	Improper comingling of accounts
Premium diversions	Illicit transfers of investment assets
Commission payment on fraudulent policy	Clean-sheeting policy application
Fee churning	Side agreements
False or overstated billings	
False premium rebates or refunds	
Ghost employee, agent, or policyholder payments	

Financial Statement Fraud

Financial	Disclosure
Overstatement or understatement of Assets:	Misleading
Investments—for example owned, valuations, rating	Inadequate
Receivables—for example, premiums or reinsurance	Improper
Revenues—for example, premiums or commissions	
Deferred policy acquisition costs	

---

[19]   Con Artist Hall of Infamy, www.thehallofinfamy.org; M.A. Kabay, "The Equity Funding Fraud," *Network World Security Newsletter,* January 21, 2001, www.networkworld.com.

[20]   Similar in presentation format to "Financial Fraud Schemes by Category" presented by the Association of Certified Fraud Examiners, Inc., *2008 Report to the Nation on Occupational Fraud Abuse* (2008), adapted simply for purposes of illustrating, by fraud category, fraud schemes affecting the insurance industry.

Understatement or Overstatement of Reserves:

    Premium Reserves—for example
        unearned premiums
        premium deficiency

    Loss Reserves—for example
        known claims
        incurred but not reported

    Policy or Contract Benefit Reserves

    Payables—for example, reinsurance, agent commissions, and so on

Overstatement or Understatement of Costs:

    Policy related—for example, underwriting, commissions, reinsurance, other expenses

    Claim related—for example, loss, loss adjustment, reinsurance, legal

Manipulation:

    Related party transactions

    Assumptions—for example, revenue recognition, actuarial reserve calculations, capital ratio, investment valuation

Corruption or Prohibited Practices

Corruption	Prohibited Practices
Claim schemes—for example, staging, collusion, and so on	Bribery/Illicit gratuities
Preferential benefit, —for example, related party transactions	Money laundering
Kickbacks, —for example, directed payments to third parties or side agreements with doctors, repair shops, and so on	Backdating
Coercion in policy-related sales practices	Clean-sheeting application
Bid rigging—for example, obtaining false policy premium bids	

Policy-Related Fraud Schemes

Insurance policies are sold to businesses, groups, or individuals. As described previously in this chapter, insurance policies may be sold to policyholders by agents or directly by an insurance company or with the involvement of a broker. Brokers and agents working for an insurance company generally receive a commission or fee income upon the sale of an insurance policy and no policy renewal. Brokers or agents may assist a policy applicant in completing the policy application and may also provide ancillary services to a policy owner or contract owner.

In addition, various insurance company employees (for example, underwriters, claims adjusters, or data processing employees) or third parties may be engaged to facilitate the administration, underwriting, or claims processes associated with an issued policy. Depending on the type of policy, a number of other "vendors" also may be involved in the policy issuance and claims adjudication processes, including doctors, valuation firms, repair shops, physical therapists, and hospitals.

Policy-related fraud can occur during policy issuance, a claim or benefit event, policy administration, or through policy or claim related fees and expenses. Fraudsters can include policyholders, claimants, beneficiaries, employees, and providers. Those parties may act individually or in collusion with others, including "independent" third parties such as theft rings, gangs, or friends. For example, fraud in the life insurance industry often involves policies with death benefits ranging into the millions, and fraud related questions range from covering the facts related to the original policy purchase, insurable interest of beneficiaries, and the cause of death to questioning whether there even was a death.

Policy-related fraud schemes can also be perpetrated by parties representing a fake insurance company, parties selling fake policies, sales of insurance products by unlicensed or unscrupulous companies or parties, and parties to false claims.

Insurance companies and third-party administrators generally have special investigative units that specialize in investigating unusual claims, including loss trends by type of claim, geography, and so on. Those parties are generally also familiar with working with law enforcement, regulators, and others and also with utilizing various other organizations and information resources on fraud and fraud trends, as described earlier in this chapter.

Asset Misappropriation Schemes

Clean-Sheeting Applications

Clean-sheeting is a colloquial term for presenting information in a policy application that is not reflective of all pertinent facts as requested. Clean-sheeting may include the omission of pertinent facts related to accident-history, medical conditions, property conditions, property use, work status, family status, and other requested information. Clean-sheeting may be done by the submitting applicant, an agent or broker, or an underwriter or through collusion involving two or more of such parties.

Clean-sheeting can result in a more beneficial standing for the applicant with respect to obtaining coverage, for example, obtaining higher policy limits, broadening coverage, or reducing premiums. Brokers and agents may also benefit from clean-sheeting in a number of ways, including achieving sales quotas, meeting bonus criteria, or increasing commission.

An insurance company that issues a policy pursuant to information contained in a clean-sheeted application is exposed to potential loss of revenue, increased loss payments, and increased expenses. An agent or broker who is victimized by an applicant's clean-sheeting may also suffer economic loss. An agent or broker involved in a clean-sheeting scheme may be terminated and lose his or her license. Employee involvement in such schemes is not only costly to the subject employee through loss of employment, but it is costly to the company due to related employee replacement and training costs.

Identifying potential clean-sheeting is sometimes possible through the underwriting process through review of supporting documents, site visits, and checks of third party resources (such as the Department of Motor Vehicles, employment records, property records, or confirmation). There may also be a possibility of identifying clean-sheeting by analysis of agent or broker production or commissions and their related policy loss experience and through investigations of filed claims in the claims process. The identification of possible clean-sheeting may be triggered by one application or loss that may result in an insurance company, or even the selling agent or broker, in reviewing similar applications, application resubmissions, or loss events for commonalities using names, addresses, events, geography, property, or other internal or external resources.

Data analysis to identify potential clean-sheeting may also be beneficial, but it may require analysis of unstructured data and also review of hardcopy unstructured information such as underwriter files, claim files, or agent or broker files.

Premium Diversions

Diversion of premiums is simply a form of theft. Premium diversions can occur through outright theft of premiums paid to an insurer through, among other ways, falsification of records to reflect a premium as unpaid despite payment, false reduction of a receivable, or reaging of a receivable. In each instance, cash paid is retained by the fraudster despite what the records may illustrate.

Policy records, premium and cash records, policyholder billing files, including complaints; and policy file audits are documents and records that may provide insight to the existence of a premium diversion scheme. Policyholder and contractholder confirmations are also a mechanism to identify potential theft.

Ghosts

Ghosts are invisible, nonexistent beings, which in insurance fraud may represent employees, agents, brokers, or even policy applicants or policyholders who never existed or may have been formerly associated with an insurance company but never removed from a company's records when their employment or association with the insurance company ended. Essentially, ghosts may exist in policyholder, claim, payroll, or commission systems but not in reality. Ghosts may exist in all varieties of insurance enterprises, including insurance companies, brokerages, agencies, and third-party administrators.

In many cases, ghosts are paid regularly and will continue to be paid if the fraud is not caught. The fraudster may be a former or current employee, broker, or agent, and he or she may or may not be specifically identifiable. Ideally, a company wants to catch the ghost along with his or her creator or benefactor confessing to receiving payments inadvertently or the party involved with enjoying the payroll commission, premium, or claim diversion.

Ghosts may be identified through, among other means, payroll or commission audits; matching records of current and former employees, brokers, or agents with payroll or commission disbursements; matching broker or agent files with licensing records; matching records between payroll, human resources, and accounting; policyholder confirmations; matching Social Security numbers to public Social Security data bases and prior policy data bases; or matching names to motor vehicle records insured payroll systems. Ghosts may also be identified by sweeping policy and claim records for commonalities, such as similar names, addresses, Social Security numbers, employment, to other policy records and employee data. It is also important to understand access of personnel to various records and cash and data change authorities to assess segregation of duties.

False Claims and Claim-related Payments

Insurance enterprises are exposed to false payments primarily related to claim-related payments. False payments can occur as a result of false claim filings, false loss-related expense billings, and misrepresentations.

False claims can also be presented by vendors for performing work that was not in fact performed, inadequately performed or not required, or for performing work at inflated rates beyond an original quote. Those false claims can be originated by the policyholder, a vendor, or through collusion (for example, a vendor and claimant) and are not infrequent in instances of auto repair, home repair or restoration, and building repair and restoration.

Insurance providers, including third-party administrators, lose in at least two ways: loss of cash and increased reserve requirements. False claim payments are cash losses, be they to a claimant, provider, or beneficiary (or through diversion by an employee). But claim payment history is also factored into how reserves are calculated for reporting in a company's financial statements. Overstated claim payments, including loss adjustment expenses, generally result in higher reserves being required to be held by an insurer.

Detection may be facilitated through the claim investigation/adjudication process or claim audits conducted at the insurance company of loss adjusters, claim files, third party administrators, and also claimants. Data analytics may also be a source to identify anomalies that indicate further analysis of experience with types of injuries, claimants, providers (for example, chiropractors, doctors, or physical therapists), matching types and dates of service by type of loss and date of loss period and by loss adjuster file adjudication statistics. Claimant investigations may be warranted and generally can involve visits to the claimant or the claimant's place of work to ascertain that the claimant is not working at the place of injury, although the claimant could possibly be working elsewhere.

False and Inflated Claims

False and inflated claims can arise in a variety of ways, as described in the prior section as regards to workers' compensation, disability, or bodily injury claims. False claims also occur in property, liability, life, and other types of insurance as a result of, among other things, staged events, false documentation, value inflation, or falsified work.

> ### Example
>
> *Bill Wilson suffered an injury at XYZ Company's warehouse where he was lifting boxes. As a result of his injury, Bill was covered by workers' compensation. Bill sought medical attention for his injury, and Bill's doctor recommended physical therapy for his back. Bill was not familiar with how to find a physical therapist, so he asked around for some names of therapists, including from his doctors and friends. Given his injury, Bill contacted a therapist his doctor had recommended who was close to his home. Bill subsequently returned to work, with the approval of his doctor, four weeks after his injury and discontinued receiving any therapy. However, unbeknownst to Bill, his physical therapist continued to submit bills to his insurer, and Bill's doctor continued to support those bills by reporting that physical therapy was still necessary.*

Workers' compensation, disability, and bodily injury claims fraud often occur when the condition of the injured party is falsely reported or the duration of the injury is falsely claimed.[21] However, claim fraud can involve participation of others through claim payment diversions or duration inflation initiated by the insured, in collusion with a claimant a provider or others, or, as illustrated in the example, through the acts of a provider and others.

It is important for an investigator to fully understand the circumstances and parties involved with the subject claim. Some of the considerations related to claim fraud involving workers' compensation, disability, and bodily injury claims include the following:

- False reporting of the injury either by the claimant or in collusion with a medical provider
- False reporting of continued disability either by the claimant or in collusion with a medical provider
- False reporting of injury or party injured either by the claimant or other party involved in or aware of an accident or in collusion with the claimant
- False billings by a provider for services rendered, either individually or in collusion with the claimant
- False coding by a provider

Staged Events

A staged event occurs when an event is planned and executed for the purpose of deception and unlawful gain. Vehicle theft, vehicle accidents, break-ins, arson, and death (among others) can all be affected through staging. It is not uncommon for a staged event to involve the

---

21 There are several laws that companies, and their insurance providers, need to be aware of with respect to those types of coverage, and consideration of the underlying insurance policy's provisions is also important.

claimant and another party, but staged events can not only involve an unwitting policyholder but a willing policyholder (for example, theft of an art object that in fact is an unknown fake or the death of a policyholder by disappearance or through collusion with a named beneficiary).

For example, a vehicle collision may result in fault being placed on a policyholder in a staged event and the then "damaged" third-party vehicles obtaining work at repair shops that colluded in the event.

Example

Travel through the city was always difficult, but tourist season was an opportunity for even more accidents, especially for cars that were exiting rental car ramps. It was especially interesting when the same type of accident scene appeared to occur at each car rental site. A car always seemed to appear at the wrong time and be side swiped. The witnesses all seemed to support the same story: the rental car driver pulled out too fast at the corner as the light changed. It took a while to realize that three or four witnesses were always around and saw the accident sites by the rental car agencies. Amazingly, the vehicle identification numbers of the cars were different, but three similar names appeared either as drivers or witnesses, and although the license plates never seemed to match, the damaged car owners lived in areas similar to the incident witnesses.

Arson

Arson is the actual or attempted malicious and deliberate burning of a physical asset. Arson can, but may not, be related to an insurance fraud, and property insurance policies have specific provisions that address arson. The United States Fire Administration in its November 2009 report on intentional fires noted that more than 210,000 fires are intentionally set each year and that those fires result in, approximately

- 375 deaths,
- 1,300 injuries, and
- $1 billion of direct property loss (buildings and automobiles).

However, arson related to insurance fraud, based on information from the III, has been declining, in part because of efforts by the United States Fire Administration to fund antifraud programs. An III November 2010 article also noted that an Insurance Research Council study indicated that only about 14 percent of arson suspects were motivated by a desire to defraud an insurance company.[22] Still, even at 14 percent, the fraud related losses are significant.

---

[22]   Insurance Information Institute (III), "Arson," last modified January 2012, www.iii.org.

Arson fraud may involve personal or commercial property, and it may be committed directly or indirectly by an insured party. Arson can occur for a number of reasons, including an attempt by an owner to recover value on unused or underused business property where the coverage value is more beneficial or homes with mortgage values in excess of the home value on property that is owned but not used or to disguise an uninsured loss with an insured loss.

As noted previously, not all intentionally set fires are arson. Some fires are controlled fires for example, clearing farmland, or forests. There have been instances however when arson fraud has occurred in situations involving a controlled fire burn.

Example

It had been a great last year for the farm, and Farmer Unknown had decided that he would expand his west fields the following year and purchased an adjoining abandoned farm. That purchased farmland unfortunately had some abandoned buildings that blocked the planned new fields. As was typical each year, Farmer Unknown informed the local authorities that he would be clearing his west field by burning the field using a controlled fire. Using the controlled burn process he always used, Farmer Unknown cleared his west field. However, after having gotten through that process, Famer Unknown decided to let the fire burn over to the abandoned buildings to save him the cost of teardown and help with the new planting costs—after all, those buildings were insured.

Underwriters and claims departments, including SIU, look for fraud when a fire is reported related to a submitted application or in reviewing a claim filing involving a fire. Reports filed by firefighters, police, and other observers, if any, are some of the factors that are considered in reviewing a claim file, particularly to assist in identifying factors that may be indicative of arson (for example, a normally closed building having windows propped open, smell of gasoline or other incendiary device, unusual activity around a building at odd hours, and so on). Other indicators will also be explored to assess potential indicators that a fire is other than accidental including the financial history or condition of the business or individual, associations with other groups or people, or threats by other parties. Investigating arson cases takes special skills and needs to start quickly to avoid evidence being destroyed.

Property Theft

Thefts of property can also result in inflated claims as a result of falsified valuations prepared by policyholders and claimants, either individually or in collusion with valuation experts or other parties. Investigation at the time of policy issuance or a loss event is critical to obtain documents and site information and observations, particularly with respect to property values, business values, security environment, theft patterns, and ownership history.

Fraudulent Financial Reporting Schemes

Fraudulent financial reporting and transaction schemes may be influenced by internal or external factors. Those factors may adversely affect financial statement amounts or disclosures and also decisions about a company by, among others, investors, rating agencies, and regulators. Various pressures that may exist are included in the following table.

Business Pressures	Internal Pressures	Financial Pressures
Increased competition	Compensation programs	Contract or debt requirements
Regulatory oversight	Unrealistic goals or expectations	Focus on earnings or surplus
Need to access capital markets	Ineffective processes, systems, and controls	Rating or analyst expectations
Global expansion	Complex organization structure	Complex transactions

As described previously, insurance companies are required to file financial statement information with state insurance regulatory agencies at least quarterly and to annually submit audited financial statements prepared in accordance with the statutory basis of accounting. In addition, state insurance regulations require additional financial information be submitted for, among other reasons, rate monitoring, premium taxes, or loss experience monitoring; solvency; structural changes; and dividend approvals. Generally, all financial information submitted to state insurance regulatory agencies is on a statutory basis of accounting.[23]

As described previously in this chapter, insurance companies and other insurance-related enterprises may report financial information in accordance with GAAP or International Financial Reporting Standards (IFRS). Those entities that are required to comply with SEC reporting requirements because the company or its parent is a registered stock company, issues public debt, or sells products that are required to be registered as security products are also subject to the related SEC rules and regulations related to reporting and disclosure. Companies that operate globally or are registered on other non-U.S. exchanges may be required to report information in accordance with the respective country's requirements, which may be GAAP, IFRS, or a local-basis of accounting, and to comply with the respective country's rules and regulations related to reporting and disclosure.

Various rules and regulations also exist related to financial reporting and transactions for complex organizations and transactions by and between related parties. With respect to insurance companies, those rules and regulations include state insurance rules and regulations for individual companies and any holding companies. A holding company may be either an insurance company or a noninsurance company. Related parties, similar to all industries, are relationships between brother or sister companies, parent or subsidiary companies, and

---

[23] Statements of Statutory Accounting Principles are a series of NAIC publications that provide accounting and reporting guidance to regulators, auditors, and preparers of financial statement of insurance companies with respect to the statutory-basis of accounting.

individuals within the corporate structure. Those complex structures need to be considered in evaluating risks and allegations of fraud or misconduct.

Financial statements are generally affected by all types of fraud, either directly or indirectly. For example, as described previously, asset misappropriation, such as issuance of fake policies, can affect a company's revenue, or the filing of false claims can affect loss costs and loss reserves. Those false policies or claims may be internally or externally generated and otherwise properly recorded as issued policies or submitted claims. Although they affect revenue or losses or benefits and reserves, such recording of falsified policies or claims may not be intentional fraud or misconduct by a company, unlike the case with Equity Funding that was a scheme to inflate sales and revenue for purposes of presenting false results to the external markets.

Earnings, or net income (or, possibly, comprehensive income), is a key consideration for insurance companies, particularly with respect to GAAP-basis financial statements and investors. However, surplus is a key driver for insurance companies from a statutory and insurance regulatory perspective. Earnings, generally, is defined similarly to other industries. Surplus, for insurance companies, is defined as follows:

> The total of an insurance company's capital stock, paid-in and contributed capital, and unassigned surplus/deficit, less the insurer's admitted assets determined in accordance with statutory accounting principles. Stated more simply, surplus is the excess of an insurance company's total admitted assets over its reserves and other liabilities.

Some of the distinctions between the determinations of surplus as compared to earnings are set forth in box 7–3.

Box 7-3: Surplus Versus Earning

Surplus	Earnings*
Assets are limited to those assets that are "admissible" pursuant to statutory accounting principles (SAP).[†]	No similar distinction between asset types.
Assets are valued based on SAP. Investments are valued in consideration of guidance provided by the National Association of Insurance Commissioners' Capital Markets & Investment Analysis Office (formerly known as the Securities Valuation Office). Bond values, generally, may be amortized cost and stocks at market value, except for investments in subsidiaries.	Valuation allowances are recorded for diminutions in certain asset values based on U.S. generally accepted accounting principles (GAAP) guidance. Investments are, generally, carried at market, or fair, value. Investments in subsidiaries are, generally, consolidated.
Policy-related claim liabilities are based on product type and SAP related guidance.	Policy-related claim liabilities are based on product type and GAAP related guidance.

Policy-related reserves are based on product type and related statutory guidance.	Policy-related reserves are based on product type and related GAAP guidance.
Policy issuance related expenses are recognized as incurred.	Policy issuance costs are deferred and amortized based on product type and GAAP guidance.

* U.S. generally accepted accounting principles (GAAP) guidance is provided in various Financial Accounting Standards Board publications. International Financial Reporting Standards (IFRS) guidance is not being considered in this table; such guidance may vary from GAAP and specific IFRS guidance should be consulted as appropriate.

† Statutory accounting principles are the accounting rules that insurance companies must follow in preparing and filing financial statements with state insurance departments. The National Association of Insurance Commissioners has issued, effective as of January 1, 2001, a series of publications that provide accounting and reporting guidance to regulators, auditors, and examiners of insurance companies referred to as Statements of Statutory Accounting Principles.

It is important when assessing alleged that fraud both bases of accounting are considered and evaluated. In addition, with the emergence of international accounting standards, other dissimilarities may arise.[24]

A number of similarities exist in the types of financial reporting and transaction fraud schemes that can occur in the insurance industry to those that can occur in other industries, including the following:

- Preparing fraudulent top-side and other journal entries
- Overstatement of assets
- Manipulation of estimates
- Revenue inflation
- Expense deflation
- Manipulation of incentive, or contingent, compensation calculations

Each of those similar types of schemes, described in other chapters for other industries, should be considered in investigations involving insurance companies, with the added twist of consideration with respect to the subject basis of accounting (for example, SAP basis and GAAP basis).

In assessing allegations of financial reporting and transaction related fraud or misconduct, it is also important to understand the subject company's reporting and disclosure requirements, that is, statutory, GAAP, IFRS, and so on, and the company's organizational structure and overall operations, and inter-company or related-party relationships.

---

[24] The emerging international accounting standards are not addressed in this chapter. In addition, the tax basis of accounting is also not addressed in this chapter.

Some examples of financial reporting and transaction fraud schemes for consideration specifically with respect to insurance companies are presented in the following sections.

Overstatement of Assets

Insurance Company A was under pressure to demonstrate that it had sufficient assets to support its capital and surplus requirements. To "shore-up" its assets, Company A decided to sell certain lower rated, illiquid, private placement bonds for cash. There had been minimal open market valuations for the private placement securities, so management decided it would need to establish a market value. Company A approached a private placement broker to assist in the sale transaction, and the broker prepared an analysis of the subject bonds and determined that although the bond portfolio had been purchased at $1 million par value, the lack of liquidity, among other factors, indicated a market valuation of $750,000. Based on this analysis, the insurance company management decided to "sell" the subject bond portfolio to a noninsurance sister company at its original cost.

Surplus or Earning Management

Similar to prior years, the company actuary prepared a number of models to assist in the evaluation of the company's reserve requirements based on a variety of assumptions. Those assumptions considered included the various company products, claims experience, current environment, and trends related to litigation, catastrophic events, demographic, and reinsurance arrangements. Based on the actuarial analysis, the recommended reserve to be recorded by the company was the mid-point of the range of reserve scenarios the actuary had developed. However, when evaluating the company's earnings trends and performance bonus calculation, it was discovered that the recording of the recommended midpoint would cause a negative earnings trend that would also adversely affect bonuses and reduce surplus levels to below the targeted surplus level. As a result, executive management decided that the recorded reserve should be adjusted to reduce the amount by 15 percent to allow it to meet its targets, and a top-side adjustment was made by the CFO. Top management was pleased and communicated to the board and analysts that their reserving approach was consistent with prior years.

Reinsurance

Company A needed to stem some of the initial adverse effects of its new product line sales. After considering various alternatives, Company A management approached Company B to enter into a reinsurance agreement. Numerous memos and e-mails were sent between the companies, and ultimately the terms were set forth that Company B would assume 50 percent of the business on a quota-share basis with a guaranteed recapture of the subject business by Company A after three years. Company A also agreed to guarantee Company B a 15 percent profit margin above any actual experience related to the business held by Company B. Company A's reinsurance group executed the contract, but the written contract, filed with the state, did not disclose, and the accounting for the reinsurance contract did not reflect, Company A's obligation to recapture the business and pay the 15 percent guarantee.

Deferred Acquisition Costs

Pursuant to GAAP accounting, Company A had capitalized, and was amortizing, its policy issue related costs (policy acquisition costs) for its variable life insurance products. Each year the actuarial group prepared an analysis of the recoverability of those costs, and adjustments were made to assumptions based on such analysis. However, in the most recent year, it was noted that the interest and surrender assumptions were out of line with actual experience. On further review, it was discovered that the data that had been provided to the actuaries was not accurate and had not been reconciled to either the investment data or the policy data for years. The revised data indicated that the deferred acquisition costs would not be recoverable as originally anticipated, and that a recommendation to unlock the original assumptions and record a write-down was necessary. The decision to do so was fraught with repercussions, so the recommendation was to smooth the write-down and changes over three years.

Management Agreement Related Schemes

Holding Company B was a holding company whose various holdings included insurance and noninsurance enterprises. One of its largest holdings was an insurance company (Company X) that historically had been the primary source of cash for Holding Company B. Unfortunately Company X had suffered significant losses and, as a result, was facing issues with meeting the regulatory requirement to allow it to pay its normal dividend to its parent company. Recognizing that to be the case, Holding Company B management established a new company (NewCo), wholly owned by Holding Company B, that would provide certain information technology related management services to its insurance company holdings for a monthly fee. The agreement was effected and provided to the state insurance regulator, but Holding Company B failed to disclose that NewCo had no employees with the requisite skills, and that all technology systems and services were embedded within Company X. Monthly fees were paid by each of the insurance companies to NewCo, which, in turn, paid a dividend to Holding Company B each month. NewCo's only employees were employees and management of Company X. Company X properly disclosed the existence of the intercompany management agreement and accounted for the expenses paid each month, but it provided no other significant information.

Corruption Schemes

Corruption schemes are schemes that involve corrupt or prohibited practices. As described previously, corruption schemes may be similar across a number of industries. In addition, frauds related to asset misappropriation and financial accounting and reporting, including disclosure, may also involve corrupt or prohibited practices.

Bid-rigging

In the early 2000s, various insurance regulatory agencies and state attorneys general investigated allegations of bid-rigging within the insurance industry involving various insurance companies and brokers. Bid-rigging involves the involvement of at a minimum three parties, for example, two insurance companies and a broker coordinating the scheme, and typically involves business-related insurance, but it may also involve a business seeking the insurance coverage. Essentially, bid-rigging involves obtaining premium bids for offered coverage with a tacit agreement that only the planned insurer will submit the winning bid and the other bid will be a proxy bid, with an implicit understanding that the next bid for coverage will be "won" by the proxy bidder.

The Impact of Fraud on the Insurance Industry

Measuring insurance fraud is extremely difficult for a number of reasons, including the variety of insurance frauds that occur, the variety of organizations that monitor only discrete types of insurance fraud (for example, select insurance coverage areas and certain types of fraudsters), the variety of insurance policies, and the lack of a centralized reporting and monitoring system for insurance fraud.

The following snapshot of the cost of insurance fraud, based solely on a select few of those insurance company organizations previously identified, illustrates a multi-billion dollar "fraudster industry" that exists to the detriment of the insurance industry:

- In 2005, the Coalition Against Insurance Fraud estimated that insurance fraud cost the industry approximately $80 billion.[25]
- The Insurance Information Institute has estimated that fraud affecting the property or casualty insurance industry is approximately 10 percent of all loss and loss adjustment expenses incurred by at industry.[26]
- The NHCAA has estimated that fraud-related health losses range from $70 billion to $234 billion per year,[27] a great portion of which is covered by health insurance provided by employers, public sources (for example, Medicaid or Medicare), or purchased by individuals.

---

[25] Coalition Against Insurance Fraud, accessed April 2011, www.insurancefraud.org. The Coalition Against Insurance Fraud is a national alliance of consumer groups, public interest organizations, government agencies, and insurers devoted to fighting fraud within the insurance industry and serving as an anti-fraud watchdog.

[26] III, accessed April 2011, www.iii.org. III is a member organization that is a source for information, analysis, and referral on the insurance industry.

[27] National Health Care Anti-Fraud Association (NHCAA), accessed April 2011, www.nhcaa.org. NHCAA is a national organization focused exclusively on fighting against healthcare fraud. A member organization, NHCAA is a comprised of, among others, private health insurers and law enforcement and regulatory agencies involved with or having jurisdiction over healthcare fraud.

Considerations in Identifying Fraud Schemes

Investigating fraud in the insurance industry requires not only an understanding of fraud investigations but also an understanding of the insurance industry. This chapter has presented a brief highlight of the industry and various fraud considerations. It is important to understand that investigating insurance fraud may require specialized operational and technical skills, including legal, accounting, and actuarial skills, in addition to core investigative skills, inclusive of forensic technology skills.

It is also important to understand that fraud categories can overlap in a fraud scheme. Finding fraud is not always straight forward. Prevention, detection, and monitoring are important, and internal controls, tone at the top, hiring screening, vendor screening, data analysis, and document gathering and retention are important considerations. But, it is important to listen to and analyze tips, complaints, and notifications (from industry sources and law enforcement), ask questions, and obtain support. A key mistake can occur when a tip or complaint is passed off as being nothing more than a disgruntled employee, agent, broker, policyholder, beneficiary, vendor, and so on or simply a "human resource issue."

Government Fraud

Patrick Chylinski, CFE
Lynda Hartzell, CPA/CIA, CFE
Todd E. Sigler, CPA/CFF, CFE
Debra K. Thompson, CPA/CFF, CFE

In essence, government and public sector fraud can be defined as intentional acts that cause financial harm to a government entity, agency, or program at the federal, state, or local level. Government-related fraud frequently involves some type of asset misappropriation scheme, procurement fraud, false claims, or corruption. Although many of the same motivating factors and techniques found in private sector fraud cases translate to government and not-for-profit schemes, there are some unique issues that set this area apart. These will be explored in the section titled "Distinguishing Factors and Methods" of this chapter.

Regardless of how public sector schemes are perpetrated, one could argue that government fraud is a more far-reaching problem than private sector fraud, because all taxpayers provide funding for government operations and the intended use of government funds is to serve a public good. In addition, the government has to dedicate sizable, publicly funded resources to prevent, detect, and prosecute fraud. Thus, government fraud can be particularly troubling, because the solvency and financial health of federal, state, and local public sector programs is essential to a well-functioning society.

This chapter will focus on the following areas related to government fraud:

- Selected fraud related statutes and laws
- Distinguishing factors and methods
- Types of government fraud
- Government agencies that work to prevent, investigate, or prosecute fraud

Selected Fraud Related Statutes and Laws

Federal Acquisition Regulation

The Federal Acquisition Regulation (FAR) is a substantial and complex set of rules governing the federal government's purchasing process.[1] The requirements for government agencies are set forth in *Territories and Insular Possessions, U.S. Code* (USC) Title 48. 48 USC regulates the three phases the government goes through to enter a purchase contract:

- *Need recognition (Part 7)*. This phase includes planning of acquisitions upon determination that a need exists within an agency. Decisions are made about whether to use a commercial or a government source and whether to lease or purchase an asset. Written acquisition plans are prepared and are to address all the technical, business, management, and other significant considerations that will control the acquisition. The plan must address prospective sources for the needed property or services and how competition will be sought, promoted, and sustained throughout the course of the acquisition.

- *Contract formation*. Subchapter C details contracting methods and contract types, including bidding and negotiation processes. Simplified acquisition processes exist for those contracts whose dollar amounts are below a certain threshold. Even under the simplified acquisition process, the government agency has an obligation to promote competition for the awarding of the contract and must ensure that it attempts to get a fair and reasonable price for any goods or services it acquires. A process involving sealed bids is required in some circumstances. Contracts may also be awarded based upon negotiation in which sealed bids are not used. Regardless of the method used to award contracts, the agency has an obligation to acquire a cost-effective solution that will meet its needs.

- *Contract administration*. The winning bidder must comply with a whole gamut of rules in performing services for the government. Those seeking more information on the requirements should consult the information provided regarding 48 USC on the U.S. Government Printing Office's website (http://ecfr.gpoaccess.gov. Title 48 – Federal Acquisition Regulations System.)

In addition to detailed contracting requirements, there are a number of safeguards and prohibitions built into 48 USC. The safeguards generally address the conduct of government employees and the companies that interact with those employees. The safeguards are addressed in Part 3 of the regulations, Improper Business Practices and Personal Conflicts of Interest. See the section titled "Procurement Integrity Act" later in this chapter.

The Department of Defense has its own implementation of the acquisition regulations. Information on this topic can be found at www.acq.osd.mil/dpap/dars/about_dfarspgi.html.

---

[1]   http://ecfr.gpoaccess.gov/. Title 48 – Federal Acquisition Regulations System.

Qui tam

The False Claims Act (FCA) (*Money and Finance*, USC Title 31, Section 1379) provides for qui tam suits. It also requires the whistleblower to follow a detailed process with the justice department or attorney general. The key elements of this process are as follows:

- The person wishing to provide evidence is called a "relator," and the relator must be represented by counsel.
- The qui tam complaint must be filed under seal, meaning that all records relating to the case are kept on a secret docket by the clerk of the court. Copies of the complaint are given only to the United States Department of Justice, the local United States Attorney's Office, and the assigned judge in district court, although authorization for further release may be sought through the court. The complaint and filings are maintained under seal for 60 days.
- At the same time the complaint is filed, the relator, through counsel, must furnish to the Department of Justice a disclosure statement setting forth substantially all of the evidence the relator has in his or her possession pertaining to the allegations in the complaint.
- The attorney general or a Department of Justice attorney must investigate allegations of violations of the FCA, and he or she will work with other law enforcement officials as appropriate. In cases in which the state is the victim, state attorneys general with this type of expertise may get involved and work closely with federal agencies.
- Several options can be pursued after or during the investigation. The Department of Justice can

  — intervene and express the intent of the government to participate as a plaintiff;
  — decline to intervene, and the relator and his or her counsel can prosecute on behalf of the United States without the United States being a party to the action;
  — dismiss the relator's complaint;
  — settle the qui tam action with the defendant prior to an intervention decision; or
  — advise the relator that the department intends to decline intervention.

- Upon intervention approval, the department files a notice of intervention, setting forth the specific claims on which the United States is intervening. It also files a motion to unseal the complaint.
- After the complaint is unsealed, the relator, through his or her counsel, must within 120 days serve his or her complaint upon each named defendant.
- The defendant then has 20 days to file an answer or motion. The discovery process under Federal Rules of Civil Procedure commences shortly thereafter.[2]

The FCA rewards whistleblowers by allowing them to receive a share of an award for cases that expose government fraud.

---

[2]   See Department of Justice, *False Claims Act Cases: Government Intervention in Qui Tam (Whistleblower) Suits*, www.justice.gov/usao/pae/Documents/fcaprocess2.pdf.

Conspiracy to Defraud the United States

Crimes and Criminal Procedure, USC Title 18, Section 371, "Conspiracy to Commit Offense or Defraud the United States," addresses actions that are meant to cheat the government out of money or property, obstruct government activity, or make wrongful use of governmental instrumentality. These cases require the prosecution to prove the traditional elements of conspiracy, including an illegal agreement, criminal intent, and proof of an overt act in furtherance of the conspiracy.[3] The *United States Attorneys' Manual* states the following:

> The intent required for a conspiracy to defraud the government is that the defendant possessed the intent (a) to defraud, (b) to make false statements or representations to the government or its agencies in order to obtain property of the government, or that the defendant performed acts or made statements that he/she knew to be false, fraudulent or deceitful to a government agency, which disrupted the functions of the agency or of the government. It is sufficient for the government to prove that the defendant knew the statements were false or fraudulent when made. The government is not required to prove the statements ultimately resulted in any actual loss to the government of any property or funds, only that the defendant's activities impeded or interfered with legitimate governmental functions.[4]

Procurement Integrity Act

The Procurement Integrity Act "prohibits the release of source selection and contractor bid or proposal information. Also, a former employee who served in certain positions on a procurement action or contract in excess of $10 million is barred for one year from receiving compensation as an employee or consultant from that contractor."[5] The purpose of this act, as with many of the laws discussed in this chapter, is to safeguard the financial interests of the U.S. government, as well as to protect the integrity and fairness of the procurement process. The Department of Justice provides an outline of this act at www.justice.gov/jmd/ethics/procureb.htm.

FCA (criminal)

Key elements for prosecution under 18 USC 287 include the following:

1. Government must establish that the defendant

   a. made or presented a false, fictitious, or fraudulent claim to a department of the United States;

   b. knew such claim was false, fictitious, or fraudulent; and

---

[3] Department of Justice, *Criminal Resource Manual*, sec. 923, www.justice.gov/usao/eousa/foia_reading_room/usam/title9/crm00923.htm.

[4] *Id.*

[5] Department of Justice, "Procurement Integrity Act," www.justice.gov/jmd/ethics/procurea.htm.

c. did so with the specific intent to violate the law or with a consciousness that what he or she did was wrong.

2. Under 18 USC 287, there may not be a requirement that the statements or claims be material. The U.S. courts of appeal are split on this issue.
3. Under case law, it is clear that specific intent to defraud is not required for conviction under this section. U.S. courts of appeal are divided about whether willfulness is an essential element of the crime.
4. The false claim must be presented (intent to present is not sufficient), and it must be presented to the government.[6]

FCA (civil)

31 USC 3729 states, in part, the following:

Liability for Certain Acts.—

(1) **In general**.— Subject to paragraph (2), any person who—

(A) knowingly presents, or causes to be presented, a false or fraudulent claim for payment or approval;

(B) knowingly makes, uses, or causes to be made or used, a false record or statement material to a false or fraudulent claim;

(C) conspires to commit a violation of subparagraph (A), (B), (D), (E), (F), or (G);

(D) has possession, custody, or control of property or money used, or to be used, by the Government and knowingly delivers, or causes to be delivered, less than all of that money or property;

(E) is authorized to make or deliver a document certifying receipt of property used, or to be used, by the Government and, intending to defraud the Government, makes or delivers the receipt without completely knowing that the information on the receipt is true;

(F) knowingly buys, or receives as a pledge of an obligation or debt, public property from an officer or employee of the Government, or a member of the Armed Forces, who lawfully may not sell or pledge property; or

(G) knowingly makes, uses, or causes to be made or used, a false record or statement material to an obligation to pay or transmit money or property to the Government, or knowingly conceals or knowingly and improperly avoids

---

6   Department of Justice, *Criminal Resource Manual*, sec. 922, www.justice.gov/usao/eousa/foia_reading_room/usam/title9/crm00922.htm.

or decreases an obligation to pay or transmit money or property to the Government, is liable to the United States Government for a civil penalty of not less than $5,000 and not more than $10,000, as adjusted by the Federal Civil Penalties Inflation Adjustment Act of 1990[7]

The Fraud Enforcement and Recovery Act of 2009 (FERA), signed into law on May 20, 2009, strengthened the FCA in a number of ways and broadened its application to include the Troubled Assets Relief Program (TARP) and the American Recovery and Reinvestment Act of 2009 (ARRA).[8]

Fraudulent Claims (Contract Disputes Act of 1978)

Public Contracts, USC Title 41, Section 601, *et seq.,* applies to all of the following:

1. Executive agency contracts for the procurement of property other the real property; the procurement of services; the procurement of construction, alteration, repair, or maintenance of real property
2. Tennessee Valley Authority contracts which contain a disputes clause requirement that a contract dispute be resolved through an agency administrative process
3. Foreign government of international organization contracts (unless the determination is made by the head of the agency that application of this chapter to the contract would not in the public interest)[9]

41 USC 604 states the following:

If a contractor is unable to support any part of his claim and it is determined that such inability is attributable to misrepresentation of fact or fraud on the part of the contractor, he shall be liable to the Government for an amount equal to such unsupported part of the claim in addition to all costs to the Government attributable to the cost of reviewing said part of his claim. Liability under this subsection shall be determined within six years of the commission of such misrepresentation of fact or fraud.[10]

Program Civil Fraud Remedies (cases less than $150,000)

31 USC 3801, *et seq.;* 31 USC 3802 states, in part, the following:

---

[7]   *Money and Finance, U.S. Code* (USC) Title 31, Section 3729, www.law.cornell.edu/uscode/text/31/3729.

[8]   Cooley Godward Kronish LLP, "Fraud Enforcement and Recovery Act Expands the False Claims Act," *Legal Update* (July 2009), www.lorman.com/newsletter/article.php?article_id=1297&newsletter_id=274&category_id=8&topic=LIT.

[9]   *Public Contracts,* 41 USC 602, http://codes.lp.findlaw.com/uscode/41/9/602.

[10]   41 USC 604, http://codes.lp.findlaw.com/uscode/41/9/604.

§ 3802. False claims and statements; liability

(a)

(1) Any person who makes, presents, or submits, or causes to be made, presented, or submitted, a claim that the person knows or has reason to know—

(A) is false, fictitious, or fraudulent;

(B) includes or is supported by any written statement which asserts a material fact which is false, fictitious, or fraudulent;

(C) includes or is supported by any written statement that—

(i) omits a material fact;

(ii) is false, fictitious, or fraudulent as a result of such omission; and

(iii) is a statement in which the person making, presenting, or submitting such statement has a duty to include such material fact; or

(D) is for payment for the provision of property or services which the person has not provided as claimed, shall be subject to, in addition to any other remedy that may be prescribed by law, a civil penalty of not more than $5,000 for each such claim. Except as provided in paragraph (3) of this subsection, such person shall also be subject to an assessment, in lieu of damages sustained by the United States because of such claim, of not more than twice the amount of such claim, or the portion of such claim, which is determined under this chapter to be in violation of the preceding sentence.

(2) Any person who makes, presents, or submits, or causes to be made, presented, or submitted, a written statement that—

(A) the person knows or has reason to know—

(i) asserts a material fact which is false, fictitious, or fraudulent; or

(ii)

(I) omits a material fact; and

(II) is false, fictitious, or fraudulent as a result of such omission;

(B) in the case of a statement described in clause (ii) of subparagraph (A), is a statement in which the person making, presenting, or submitting such statement has a duty to include such material fact; and

(C) contains or is accompanied by an express certification or affirmation of the truthfulness and accuracy of the contents of the statement, shall be subject to, in addition to any other remedy that may be prescribed by law, a civil penalty of not more than $5,000 for each such statement.

Major Fraud Act (cases over $1M)

18 USC 1031 states, in part, the following:

§ 1031. Major fraud against the United States

(a) Whoever knowingly executes, or attempts to execute, any scheme or artifice with the intent—

(1) to defraud the United States; or

(2) to obtain money or property by means of false or fraudulent pretenses, representations, or promises, in any procurement of property or services as a prime contractor with the United States or as a subcontractor or supplier on a contract in which there is a prime contract with the United States, if the value of the contract, subcontract, or any constituent part thereof, for such property or services is $1,000,000 or more shall, subject to the applicability of subsection (c) of this section, be fined not more than $1,000,000, or imprisoned not more than 10 years, or both.[11]

On May 20, 2009, President Barack Obama signed into law the FERA. This act expanded the applicability of this law to include not only fraud in government procurement but also to grants under the ARRA, transactions under the TARP, and any "other form of federal assistance."[12]

Fraud and False Statements (criminal)

18 USC 1001 states the following:

(a) Except as otherwise provided in this section, whoever, in any matter within the jurisdiction of the executive, legislative, or judicial branch of the Government of the United States, knowingly and willfully—

(1) falsifies, conceals, or covers up by any trick, scheme, or device a material fact;

(2) makes any materially false, fictitious, or fraudulent statement or representation; or

(3) makes or uses any false writing or document knowing the same to contain any materially false, fictitious, or fraudulent statement or entry;

shall be fined under this title, imprisoned not more than 5 years or, if the offense involves international or domestic terrorism (as defined in section), imprisoned not more than 8 years, or both. If the matter relates to an offense under chapter 109A, 109B, 110, or 117, or section 1591, then the term of imprisonment imposed under this section shall be not more than 8 years.

---

[11] 18 USC 1031, www.law.cornell.edu/uscode/pdf/uscode18/lii_usc_TI_18_PA_I_CH_47_SE_1031.pdf.

[12] "Fraud Enforcement and Recovery Act of 2009," last modified April 24, 2012, http://en.wikipedia.org/wiki/Fraud_Enforcement_and_Recovery_Act_of_2009.

Truth in Negotiations Act (Armed Forces, USC Title 10, Section 2306a)

Title 10, Subtitle A, Part IV, Chapter 137 of the USC addresses the requirements for procurement by the U.S. Armed Forces. Excerpts of 10 USC 2306a state the following:

(a) Required Cost or Pricing Data and Certification.—

(1) The head of an agency shall require offerors, contractors, and subcontractors to make cost or pricing data available as follows:

(A) An offeror for a prime contract under this chapter to be entered into using procedures other than sealed-bid procedures shall be required to submit cost or pricing data before the award of a contract if—[certain monetary thresholds and conditions are met]...

(B) The contractor for a prime contract under this chapter shall be required to submit cost or pricing data before the pricing of a change or modification to the contract if—[certain monetary thresholds and conditions are met]...

(C) An offeror for a subcontract (at any tier) of a contract under this chapter shall be required to submit cost or pricing data before the award of the subcontract if the prime contractor and each higher-tier subcontractor have been required to make available cost or pricing data under this section and—[certain monetary thresholds and conditions are met]...

(D) The subcontractor for a subcontract covered by subparagraph (C) shall be required to submit cost or pricing data before the pricing of a change or modification to the subcontract if—[certain monetary thresholds and conditions are met]...

(2) A person required, as an offeror, contractor, or subcontractor, to submit cost or pricing data under paragraph (1) (or required by the head of the agency concerned to submit such data under subsection (c)) shall be required to certify that, to the best of the person's knowledge and belief, the cost or pricing data submitted are accurate, complete, and current.

Bribery of Public Officials (criminal)

Excerpts of 18 USC 201 state the following:

Anti-Kickback Act of 1986: According to the *United States Attorneys' Manual*, 41 USC 51, *et seq.*, accomplished the following:

- Closed loopholes in the previous anti-kickback laws.
- Expanded the definition of prohibited conduct, making the law a more useful prosecutorial tool.

- Made the law applicable to a broader group of persons involved in government subcontracting.

Prosecutions under these statutes must establish the following:

- *Prohibited conduct.* The statute states that "… attempted as well as completed "kickbacks," which include any money, fees, commission, credit, gift, gratuity, thing of value, or compensation of any kind. The act also provides that the inclusion of kickback amounts in contract prices is prohibited conduct in itself."
- *Purpose of kickback.* The purpose must relate to improperly obtaining or rewarding favorable treatment.
- *Recipient of kickback.* Kickbacks must have been made to "… prime contractors, prime contractor employees, subcontractors, and subcontractor employees. These terms are defined in the Act."
- *Type of contract.* The exchange must involve some type of government contract.
- *State of mind.* The persons must have knowledge and willfulness.[13]

Sherman Antitrust Act and other antitrust laws (collusive bidding prohibited) (Commerce and Trade, USC Title 15, Section 1–7)

The Sherman Antitrust Act, passed in 1890, was the first measure designed to prohibit trusts and monopolies. It has been supplemented by the Clayton Antitrust Act, the Robinson-Patman Act, and the Celler-Kefauver Act, among others. The Sherman Antitrust Act authorized the federal government to dissolve trusts (and other combinations that could restrain trade or commerce) and established penalties for persons convicted of establishing the combinations.[14]

On the matter, the Antitrust Division of the Department of Justice writes the following:

> The goal of the antitrust laws is to protect economic freedom and opportunity by promoting free and fair competition in the marketplace.
>
> Competition in a free market benefits American consumers through lower prices, better quality and greater choice. Competition provides businesses the opportunity to compete on price and quality, in an open market and on a level playing field, unhampered by anticompetitive restraints. Competition also tests and hardens American companies at home, the better to succeed abroad.
>
> Federal antitrust laws apply to virtually all industries and to every level of business, including manufacturing, transportation, distribution, and marketing. They prohibit a variety of practices that restrain trade, such as price-fixing

---

13   Department of Justice, *Criminal Resource Manual*, sec. 927, www.justice.gov/usao/eousa/foia_reading_room/usam/title9/crm00927.htm.

14   The Linux Information Project, "The Sherman Antitrust Act," www.linfo.org/sherman.html.

conspiracies, corporate mergers likely to reduce the competitive vigor of particular markets, and predatory acts designed to achieve or maintain monopoly power. [15]

The Antitrust Division's website [16] contains additional information on the application of various antitrust laws.

(b) Whoever—

    (1) directly or indirectly, corruptly gives, offers or promises anything of value to any public official or person who has been selected to be a public official, or offers or promises any public official or any person who has been selected to be a public official to give anything of value to any other person or entity, with intent—

        (A) to influence any official act; or

        (B) to influence such public official or person who has been selected to be a public official to commit or aid in committing, or collude in, or allow, any fraud, or make opportunity for the commission of any fraud, on the United States; or

        (C) to induce such public official or such person who has been selected to be a public official to do or omit to do any act in violation of the lawful duty of such official or person;

    (2) being a public official or person selected to be a public official, directly or indirectly, corruptly demands, seeks, receives, accepts, or agrees to receive or accept anything of value personally or for any other person or entity, in return for:

        (A) being influenced in the performance of any official act;

        (B) being influenced to commit or aid in committing, or to collude in, or allow, any fraud, or make opportunity for the commission of any fraud, on the United States; or

        (C) being induced to do or omit to do any act in violation of the official duty of such official or person;

    (3) directly or indirectly, corruptly gives, offers, or promises anything of value to any person, or offers or promises such person to give anything of value to any other person or entity, with intent to influence the testimony under oath or affirmation of such first-mentioned person as a witness upon a trial, hearing, or other proceeding, before any court, any committee of either House or both Houses of Congress, or any agency, commission, or officer authorized by the laws of the United States to hear evidence or

---

[15] Department of Justice, Antitrust Division, "Mission," www.justice.gov/atr/about/mission.html.

[16] Department of Justice, Antitrust Division, www.justice.gov/atr/index.html.

take testimony, or with intent to influence such person to absent himself therefrom;

(4) directly or indirectly, corruptly demands, seeks, receives, accepts, or agrees to receive or accept anything of value personally or for any other person or entity in return for being influenced in testimony under oath or affirmation as a witness upon any such trial, hearing, or other proceeding, or in return for absenting himself therefrom;

shall be fined under this title or not more than three times the monetary equivalent of the thing of value, whichever is greater, or imprisoned for not more than fifteen years, or both, and may be disqualified from holding any office of honor, trust, or profit under the United States.

(c) Whoever—

(1) otherwise than as provided by law for the proper discharge of official duty—

(A) directly or indirectly gives, offers, or promises anything of value to any public official, former public official, or person selected to be a public official, for or because of any official act performed or to be performed by such public official, former public official, or person selected to be a public official; or

(B) being a public official, former public official, or person selected to be a public official, otherwise than as provided by law for the proper discharge of official duty, directly or indirectly demands, seeks, receives, accepts, or agrees to receive or accept anything of value personally for or because of any official act performed or to be performed by such official or person;

(2) directly or indirectly, gives, offers, or promises anything of value to any person, for or because of the testimony under oath or affirmation given or to be given by such person as a witness upon a trial, hearing, or other proceeding, before any court, any committee of either House or both Houses of Congress, or any agency, commission, or officer authorized by the laws of the United States to hear evidence or take testimony, or for or because of such person's absence therefrom;

(3) directly or indirectly, demands, seeks, receives, accepts, or agrees to receive or accept anything of value personally for or because of the testimony under oath or affirmation given or to be given by such person as a witness upon any such trial, hearing, or other proceeding, or for or because of such person's absence therefrom;

shall be fined under this title or imprisoned for not more than two years, or both.

Laws Related to the Federal Income Tax

The IRS lists on its website a number of laws related to income tax, indicating further that the list in this section is not all-encompassing (see the following sections for further discussion).

Title and Section	Definition
Title 26 USC § 7201 **Attempt to evade or defeat tax**	Any person who willfully attempts to evade or defeat any tax imposed by this title or the payment thereof shall, in addition to other penalties provided by law, be guilty of a felony and, upon conviction thereof: • Shall be imprisoned not more than 5 years • Or fined not more than $250,000 for individuals ($500,000 for corporations) • Or both, together with the costs of prosecution
Title 26 USC § 7202 **Willful failure to collect or pay over tax**	Any person required under this title to collect, account for, and pay over any tax imposed by this title who willfully fails to collect or truthfully account for and pay over such tax shall, in addition to penalties provide by the law, be guilty of a felony • Shall be imprisoned not more than 5 years • Or fined not more than $250,000 for individuals ($500,000 for corporations) • Or both, together with the costs of prosecution
Title 26 USC § 7203 **Willful failure to file return, supply information, or pay tax**	Any person required under this title to pay any estimated tax or tax, or required by this title or by regulations made under authority thereof to make a return, keep any records, or supply any information, who willfully fails to pay such estimated tax or tax, make such return, keep such records, or supply such information, at the time or times required by law or regulations, shall, in addition to other penalties provided by law, be guilty of a misdemeanor and, upon conviction thereof: • Shall be imprisoned not more than 1 years • Or fined not more than $100,000 for individuals ($200,000 for corporations) • Or both, together with cost of prosecution
Title 26 USC § 7206(1) **Fraud and false statements**	Any Person who… (1) Declaration under penalties of perjury - Willfully makes and subscribes any return, statement, or other document, which contains or is verified by a written declaration that is made under the penalties of perjury, and which he does not believe to be true and correct as to every material matter; shall be guilty of a felony and, upon conviction thereof; • Shall be imprisoned not more than 3 years • Or fined not more than $250,000 for individuals ($500,000 for corporations) • Or both, together with cost of prosecution
Title 26 USC § 7206(2) **Fraud and false statements**	Any person who…(2) Aid or assistance - Willfully aids or assists in, or procures, counsels, or advises the preparation or presentation under, or in connection with any matter arising under, the Internal Revenue laws, of a return, affidavit, claim, or other document, which is fraudulent or is false as to any material matter, whether or not such falsity or fraud is with the knowledge or consent of the person authorized or required to present such return, affidavit, claim, or document; shall be guilty of a felony and, upon conviction thereof: • Shall be imprisoned not more than 3 years • Or fined not more than $250,000 for individuals ($500,000 for corporations) • Or both, together with cost of prosecution

Title and Section	Definition
Title 26 USC § 7212(A) **Attempts to interfere with administration of Internal Revenue laws**	Whoever corruptly or by force endeavors to intimidate or impede any officer or employee of the United States acting in an official capacity under this title, or in any other way corruptly or by force obstructs or impedes, or endeavors to obstruct or impede, the due administration of this title, upon conviction: • Shall be imprisoned not more than 3 years • Or fined not more than $250,000 for individuals ($500,000 for corporations) • Or both
Title 18 USC § 371 **Conspiracy to commit offense or to defraud the United States**	If two or more persons conspire either to commit any offense against the United States, or to defraud the United States, or any agency thereof in any manner or for any purpose, and one or more of such persons do any act to effect the object of the conspiracy, each: • Shall be imprisoned not more than 5 years • Or fined not more than $250,000 for individuals ($500,000 for corporations) • Or both*

* IRS, "Related Statutes and Penalties—General Fraud," www.irs.gov/compliance/enforcement/
article/0,,id=106790,00.html

Program fraud (18 USC 666)

According to the *United States Attorneys' Manual*, 18 USC 666 was enacted to protect the integrity of money distributed through federal programs. It is designed to facilitate the prosecution of those who steal money or otherwise divert property or services from state and local governments or private organizations that receive large amounts of federal funds.[17]

The Antideficiency Act (31 USC 1341, et seq.)

The Antideficiency Act prohibits a government employee from spending money or creating obligations in excess of the amounts available under an appropriation. They also may not accept voluntary services or employ persons when not authorized by law, except in cases of emergency involving the safety of human life or the protection of property. Federal employees who violate this law may be subject to both administrative sanctions in relation to their employment status and penal sanctions including fines, imprisonment, or both.[18]

Embezzlement of Government Property (18 USC 641)

This is the primary statute aimed at protecting government property. It makes the unauthorized taking, destruction, or use of government property a criminal offense. According to the *United States Attorneys' Manual*, the elements to the crime of embezzlement of government property are as follows:

---

[17] Department of Justice, *United States Attorneys' Manual*, ch. 9-46.000, www.justice.gov/usao/eousa/
foia_reading_room/usam/title9/46mcrm.htm.

[18] U.S. Government Accountability Office (GAO), "Antideficiency Act Background," www.gao.gov/
legal/lawresources/antideficiencybackground.html.

- A trust or fiduciary relationship must exist between the defendant and the property owner.
- The property must fall within property covered by the statute. Such property includes "any record, voucher, money, or thing of value of the United States or any department or agency thereof, or any property made or being made under contract for the United States or any department or agency thereof."[19]
- The property must have come into the possession of the defendant by virtue of the defendant's employment.
- The property belonged to the United States.
- The defendant's actions with respect to the property constituted a fraudulent conversion or appropriation to his or her own use.
- The defendant acted with the intent to deprive the owner of the use of the property.

Although the defendant must act with the intent to deprive the owner of the use of the property, no requirement exists that the intent be to permanently deprive the owner of the use of his or her property. Therefore, even if the defendant intends to return the property, a crime has still been committed.[20]

Distinguishing Factors and Methods

The clearest distinguishing feature of public sector fraud is the domino effect. In fact, when funds are taken or diverted from a government entity or program, the resulting budgetary hole can result in less money available for other services and programs. This, in turn, can lead to increases in taxes and fees as the government takes steps to replace the revenue lost to fraud.

Another key difference in public sector fraud is its potentially massive size and scope. Successful fraud schemes rely on the existence of two key elements: the presence of financial resources and the opportunity to obtain some portion of those resources. Government entities and programs provide fertile ground on both fronts. For example, trillions of dollars flow in and out of federal, state, and local government entities each year, so siphoning even a small percentage of that money adds up to big money for fraudsters. And, because of the size and complexity of many government agencies, those looking to commit fraud can often find ample opportunity to do so.

Although big picture fraud schemes, such as asset misappropriation or corruption, can take place in any setting, these methods take on slightly different characteristics when used in the public sector. A key reason for this is because taxpayers are the end-users of government services or the recipients of government collected funds. For example, asset misappropriation schemes that are unique to the public sector include tax fraud, program fraud, and false

---

[19] Department of Justice, *Criminal Resource Manual*, sec. 1643, www.justice.gov/usao/eousa/foia_reading_room/usam/title9/crm01643.htm#1643.

[20] Department of Justice, *Criminal Resource Manual*, sec. 1638, www.justice.gov/usao/eousa/foia_reading_room/usam/title9/crm01638.htm.

claims targeted at government programs. An overview of these and other schemes are covered in more detail later in this chapter.

Table 8-1 highlights how fraudulent activities affect the public and private sectors.

Table 8-1: Impact of Fraudulent Activities in Private and Public Sectors

Factor	Description	Government Related Fraud vs. Private Sector Fraud
Motivation	Opportunity, pressure, rationalization	Similar*
Techniques	Asset misappropriation, corruption, fraudulent disbursements	Similar
Source of Funds	Taxpayer vs. private	Different
Fraud Type	Corruption, procurement fraud & false claims vs. asset misappropriation & financial statement fraud	Different
Perpetrators of fraud	Inside vs. outside the organization	Different
Scope of fraud	Relatively limited vs. widespread impact	Different

* www.acfe.com/article.aspx?id=4294970127

As outlined in table 8-1, the motivations for illicit acts in private business and government are often the same, as are some techniques and schemes used for their perpetration. However, public sector fraud tends to be more heavily weighted in the areas of corruption, procurement fraud, and false claims, while private sector schemes tend to cluster around the areas of asset misappropriation, corruption, and financial statement fraud. In addition, government fraud is most frequently perpetrated by outsiders, such as recipients of public funds, vendors selling goods or services, or contractors working with a public sector agency. This differs from a conventional business, in which fraud tends to take place at the hands of employees or executives on the inside of a company or organization.

Types of Government Fraud

For purposes of this chapter, government fraud can be broken down into six main categories:

1. Asset misappropriation
2. Procurement fraud
3. Tax fraud
4. Program fraud
5. False claims
6. Corruption

The following sections provide a closer look at each of these schemes within a public sector environment.

Asset Misappropriation

Asset misappropriation is the theft or misuse of cash or other assets from an intended recipient or for an intended purpose. Forms of asset misappropriation are addressed in chapter 3, "On- and Off-the-Books Fraud Schemes." Although asset misappropriation may be less prevalent in the public sector, it still bears watching as an opportunity for fraudsters. Some examples of prevalent asset misappropriation schemes in the public sector are

- personal purchases (such as those made by government issued procurement cards),
- expense reimbursement schemes (such as expensing personal travel items as government-related), and
- misuse of government-issued assets (such as automobiles or computers).

As the following excerpt demonstrates, asset misappropriations by employees are similar in the public and governmental sectors.

Example

A California federal court sentenced a former postal sales associate to 2 years in prison for embezzling $426,065 in postal money orders from October 2003 to July 2005. The former associate admitted he engaged in a scheme to issue postal money orders to himself by falsely recording them as customer purchases. He used the money for personal expenses and gambling.*

---

* U.S. Postal Service Office of Inspector General, "Convicted Former Postal Worker Ordered to Repay $410,000 to the Postal Service," www.uspsoig.gov/inv_embezz.htm.

Procurement Fraud

Procurement is a significant source of public sector fraud because the federal government is a major purchaser of goods and services. Entities such as the General Services Administration (GSA), Department of Defense (DOD), and the National Aeronautics and Space Administration (NASA) contract for and purchase billions of dollars of goods and services each year. And as a share of gross domestic product, U.S. government spending has been increasing for more than 50 years and totals approximately 40 percent of the entire U.S. economy.[21] This provides ample opportunity for fraudsters to commit illicit acts.

Procurement fraud relates to schemes that seek to benefit from government processes to acquire goods and services. External contractors can attack the procurement process at multiple stages, including the request for bid (or pre-bid) phase, bidding, fulfillment, and billing. Consider the following example:

---

[21] usgovernmentspending.com, "US Government Spending Chart Factory," www.usgovernmentspending.com/spending_chart_1950_2015USp_F0t.

The federal government spends a tremendous amount of taxpayer dollars each year on construction, much of which is funneled through the various stages of procurement. In 2009, the U.S. military alone spent approximately $15 billion on construction.[22] Fraud schemes prey on government construction programs from the request for bid stage all the way to project completion via such schemes as bidding fraud, bribes, kickbacks, overcharging, providing substandard materials, or workmanship and billing scams.

Although procurement fraud overall is not unique to government fraud, certain factors in the execution of this type of fraud are particular to government and public sector fraud, including the size or amount of the fraud, pervasiveness or scope of the fraud, number of participants, or involvement of foreign governments or nationals.

Example

In 2011, a North Carolina man was sentenced in federal court for his role in a conspiracy to defraud the federal government of more than $225,000. Jeffrey Blake, the founder of M&A supply, was an approved goods and services vendor to the federal government. He obtained more than $225,000 in payments for fraudulent claims based on inflated invoices for shipping expenses.*

---

* Department of Justice, "North Carolina Man Pleads Guilty to $225,000 Scheme to Defraud the Federal Government," news release, September 29, 2010, www.justice.gov/usao/mow/news2010/blake.ple.htm.

In addition to the examples noted previously in this chapter, procurement fraud can also take the form of collusion, when several parties agree to take collective action for fraud-related gains. Collusion in procurement fraud can take a number of forms, including the following:

- *Price fixing.*[23] This is an agreement among competitors to raise, fix, or otherwise maintain the price at which goods or services are sold. It is not necessary that competitors agree to charge exactly the same price or that every competitor in a given industry join the conspiracy. Price fixing can take many forms, such as agreements to establish price discounts, hold prices firm, eliminate or reduce discounts, adopt standard price formulas, maintain similar price differentials, set minimum fee or price schedules, fix credit terms, or not advertise prices. Any of these agreements that restrict price competition are a violation of the law. Antitrust laws were discussed in the previous section.

---

[22] War Resisters League, "Where Your Income Tax Money Really Goes," www.warresisters.org/pages/piechart.htm.

[23] Department of Justice, "Price Fixing, Bid Rigging, and Market Allocation Schemes: What They Are and What to Look For," www.justice.gov/atr/public/guidelines/211578.htm.

- *Bid rigging.*[24] Conspiring competitors effectively raise prices when purchasers, often federal, state, or local governments, acquire goods or services by soliciting competing bids. Almost all forms of bid-rigging schemes have one thing in common: agreement among some or all of the bidders that predetermines the winner, thus limiting or eliminating competition. As with most fraud schemes, big rigging is not unique to the government. However, due to the lack of direct financial stake on the part of the government's contracting officers (they are rarely held financially accountable for errors or oversights), bid rigging (in its various guises discussed subsequently) can be a particularly costly fraud when perpetrated on the government, and it can also have a particularly deleterious effect upon the public's perception of the efficacy and efficiency of government when these frauds are uncovered. The U.S. Department of Justice has stated that "when competitors collude, prices are inflated."[25] Public purchasers, and ultimately the taxpayers, are cheated, and for these reasons, bid rigging is illegal in the United States. Bid rigging can take many forms, and it usually falls into one or more of the following categories:

    — *Bid suppression.* In bid suppression schemes, one or more competitors who otherwise would be expected to bid agree to refrain from bidding or withdraw a previously submitted bid. This ensures that the designated winning competitor's bid will be accepted.

    — *Complementary bidding.* Complementary bidding (also known as "cover" or "courtesy" bidding) occurs when some competitors agree to submit bids that are either too high to be accepted or contain special terms not acceptable to the buyer. Complementary bidding schemes are the most frequent form of bid rigging, and they defraud purchasers by creating the appearance of competition to conceal secretly inflated prices.

    — *Bid rotation.* In bid rotation schemes, all conspirators submit bids but take turns being the low bidder. A strict bid rotation pattern defies the law of chance and suggests collusion is taking place.

    — *Subcontracting.* In exchange for agreeing not to bid or submit a losing bid, a vendor can be rewarded with subcontracts or supply contracts from the winning bidder in the fraud scheme. In some cases, a low bidder will agree to withdraw its bid in favor of the next lowest bidder in exchange for lucrative subcontract arrangements.

    — *Product substitution.* This scheme involves providing substandard parts or materials in lieu of the expected or contractually agreed upon supplies.

---

[24] *Id.*

[25] Robert E. Connolly Esq., U.S. Department of Justice, *Big Rigging – It Happens: What it is and What To Look For, An Antitrust Primer For Procurement Professionals* (October 2009), 1.

- *Market division.*[26] Market division or allocation schemes are agreements in which competing firms allocate specific customers or types of customers, products, or territories among themselves. For example, one competitor will be allowed to sell to—or bid on—contracts let by certain customers. In return, that competitor will not attempt to make sales or bid on contracts let by customers allocated to the other competitors. In another version of this scheme, competitors agree to sell only to customers in certain geographic areas, while refusing to do business with customers in geographic areas allocated to other firms in the conspiracy.

Example

On December 21, 2011, Kaman Precision Products Inc. was instructed to pay the United States $4.75 million to settle allegations it knowingly substituted nonconforming fuses in "bunker-buster" bombs. This illegal product substitution could have created a hazard for military personnel and caused misfires of the warheads.[*]

[*] Department of Justice, "Florida-Based Defense Contractor Pays US $4.75 Million to Resolve Allegations Related to Defective Bomb Fuzes," news release, December 21, 2011, www.dodig.mil/IGInformation/IGInformationReleases/DOJKaman.pdf.

Example

The Department of Justice announced on November 11, 2011, that Sea Star Line LLC agreed to plead guilty and pay a $14.2 million criminal fine for its role in a conspiracy to fix prices in the coastal water freight transportation industry. Sea Star Line and the co-conspirators agreed during meetings and communications to allocate customers of Puerto Rico freight services and to rig bids and fix the rates and surcharges to be charged to purchasers of water transportation between the continental United States and Puerto Rico.[*]

[*] Department of Justice, "Florida-Based Sea Star Line LLC Agrees to Plead Guilty and Its Former President Is Indicted for Price Fixing on Coastal Freight Services Between the Continental United States and Puerto Rico," news release, November 17, 2011, www.dodig.mil/IGInformation/IGInformationReleases/SeaStarPR111711.pdf.

The aforementioned categories of bid rigging do not reflect all the possible ways that bid rigging in a government or public sector occurs, and in fact some schemes have elements of several bid rigging methods.

---

[26] Department of Justice, "Price Fixing, Bid Rigging, and Market Allocation Schemes: What They Are and What to Look For," www.justice.gov/atr/public/guidelines/211578.htm.

Example

In July 2011, J.P. Morgan settled complaints brought by the Securities and Exchange Commission (SEC), IRS, bank regulators, and 25 state attorneys general that a division of its bank made at least 93 secret deals with companies that handled the bidding processes in 31 states to sell bond offerings to cities and counties. Those deals allowed the bank to review the competing offers and deprived the various governmental entities a true competitive process that would produce the best return on their investments. A *USA Today* article reported that "Bank of America and UBS have agreed to settlements based on similar municipal bid-rigging charges brought by federal and state authorities. Bank of America agreed in December to pay more than $137 million. UBS agreed in May to pay more than $160 million.'"

—————

*   Daniel Wagner, JPMorgan pays $228M to settle bid-rigging charges," *USA Today,* July 7, 2011, www.usatoday.com/money/companies/regulation/2011-07-07-jpmorgan-bid-rigging_n.htm.

Although collusion is common in procurement fraud, noncollusion schemes are also a useful means through which fraudsters can achieve their illegal goals. Some examples of noncollusion activity include the following:

- *Pre-bid or pre-request fraud.* To obtain products or services, the government often seeks competitive bidding, project proposals, or sole source (no-bid) requests. Pre-bid fraud can be major problem in no-bid situations. In these cases, an entity or individual may be in a position to contract without competition, opening the door for overcharges on products or services. Pre-bid fraud in a competitive bidding situation can occur when someone uses insider information to gain an advantage over other entities or individuals that might also bid or propose on a project. This can also lead to contracts in which the government overpays for products or services.
- *Fulfillment fraud.* Fulfillment fraud often involves a vendor that supplies substandard products or services to government agencies or a provider that doesn't deliver what was called for in a contract. These illicit practices can result health and safety risks, in addition to potentially greater expense to replace substandard products or services originally received. An example of a very similar scheme is detailed in the "bunker-buster" fuse example cited previously.
- *Billing schemes.* Billing schemes often take the form of progress payment fraud, overcharging, or mischarging. Progress payment fraud refers to a scheme in which a vendor or contractor submits progress bills for work or material that has not yet been provided, therefore receiving payment in advance of what has been provided or called for in the contract. An example of this type of government fraud is when a contractor falsifies labor charges under a contract and then submits a progress payment request based on attaining this fraudulent milestone. Overcharging or mischarging can be accomplished by invoicing for a higher price than was agreed to or is allowed under the contract, misstating the quantity that was provided, or including expenses that are not allowed under the contract.

Example

On September 3, 2011, Ann Warwick was sentenced to 5 years' probation with 10 months to be served in home detention with electronic monitoring for making false statements in connection with the hours she worked on a National Security Agency contract. She was also ordered to pay restitution of $108,780.46. In total, Warwick submitted false timesheets which claimed that she had worked a total of 836 hours more than she had in fact worked.*

---

* Department of Justice, "Former NSA Contractor Sentenced F=for Making False Statements on Time Sheets Causing NSA to Overpay by More Than $108,780," news release, September 30, 2011, www.justice.gov/usao/md/Public-Affairs/press_releases/press08/FormerNSAContractorSentencedforMakingFalseStatementsonTimeSheets.html.

Tax Fraud

The tax system is a major channel for government fraud because taxes are the main source of revenue for public sector entities and programs. Generally, tax fraud occurs when a person or company does not file a required return, does not report or underreports income, or falsifies expenses. In a previous section, a partial list of relevant laws was provided.

Although fraud perpetrated on the IRS does not cover all tax schemes, the agency's specific fraud categories do summarize the most prevalent types of individual tax scams, which include the following:[27]

- *Foreign trust tax schemes.* The foreign trust scheme usually starts off as a series of domestic trusts. This set-up is used to give the appearance that a taxpayer has turned his or her business and assets over to a trust and is no longer in direct control of those accounts. However, once these assets are transferred to the domestic trust, the income and expenses are passed to one or more foreign trusts, typically in tax haven countries where the trust can avoid payment of U.S. taxes.

- *International business corporations.* In this scheme, taxpayers use the name of their business to establish an international business corporation (IBC) and a bank account in a foreign country. When customer checks are received, the fraudster sends them to the foreign bank, which uses its correspondent account to process the checks in a way so the funds never appear to have been sent offshore. Once the checks clear, the taxpayer's IBC account is credited for check payments, and the fraudster benefits from unreported income.

- *False billing schemes.* In this fraud, an individual works with a local "promoter" to arrange an offshore IBC and bank account. When the promoter invoices the fraudster's company for goods allegedly purchased, the taxpayer then sends payment to the IBC, which is deposited as unreported income into a joint account held by the IBC and the taxpayer. This individual then takes a business deduction based on that payment, thereby reducing taxable income.

---

27 IRS, "Program and Emphasis Areas for IRS Criminal Investigation," www.irs.gov/compliance/enforcement/article/0,,id=130611,00.html.

In addition to tax schemes, fraudsters often seek to skirt tax payments by misusing the bankruptcy system. According to the U.S. Bankruptcy courts, there were 1.4 million and 1.6 million filings in the years ended September 30, 2009, and September 30, 2010, respectively.[28] This high number of filings makes illicit acts inevitable. In fact, the FBI estimates that 10 percent of U.S. bankruptcy cases involve fraud.[29] A pair of studies conducted by U.S. Bankruptcy Judge Steven Rhodes found that 99 percent of a random sample of consumer bankruptcy cases contained errors or problems. Just as troubling, fully 38 percent of assets administered by bankruptcy trustees in Rhodes's district had not been disclosed in the debtor's initial bankruptcy filing.[30]

In addition to individual tax fraud, corporations also have ways to cheat the government revenue system. *Corporate fraud* is defined by the IRS as violations of the Internal Revenue Code and related statutes by large, publicly traded (or private) corporations or by their senior executives.[31] This type of illicit activity is often not solely related to taxes, but rather is an additional fraud that flows out of other schemes by corporations or their officers.

Example

In 2010, Timothy Huff was sentenced to 50 months in prison and 3 years of supervised release. Huff, formerly CEO of GlobeTel Communications, pleaded guilty to a conspiracy to commit securities fraud and to defraud the United States, the Treasury Department, and the IRS.

In case filings, it was reported that Huff and his co-conspirators caused GlobeTel to report fictitious revenue, both on its books and in periodic filings with the SEC. Huff and other corporate fraudsters created fraudulent invoices and technical documents, known as call detail records (CDRs) that appeared to corroborate the company's fictitious revenue. GlobeTel executives provided the fraudulent CDRs and invoices to the firm's independent auditors, seeking to mislead them into believing that GlobeTel had received more than $22 million in fraudulent revenue. Additionally, Huff and one other executive failed to have Forms 1099 issued for a fraudulent stock sale of $980,500 and failed to report the proceeds of the stock transaction on their personal tax returns for 2001 through 2004.[*]

---

[*]   IRS, "What is Corporate Fraud?" www.irs.gov/compliance/enforcement/article/0,,id=121468,00.html.

Other tax evasion schemes used by corporations include the following:

- *Pyramiding. Pyramiding* of employment taxes is a fraudulent practice in which a business withholds taxes from employees but intentionally fails to remit them to the IRS. Businesses involved in pyramiding frequently file for bankruptcy, because they want to discharge the accrued liabilities and start a new business under a different name.

---

[28]   James C. Duff, *Judicial Business of the United States Courts: 2010 Annual Report of the Director*, (2010), www.uscourts.gov/uscourts/Statistics/JudicialBusiness/2010/judicialbusinespdfversion.pdf.

[29]   Noreen Clancy and Stephen J. Carroll, *Identifying Fraud, Abuse, and Error in Personal Bankruptcy Filings* (2007) www.justice.gov/ust/eo/public_affairs/reports_studies/docs/Fraud_and_Abuse_Study_Rand.pdf.

[30]   *Id.*

[31]   IRS, "What is Corporate Fraud?" www.irs.gov/compliance/enforcement/article/0,,id=121468,00.html.

- *Leasing.* Although employee leasing is a legal business practice, it is sometimes subject to abuse. *Employee leasing* is the practice of contracting with outside businesses to handle all employment-related administrative, personnel, and payroll concerns. In some instances, employee leasing companies fail to pay collected employment taxes (such as Social Security, federal, or state taxes) to the IRS. Instead, these taxes can be spent by fraudsters on business or personal expenses.
- *Paying employees in cash.* Paying employees in cash is a common method of evading income and employment taxes. This commonly results in lost tax revenue and the long-term risk of reduced or lost Social Security or Medicare benefits for the employee.
- *False or unfiled payroll tax returns.* The use of false payroll tax returns, which understate the amount of wages on which taxes are owed, or failure to file employment tax returns are two methods commonly used by companies to evade employment taxes.

While fraudsters (and other types of criminals) are often reluctant to disclose to the IRS the proceeds of their illicit activities, failing to do so is a crime.

Example

According to court documents, from 2003 to 2006, Roseberry owned and operated a drywall business as a sole proprietorship under the name of Western Wallboard or Bustos Drywall. During this time period, he evaded or failed to remit more than $1 million in employment and income taxes owed to the IRS in connection with the 350 employees of the firm. He also significantly underreported total wages and employment taxes due to the IRS, while collecting more than $236,000 in income taxes that he did not remit to the IRS.*

---

* IRS, "Examples of Employment Tax Fraud Investigations - Fiscal Year 2011," www.irs.gov/compliance/enforcement/article/0,,id=228085,00.html.

Fraud in Health and Human Services Programs

Numerous programs are funded by the government to provide help for those who need assistance with healthcare, child care, housing, and food. Fraud in such programs may include the following activities and schemes:[32]

- Crimes or gross misconduct committed by Health and Human Services (HHS) employees or contractors
- Conflicts of interest on the part of HHS department employees
- Cost overruns in HHS programs or initiatives due to mismanagement
- False applications for HHS contracts or grants
- Failure to provide the services or products for HHS grants or contracts

---

[32] Office of Inspector General, U.S. Department of Health and Human Services, "Report Fraud," http://oig.hhs.gov/fraud/report-fraud/index.asp.

- False or fraudulent claims submitted to Medicare or Medicaid
- Kickbacks or inducements for referrals by Medicare or Medicaid providers
- Medical identity theft involving Medicare and or Medicaid beneficiaries
- Door-to-door solicitation of Medicare or Medicaid beneficiaries
- Misrepresentation of Medicare private plans
- Fraud or waste in ARRA grants

Example

In 2007, an Arizona woman was sentenced to 2 months in county jail for illegally using food stamps. The woman made false statements on welfare applications on 10 different occasions between August 2000 and September 2004. On the applications, she misstated her income and the number of children she had and failed to tell the Arizona Department of Economic Security that she already received substantial adoption payments. She pleaded guilty to fraudulent schemes and practices and was sentenced to 3 years' probation and ordered to pay $54,725 in restitution.*

* California Department of Health and Human Services, "Welfare Fraud Stories," www.dss.cahwnet.gov/fraud/PG270.htm.

FCA

False claims are a major opportunity for government fraud, and they can take place within the context of other schemes already discussed (such as welfare or procurement fraud). Fraud investigators should bear in mind that the FCA makes it illegal to present a false claim in an effort to defraud the government.

Example

In August 2010, Hewlett-Packard Co. (HP) agreed to pay the United States $55 million to settle claims that the company defrauded the GSA and other federal agencies by knowingly paying kickbacks, or "influencer fees," to systems integrator companies in return for recommendations that federal agencies purchase HP's products.

The allegations that HP improperly paid kickbacks were first made in a lawsuit filed by whistleblowers Norman Rille and Neal Roberts in 2004. Under the qui tam provisions of the FCA, private citizens may file actions for fraud on behalf of the United States and share in any recovery.

The United States has settled kickback allegations similar to those made in this case in matters involving IBM for $2.9 million, Computer Sciences Corporation for $1.37 million, and PricewaterhouseCoopers for $2.3 million. In addition, these same allegations were a part of a settlement with EMC Corporation, which totaled $87.5 million.

Corruption

Corruption is the use of one's position, status, or relationships in a wrongful or abusive way to gain some sort of benefit. Corruption is addressed in chapter 3 of this book. The FBI defines *corruption* as "a breach of trust by federal, state, or local officials—often with the help of private sector accomplices."[33]

A typical form of corruption is the acceptance of a bribe by a public official or employee in exchange for an action that will provide a benefit to the person or entity paying the bribe. Corruption is an abuse of power and a violation of the public trust, and it can create situations in which government agencies overpay for products or services. In fact, for the following reasons, the FBI considers corruption its top investigative priority because of its potential for significant damage in public and private sector organizations:

> Public corruption poses a fundamental threat to our national security and way of life. It impacts everything from how well our borders are secured and our neighborhoods protected...to verdicts handed down in courts...to the quality of our roads, schools, and other government services. And it takes a significant toll on our pocketbooks, wasting billions in tax dollars every year.[34]

Corruption can take many forms, including the following:[35]

- Bribery
- Extortion
- Embezzlement
- Kickbacks
- Natural disaster corruption (diverting funds meant for disaster relief for personal gain)
- Illegal gratuities
- Self-dealing or related party dealings and transactions

---

[33] Federal Bureau of Investigation (FBI), "Public Corruption: Why It's Our #1 Criminal Priority," March 26, 2010, www.fbi.gov/news/stories/2010/march/corruption_032610.

[34] FBI, "Public Corruption," www.fbi.gov/about-us/investigate/corruption/public_corruption.

[35] FBI, "Public Corruption: Why It's Our #1 Criminal Priority," March 26, 2010, www.fbi.gov/news/stories/2010/march/corruption_032610.

Example

A Tennessee sheriff was prosecuted for drug conspiracy, money laundering, and extortion charges. The sheriff, Billy Long, was accused of operating a "shakedown" of local business owners, which included threats to close down stores of those who had promised campaign contributions, but had not yet paid the full amount of the pledges. In addition, Long provided protection and assistance to move hundreds of thousands of dollars in drug trafficking proceeds from Mexico into Tennessee. During this time, he provided a badge and gun to a convicted felon, who helped him commit various crimes. Shortly after his arrest in November 2008, Long resigned his position, pleaded guilty to the offenses, and received a 14-year prison sentence.[*]

---

[*] United States Attorney's Office, Eastern District of Tennessee, "Public Corruption," www.justice.gov/usao/tne/public_corruption.html.

Government Agencies That Work to Prevent, Investigate, or Prosecute Fraud

At all levels, government entities spend enormous sums of money to combat fraud. At the forefront of that effort are a number of key agencies involved in investigating, preventing, and prosecuting schemes:

- *Government Accountability Office (GAO).* The GAO works at the direction of Congress to determine whether federal funds are being effectively spent and investigate allegations of illegal or improper activities.[36] The GAO has more than 3,000 employees and a budget of more than $571 million dollars (figures for 2010).[37] The GAO also has a program called FraudNet, a forensic audit and investigative tool that facilitates the reporting of fraud, waste, abuse, or mismanagement of federal funds.[38]
- *Inspector General offices.* In addition to its outside investigative work, the GAO has its own Office of Inspector General, which investigates potential fraud, waste, or abuse of GAO resources.[39] Most other major federal agencies, including the State Department, HHS, DOD, and NASA all have inspector general offices that monitor possible illicit schemes in those government operations.
- *Other federal players.* The FBI, SEC, and the Department of Justice are also key players in the federal government's efforts to prevent, detect, and prosecute fraud.

---

[36] GAO, "About GAO," www.gao.gov/about/index.html.
[37] GAO, "GAO at a Glance," www.gao.gov/about/gglance.html.
[38] GAO, "FraudNet/Reporting Fraud," www.gao.gov/fraudnet/fraudnet.htm#federal.
[39] *Id.*

- *State agencies.* States also have various agencies and programs aimed at combating the fraud problem. For example, the California Justice Department, through the Office of the State Attorney General, has a corporate fraud section that monitors various types of financial wrongdoing. This dedicated fraud resource has a false claims unit, which investigates and prosecutes fraudsters who attempt to illegally obtain funds or resources from the state.[40] Within the attorney general's office, the corporate fraud section coordinates its efforts with consumer protection, antitrust or business competition, charities, and Medi-Cal fraud or elder abuse units.[41]

Resources for More Information

U.S. Department of Health and Human Services (HHS), Office of Inspector General	http://oig.hhs.gov/
HHS, Stop Medicare Fraud	www.stopmedicarefraud.gov/
U.S. Government Accountability Office, Fraudnet and fraud reporting	www.gao.gov/fraudnet/fraudnet.htm
U.S. Department of Justice, Fraud Section	www.justice.gov/criminal/fraud/
National Aeronautics and Space Administration, Office of Inspector General	http://oig.nasa.gov/hotline.html
U.S. Department of State, Office of Inspector General	http://oig.state.gov/
U.S. Department of Defense, Office of Inspector General	www.dodig.mil/hotline/index.html
U.S. Department of Agriculture, Risk Management Agency	www.rma.usda.gov/aboutrma/fraud.html
U.S. Department of Agriculture, Office of Inspector General	www.usda.gov/oig/index.htm
U.S. Department of Transportation, Office of Inspector General	www.oig.dot.gov/
U.S. Department of Commerce, Office of Inspector General	www.oig.doc.gov/Pages/default.aspx
General Services Administration, Office of Inspector General	www.gsaig.gov/
Federal Reserve, Office of Inspector General	www.federalreserve.gov/oig/
U.S. Postal Service, Office of Inspector General	www.uspsoig.gov/
U.S. Social Security Administration, Office of Inspector General	www.socialsecurity.gov/oig/
U.S. Department of Labor, Office of Inspector General	www.oig.dol.gov/hotlinemain.htm
Federal Communications Commission, Office of Inspector General	www.fcc.gov/office-inspector-general
Federal Acquisitions Regulation	www.acquisition.gov/far/index.html
Federal Bureau of Investigation – Corruption Information	www.fbi.gov/about-us/investigate/corruption
False Claims Act Information	www.taf.org/whyfca.htm

---

[40] California Department of Justice, Office of the Attorney General, "False Claims Unit," http://ag.ca.gov/cfs/falseclaims.php.

[41] California Department of Justice, Office of the Attorney General, "Corporate Fraud Section," http://ag.ca.gov/cfs/index.php.

Gaming Fraud

Lynda Hartzell, CPA/CFF, CFE

Introduction

Gaming is very prevalent in the United States and other countries. Some companies involved in gaming are large, multi-national companies that offer a wide variety of hotel, gaming, entertainment, dining, and retail shopping options. On the other hand, gaming may also be operated by much smaller entities, including branches of government, Native American tribes, partnerships, and sole proprietorships. Any of these entities may be susceptible to a range of fraudulent activities, including asset misappropriation, fraudulent financial statements, and records and corruption or prohibited practices.

The opportunity for fraud activity may be heightened in the gaming industry, due to the presence of large volumes of cash and the fact that in some departments, individual transactions between the operating company and its customer are not recorded. Because summary information is compiled on a shift or daily basis, it is very possible that weak controls can allow revenue to be diverted without it ever being recorded by the operator. Generally speaking, the main fraud threats to any gaming operation are the following:

- **Employees.** Given the state of the current job market, economic pressures upon employees may be very high, given the potential for losing one's job and the demands (including decreased pay and benefits and increased workloads) imposed upon the remaining employees. In fact, it is not difficult for an employee to rationalize that because the gaming company is making "easy money" from customers, the worker deserves more than just what he or she earns.

- **Executive leadership.** Companies may commit fraudulent acts to reduce their tax burden (including gaming taxes), mislead investors or creditors, or achieve bonuses. In the context of financial statement reporting, there may be a motivation among company executives to report higher income from gaming operations. Conversely, from a gaming tax reporting perspective, the motivation would typically be to understate gaming revenue. Although legitimate differences exist that can make complete reconciliation between taxable gaming and financial statement revenues a bit cumbersome, clearly variances that cannot ultimately be reconciled are cause for alarm.

- *Customers*. Patrons of a gaming enterprise may also perpetrate fraud against the company, via theft of company property, cheating, or credit fraud (many operators offer their customers the ability to wager on credit extended directly by the company to the customer).

In the larger picture, many gaming companies are under extreme financial pressure, which has forced several of them to declare bankruptcy or abandon incomplete construction projects in which millions of dollars had been committed or expended. When customers spend less money, gaming operators large and small are forced to cut staff and consolidate or outsource functions, which can have a negative effect on operational and financial reporting controls. For that reason, a heightened risk of financial statement fraud exists among gaming operators, as borrowers are challenged to meet debt-related covenants. Economic uncertainty has also created an elevated risk for fraud related to construction or bankruptcy. Corruption risk may be quite high for companies doing business in other countries and seeking to expedite government approvals for new projects. Such endeavors, which become very important in the face of declining domestic revenue streams, may cause some gaming executives to run afoul of the Foreign Corrupt Practices Act.

The professional standards issued by the AICPA provide excellent guidance to financial statement auditors on general fraud risk factors (codified primarily in AU section 316, *Consideration of Fraud in a Financial Statement Audit*, [AICPA, *Professional Standards*]). In addition, AICPA Audit and Accounting Guide *Gaming* provides a solid overview of financial statement issues related to gaming and good background information for fraud investigators less familiar with the casino environment.[1]

Due to the unique nature of gaming, the industry is also susceptible to specific types of fraud schemes. For that reason, this chapter will cover the following topics on gaming fraud:

- Regulatory environment and history
- Credit or cage operations fraud
- Table games department fraud
- Slot department fraud
- Bingo department fraud
- Keno department fraud
- Race book and sports pool fraud

Regulatory Environment and History

The gaming industry tends to be a vital source of tax revenue for jurisdictions in which it operates which is why authorizing bodies, such as state legislatures, understand that significant oversight of the gaming industry is essential to maintain public confidence and ensure the proper collection of taxes. This oversight places considerable pressure on gaming companies to operate in an appropriate manner.

---

[1]   AICPA Audit and Accounting Guide *Gaming*.

In Nevada, for example, licensees are subject to numerous gaming regulations and reporting requirements. For example, larger operators are required to engage independent accountants to review or audit their financial statements and perform compliance tests. Many operators are required to have an internal audit function, and some companies must also have compliance committees to monitor overall compliance efforts. Nevada casinos (and casinos operating elsewhere) are also subject to anti-money laundering and anti-terrorist financing laws. Additionally, state regulatory agents can appear on an unannounced basis to perform audits or inspections.

Unlike those employed in less-regulated industries, gaming workers may have a heightened sense of risk attached to being caught in illicit activities. A job applicant with a history of criminal actions involving gaming may not be able to find employment in the industry. Even if a gaming operator was willing to hire a person with a questionable past, regulatory authorities may block the action through the registration, approval, or licensing process.

Applicants for gaming licenses, which can include key executives as well as owners, are subjected to extensive and intrusive background checks paid for by the company seeking the license. Disciplinary action is possible when a licensee fails to exercise proper oversight, and fines against operators are fairly common and can be very substantial. In extreme cases, a gaming license can be revoked. Therefore, although the inherent risks of fraud in the gaming industry are high, the controls *may* serve to reduce overall risk. These controls include the operator's own "tone from the top" governance, as well the regulatory structure in a given geographic location (bear in mind that regulatory oversight can vary considerably among jurisdictions).

Because Nevada has significant and lengthy experience with gaming, a brief review of its regulatory history may help underscore the need for proper governance and controls. Although many other jurisdictions have since embraced gaming, many of those states and countries still seek the advice of Nevada regulators when dealing with tough issues.

Although gaming in unregulated form existed in Nevada as far back as the 1800s, it was regulated only at the local and county levels until 1945. At that time, regulation shifted to the state level. One year later, the state imposed a 1 percent fee on gross gaming revenue (today, that fee is levied on a tier system, with a maximum rate of 6.75 percent).

Drawn by its lucrative nature, many "rough characters" got involved in Nevada gaming in the 1950s (including organized crime). Because gaming had become significant to Nevada's economic well being, the state created a Gaming Control Board in 1955. This oversight body makes recommendations on licensing matters, and it is responsible for the day-to-day oversight of gaming in the state.[2] In 1959, the Nevada legislature passed the Gaming Control Act. This led to the creation of the Nevada Gaming Commission, which remains to this day the final arbiter of gaming licensing matters.

The Gaming Control Board consists of three members, each of whom is appointed by the governor to four-year terms. The Nevada Gaming Commission consists of five members, who are also appointed to four-year terms by the governor. A key distinction between the

---

[2]   Nevada Resort Association, "History of Gaming in Nevada," accessed December 13, 2011, http://nevadaresorts.org/docs/history/.

two entities is the degree of involvement: Board members are full-time appointees who direct the organization's day-to-day activities; commission members are part-time appointees who often have substantial outside business commitments (see Nevada Revised Statutes [NRS] 463 for the Gaming Control Act and NRS 463.022–.085 for composition of the two entities).

Under the current regulatory structure, the commission is empowered to adopt regulations that govern gaming. Although suggestions for new regulations may come from industry representatives, the board, or other sources, the commission must actually adopt the regulations. For example, the Nevada legislature recently passed a bill mandating that the commission adopt regulations for interactive gaming (that is, Internet gaming). The board's senior staff, working with the state attorney general's office, was responsible for identifying potential areas in need of new policies and recommending a set of draft regulations for the board and commission to consider at public meetings. Along the way, extensive input was sought from gaming industry representatives and other interested parties. As the final decision maker, the commission voted on and passed contents of the final regulations (note that if future changes to the regulation are proposed, those revisions would be subject to the same review and voting process).

Throughout Nevada's gaming industry, the following key factors have driven the need for regulation revisions:

- *New technologies.* This involves tools created by the industry, such as hand-held "mobile gaming" devices. Although the industry initiated regulation discussions to facilitate this new activity, the board and industry leaders collaborated on a framework that would allow the activity to proceed in a safe and auditable fashion. This included the amending of various commission regulations.

- *Perceived risk issues.* Due to specific instances in which gaming operators went out of business before paying all amounts due to patrons, the board drafted and the commission passed strict regulations requiring gaming operators to maintain specific cash and restricted reserves (see Nevada Gaming Commission Regulations 6.150 and 22.040).

- *Streamlined reporting.* Currently, Nevada requires "key employees" in a casino or other gaming operation to be reported to the board (see Nevada Gaming Commission Regulation 3.100[3]). This rule was designed to expedite evaluations of employees holding gaming positions where additional scrutiny might be important. However, in response to industry concerns, the board drafted (and the commission adopted) regulation changes that substantially reduced the reporting requirements after carefully considering what information was valuable from a regulatory perspective and which parts of the existing regulatory requirements could be removed without sacrificing proper oversight.

---

[3] All regulations are available at http://gaming.nv.gov/stats_regs.htm.

One of the more relevant regulations in Nevada's gaming industry requires licensees to submit a written system of internal control to the board. After years of using an internal control review process that was both lengthy and cumbersome, the Nevada Gaming Commission adopted Regulation 6.090 in the mid-1980s. Under this rule, licensees above a certain revenue range are required to follow minimum internal control standards (MICS),[4] which identify specific control objectives each gaming operator must achieve. At the same time, operators have the freedom to design their own controls, so long as the internal systems meet MICS objectives. Some of the significant provisions of Nevada Gaming Commission Regulation 6.090 are noted as follows:[5]

- The board publishes MICS.
- A licensee must submit to the board a written system of internal control, and this system must comply with the standards. The system can only deviate from such standards if the licensee has obtained a "variation" from one or more specific standards.
- The written system must provide a specific description about how the control objectives found in the MICS are achieved.
- The system must also be designed to address safeguarding of assets and the proper authorization of transactions. Further, the system must also be designed in a way that provides reasonable assurance with regard to financial reporting.
- An applicant must have its system reviewed by a CPA firm, and both the CPA firm and the key executives must attest to the fact that the system complies with the MICS.
- Established licensees must have the same CPA who performs the financial statement audit report annually on the system's compliance with the MICS.
- The licensee must have an internal audit function (in-house or outsourced) that also reports on MICS compliance.

The use of MICS has been emulated by various jurisdictions, including the National Indian Gaming Commission (NIGC), which oversees tribal gaming. Information on the NIGC's MICS can be obtained at www.nigc.gov/Laws_Regulations/Commission_Regulations/Minimum_Internal_Control_Standards.aspx. Although smaller operators in Nevada do not face the reporting requirements established by MICS, they must follow what are known as internal control procedures.[6,7]

A different approach to internal control requirements may also be taken by the regulators. One of the newer gaming jurisdictions in the United States, Pennsylvania, addresses its requirements for internal controls in Pennsylvania Gaming Control Board Regulations (Title 58, Pa. Code, Part VII) Section 465a. Although the control objectives embodied within

[4] Nevada's minimum internal control standards (MICS) may be viewed at http://gaming.nv.gov/internal_control_info.htm.

[5] Nevada Gaming Commission Regulation 6.090, http://gaming.nv.gov/stats_regs.htm.

[6] Nevada Gaming Commission Regulation 6.100.

[7] Nevada Gaming Commission and State Gaming Control Board, "Internal Control Procedures—Group II Licensees," http://gaming.nv.gov/internal_control_group2.htm.

this regulation are similar to those found in Nevada's Regulation 6.090, the administrative requirements relating to written systems of internal control are somewhat different. A copy of the regulation is available at http://gamingcontrolboard.pa.gov/files/regulations/Final_Regulations_Master.pdf.

Forensic accountants should remember that no system of internal control, including one designed in accordance with standards or regulations, can provide more than reasonable assurance with regard to the control objectives. In fact, internal control standards should be viewed as an ongoing learning process, because new cases of fraud often provide the impetus for new standards or regulations. With that in mind, investigators should exercise extreme care when evaluating gaming fraud and ensure that regulators are *never* left out of the loop. A gaming licensee should immediately contact regulatory authorities whenever criminal activity is suspected. This approach not only improves the odds that wrongdoers will be successfully prosecuted, but it also makes other licensees aware of imminent fraud threats that could affect their operations.

When performing financial statement audits, forensic accountants must be guided by AICPA *Professional Standards*. In addition, the counsel of a qualified gaming attorney should be sought when questions arise about a licensee's responsibilities regarding fraud discovered within its operations. This can help the investigator gain a better understanding of the legal aspects of gaming fraud in a specific situation.

In the following discussion of fraud scenarios unique to gaming, some examples are fictional, and some details have been changed in others to protect the identity of the gaming property. Some scenarios are actually amalgamations of multiple cases, which are included to help demonstrate various fraud risk factors.

Credit or Cage Operations Fraud

In most casinos, customers may gamble on credit by using documents referred to as *markers*. Markers are multi-part forms: The original is a negotiable instrument that proves the debt, and other parts of the form are used to record the issuance and payment of the marker. Because casino credit is considered high-risk, a gaming company should establish the patron's creditworthiness and conclusively verify his or her identity. Failure to exercise sound judgment in the issuance of markers can mean substantial losses to the company. Strong internal controls are also needed to ensure the physical custody of markers, as well as proper recording of collections on outstanding instruments.

The following sections provide sample fraud cases that involve casino credit, along with suggested controls and discovery or audit methods.

Fictitious Personal History and Credit Information Supplied by Patron

Consider the following example:

Example

A player well known in Las Vegas as a "high roller" who always paid his debts convinced a local casino to sponsor a group of purported "high rollers," who provided false names and credit information to obtain thousands of dollars in casino credit. This player, acting as a representative, personally guaranteed the other players' debt. Thus, proper credit checks were not performed, and the personal history of these players was not verified prior to extending credit at the first casino. Other casinos, using a local credit record service, acquired knowledge of these customers' credit histories at the first gaming location and also extended casino credit without any of the other required credit checks. Ultimately, more than $1 million in casino credit was extended—but never repaid.

Recommended Controls to Minimize Fraud

A gaming company should always perform a proper credit check, and funds should not be advanced until the operator has independently verified the identity and creditworthiness of the patron. To facilitate timely credit availability, procedures may be established allowing the customer to provide such information prior to arrival, with final verification (such as request for identification) completed upon the customer's arrival. If satisfactory credit checks cannot be performed, a deposit of front money should be obtained from the patron prior to the preparation of markers. The casino then has funds on deposit that can be used to cover the markers if the patron does not repay the markers from his or her winnings or with other assets.

Discovery or auditing Methods

Any large, unpaid marker could indicate that proper credit checks were not performed in advance. Although internal audit and compliance staff should routinely ensure that casino credit procedures are followed, they also should review evidence to *verify* performance of proper checks and documentation. The mere notation that a credit check was performed does not prove that it was performed, nor does it prove that the check showed credit-worthiness.

Before a gaming operator abandons collection efforts and writes off bad markers, an independent third-party should conduct a thorough review of the transaction in question. It is important to understand that chips (not cash) should be given to a customer when markers are signed. Internal play records may be able to substantiate whether chips were wagered at the gaming table or whether the chips were just redeemed at the cage. If gaming activity is not verifiable, a strong possibility exists that the chips were redeemed for cash, and a high likelihood exists that the cage employee received money in exchange for participating in the fraud (because good controls would suggest that a cashier not redeem the chips without verification with the pit). Additional information should be sought through interviews whenever possible.

In general, a casino should establish controls in the cage and pit to minimize the risk of a patron "walking" with chips.[8] The surveillance department may also help reduce these risks through monitoring patron chip redemption activity and providing video recordings to fraud investigators (if the investigation is undertaken in a very timely manner). In addition, prompt reviews of aging receivables by the accounting department (or other departments independent of the cage) may help alert management to the possibility of fraudulent marker transactions.

Employee Use of Known Customers' Credit History

Consider the following example:

Example

A casino employee, who had access to customer credit information, provided this detail to several accomplices. These accomplices then worked with the employee, who issued credit in the normal manner using the names of legitimate customers. After credit was issued, the employee fraudulently recorded a repayment of credit issued, and the accomplices retained the proceeds. Although the full amount of the fraud could not be proven conclusively, it is estimated that the house was defrauded for hundreds of thousands of dollars.

Recommended Controls to Minimize Fraud

This case highlights a number of control deficiencies. First, it is important for gaming companies to properly control access to customer information. Ideally, once a credit application has been entered into the system and is approved by management, software controls should make it difficult for cage cashiers or pit clerks to view full customer data. In addition to reducing potential loss of money on credit, this step can minimize the company's contribution to customer identity theft. As a side note, gaming databases should encrypt customers' personally identifiable information (such as Social Security numbers), rather than using clear text in sensitive fields.

Although the use of accomplices made this fraud possible when it would otherwise have been very difficult, it could still have been prevented by using reasonably simple steps. All large transactions should be approved by a supervisor who checks identification and compares the signature on the marker to the signature on file. In addition, controls over payments were apparently quite lax, because the pit and the cage are the only two places payments are typically accepted while a customer is on property. When a patron repays credit in the pit, the payment slip should be completed by someone other than the dealer (to attest to the payment), and then inserted into a drop box by the dealer. Otherwise, it would be easy for

---

[8]   *Walking with chips* means that a patron obtains chips but does not use them in a gaming transaction.

someone to record a payment that never happened. The potential for recording a false payment exists because customer chip payments are placed in the chip tray, and the chip inventory is tracked only at the beginning and end of each shift. There is no record of individual transactions. On the other hand, if a payment were accepted at the cage, it would cause the cage to be out of balance, because there would be no assets to support the amount of the payment.

Discovery Or auditing Methods

When this type of fraud is suspected, randomly confirming some patron credit activity (even if a zero balance exists) might be very helpful. Once a suspected time frame has been identified, a fraud investigator should check credit issuances against other evidence that may prove if customers were at least on the property (based on hotel or other records). Armed with that detail, the investigator can use a more targeted approach to identify suspects who were present during the time frame in question.

Analytical procedures are useful in initially identifying the posting of false payments. Posting payments that never occurred should cause the pit's hold percentage to be very low for the shift in which the alleged payment was recorded. Although low hold percentages may not conclusively prove marker fraud, casino personnel independent of the table games and cage departments should always analyze statistics and maintain detailed records on the conclusions reached during the follow-up performed.

If the fraudulent payment was posted at the cage, that payment should cause the cage to be out of balance (though this might have been hidden by improper counts of chips). A thorough count of the cage chips would disclose this problem. Surprisingly, there have been instances when the cage balance has been manipulated and out of balance for some time, only to be discovered during a subsequent reconciliation to general ledger accounts. Never underestimate the creativity of employees who may be very adept at detecting weaknesses in internal controls. Counting the cage without checking the chip trays is akin to performing a merchandise inventory count without checking to see if the cartons are full or empty.

A daily review of management reports, followed by a "show me" approach by internal staff performing follow-up, is far more effective than perfunctory reviews done to satisfy regulatory requirements. Follow-up in response to low hold percentages could include a review of all marker transactions related to tables where the hold percentage is low, as well as interviews of cage and pit personnel regarding any unusual activity. Even when investigations are performed some time after a fraud has occurred, some possibility exists that detailed reviews of issuance and payment activities could disclose irregularities and lead to employees involved in a scam.

Improper Voiding of Markers

Markers may occasionally need to be voided because of an input or preparation error. However, a marker should never be voided if the chips were given to the customer. To allow voiding of a marker when the credit was actually extended is tantamount to posting a false payment. For these reasons, voids should arouse additional scrutiny and be very tightly controlled.

In general, local regulatory authorities may provide detailed requirements for internal control procedures to be used when a marker is voided (though the degree of concern may vary based on how casino credit affects gaming taxes). Regardless of regulatory requirements, to protect its assets a gaming company should establish strong procedures over voids, ensuring that no single individual can void a marker transaction without the involvement of another employee and without sufficient explanation. To mitigate the most egregious risks, a cage employee should not be permitted to void a marker issued in the pit.

Other Issues in the Casino Cage

The cage is the hub of all casino activity. Cash flowing into the property from gaming activity typically flows through the cage, which then serves as the in-house "bank" to retail outlets and other areas where cash is needed. Bank deposits are also compiled from the cage. Furthermore, chips are transferred between the cage and the pit. Given its function within the casino, the cage can be ripe for fraud for the following reasons:

- Losses can occur when patrons using their own identity are given credit, despite a lack of ability to repay the debt. To address this issue, gaming operators must ensure that cashiers have very little power to establish credit lines and the transactions they do perform are subject to review and oversight. This prevents cashiers from misappropriating assets, because they cannot give money to customers who should not have it.

- All *employee* transactions should be carefully controlled. For example, no cashier or other cage employee should have the ability to cash checks or otherwise obtain cash without the involvement of a supervisor. In turn, supervisory employees also should not be able to perform transactions on their own behalf. When inspecting the cage to verify funds, close attention should be paid to any items when an employee was the principal in a transaction.

- The cage should be treated as a "sterile" area, making it difficult to conceal cash, chips, or other items of value. This means no employee handbags or similar items should be in the cage. Also storage cabinets and boxes should be carefully controlled, because they may be useful for stashing cash or fraudulent paperwork. In addition, gaming operators should conduct surprise counts, during which employees are asked to count down funds accountable to their shift and move items in their immediate area to show that the spaces contain only permissible items. Note that the employee—not the auditor or fraud investigator—should be the one handling money and other items in this check. When completed, all actual cash and cash representatives (such as chips and payout receipts) making up the cage balance should be carefully tied to shift-specific accountability documentation. Furthermore, the cage documentation should be reconciled to general ledger accounts. When employees know they are subject to surprise counts, they will be less inclined to misappropriate assets.

- Most cages use written procedures for performing cash transactions and for computing the proper balance for each shift. Auditors and fraud investigators asked to review cage operations should always take time to review these written procedures.

Additionally, the investigators should ask employees not thought to be involved in fraudulent activity to explain (or demonstrate) how routine transactions are typically handled, including end-of-shift counts. The auditor or investigator should not hesitate to ask as many questions as needed, such as, "What paperwork would I use to verify this number if I needed to?" In that fashion, the auditor or investigator can better identify any unusual flow of money in or out of the cage and can more effectively determine the approximate amount and timing of cage asset losses.

Table Games Fraud

Before attempting to explain frauds that can occur in the table games area, it is important to understand some key terms and revenue flow in that department. Bear in mind that precise regulatory definitions will not match the simplified terms provided in the following sections.

Drop Box

Each gaming table has a locked container in which cash receipts and paperwork in support of transactions are placed. The box is secured to the table by a lock, and a separate lock secures the contents. A slot on the top of the table enables the dealer to place cash or other items into the box without having access to box contents. When no dealer is present, the slot opening should be secured.

To help maintain good internal controls, the dealer must be the only employee placing anything in the drop box, because a supervisor should approve most transactions, and the dealer's involvement ensures that the transaction actually occurred. The contents of the drop boxes are tallied in the count room, where cash is removed and recorded and paperwork is compared to records created elsewhere for verification purposes. Cash in the drop box is one component of "table games win," which is typically measured on a by-shift and by-table basis.

Table Games Win Computation

Win, or revenue from the table games wagering, can be computed as follows for a given shift:

> *Cash in drop box*
>
> *Plus markers issued but not paid*
>
> *Equals total drop*
>
> *Plus or minus net transfers of chips (fills are subtracted, credits are added)*
>
> *Plus or minus net change in the chip tray inventory (the beginning inventory is subtracted, the ending inventory is added)*
>
> *Equals gross gaming revenue or win*

Chip Tray

Each gaming table will also have a chip tray. Chips represent value that can be used within the gaming establishment; they are not legal tender and should not be used for nongaming transactions. The dealer uses chips to pay winning wagers and give to wagering customers in exchange for cash or markers. Chips are made in various denominations defined by different colors, which helps facilitate rapid computation of the chips' dollar value at the table (or in the cage). Distinguishing chip value by color helps to ensure that winners are properly paid and to otherwise enable security and surveillance personnel to provide proper oversight. For the house, it is much easier for supervisory and surveillance or security personnel to provide proper oversight if they can easily determine the value of chips used in any transaction.

At the start and end of each shift, the total value of chips in the tray must be counted and documented in a secure manner. Any change in the chip balance is a component of gaming win and is affected by customer wagering, payment of winning wagers, exchange of cash for chips, and the issuance of chips in marker transactions. In addition, chip tray inventory is affected by fills and credits, which are exchanges between the gaming table and the casino cage (or some auxiliary bank used for that purpose). For those reasons, it is critical that chip counts be done accurately, because there is no running detail of transactions during a shift. Although some tables operate almost continuously, good internal controls require trays to have locking covers, which prevent theft of chips when the table is not in use.

Fills and Credits

Although the cage is accountable for cash on the casino floor (though some of it may be physically located in other areas of the gaming property), it is also ultimately accountable for chips used for table games.

To maximize accountability over casino assets, transfers of chips between tables and the cage are strictly controlled. A transfer from the cage to a table is called a *fill*, which is documented on a fill slip generated either manually or by computer. A *credit* is a transfer from the gaming table to the cage, and it is controlled in the same fashion via a credit slip. Credit slips may also be used to transfer markers issued at the table to the cage (if the patron does not repay the marker in the pit).

Typically, the fill and credit forms will be signed by the cashier to verify movement in and out of the cage, as well as by an independent party who physically transfers the chips across the floor (sometimes referred to as the "runner"). In addition, the pit supervisor[9] who witnesses the transaction and the table dealer will also sign the form. A copy of the fill or credit slip is then placed in the drop box. At the end of each shift, the count team compares the fill and credit forms to records created in the cage. This set of controls helps ensure that fill and

---

[9]   The *pit* is the common term for a table games area consisting of several gaming tables where the seats for players are on the outside of the pit, and the dealers and other pit employees are on the inside. A given casino may actually have several pits which are essentially areas under the supervision of individual supervisors and higher level supervisory people who sometimes are called *pit bosses*. A *pit clerk* is a person who performs recordation functions within the pit.

credit transactions actually occurred in the table games department—and were not merely a manipulation of cage balances.

Because transactions with customers are not individually recorded, the table games area is highly dependent upon "people watching people" controls. An auditor or fraud investigator will never be able to use documentation to prove that the win (or loss) recorded for a given table accurately reflects wagers made by patrons or payments made to winning patrons. And, auditors and investigators will be even less able to verify that all winnings were paid in accordance with house rules, as opposed to the dealer "giving away the store" in hopes of personal gain.

However, this does not mean that table games fraud never leaves a trail. For instance, a casino computes gaming win as a percentage of drop, and games such as blackjack, baccarat, or craps tend to hold certain percentages over time. Composite data on gaming win is available from specific regulatory agencies. Although luck is a huge factor in determining short-term performance, a depressed hold percentage over a long period of time may indicate fraudulent table games activity. When this occurs, a vigilant gaming operator will monitor performance trends tied to tables under a given supervisor's or dealer's control, often through reviews of surveillance recordings and discussions with other casino personnel.

Because most evidence of fraud would be indirect, gaming operators often work with the law enforcement arm of their regulatory agency to develop a case for prosecution. Although actual losses may be very hard to establish with certainty due to the absence of documentation, fairly solid estimates may be developed.

The following sections provide an overview of employee-related frauds that may occur in the table games area.

Frauds Involving Scheduled Counts

Fraud can be perpetrated during scheduled counts. Before discussing the frauds that can occur, some background information on proper controls is provided.

The count of drop box proceeds should be conducted by employees who are independent of the table games and cage departments. Drop boxes are removed from the tables at the change of each shift and transported by people independent of the table games department (usually by a security guard). Although one key is needed to release a table box (the "release key"), a second is required to remove the contents (the "contents key"). For that reason, the transport team should never have access to contents keys, because that restriction will prevent any removal of cash before the drop box reaches the count room. Once in the count room, all drop boxes should be locked in special cabinets until the actual count begins. At that time, the count team obtains the contents keys from wherever they are stored. Good internal controls demand that this storage unit require two separate keys to open, with each key maintained by a different department. Typically, the department housing the locked container provides the involvement of a third department, thus strengthening the controls.

The count team should open each table games box individually using the contents key. The box should then be shown to other count team members and to surveillance cameras to prove that everything has been removed. Once cash is counted and verified, one team member enters the amount of cash and information from fill and credit slips into a computer program designed to record count information. By comparing the fill and credit information coming out of the drop boxes to the information generated in the cage, the potential for undetected manipulation of cage balances is reduced.

As previously discussed, one important control feature for markers is that both issuance and payment are documented on various parts (copies) of the marker form. If the marker is issued by the pit, then the issue slip is placed in the table's drop box. If payment occurs in the pit, then the payment slip is dropped in the box. The count team is responsible for either entering data from the issuance and payment forms or comparing it to amounts already recorded. As with fill and credit slips, this comparison is an important element of internal control. Similarly, the opening and closing chip inventory numbers should also be verified. By using all of this information, a win amount per table can be computed while the count is in progress.

When all drop boxes have been counted, the cash amounts for each one should be tallied. Then, the total amount from all boxes should be verified against total cash in the count room. All count team members should be involved in performing this reconciliation (counting or watching the count) and should sign attesting to the final amounts. When the count team has counted and verified all drop box contents, the currency is brought to the cage. Once there, the cage cashier must recount the currency, sign the count sheet attesting to the amount, and assume responsibility for the funds. Breakdowns in any required controls can lead to inaccurate count documentation or open the door to later alteration to conceal fraud. As previously noted, cash receipts at tables have little documentation, meaning that the cash drop's reliability is heavily dependent upon key table, transport, and count room controls.

Count room frauds can include the following:

1. *Undercounting drop box contents.* Although this would require collusion or inattention on the part of other count team members, it is possible for the person opening a drop box to not record some of the cash in a box (or a series of boxes). However, to profit from this activity, the fraudster needs a means to remove the unrecorded cash. Although surveillance and a sterile count room environment can minimize the risk, inattention or understaffing can eliminate the control value.

   To detect any skimming of cash proceeds, pit personnel often keep a record of large cash transactions. Although this is not sufficient to perform a reconciliation, it may show the theft of large denomination bills. For example, if the casino's policy calls for a shift supervisor to record $100 bills placed in the drop box and none appear on the count sheet, then it is appropriate to suspect count room theft. To further reduce the prospect of skimming, the count team should be large enough to ensure that inattention by one person is not enough to ruin overall control. In addition, the count team members should be rotated frequently, reducing the potential for conspiracy within a small group of people who frequently perform the count together. Overall, if management notes negative trends in revenue or hold percentages, it is wise to review count controls, looking particularly at any hidden association among count team members (or between a count team member and cage employees).

2. *Alteration of count documents.* Another avenue for fraud involves the alteration of count documents, which may enable a cage cashier to divert funds—either directly from the drop or to cover up another fraud—by lowering the total amount of cash for which the cashier is responsible. Because the total drop must agree with the total from individual box counts, a fraudster must make alterations in at least two places to make this scam work. For instance, a careful recomputation of the "stiff sheet" (an informal name for a traditional master summary of the table games count) may show that the numbers do not add up. The in-house accounting staff is in the best position to note this red flag. Additionally, it is also important that the accounting department compare cash recorded by the count team to the cage accountability document, which will show count proceeds coming into the cage. If no one checks these discrepancies, a knowledgeable cashier could simply use a different number than that recorded by the count team—without making any alterations to the actual stiff sheet.

   Specific policies and practices can reduce the likelihood of alterations leading to skimming or larceny. For example, the use of correction fluid or tape on any manual count documents should be prohibited. Instead, count team employees may line through the original recorded amount (ensuring the original entry is still legible), clearly record a new amount, and then have two people initial the change. For a computerized count report, for which corrections involve the use of passwords, the password controls should be set up so that a person in custody of the cash cannot change count documentation without verification by another individual.

   When the count team has finished its work, specific controls should be in place for transmitting original documentation to the accounting department. This may involve a direct transfer by the count team or securing the count documentation in a locked area for retrieval by the accounting department. The latter is an acceptable alternative in situations when the count is completed before the accounting department staff has arrived for work. In any of these scenarios, cashiers should then receive summary documentation or a copy of the full count sheet in order to support the increase in cage funds arising from soft count proceeds. They should never have possession of the original documents.

3. *Re-creation of count documentation.* As an example, assume a cashier and an accounting clerk were in collusion. They conspired to change the records after a completed count, allowing the cashier to remove excess funds. The drop numbers were altered and the signatures of count team members were forged, so everything appeared to be in order. The collusion in this example demonstrates one of the major limitations to internal controls, because the normal "segregation of duties" between the post-count audit, cashiering function, and count team was subverted. A full analytical review, using steps detailed previously in the discussion of undercounting drop box contents may be of some value in detecting this type of fraud.

Frauds Risks Related to Inadequate Key Controls

Without proper key controls, a fraudster may either remove drop box contents or perform undocumented counts. For that reason, it is crucial for gaming operators to perform frequent and thorough reviews of the controls over the sensitive keys in the table games department. Some risks associated with poor controls over keys are described subsequently, as are some additional safeguards that in addition to the key controls help to mitigate fraud risk.

If the drop team has access to the contents keys while performing the drop, it would be possible for them to remove cash. Additional potential safeguards against this happening include surveillance and the composition of the drop team itself.

If the access to the stored, full drop boxes is improperly controlled, boxes can be removed from the storage area such that the box contents are never recorded by the count team. One additional safeguard is the fact that boxes are to be numbered according to table game number and shift. If proper procedures are being followed in the count room and in the accounting department, the missing box should be easily detected. If, however, the key control problems allowed access to the contents key, then there would be no reason for the perpetrator to risk this detection. He or she could merely remove some portion of the cash. It may also be possible for documents critical to the computation of win or verification of marker payments to be inserted, making it possible to falsify the documents.

If access to stored, empty drop boxes is improperly controlled, falsified sensitive documents affecting the computation of win can be inserted.

It would be theoretically possible for an entirely separate, undocumented count to occur when the proceeds were never recorded in the books of the gaming company. This would need to involve high-level management in order for it to be unnoticed, so it would be more likely to be a case of wholesale fraud against the taxing authorities, possibly involving organized crime linkage.

In addition to evaluating the controls over the keys in daily use, it is also important to evaluate controls over any duplicate keys the company may maintain for emergencies. The controls over those keys should be carefully checked, because it is possible that authorized duplicates may have fallen into the hands of unscrupulous employees. For that reason, all known key custodians should be interviewed to uncover unusual activity, such as extended delays in returning keys. Access logs, if maintained, may also provide valuable leads.

Fraudulent Fills

A false fill occurs when an employee does not deliver chips from the cage to a table. Instead, the employee takes the chips and later redeems them (or has an accomplice redeem them) at the cage. Ordinary controls designed to prevent such outright theft of assets include the following:

- Requiring that fills be transported by a security guard or other party who is independent of both the cage and the pit
- Requiring several signatures on the fill slip form, including that of the dealer

- Requiring that a restricted copy of the fill slip be maintained, with one copy of the slip placed in the drop box *by the dealer*
- Requiring that the count team compare cage-generated records to fill slips found in the drop box
- Designing the drop box so that when the dealer is not present at the table, the surface slot is not accessible

If these controls are in place, but fraudulent fills are still suspected, the investigator can use other tools to help uncover the problem. For example, if the dealer's signature on a fill slip appears to not be genuine, fraud may be suspected. If the chip inventory change is unreasonable given other records of activity, the auditor or investigator should check the timing of the fill. A fill occurring while the table was closed is a clear red flag for possible fraud. Finally, investigators should note that a lack of care in verifying the chip amount brought to the table could permit a security guard to steal part of the fill.

Dealer Fraud

Dealers conduct table games, sell chips to players, collect chips from losing players, and pay winners. In this role, they can steal from casinos by not conducting games properly, paying more than they should (or paying losing bets), and allowing players to retain chips they should have lost. Because tipping dealers is a very common practice, dealers are also subject to bribes from patrons who can incentivize a dealer to allow the patron unfairly beat the house. This type of collusion can take several forms, such as dealers passing signals to a patron on a blackjack hand or a dealer arranging cards to help a given player win.

Although on-floor supervisors and attentive surveillance practices help minimize these risks, these controls may be inadequate on a busy night. For that reason, dealers should be thoroughly trained to use proper hand movements visible to house surveillance and to floor personnel. In addition, a tip pool among dealers may lessen the motivation to illegally reward players, and the use of automatic shufflers reduces the risk of a dealer influencing a game. In general, statistical anomalies will point to the potential for dealer fraud, but only live observations or surveillance recordings will definitively reveal the problem.

Detecting Fraudulent Activity

In addition to the follow-up procedures already enumerated in this chapter, some tools can be employed to evaluate whether fraud may be occurring, including the following:

1. *Salting the drop boxes.* This is a procedure wherein bills are recorded by serial number and then used at the gaming tables. If the count is being conducted honestly, the "salted" bills should show up in the count.
2. *Turning up surveillance, security, and floor supervision.* On occasion, surveillance and security staff can be alerted to watch for suspicious activity (even if no imminent threat exists). Pit supervision can be also increased, with additional attention paid to estimating the drop based on cash activity at the table.

3. *Performing surprise count observations.* This exercise should be conducted periodically, even when fraud is not suspected. The count team should be asked to complete the count of any open boxes, after which proceeds in the room should be reconciled to recorded amounts. Although this would not uncover any money removed prior to the count, it could reveal a situation in which box counts were not accurately recorded. Additionally, the observation should include a thorough search of any potential hiding places. In cases when fraud is suspected, it may be better to covertly perform a series of count observations from the surveillance room to avoid alerting suspects.

4. *Evaluating lifestyle issues.* If employees who have potential access to drop proceeds appear to be living beyond their means, closer scrutiny of those employees and their activities is warranted. Auditors or fraud investigators should pay close attention to any groups that work together frequently enough to suggest risk of collusion. If suspicious activity is identified, investigators should consider checking personnel records or social media sites to uncover any previously undisclosed associations among employees.

Slot Department Fraud

Modern slot machines certainly do not resemble the "one-armed bandits" of early gaming days. However, people both outside and within a casino can still find ways to "rob the bandits." Although this chapter will not cover slot machine cheating, it will address various slot games frauds committed by employees.

In general, there are several avenues, including the following, through which money can be diverted from the slot department:

- The machine's programming can be altered, allowing it to pay more than it is supposed to or pay when no winnings are due. A casino could also tamper with a machine's programming in order to cheat customers.
- Employees can steal money (either coins or currency) from machines.
- Money can be taken due to improper drop and count procedures.
- Tickets used for cashless wagering can be manipulated or altered, causing the casino to pay money it does not owe.
- Hand-paid jackpots can be allocated improperly, or entirely false jackpot forms can be prepared.
- Evasion of gaming tax payments can occur, especially when there are slot games on the floor not shown on the operator's analytical reports.
- Larceny can occur when slot department funds are not properly accounted for or controlled.

Overview of Slot Machine Terminology and Revenue Cycle

To aid understanding of slot frauds, a review of the revenue cycle for slot machines is necessary (the following simplified definitions may not correspond to specific regulatory or statutory definitions).

Slot wagering may be conducted with coins, tokens, currency, wagering vouchers, or electronic transfers. At one time, tokens were commonly used in lieu of coins for denominations of $1 or higher. However, coin and token based wagering has greatly diminished.

Unless machines are completely coinless, they require a *hopper*, which is a large container that contains coins or tokens used to pay out jackpots. The casino must provide the coins or tokens, and the amount supplied by the operator is called a *hopper load* (customer coins and tokens also go into the hopper). Once a hopper has reached capacity, its contents are diverted to a separately keyed drop bucket, which is in a cabinet below the slot machine. The money in the drop bucket is called the *coin drop*, and the count of that money is called a *hard count*. When jackpots deplete the hopper, fills are made to the slot machines. Hand-paid jackpots are necessary in many cases, because some payouts are too large to pay from the hopper.

Slot machines are typically equipped to accept currency which may be legal tender or tickets. If the customer uses a ticket, any payout may be made in similar form, allowing the customer to insert the payout ticket as a wager into another machine or redeem the ticket at the casino cage or kiosk designed to dispense cash. When either cash or tickets are inserted into a slot game, the player receives electronic credits that are displayed on a meter. The customer then wagers those credits and cashes them out when done playing. The currency acceptor drop boxes (also referred to as bill validator cans) hold both vouchers and legal tender and are keyed separately from the slot machine cabinets. The contents of these boxes are typically counted in the same room as the table games drop (the "soft count room"), although the counts must be performed in a fashion that prevents the commingling of funds from the two counts.

To facilitate slot wagering, a customer may also open a wagering account, in which the money is put on deposit at the cage and credits may be sent electronically to the machine. At the conclusion of play, those credits may be transferred from the slot machine back to the account.

The computation of revenue from slot wagering is explained in box 9-1.

Box 9-1: Slot Revenue Computation

Add Drop:

Cash and tickets removed from the currency acceptors, and

Coins removed from the drop buckets, and

Electronic transfers to the slot machines from wagering accounts

Equals total drop

Subtract Deductions:

Tickets issued by the machine (representing payouts), and

Fills to the machine (coins or tokens placed in the hoppers), and

Hand-paid jackpots (cash paid from other areas of accountability), and

Electronic transfers from the slot machine to wagering accounts

Equals total deductions

Plus or minus change in hopper balance (add if hopper increased, subtract if hopper decreased)*

Equals Revenue

---

* As a practical matter, the change in the hopper balance is ignored in statistical reports because it is measured only infrequently. Estimates of the total hopper loads on the floor may be needed at the close of financial reporting periods or may be performed periodically for reporting to the taxing authorities.

Slot Machine Technical Standards

Technical standards are used in many jurisdictions to establish requirements gaming equipment manufacturers use when designing their products. Without public confidence that slot machines are fair, this form of gaming activity would quickly lose its popularity. Additionally, regulators need this assurance, because they impose a tax on slot revenue. Finally, operators face less risk of economic loss when only properly designed equipment is placed on the floor.[10]

Slot machine technical standards are designed to ensure

- the randomness of game outcome.
- the integrity of the devices themselves, minimizing the possibility of tampering.

---

[10] Nevada's technical standards can be viewed at: http://gaming.nv.gov/stats_regs_history.htm#tech_standards.

- the continuous operation of equipment.
- that proper metering of transactions takes place, which provides an audit trail and a basis for analysis of machine performance.

Depending on the jurisdiction, regulators may have their own labs, or they may use independent labs that are subject to the regulator's oversight. A combination of approaches may also be used within a given jurisdiction. Following are links to pertinent sections of selected gaming authority websites wherein technical standards for slot machines are addressed:

- Colorado: www.colorado.gov/cs/Satellite/Rev-Gaming/RGM/1213781235654
- Mississippi: www.mgc.state.ms.us/lab/lab.html
- Missouri: www.mgc.dps.mo.gov/
- Nevada: http://gaming.nv.gov/tech_main.htm

Slot Machine Fraud Scenarios

The following sections provide a closer look at eight common slot frauds, with possible control steps to minimize illicit activity.

Machine Tampering

As previously mentioned, most modern slot machines are software driven, so tampering typically involves programming alterations. Some forms of known slot machine tampering include:

- Changing the erasable programmable read-only memory (EPROM) (computer chips containing program information) in such a way that randomness is altered and higher-paying outcomes (such as a royal flush on a video poker machine) are never paid
- Changing the EPROMs to add unauthorized jackpots not built into the approved program
- Altering software controls for the currency acceptor, which may then treat (for example) a $1 bill as a $10 bill

Potential controls. In general, slot machine tampering by employees is made possible through weak controls, poor surveillance practices, and insufficient testing of EPROMs. Although EPROMs are tested and approved by gaming laboratories, the ongoing integrity of this programming is in the hands of the casino operator. The following are some recommended (or in some jurisdictions, required) controls:

- Requiring that the slot machine cabinet (where all components critical to machine functioning are housed) be locked and ensuring that proper controls over this cabinet key
- Requiring (in some cases) that EPROMs be sealed in a separate compartment within the cabinet, making access to the EPROMs detectable

- Controlling access to EPROM duplicating equipment and EPROMs not yet installed
- Requiring that EPROMs in slot machines periodically be compared against chips approved for use
- Ensuring sufficient surveillance over the slot machine area
- Using monitoring systems to identify times when the slot machine door cabinets are open, and then using either surveillance or floor supervision to monitor technician activity
- Checking the EPROMs to ensure they have not been altered before paying out large jackpots

Modern slot machine technology allows software to be downloaded from a server to an individual device. In such "system-based gaming," the focus of fraud investigations often shifts to controls at the server level and to computer media located in the machines. When Nevada authorized server-based, system-supported, and mobile gaming, it had to present an interim approach to standards while working to bring the overall regulations up to date. To do this, the Gaming Control Board issued a whitepaper that addressed interim controls, which remains a valuable tool for understanding how these systems function.[11]

Detecting fraud. Analytical review is a major tool for detecting slot machine fraud. Modern systems produce analytical reports in automated form. Each machine is designed by its manufacturer to hold a certain percentage of the amounts wagered. This means that for every dollar wagered, a certain percentage will be paid out over time, with the remainder held by the casino (the hold percentage). Bear in mind that a hold percentage may be as low as 2 percent, meaning that the machine is designed to pay back 98 percent of amounts wagered. Deviations between the theoretical hold and actual hold are cause for investigation, particularly if the deviation persists despite substantial machine play over an extended time period. A machine that is under-holding may indicate theft, while significant over-holding may indicate some form of tampering in which customers are being cheated. In addition to checking deviations in hold percentage, investigators should also look for any excessive opening of slot machine cabinets where no fill (or repair) is being performed. This may be a possible indication of fraud. And, a routine comparison of EPROM programming to an approved system may disclose improper alterations.

For slot machines for which player skill is a factor, such as video poker machines, the par hold percentage is actually a range. If a skill machine is placed in a location that is frequented by highly skilled players, that machine will likely hold less than the same machine placed in an area catering to less experienced players. Thus, an independent investigator should always ask to see the manufacturer's par sheets, which can help the investigator make an informed judgment on proper comparison benchmarks. A valid selection is highly dependent upon knowledge of the casino's clientele.

---

[11] State of Nevada Gaming Control Board, *Audit and Control of Mobile Gaming Systems, System Based Games, and System Supported Games* (October 30, 2007), http://gaming.nv.gov/documents/pdf/ic_whitepaper_07oct30.pdf.

In contrast to table games, hold percentages for slot machines are not computed using win as a percentage of drop. The regulations and technical standards require a large number of meters, such as the coin-in meter. As a customer wagers credits on a slot machine, those credits are registered by the coin-in meter. The wagered amount, in turn, becomes the denominator for purposes of the hold percentage; win is the numerator. Depending on the age and sophistication of slot equipment, win may be calculated entirely based upon meters. With this in mind, a thorough fraud investigation should start with learning about the types of meters used in a casino's slot machines and determining whether the house routinely verified that such equipment was functioning correctly.

Theft of Money From Machines

As previously indicated, coins, currency, and tokens may all be contained in different locked areas associated with slot machines. Currency is found in currency acceptor cans, while coins or tokens are found in both the hopper and drop bucket. Slot machine money theft can technically be considered skimming if is stolen prior to a count and thus never recorded as taxable revenue. On the other hand, given the metering systems used by many slot systems, money theft may more properly be deemed larceny, because cash receipts are recorded by the slot system. In either case, the existence of numerous slot meters may provide fairly strong evidence that theft is occurring.

Most often, slot machine theft is made possible through weaknesses in key controls for the slot cabinets, currency acceptors, or drop cabinets. Consideration of the effectiveness of these controls is important for an auditor or fraud examiner when investigating possible cash theft.

Losses Due to Drop and Count Problems

Because of the number of machines that accept coins, tokens, and currency, two types of drops and counts are often performed for slot machines. The coin or token drop and count are sometimes referred to as the "hard drop and count," and the drop and count of the currency acceptor box contents may be referred to as the "currency acceptor drop and count." Because of the similarities with the table games count process, the money in currency acceptor drop boxes is subject to many of the same vulnerabilities. Before starting an investigation, it is helpful to understand pertinent technical standards for slot machine metering. Nevada frames these requirements as shown in the following box.

Technical Standard 2.040—Meters for conventional gaming devices, system supported and system based games.

1. All gaming devices must be equipped with electronic digital storage meters of at least 10 digits capable of displaying the information listed in this section on demand. These meters, listed below, must accumulate the following information in units equal to the denomination of the device or in dollars and cents. Devices configured for multi-denomination play must display the required information in dollars and cents....

    (h) Bill In. The machine must have a meter specifically labeled "Bill In" that accumulates the total value of currency accepted. Additionally, the machine must have a specific meter for each denomination of currency accepted that records the number of bills accepted of each denomination;

The following box shows Nevada's MICS requirements pertaining to the currency acceptor count.

Slot MICS # 39

The count team does not have access to bill-in amounts per the slot machine/socket ID meters until after the count is completed and the drop proceeds are accepted into cage/vault accountability. A count team member is allowed to read/record the amount from the bill in meters as long as the count team members do not have knowledge of the dollar amount of currency contained in the currency acceptor drop boxes pursuant to the bill in meters during the count process.

Slot MICS #129

At the time a drop box (coin or currency) is removed in conjunction with a slot drop, the "Drop Meters" (coin drop, bill-in, voucher in and coupon promotion in) for each slot machine dropped are read, meter amounts recorded and maintained.

Slot MICS #135

Variances, by slot machine/socket ID, noted in the reports required by MICS #134 that are in excess of the following parameters are reviewed by the accounting department:

a. For slot machines dropped, variances in excess of one percent or $100, whichever amount is greater, for each drop type (coin, bills, vouchers and coupons).

Within these requirements, the following key elements deserve special notice:

- The technical standards require the bills to be metered as they flow into the currency acceptors. To comply with the MICS, meter readings should be timed to coincide with the drop to provide comparable information.
- Second, the employees performing the count should perform it without knowledge of the meter readings.
- The accounting department should note discrepancies between the actual count and metered amounts, following up as needed.

Such procedures, if faithfully and carefully executed, can be a powerful weapon in the early detection of fraudulent activity. That said, a fraud investigator should always ask to see evidence of the procedures (and discuss methodology with the employee who actually does the work) before assuming that risks have been properly minimized. Because some gaming companies are trying to control expenses by cutting staff, telling an employee to follow a procedure is no guarantee that he or she had time to do so, much less that he or she performed those procedures with the proper skepticism or insight to identify any potential problems.

Fraud Involving Cashless Wagering

As mentioned earlier in this section, slot wagering can take place using tickets instead of currency, coin, or tokens. This form of ticket in, ticket out wagering allows customers to redeem a ticket for cash at an automated kiosk or staffed cage or use the ticket in another slot machine. Although this cashless wagering system handles all ticket accounting and validation in a central computer location, this does not immunize it from potential fraud threats. These may include the creation of a false ticket, in which the system could be "tricked" into paying, or the outright theft of tickets.

The primary controls to prevent fraud in cashless wagering systems include the following:

- *Enforcing system validation prior to payment.* Although some manual payments prior to validation may be necessary due to system issues, all paid tickets should be entered into the system just as soon as the system is up and running. Tickets paid prior to validation should be subject to additional approval processes, and records of the employee handling the transaction should be maintained. On occasions when tickets are damaged and cannot be properly scanned, additional manual evidence should be gathered prior to payment. Although a properly functioning cashless wagering system should pay a ticket with a specific serial number only once, if payments occur prior to validation, duplicate payments will not be detected until after the tickets are entered into the system.
- *Proper handling of lost or misplaced tickets.* Tickets found on the casino premises should be turned in to a secure location (such as the casino cage) for safekeeping. Employees should never have the ability to cash tickets in their possession.

False Jackpots and Fills

Arguably, the greatest risk within a slot department is false jackpots and fills. Although computerized slot monitoring systems offer some protection, they do not conclusively prove that jackpots or fill forms represent actual payments to customers. This opens the door for potential theft of assets or misstatement of taxable revenue.

When a jackpot is won, it is important to first establish that it is a customer win. For example, if the fill or jackpot form is automatically generated by a computerized system, it is possible the software has an override feature, which allows a system user to enter a false payout. Even when the computerized system appears accurate, it is important that witnesses visually verify the jackpot win and for the person disbursing the cash to attest that it was given to a patron. Finally, the completed jackpot documents should be routed in a manner that prevents an employee from creating a false jackpot form, forging signatures, and misappropriating cash.

In Mississippi, the internal control requirements for jackpot payouts are directly addressed in the following state regulations:[12]

Section 3. Jackpot Payout Procedures.

(a) Payouts for jackpots must be authorized by a Slot Attendant or a Slot Supervisor actually observing the jackpot combination on the machine.

(b) The information which shall be included on every jackpot payout slip and in all stored data for each jackpot payout is the:

    (1) casino name and location;

    (2) number of the slot machine on which the jackpot was registered;

    (3) reprinted or concurrently-printed sequential number of the jackpot payout slip;

    (4) total amount of the jackpot;

    (5) winning combination of reel characters constituting the jackpot or the type of other payout (e.g. cancel credit, short pay, bonus, etc.);

    (6) date and time;

    (7) amount to be paid;

    (8) slot booth number, if applicable, from which the amount is to be paid; and

    (9) signature lines.

(c) All remuneration paid to a patron as a result of winning a jackpot shall be disbursed by the cashier directly to a Slot Attendant or Slot Supervisor who shall transport the winnings directly to the patron.

---

[12] Mississippi Gaming Commission Regulations adopted through July 25, 2010, accessed December 26, 2001, www.mgc.state.ms.us.

(d)   Signature Requirements:

    (1)   Computerized Jackpot Payouts.

Signatures, attesting to the accuracy of the information contained on the original and duplicate of the jackpot payout slip, shall be of the Slot Attendant or Slot Supervisor who prepared the payout slip and a cage cashier. A verifier must attest to by signature any Jackpot payouts in excess of $1199.99. A manager must attest to the payout by signature if the amount of the jackpot is in excess of $5,000.00. The Commission must be notified prior to payments of a jackpot of $100,000.00 or greater. A Manager is defined as a Slot Supervisor, Slot Manager, Slot Director, Casino Shift Manager, Vice President of Slots, Assistant General Manager and/or General Manager.

Supplemental slot payout procedures may be used for jackpot payouts less than $1,200. This procedure will not apply to system override and manual procedures. For supplemental payout procedures where the licensee does not print the jackpot payout slip prior to payment, a payout request slip must be utilized. The payout request slip must contain the same information required on the jackpot payout slip. The payout request slip must be signed by the Slot Attendant and a verifier witnessing the payout.

Procedures for replenishment of supplemental jackpot payout funds must comply with all other requirements of this regulation. Licensees utilizing payout request slips must attach the payout request slip to the duplicate copy of the jackpot payout slip.

    (2)   Override Jackpot Payouts.

System overrides must be authorized by a Slot Supervisor or Slot Manager. All override jackpot payout slips shall be marked in a way that identifies the payout as an override. Signatures attesting to the accuracy of the information contained on the original and duplicate of the override payout slip shall be of the Slot Supervisor or Slot Manager who prepared the override payout slip and cage cashier. A verifier witnessing the jackpot payout to the patron must sign the original override jackpot payout slip.

    (3)   Manual Jackpot Payouts.

Manual jackpot payout slips must be authorized by a Slot Supervisor or Slot Manager. All manual jackpot payout slips shall have the reason for the manual payout. Signatures attesting to the accuracy of the information contained on the original, duplicate and triplicate copies of the manual jackpot payout slip shall be of the cage cashier who prepared the payout slip and Slot Supervisor or Slot Manager.

A verifier witnessing the payout to the patron must sign the original manual jackpot payout slip.

(e)   The original jackpot payout slip shall be deposited into a locked box only accessible by Accounting. The duplicate jackpot payout slip shall be retained by the cashier for end of shift reconciliation and forwarded to Accounting daily. The triplicate copy of the manual jackpot payout slip will be retained in the locked dispenser to be removed by Accounting or Security personnel.

Still, control breakdowns can and do occur, because an effective routing structure for slips is often difficult for some licensees to achieve. In Nevada, the control objectives for forms routing are defined as follows:

66. Manual and computerized payouts, including jackpots, fills, cancelled credits, short pays exceeding $10 and promotional payouts exceeding $100 that are deducted from gross gaming revenue, are controlled and completed in a manner that precludes any one individual from initiating and producing a fraudulent payout form, obtaining the funds, forging signatures on the payout form, routing all parts of the form, and misappropriating the funds.

Note 1: Acceptable procedures in meeting the requirements of MICS #66 include the following:

- Funds are issued either to a second verifier of the payout (i.e., someone other than the individual who generated/requested the ticket) or to two individuals concurrently (i.e., the generator/requestor of the form and the verifier of the payout). Both individuals witness the payout, or
- The routing of one part of the completed form is under the physical control (e.g., dropped in a locked box) of an individual other than the individual that obtained/issued the funds and the individual that obtained/issued the funds must not be able to place the form in the locked box, or
- Some other procedure which provides at least the same level of control as discussed in this note.

Historically, many frauds involving poor routing practices have involved forged signatures. This was particularly true when jackpots used only manual forms and analysis capabilities were less sophisticated. Today, however, it remains important to monitor both placement of—and access to—these forms in locked containers. This means the gaming operator must have sound segregation of duties, such that an employee with access to slot department funds cannot also place (or retrieve) the completed forms in the locked container. This separation of functions is critical to preventing signature forgery, thus reducing the probability that false jackpots will be an avenue for cash misappropriation.

When investigating possible fraudulent jackpots, the best place to start is with a thorough review of the payment process, examining such issues as the following:

- Custody of manual forms
- Access to the computerized system
- Procedures for releasing funds from the fund custodian
- Access to various parts of completed forms, from the time the form is generated to the point at which completed forms are sent to the accounting department.
- Any and all verification work done by the accounting department

The existence of possible jackpot schemes may be discovered by an observant employee, such as an in-house slot auditor who notes unusual trends, patterns, or anomalies when auditing payout forms. However, a broader analytical review is the more likely vehicle for detecting red flags. Because a smart fraudster would be unlikely to tap a single machine over and over, investigators may find it more effective to examine trends, such as those within a specific casino area overseen by particular slot department supervisor. Or, if an examiner notes discrepancies between jackpot meter totals and the dollar value of jackpot forms, it is wise to take a closer look at jackpot forms and signatures pertaining to the machines in question.

Machines Not in the Records

Although such a scheme would require substantial planning, it is possible for a casino to have machines that do not appear on the slot analysis report, which is the primary record supporting the slot revenue figures on reports filed with taxing authorities. Typically, auditors employed by the taxing authority may include a full count of machines on the floor, which is reconciled to the slot analysis report. Thus, if some machines are not in that report, it may indicate that employees have found a way to profit from unauthorized slot winnings or that management is attempting to defraud the taxing authorities. In either case, regular spot checks to reconcile actual machine counts with the slot analysis report are the most likely avenue of detection.

Fraud in Customer Loyalty Programs

Customer loyalty programs are very prevalent, and gaming companies use these incentive tools to drive increased business. Players may accumulate points toward rewards, most commonly through slot play. Rewards may consist of free wagering opportunities, discounts on amenities or merchandise, or upgraded services. Most often, customers sign up for a loyalty program at a casino property where designated employees are authorized to set up new player accounts or make adjustments to the accounts. Typically, loyalty programs are facilitated through the use of some type of player card and an associated personal identification number (PIN).

Fraud using loyalty programs can involve the following:

- Unauthorized additions to a player's account, which may result in a player being awarded items of value to which he or she was not entitled
- Theft of a customer's points, which may be illicitly used by an employee for personal gain

To minimize these fraud risks, gaming operators must ensure that supervisory employees are involved in any redemption of points not handled through an automated process. Supervisors must also approve any adjustments to a player's account, other than automated additions or deletions generated through play or qualifying purchases.

Automated customer loyalty systems also require internal controls. For example, consider a fraud case that involved the theft and use of unencrypted PIN information and customer play history. A group of perpetrators, including at least one casino employee, targeted the accounts of less active players to create new loyalty cards. The points from those cards were then used at slot machines. Once fraud was suspected, the gaming company used sophisticated data mining techniques to identify these accounts and evaluate point usage. Local regulators, working in cooperation with gaming company personnel, then arrested one of the perpetrators, who had in his possession several player club cards. Through a careful study of associations, additional arrests were made. This example illustrates the importance of computer security controls, as well as the need to encrypt database fields containing highly sensitive information.

Larceny of Slot Funds

Although cash, coins, and tokens may be located within different areas of accountability, regular transfers take place between these areas and the main cage or vault. These transfers serve to restore the balance of cash, coins, or tokens to proper levels, and each transfer is typically documented to allow reconciliation to take place. When each area of accountability, such as a slot booth, is maintained on an imprest basis,[13] risk is minimized. However, that risk rises if the balance floats, with increases and decreases supported only by paperwork reflecting various transactions. This underscores the importance of surprise inspections and counts as a sound internal control feature. As previously noted, when potential fraudsters discover lack of such oversight, they often devise a way to take advantage of the situation.

Bingo Fraud

Bingo is a game played for fun by many groups. Whether bingo is played using traditional cards or computer equipment, the game's basic structure remains the same. Bingo is played on a grid, with the letters B-I-N-G-O across the top of five columns. Numbers fill the remaining rows. The numbers are randomly selected, often by balls blown into tubes, or by a random number generator. As selected numbers are called, players mark (or "cover") corresponding numbers on their cards. In some forms of bingo, the winner is the player who covers all numbers on his or her card first. Other bingo games may involve covering a line

---

[13] On an imprest system, a fixed amount is maintained at all times and only the composition changes.

down a column, across a row, or in a pattern representing a letter of the alphabet. The winning design or pattern is known to all players in advance, as is the prize to be won.

Revenue computation in bingo is very simple. Player cards are sold at the "counter"[14] and winning payouts are made by bingo agents working the floor. The difference between card sales and payouts is revenue. Because the winning amount is typically fixed, the bingo operator's goal to sell as many cards as possible. Although it is common for individual games or sessions to be operated at a loss, the larger objective is to use bingo to drive additional foot traffic through the property (in the hope that bingo players will spend money in restaurants or on other gambling opportunities).

In bingo, fraud may occur when the number selection process is altered to favor certain players, when payments are improperly made, or when funds are stolen. Because bingo is a social activity, it is unlikely that a person who did not actually win would get paid. Thus, many internal control standards focus on controlling access to the balls (or the random number generator), which ensures the integrity of number selection. For instance, because the weight and structure of balls may affect how likely they are to be blown into selection tubes, it is important that the balls be inspected prior to use. Most remaining controls are designed to ensure accurate recording of card sales and secure oversight over funds in the bingo room.

Although bingo fraud is not thought to be prevalent, it is possible. For an investigator, analytical review offers only limited value because the win-to-write[15] percentage varies considerably depending upon the volume of play. However, noteworthy downward trends in the write may indicate that bingo card sales are not being accurately recorded. Payout amounts should be predictable. If the total payouts do not appear to be reasonable, follow-up should be performed.

Keno Department Fraud

In many ways, keno is similar to bingo. Keno is played with 80 balls, numbered 1–80. Keno tickets have the same 80 numbers, and players make their own number selections. In manual systems, a keno writer records player selections on a ticket, which is the official document for determination of win or loss. The player is supplied with a matching copy of that ticket. However, most operators today use computerized keno systems in which selections are recorded in a database and the player receives a printed ticket as a receipt.

A simple wager is described as follows:

> Assume a player wagers $1 on an 8-spot ticket. This means the player selected and marked 8 of the numbers. Only 20 of 80 numbers will actually be drawn in any game. The player hopes to match as many of his 8 spots with the ball draw as possible. The more he matches, the higher the payout. Any number of players can participate, and winnings by one player do not affect the winnings of others.

---

[14] In Nevada, Bingo, Keno, and race and sports wagering are all referred to in Nevada Gaming Commission Regulation 6.110 as "counter games" due to the nature of the facility at which wagering opportunities are sold. In all three cases, the player makes his or her purchase and then goes elsewhere to wait for the outcome of the game. Modern technology, however, does permit the sale of wagering opportunities to occur elsewhere as well.

[15] *Write* is the term used to describe the amount of money collected in counter games.

Because of the similarities between keno and bingo, some of the risks are similar. These risks include the following:

- Tampering with game outcome
- Accepting wagering after the game is in progress or the outcome is known
- Altering the wager amount
- Altering ticket number selections
- Making improper payment on tickets

A key advantage in keno is the existence of an audit trail for all customer transactions, because all wagers, payouts, and game outcomes are recorded. Therefore, keno is one of the most "audit friendly" forms of wagering. Keno fraud would show up in a casino's win-to-write statistics (assuming the fraud was significant in relation to the volume of play), and any illicit activity should be detectable through daily audit procedures. In casino-based keno (as opposed to a lottery), several general areas of control are crucial, and they are briefly described in the following sections in relation to the associated fraud risks.

Prevention of Game Tampering

As with bingo, the randomness of a physical ball draw can be altered by tampering, which means controls must be in place to regularly inspect and safeguard the balls. In addition, a keno department employee should enter all ball draw information, with surveillance cameras also recording each draw as it occurs. When verifying the game outcome prior to payment of very large wagers, the surveillance recordings are key evidence of the actual ball draw. On the other hand, when random number generators are used, the controls should meet the same standards as those applied to other gaming devices (such as slot machines). Because random number generators are automated, the results of each draw should be instantly relayed to the computerized keno system.

Prevention of Wagering After the Game Is in Progress or the Outcome Is Known

With manual ticket systems, in which tickets could potentially be submitted after the results are known, risk can be mitigated through a system of ticket sequencing and microfilming that produces a "game opening ticket" and a "game closing ticket." Alternatively, tickets could be written using machines that retain a restricted copy in continuous form. All game opening and game closing information would appear on that restricted copy. In modern keno systems, the computer ensures that the game is closed properly before the ball draw takes place. However, the effectiveness of such wagering cut-off controls is dependent upon controls over the system itself.

A separate potential fraud occurs when a ticket, accepted after the start of the ball draw, is a loser that a player then seeks to void after the game's completion. This risk can be mitigated by strong ticket voiding controls.

For example, Wisconsin's MICS for Indian gaming state the following:

(4) When it is necessary to void a ticket, the void information shall be inputted in the computer and the computer shall document the appropriate information pertaining to the voided wager (e.g., void slip is issued or equivalent documentation is generated).

(5) Controls shall exist to prevent the writing and voiding of tickets after a game has been closed and after the number selection process for that game has begun …

(8) A Keno ticket may not be voided or changed once the Keno computer system has been locked out for the start of the game. Each Keno computer system shall be capable of maintaining, on a daily basis, a list of voided Keno tickets for each Keno workstation.[16]

Preventing Alteration of the Wager Amount or Number Selections

The risk of altering a wager amount or number selection are discussed together, because both risks are controlled the same way. One of the primary controls to prevent such activities is the existence of a restricted copy, which is inaccessible to keno employees who could directly profit from an alteration. One of the best ways to prevent substantial losses in the keno department is to ensure that an employee from another area of the casino regularly inspects the restricted copy prior to payment on large winning tickets. A second good control includes requiring auditing staff to conduct daily sample inspections of restricted copies at various payment thresholds. Additionally, restricted ticket copies should periodically be added up (or "footed") and compared to other records, which serves to validate the write amount recorded elsewhere.

Prevention of Improper Payment of Tickets

Internal control requirements adopted by various jurisdictions specify procedures to prevent improper payments. The relevant Nevada MICS (Version 6) for computerized systems are as follows:

Winning Ticket Verification and Payment

14. The ticket number of the ticket presented for payment is input/scanned into the computer for payment through the computer system, and the payment amount indicated by the computer is paid to the patron.

15. Procedures are established to preclude payment on tickets previously presented for payment, unclaimed winning tickets (late pays) after a period of time specified by management, voided tickets, and tickets that have not yet been issued.

---

[16] State of Wisconsin Division of Gaming, Office of Indian Gaming and Regulatory Compliance, *Minimum Internal Control Standards*, Section 17—Keno, accessed December 28, 2011, www.doa.state. wi.us/category.asp?linkcatid=823&linkid=117&locid=7.

16. All payouts are supported by the customer (computer-generated) copy of the winning ticket, and the payout amount is either indicated on the customer ticket or a payment slip is issued.

17. A manual report is produced and maintained documenting any payments made on tickets which are not authorized by the computer, including payments exceeding the aggregate payout limit.

18. For payments made on tickets which are not paid through the computer system, supervisory personnel must authorize the payment and sign the ticket at the time of payment.

Note: Appeasement payments (e.g., nonwinning ticket payouts resulting from a customer complaint or writer error) are not deductible from gross gaming revenue.

19. Winning tickets in excess of a specified dollar amount (not to exceed $10,000 for locations with more than $5 million annual keno write and $3,000 for all other locations), including such payout on a single winning game contained within a multi-race ticket, also require the following:

    a. Approval of management personnel independent of the keno department with signature evidencing approval.

    b. Reviewing the recording of the rabbit ears to verify the legitimacy of the draw and the accuracy of the ball draw results (for rabbit ear systems only).

    c. Comparison of the winning customer copy to the computer reports.[17]

    d. Regrading of the customer copy using the payout schedule and ball draw results.

    e. Performance of all of the above is documented and maintained.

20. When the keno game is operated by one person, all winning tickets in excess of an amount to be determined by management (not to exceed $1,500) must be reviewed, authorized and ticket signed by a keno supervisor (who did not write the ticket), or by someone independent of the keno department prior to payment.

---

[17] In a computerized system, the report serves as the restricted copy. Standards applicable to manual systems (which no longer are used in Nevada), previously specified that a comparison be made to the restricted copy, in whatever form it existed for a given operator.

Race Book and Sports Pool Fraud

Wagering on animal racing and sporting events is legal in some jurisdictions and may take place within a casino environment. Recent changes to Nevada regulations allow wagering to take place on events other than animal racing and sports.[18]

Race and sports wagering are both "counter games" like bingo and keno. Revenue is computed as write less payouts on winning wagers. Many of the same risks that exist in keno also exist in race and sports wagering, such as the possibility of wagers being taken late or losing wagers being voided. Manual record-keeping systems are not permitted for Nevada licensees; all book operators are required to use computerized systems.

One of the key risks associated with sports betting is potential game fixing. Although this is not something regulators can fully control, it does tend to shape public and regulatory policy. For example, it is not permissible to accept wagers on amateur events, nor is it permissible to accept bets from coaches or participants in events for which wagers are accepted. To further address this concern, licensees in Nevada are required to report to the Gaming Control Board suspicious wagering activities.[19] In animal racing, events often take so little time that accepting wagers even slightly past the start of the race could enhance the bettor's odds of predicting the outcome. This issue is addressed extensively in Nevada Gaming Commission Regulation 22.

It is vital that the outcome of wagering opportunities be verifiable. Not only does this ensure that operators pay the proper winners, it also helps resolve disputes between bettors and operators while clearly establishing which payouts are deductible for tax purposes. As new race books and sports pool options arise, the ability for gaming operators to verify results years after the event (for purposes of regulatory authority audits) is crucial. In anticipation of this problem, the Nevada Gaming Commission established the following in Regulation 22.120:

> 2. A request for approval to accept wagers on an event other than a horse race, greyhound race, or an athletic sports event shall be made by a book on such forms approved by the chairman, and shall include:
>
> (a) A full description of the event and the manner in which wagers would be placed and winning wagers would be determined.
>
> (b) A full description of any technology which would be utilized to offer the event.
>
> (c) Such other information or documentation which demonstrates that:
>
> (1) The event could be effectively supervised;
>
> (2) The outcome of the event would be verifiable;

---

[18] Race and sports wagering in Nevada is governed by Nevada Gaming Commission Regulations 20, 21, 22, 26, 26A, 26B, and 26C. The new provision for "other events" is covered in Regulation 22.120. Although there are MICS pertaining to race and sports wagering, a more succinct presentation of the essential risks can be performed using Regulation 22.

[19] Regulation 22.121.

(3)   The outcome of the event would be generated by a reliable and independent process;

(4)   The outcome of the event would not be affected by any wager placed;

(5)   The event could be conducted in compliance with any applicable
laws; and

(6)   The granting of the request for approval would be consistent with the
public policy of the state.

(d)   Such additional or supplemental information as the chairman may require.

The decision whether to grant approval to accept wagers on an event
other than a horse race, greyhound race, or an athletic sports event shall be
based on all relevant information including, but not limited to, the factors
in subsection 2(c) of this section. The chairman may subject any technology that would be utilized to offer the event to such testing, investigation
and approval process as he deems appropriate.

The state of Nevada continues to refine its administrative policies regarding Regulation
22.120 and posts information on its website (www.gaming.nv.gov). This remains an evolving area to watch by both regulators as well as those interested in issues surrounding gaming
fraud.

10

Securities and Investment

Scott M. Richter, CPA/ CIA, CFE

Introduction

Whether in a bear or bull market, recession or boom economy, one thing is for certain: securities and investment fraud is ever-present. In fact, some investment fraud schemes have been around for more than 100 years. With that in mind, it is wise for forensic accountants to remember that although the tools and technologies fraudsters use to ensnare victims may change, the underlying scam is often the same.

This chapter will focus on the following securities investment frauds:

- Ponzi schemes
- Pyramid schemes
- Boiler room operations (the "pump and dump")
- Unregistered and unlicensed brokers and investment advisers

Ponzi Schemes

The Ponzi scheme has become a well-honed talking point in popular culture. That's a positive development for many American households because, to current or aspiring Ponzi schemers' dismay, people have become more skeptical about where and with whom they invest their money. While much has been published on Ponzi schemes in recent years, the content often fails to make clear the history, key elements, red flags, and linkages to bankruptcy contained in virtually every Ponzi scheme. This chapter will discuss all of those elements in more detail.

History

The Ponzi scheme is named after Carlo "Charles" Ponzi, who in 1919, devised a simple investment vehicle. Effectively, Ponzi planned to take advantage of weakening foreign currencies by purchasing international postal coupons overseas that could be redeemed for U.S. postage stamps. He would then sell the U.S. stamps and make a profit. However, Ponzi was unable to reap any meaningful profits due to the bureaucracy and administrative burden involved in redeeming these coupons.

Instead of abandoning this unsuccessful (but legitimate) investing method, Ponzi refined his pitch to potential investors, saying he could return a 50 percent profit on their investment in 45 days or double their money in 90 days. Ponzi advised investors that he would achieve such returns through a "network of international agents," who would purchase the postal reply coupons on his behalf. He withheld further details of how he would achieve such returns "due to competitive reasons." In reality, Ponzi was merely paying off early investors with new investors' funds while making no new purchases of postal reply coupons.

In the short 8-month duration of his scheme, Ponzi collected as much as $15 million from 40,000 investors. News reports at the time described huge crowds lined up outside Ponzi's Boston office waiting to invest. However, after the scheme unraveled, Ponzi was $7 million in debt, with assets that included a mere $61 in postal reply coupons. In the decades since Ponzi launched this brazen scam, thousands of other fraudsters have pursued schemes with the same common denominator: earlier investors are paid off with funds from new investors. Today, the legal definition of a *Ponzi scheme* is simply, "a phony investment plan in which monies paid by later investors are used to pay artificially high returns to the initial investors, with the goal of attracting more investors."[1]

Although many people tend to use the terms "Ponzi scheme" and "pyramid scheme" interchangeably, there is an essential difference between the two. In a Ponzi scheme, the fraudster (and perhaps his or her agents), serve as the operational hub into which all investor monies flow.

As described more fully in the next section of this chapter, a pyramid scheme is specifically designed for early investors (top levels of the pyramid) to collect their returns from new investors (lower levels of the pyramid). In fact, some operators of pyramid schemes even use that term with investors, telling them that their returns are solely dependent on the recruiting of new participants.

Because Ponzi schemes are dependent on new investors to pay earlier investors, by definition they are mathematically doomed to fail. Like pyramid schemes, they will eventually reach a point at which there are no more new investors in existence to fund investment returns and returns of capital to existing investors. But Ponzi schemes usually collapse sooner than that, largely because

- the scheme reaches a point at which the fraudster can no longer recruit new investors and not enough funds are available to pay existing investors.
- the fraudster decides to close the scheme and abscond with investors' money before the fund fully collapses or is uncovered by outside parties.
- the fraudster is exposed in some way, such as through investigation by regulators, by bad press, or by skeptical or suspicious investors. Market or economic conditions force investors to withdraw their returns or initial capital, which fatally destroys the liquidity of the scheme. In fact, many Ponzi schemes have unraveled within the past few years as a result of the global financial downturn.

---

[1]   *Alexander v. Compton*, 229 F.3d 750, 759n1 (9th Cir. 2000).

Key Elements

Because virtually all Ponzi schemes have the same characteristics, those elements can serve as red flags to potential investors. This section will discuss the most common key elements.

Above-market or Guaranteed Return

In order to entice prospective investors, the Ponzi schemer must offer an above-market or guaranteed investment return. However, the fraudster will likely offer only a "reasonable" above-market rate, so as not to attract suspicion or unwanted attention. One of the primary reasons Charles Ponzi's scheme failed so quickly is the attention it received for guaranteeing outlandish returns.

To "sweeten the pot" for current investors, a fraudster may use some creative tools. For example, the Ponzi schemer will often encourage existing investors to provide favorable reviews to new investors in exchange for a commission or finder's fee. And, the fraudster also makes sure to pay returns to existing investors, thus demonstrating that the operation is "legitimate." The goal of this step is to encourage current investors to reassure prospective new investors that the "investment" is sound and that they too will be paid.

Appearance of Illegitimacy or Impeccable Reputation

Large Ponzi schemes do not tend to be fly-by-night operations, run by operators with questionable or unknown pasts. In fact, a Ponzi scheme often grows out of a legitimate operation and is run by a person with impressive credentials. A well-publicized recent example is Bernie Madoff, who co-founded the NASDAQ, was Chairman of the National Association of Securities Dealers, and founded Madoff Investment Securities. Before his long-time Ponzi scheme was exposed, he was one of the largest market makers on Wall Street. In addition, Allen Stanford of the Stanford Financial Group, once a well-respected financier and philanthropist, was recently convicted of running a multibillion-dollar Ponzi scheme.

Marketing and Exclusivity

A Ponzi scheme is not typically marketed through high pressure sales tactics. Rather, the fraudster lets the scheme sell itself through allegedly attractive investment returns and through the word-of-mouth of initial investors who often help attract new participants. The fraudster does not necessarily want a wide and diverse pool of potential investors, because that increases the probability that someone might recognize red flags, ask too many questions, or report the scheme to regulators. Instead, the fraudster creates exclusivity by targeting potential investors with common affiliations, such as the similarities in religious or social circles. For example, some of Madoff's favorite groups from which to recruit investors were the Florida-based Palm Beach County Club and Boca Pointe Golf Club, in addition to a multitude of Jewish charitable organizations.

Investor Greed

As a basic aspect of human nature, Ponzi schemes thrive on investor greed. It is important to point out that fraudsters do not need gullible or unsophisticated investors to leverage greed via a Ponzi scheme. Consider that many—if not most—of Madoff's investors were well educated and financially prudent individuals or organizations. Thus, the more successfully a fraudster can build the illusion of above-market or guaranteed returns, the more frequently he or she can leverage greed to entice people or organizations to reinvest for even higher returns.

Red Flags and Warning Signs

This section will discuss some of the most common red flags and warning signs linked to Ponzi schemes:

"Secret" or "Proprietary" Investing Formula

The fraudster will often advise investors that his or her investment strategy is secret and proprietary, and it cannot be disclosed due to competitive reasons. For instance, Madoff told investors that his strategy was to purchase option contracts for stocks of major companies he had bought. However, if Madoff had actually executed this strategy, he would have flooded the options market with trades. In reality, activity from Madoff Securities didn't register a blip on the Chicago Board Options Exchange. Years ago, Charles Ponzi also touted his "proprietary method" of generating significant investment returns from the exchange of postal reply coupons. But, according to an analysis done at the time by *Barron's* financial magazine, Ponzi's scheme would have required 160 million postal reply coupons in circulation—well in excess of the 27,000 that actually existed.

For these reasons, fraud investigators should always be wary of any "veil of secrecy" that surrounds a potential investment strategy.

Difficulty in Performing Due Diligence

For forensic accountants, the most basic of due diligence steps can quickly uncover the following red flags in a Ponzi scheme:

- Lack of audited financial statements or statements audited by an unrecognized firm too small to adequately render an opinion on the investment company
- Reluctance on the part of the investment company to divulge records or data that provide visibility into its results and operations
- Vague or undisclosed investment strategy
- Inability to realistically execute any represented investment strategy in the public markets
- Historical investment performance that is too steady and consistent from year to year, defying downward trends in the market
- Offshore presence of key operations, executives, or corporate registration with little or no justification

Ponzi Schemes and Bankruptcy

As previously discussed, it is inevitable that a Ponzi scheme will eventually collapse, leading the company through which the scheme was operated into bankruptcy. When this occurs, a trustee is usually appointed to help recover assets and distribute funds to investors who have suffered losses under the scheme. Assuming the trustee confirms that the operation was a Ponzi scheme, any payments made to earlier investors (whether profits or principal) can be legally classified as fraudulent conveyances.

Under the law, early investors who benefitted most from the scheme must pay back the bankrupt estate, unless they can demonstrate that the return of capital and profit was taken both in good faith and "for reasonably equivalent value."[2] Bear in mind that the burden of proof in this scenario is on the investor. For instance, a recent bankruptcy court decision in New York surrounding the Bayou Group hedge funds, a $450 million Ponzi scheme, ruled that investors "should have known" of the fraud, and investors who redeemed their capital and profits after becoming aware of any "red flags" could not assert a good faith defense.

Pyramid Schemes

As mentioned earlier in this chapter, a pyramid scheme is structured such that the fraudster at the top recruits participants (or "members") into the scheme for a fee. Those new members then recover that fee and realize any gains through "commissions" paid by the fraudster for recruiting additional members. Layers of the pyramid are built as new groups of members come onboard, but those at or towards the bottom of the pyramid are the least likely to recover their investment.

Unlike a Ponzi scheme, the pyramid scheme offers no products or outside investments. The commission structure and cash flow in a pyramid scheme can be structured several different ways. A simple example would be when the fraudster at the top of the pyramid receives $100 from each member to join the scheme. The fraudster than pays members a $20 commission for each new person they recruit. So, in order for a member to recover the initial investment, that person must recruit 5 new members (meaning that commissions paid on any additional recruits are profit). Meanwhile, the fraudster makes $80 for each member recruited into the scheme, simply by sitting atop the pyramid. Over time, the scheme cannot sustain itself, because there are not enough new members to join the pyramid that will allow current members to still recover their initial investment. In fact, as shown in figure 10-1, there are not enough people on Earth to sustain a large pyramid scheme.

---

[2]   Patrick M. O'Keefe, Russell D. Long, and Michael S. McElwee, "Ponzi Schemes in Bankruptcy," *ABI Committee News*, July 2007.

Figure 10-1: Pyramid Scheme Sustainability

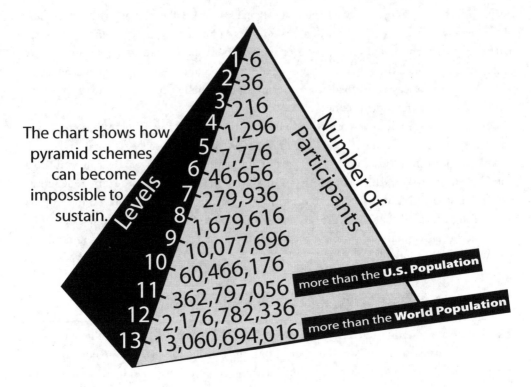

The chart shows how pyramid schemes can become impossible to sustain.

Levels

Number of Participants

1 – 6
2 – 36
3 – 216
4 – 1,296
5 – 7,776
6 – 46,656
7 – 279,936
8 – 1,679,616
9 – 10,077,696
10 – 60,466,176
11 – 362,797,056   more than the **U.S. Population**
12 – 2,176,782,336
13 – 13,060,694,016   more than the **World Population**

Source: Securities and Exchange Commission.

Though some pyramid schemes are disguised as multi-level marketing programs, not all multi-level marketing programs are illegal. For example, if a multi-level marketing program allows members to make a profit solely through sales of products and services while recovering their costs without the need to recruit new members, the program will typically be considered legitimate. On the other hand, if members of such a program are incentivized only with money or free products to recruit new members (or if members are forced to buy more product then they could realistically sell), then it will most likely be considered a pyramid scheme.

Red Flags and Warning Signs

The Internet has made it easy for promoters to market pyramid schemes. What was once largely a word-of-mouth effort is now broadcast in many different forms through online banners and spam e-mail. Although the recruiting tools through which fraudsters conduct their illicit acts may have changed, the underlying model for pyramid schemes has not. Forensic accountants should be on the lookout for the following red flags and warning signs.

Unrealistically High Investment Returns

Unlike some Ponzi schemes that promise more modest—but guaranteed—returns over time, the pyramid scheme is typically more urgent in its recruiting style. The promise of extremely high investment returns in a short period of time is a key feature of a pyramid scheme.

No Product or Service Being Sold

The tell-tale signs of a pyramid scheme are the absence of a product or service for sale or a focus on recruiting new members as the sole source of a participant's earnings.

Commissions for Recruiting New Members

When a product or service is being sold, investigators should check if a significant amount of a participant's compensation is dependent on recruiting new members. If so, it may be a pyramid scheme. In any legitimate venture, products or services offered should be available to the public, and a prospective participant should have the ability to perform due diligence on retail sales, pricing, and inventory turnover. Conversely, programs that sell primarily to their own members require significant purchases of inventory that are likely not to be sold or sell that inventory at higher than expected prices should draw a high level of scrutiny.

Regulation and Enforcement

Pyramid schemes are illegal and can be investigated and enforced by a variety of regulators. The Federal Trade Commission and Securities and Exchange Commission (SEC) have the authority to file suits, obtain injunctions, and freeze assets. In addition, the U.S. Department of Justice and U.S. Postal Inspection Service, as well as state attorneys general, can pursue criminal charges such as securities fraud, mail fraud, racketeering, and money laundering.

Boiler Room Operations (the "Pump and Dump")

In the context of investment scams, a "boiler room" can be a rented space with banks of telephones, where a collection of brokers use cold-calling and high-pressure sales tactics to sell large volumes of thinly traded stock to unwitting investors. The goal of this scam is to pump up the share price so the brokerage firm can dump a company's stock at a profit. As a result, investors are often left with nearly worthless stock, because the artificially inflated purchase price far exceeds the typical market value. In many cases, a boiler room operation is run in conjunction with the company's owners, who are seeking to boost their stock price. Because this small group usually holds significant shares of "house stock," the owners stand to reap big gains from selling those securities at the inflated price.

Micro-cap (or "penny") stock is the primary tool of the "pump and dump" scam. Micro-caps are companies with low market capitalization (generally between $50 million and $300 million), which are lightly traded on the Over-The-Counter Bulletin Board. Such

"Pink Sheet" stocks are highly volatile, and they do not have to meet minimum listing standards. Further, companies with fewer than 500 investors and less than $10 million in assets do not have to file reports with the SEC.

Boiler room operators exploit the features of micro-cap and small company stocks by being the sole source of information on the company (because no public information is usually available to potential investors). This makes it next to impossible to verify any representations made by "pump and dump" brokers, as no worthwhile due diligence can be performed by outside investors.

In the era of online media, boiler room operators are moving from cold-calling to bombarding e-mail accounts and message boards, offering investors "inside" or "pre-initial public offering " (IPO) pricing that can deliver quick returns. In fact, many of these "brokers" are not even licensed or qualified to sell securities because a sizable percentage of boiler room operations are either part of organized crime or operate out of foreign countries with little regulation and no extradition treaties with the United States.

Red Flags and Warning Signs

Lack of Financial Information or Inability to Perform Due Diligence
When viewing a potential boiler room pitch, forensic accountants should pay attention for high pressure sales tactics, a lack of reliable financial information or analysis on the company, or outright refusals by a broker to provide any due diligence material. If financial statements are available, the investigator should be wary of anything other than an unqualified audit opinion, scrutinize footnote disclosures, related-party transactions, and determine whether large amounts of stock are owned by insiders. In addition, the company's auditing firm should be vetted.

Research Those Touting the Investment
Forensic accountants should seek out any regulatory actions against the brokerage firm, its owners, or the individuals attempting to sell the stock.

Overseas Connections
Beware of firms registered or operating in foreign countries that have little or no securities regulation. In fact, one of the biggest reasons for a brokerage firm (or boiler room) to sell micro-cap stocks from a foreign country may be to avoid potential liability.

Regulation and Enforcement
Many federal regulators have an interest in "pump and dump" scams involving micro-cap stock. For civil cases, the key players include the SEC and the Financial Industry Regulatory Authority (FINRA). On the criminal side, various U.S. Attorney's offices, the Federal Bureau of Investigation, IRS, and the Department of Justice are the chief agencies prosecuting boiler room operations.

Unregistered and Unlicensed Brokers and Investment Advisers

Both federal and state regulators have complex procedures in place for the registration and licensing of brokers and investment advisers. This is for good reason, because brokers buy and sell securities on behalf of others and are defined under the Securities and Exchange Act of 1934 as "any person engaged in the business of effecting transactions in securities for the account of others." Investment advisers provide information to clients on the buying and selling of securities, often via direct conversations, newsletters, and online publications. For those reasons, most brokers must register with the SEC, in addition to joining a "self-regulatory organization," such as FINRA.

Unfortunately, headlines are often littered with stories about unscrupulous brokers and investment advisers (some registered, some not). On many occasions, these fraudsters have absconded with client funds or simply stolen investors' money via phony securities or nonexistent ventures. For example, in 2011 federal prosecutors charged Florida resident John Mattera and several other individuals with securities fraud, wire fraud, and money laundering. Mattera and the others were accused of selling pre-IPO shares in Facebook, Groupon, and Twitter—three highly valued companies for which IPOs were highly anticipated. However, Mattera or his co-conspirators owned no such shares, and funds raised from investors through this scam were transferred to personal accounts and used in support of the fraudsters' lavish lifestyles.

In addition to shady investment advisers, forensic accountants should also be aware of how investment fraud can be leveraged by everyday people. One of the unfortunate byproducts of the recent global financial downturn has been a push by some investors, particularly retirees and aging baby boomers, to recoup real estate and investment losses. According to the *Wall Street Journal*, the number of criminal complaints in 2010 involving state-level regulatory actions against investors age 50 or older was double that of the previous year. In addition, the North American Securities Administrators Association (NASAA) reported that court cases involving older investors and unregistered securities outnumbered those related to ordinary stocks and bonds by a ratio of 5-to-1. Notable cases included a 56-year old man who lost $500,000 in an investment fund marketed to older individuals. This fund, which guaranteed annual returns of 14–24 percent, turned out to be a Ponzi scheme.[3]

Red Flags and Warning Signs

Forensic accountants are in a good position to help investors and companies avoid scams such as those noted in this chapter by performing basic due diligence, as described in this section.

Checking Registration and Licensure of Brokers

A simple online resource for this task is BrokerCheck, a free tool available on FINRA's website. BrokerCheck allows users to search for brokers and obtain background reports and

---

[3]   Kelly Greene, "Boomers Wearing Bull's-Eyes," *Wall Street Journal*, December 14, 2011.

other information through a central registration depository (CRD). This securities industry online registration and licensing database can reveal whether or not a broker is properly licensed in a particular state, and if he or she has negative issues reported by regulators or investors. Information from CRD can also be requested through state securities regulators, with full contact information available from the NASAA website.

Vetting Investment Advisers

Depending on the size of assets under management, investment advisers must either register with the SEC or with securities regulators in their state using Form ADV. This form requires the investment adviser to provide information about his or her business, ownership, clients, as well as about any disciplinary actions. The form also requires the adviser to describe the services he or she offers, fee schedules, and backgrounds of professional staff. An adviser's Form ADV can be obtained online at the Investment Adviser Public Disclosure website, from state securities regulators, from the SEC, or directly from the adviser.

11

Financial Institutions Fraud

Al Kohl, CFE

Introduction

Forensic investigations of financial institutions have special challenges. First, financial institutions have unique and complex processes, procedures, and accounting methodologies, which differ greatly from other types of organizations. Knowledge of these issues is paramount in conducting a successful investigation. Second, financial institutions are heavily regulated and are supervised and examined by multiple authorities. For example, banks and savings institutions are regulated by an array of departments and agencies at both the federal and state levels. Finally, a number of federal laws and regulations govern financial institutions.

A successful forensic accountant must understand these agencies, the roles they play, their needs and concerns, and how those elements can potentially affect an investigation. By necessity, regulatory agencies often become involved in investigations or at minimum are interested in the final investigative outcome. Forensic accountants should understand that both the investigative work plan and final report may be scrutinized by these agencies. This chapter will take a closer look at accounting structures, regulatory agencies, and specific laws that affect financial institutions, including banks and credit unions.

Financial Institutions Overview

The accounting structure of banks, credit unions, and other savings institutions are known as "pass-through" entities, which borrow money and subsequently invest it. For ease of discussion, this chapter will refer to these financial entities as "banking institutions."

Generally, banking institutions raise funds by collecting deposits. Banking institutions invest these deposits in a number of ways, such as traditional loans, or allocate funds to securities or other investments. The profit a banking institution earns is determined by the *net interest spread* (the difference between the rates it pays to depositors and the rates it earns on investments). Additionally, banking institutions often earn fee revenues related to trust services, investment services, and depositor fees, such as ATM or account service charges. Larger banking institutions may also earn income from investment banking, foreign exchange, and credit card operations.

Because a banking institution's deposits (except for those held by credit unions) are owned by depositors, they are classified as a liability on the balance sheet. Conversely, a banking institution's investments, including loans, are listed as assets on the balance sheet. This can be confusing to someone not familiar with this unique accounting structure, because loans for nonbanking entities are generally considered liabilities for balance sheet purposes (because loans are usually debts—not investments—in a typical business).

When a banking institution drafts checks for customers (such as cashier's checks), payroll, or payments to vendors and suppliers, those amounts are usually transacted from the institution's own checking accounts. For that reason, the checks are classified as a liability of the banking institution for balance sheet purposes—not as an asset.

Banking institution income statements follow a different format than that of other businesses and are presented in the following order:

> Interest Income
> (less) Interest Expense
> (equals) Net Interest Income
> (plus) Non-Interest Income
> (less) Non-Interest Expense
> (equals) Income before Income Taxes

In addition to traditional financial statements, banking institutions must also report capital ratios that are specifically defined by regulatory agencies. These ratios are as follows:

- Tier-1 capital[1] to risk-weighted assets
- Total capital to risk-weighted assets
- Leverage ratio (Tier-1 capital to total average assets less goodwill and intangibles)

By definition, *risk-weighted assets* are the assets of a bank multiplied times a specific percentage depending upon the perceived risk of the asset category (as defined by the Basel Committee on Banking Supervision guidelines).[2] For example, cash is considered risk-free and therefore has a multiplier of 0, while loans and leases may be multiplied by ratios of 20 percent to 100 percent, depending on the type of loan. Therefore, the resulting balance of risk-weighted assets is higher when the banking institution has a larger percentage of riskier assets, resulting in a lower capital ratio. These capital ratios allow regulators to quickly assess and monitor the soundness of a banking institution, because they accurately reflect the entity's specific risk structure.

Credit unions are a different type of banking institution. As a nonprofit financial cooperative, a credit union is owned by its members and governed by a board of directors elected by (and from within) that membership. Usually, credit unions are formed around a common theme, such as employment with the same company or residence in the same geographic area. Credit unions accept deposits from members and use them to make loans, usually at

---

[1]   *Tier 1 capital is defined as core capital, which is the book value of equity, plus retained earnings*

[2]   Bank for International Settlements, *International Convergence of Capital Measurement and Capital Standards* (June 2006), www.bis.org/publ/bcbs128b.pdf.

favorable rates compared to banks or savings institutions. Deposits are regarded as purchases of shares in the credit union, and all net income of these institutions is paid back as dividends to members. This structure means that member deposits are not considered liabilities of the organization, as in a bank or thrift institution, but instead are classified as capital on a credit union's balance sheet.

A subset of banking institutions are known as "savings institutions" (also called savings and loans, thrifts or savings banks). Savings institutions have similar accounting structures to banks, but they specialize in real estate financing.

Role of Supervisory and Regulatory Entities Involved With Financial Institutions

Although the terms "supervision" and "regulation" are often used interchangeably, they actually refer to distinct roles. *Supervision* involves the monitoring, inspecting, and examination of organizations. The main objective of the supervisory process is to evaluate an organization's overall safety and soundness. This evaluation includes an assessment of the organization's risk-management systems, financial condition, and compliance with applicable laws and regulations.[3]

On the other hand, *regulation* involves issuing and monitoring specific laws and guidelines that govern financial organizations.[4] These regulations are designed to ensure that financial institutions operate in a safe and sound manner, in accordance with applicable law. These regulations may be in the form of rules, policy guidelines, or supervisory interpretations, which may be established under specific legal provisions or under more general legal authority.[5] This chapter will focus on how the supervisory function affects forensic investigations.

Because of their role, supervisory authorities such as the Office of the Comptroller of the Currency (OCC) or the Federal Reserve Bank (FRB) are concerned with anything that affects a financial institution's risk profile. This includes the supervisory authority's assessment of an institution's safety and soundness, including the effectiveness of the institution's officers and directors. In this role, the supervisory authority will be especially concerned about material impacts on the institution's financial statements, including any changes to a financial institution's regulatory capital ratio. When changes are noted, these authorities usually request a rapid assessment of the materiality of any forensic issue, including an understanding of any possible involvement of senior officers or directors in such an issue. As a general rule, these authorities often mandate that financial institutions perform quick, thorough, and independent investigations when such issues arise.

During a supervisory examination, issues concerning fraud, embezzlement, or other defalcations are often discovered. When this occurs, the supervisory authority may conduct its

---

[3] Board of Governors of the Federal Reserve System, *The Federal Reserve System: Purposes and Functions*, www.federalreserve.gov/pf/pdf/pf_complete.pdf.

[4] *Id.*

[5] *Id.*

own follow-up investigation or may require that the institution conduct its own review. For the latter, the supervisory authority often suggests the engagement of an outside independent forensic investigator to ensure credibility.

During this type of review, the supervisory authority may suggest or require that certain procedures be performed, and it usually requests copies of reports detailing the procedures and results of an investigation. On occasion, the supervisory authority may also request to speak directly with a forensic investigator concerning specific scope of work and procedures. Even if the financial institution engages an independent investigator, the supervisory authority may concurrently conduct its own review into the matter.

With these possibilities in mind, it is wise for the forensic investigator to assume that any report or other deliverable will likely be reviewed by the authority. That review will most likely involve an evaluation of investigative procedures, including an assessment of work quality and resulting conclusions.

After any investigation of this kind, a financial institution will almost certainly receive some feedback from the supervisory authority. In the worst case scenario, the financial institution may be hit with supervisory limitations, which may include the removal of certain directors or officers. Documents obtained by the forensic investigator may also be turned over to the supervisory authority for further review. For those reasons, before taking on this type of investigative assignment, the forensic investigator must understand the potential pressure that a supervisory authority can exert upon directors and officers of a financial institution targeted for a detailed review.

Supervisory authorities can be a tremendous source of information for the forensic investigator. A supervisory authority can sometimes assist in obtaining information from other institutions, if the investigator has verified a trail of financial transactions that point to particular outside accounts. For example, if funds have allegedly been embezzled from an account at one bank and appear to have been sent to an account at a second bank, the forensic investigator may be able gain supervisory authority to request information from the second bank to trace those transactions. That is an important resource, because such transaction information is generally not available to investigators without a subpoena.

Supervisory and Regulatory Agencies

The supervisory and regulatory bodies that oversee financial institutions are determined primarily by where the institution was chartered. Banks that are chartered nationally are called *national banks*. Banks chartered by a state are called *state banks*. Federal authorities that supervise and regulate financial institutions range from the FRB, OCC, the Federal Deposit Insurance Corporation (FDIC), and the Office of Thrift Supervision (OTS). Meanwhile, state banking departments have similar agencies that serve those jurisdictions. The following section will describe the roles of each federal agency in the supervisory and regulatory process.

Federal Reserve Bank

The FRB was founded by the U.S. Congress to perform four functions:

1. Conduct the nation's monetary policy by influencing the monetary and credit conditions in the economy, maintaining the stability of the financial system, and containing systemic risk that may arise in financial markets
2. Provide financial services to depository institutions, the U.S. government, and foreign official institutions, including playing a major role in operating the nation's payments system
3. Maintain the stability of the financial system
4. Supervise and regulate banking institutions to ensure the safety and soundness of the nation's banking and financial system and to protect the credit rights of consumers[6]

The FRB has primary supervisory authority for state banks that elect to become members of the Federal Reserve System.[7] Banks are often owned and controlled by holding companies, and the FRB has supervisory authority over these entities, regardless of whether the subsidiary bank is a national bank, state member bank, or state nonmember bank.

Office of the Comptroller of the Currency

The OCC charters, regulates, and supervises all national banks and federal savings associations. It also supervises the federal branches and agencies of foreign banks. The OCC is a bureau of the U.S. Department of the Treasury, and its examiners conduct onsite reviews of national banks and provide supervision of bank operations.[8]

Federal Deposit Insurance Corporation

The FDIC is an independent agency of the federal government, which was created during the Great Depression to protect depositors in response to thousands of bank failures that occurred during that period. The FDIC insures deposits of banks and savings associations up to certain limits established by law.[9] As the insurer, the FDIC has special examination authority to determine the condition of an insured bank or savings association for insurance purposes, regardless of whether the FDIC is the primary supervisory authority.[10] In addition, the FDIC supervises state chartered banks that are not members of the Federal Reserve System, and it examines banks for compliance with certain banking and credit related laws.[11]

---

[6] *Id.*

[7] *Id.*

[8] U.S. Department of the Treasury, "About the Office of the Comptroller of the Currency," accessed May 1, 2012, www.helpwithmybank.gov/about/index.html.

[9] Board of Governors of the Federal Reserve System, *The Federal Reserve System: Purposes and Functions*, www.federalreserve.gov/pf/pdf/pf_complete.pdf.

[10] *Id.*

[11] Federal Deposit Insurance Corporation (FDIC), "Who is the FDIC?" accessed May 1, 2012, www.fdic.gov/about/learn/symbol/index.html.

In addition to its role as supervisor and regulator, the FDIC becomes immediately involved when a financial institution is declared insolvent and is taken over by the government. An institution is generally declared insolvent by its chartering authority, such as the state division of banking, FRB, or OCC. After being appointed receiver for the failed financial institution, the FDIC conducts its own investigation into causes of the failure. This investigation includes a thorough examination of lending policies, procedures, and practices that contributed to the bank's insolvency, as well as any other functional areas that may have contributed to the failure. Additionally, the FDIC assesses actions taken by the institution's officers, directors, or other professionals who performed work on its behalf, as well as attorneys, appraisers, investment advisers, and accountants involved with the financial institution in a consultative role. If an FDIC investigation determines there is sufficient cause to prevail on a lawsuit against an officer, director, or professional entity, it will typically file a civil suit against the party as the receiver of the failed institution. The purpose of this litigation is to recover funds, which help offset taxpayer losses incurred on depositors' guaranteed accounts. As receiver, the FDIC also determines whether the financial institution will pursue claims against any directors, officers, or fidelity bond insurance policies.

Office of Thrift Supervision

The OTS's responsibilities transferred to the OCC in July 2011. As such, the OCC is now responsible for the supervision and regulation of savings associations. Savings associations include both savings and loans and savings banks, which are both commonly known as "thrift institutions." The OCC examines savings association to assess its safety, soundness, and compliance with consumer protection laws and regulations. In addition, OCC examiners monitor the condition of thrifts through off-site analysis of regularly submitted financial data, in addition to regular contact with thrift personnel.[12]

Summary of Bank Supervisory and Regulatory Authorities

Box 11-1 summarizes the supervisory responsibilities of each agency according to the type of organization.

State Departments of Banking

State chartered banks are subject to a two-tier regulatory system, involving the state regulatory agency and the FDIC. Although all banks have federal regulators, only state banks have state oversight. Federal regulation is determined by whether or not the bank is a member of the Federal Reserve System. For example, a Missouri state bank that is not a member of the Federal Reserve System would be regulated by both the Missouri state banking regulator and the FDIC. On the other hand, a California state bank that is a member of the Federal Reserve System would be jointly regulated by the California banking regulatory authority and the FRB.

---

[12]   www.occ.treas.gov/about/what-we-do/mission/index-about.html

Box 11-1: Bank Supervisory Responsibilities by Organization[*]

Type of Institution	Supervisor and Regulator
Bank Holding Company	FRB
Nonbank Subsidiary of Bank Holding Company	FRB/Functional Regulator
National Banks	OCC
State Banks	
FRB Member	FRB
FRB Non-Member	FDIC
Thrift Holding Companies	FRB
Federally Chartered Thrifts	OCC
State Chartered Thrifts	FDIC
Foreign Banks	
State-licensed	FRB/FDIC
Federally-licensed	OCC/FR/FDIC

[*] http://www.jonesday.com/files/Publication/5064ffd8-e6f6-44b1-b223-e664f0ee47c6/
Presentation/PublicationAttachment/c7adf431-6f84-4e1f-81a4-ea980cc173d5/
macdonald%20schwartz%20after%20the%20ots.pdf

In addition to federal regulatory examinations, state banking authorities conduct separate reviews of member institutions. Although this system can lead to conflicting regulatory opinions, the dual federal or state regulatory process helps ensure the safety and soundness of those financial institutions. Generally, there is no coordination of timing for state or federal regulatory examinations, though it is rare for both agencies to conduct simultaneous reviews. It is even rarer that a forensic investigator would have to deal with both agencies at the same time.

When a financial institution is being investigated for possible misappropriations or malfeasance, the bank is required to do nothing more than file a suspicious activity report (SAR) (which is discussed in more detail later in this chapter). However, as a commonplace professional courtesy, most banks will notify their federal regulator. In most fraud investigations, the forensic accountant on the case typically works only with the federal authority.

Publicly Available Information for Banking and Thrift Financial Institutions

Because financial institutions are publicly supervised and regulated, a considerable amount of data is easily available through federal regulatory agencies. This is important to understand, because this well of information may be extremely helpful to a fraud investigator. For example, if a forensic accountant needs to review historical trends for a financial institution to understand how certain metrics have changed over time, access to detailed regulatory call reports may provide insight on the trends and suggest areas of possible inquiry.

Both banks and thrift institutions are required to file monthly reports on their financial condition (known as "call reports" for banks and "thrift financial reports" for thrift institutions). The reports are required to be filed 30 days after the close of each month, and these reports can be printed or downloaded from the Federal Financial Institutions Examination Council's website. These reports present detailed analyses of the institution's balance sheet, income statement, and capital position. Additionally, sub-reports provide great detail on the makeup of a bank's loans and leases, deposits, borrowings, and investments.

Although not as detailed, the FRB requires bank holding companies it supervises to file semiannual reports on their condition. These reports are located on the National Information Center's website, which also contains bank holding company peer group reports that compare the financial condition of banks to their overall comparison groups.

For national banks, the OCC provides the following information on its website:

- Corporate applications filed by banks to apply for a national charter; merge with another bank; open, close, or relocate a branch; or engage in other innovative activities
- Evaluations of bank performance under the Community Reinvestment Act (CRA).
- Enforcement actions the OCC imposed or withdrew

On its website, the FDIC provides the following detailed statistical information on banks:[13]

- Uniform Bank Performance Reports, which analyze various financial statements, line items, and financial ratios for a particular bank against its peer group
- Banking industry statistics and the most recent industry trends
- Graphs, tables, and maps depicting economic conditions and how they change over time for any state or metropolitan statistical area
- The latest comprehensive financial and demographic data for every FDIC-insured institution

Role of Supervisory and Regulatory Entities With Nonbanking Financial Institutions

Like their bank and thrift relatives, several government and industry agencies supervise and regulate functions for investment firms and credit unions. For forensic accountants, it is important to note that only these two nonbanking areas have centralized regulatory bodies, because other nonbanking financial institutions, such as mortgage brokers, payday and title lenders, and check cashing firms, have no central oversight. The following sections provide a quick overview of the agencies that oversee credit unions and investment firms.

---

[13] FDIC, "Bank Data Guide," accessed May 1, 2012, www.FDIC.gov/bank/statistical/guide/index.html.

National Credit Union Administration

The National Credit Union Administration (NCUA) is the independent federal agency that regulates, charters, and supervises federal credit unions. With the backing of the full faith and credit of the U.S. government, NCUA also operates the National Credit Union Share Insurance Fund (NCUSIF), insuring the deposits of 92 million account holders in all federal credit unions and the overwhelming majority of state-chartered credit unions.[14]

Financial Industry Regulatory Authority

The Financial Industry Regulatory Authority (FINRA) is the largest independent regulator for all securities firms doing business in the United States. FINRA's mission is to protect investors by making sure the securities industry operates fairly and honestly. The agency touches virtually every aspect of the securities business, including registering and educating industry participants, examining securities forms, writing and enforcing federal securities laws, and providing trade reporting services. FINRA also performs regulation under contract for major U.S. stock markets, including the New York Stock Exchange, NASDAQ, and the International Securities Exchange.[15] It is also the agency primarily responsible for investigating the activities of members and associated persons for compliance with FINRA and federal and other self-regulatory organization rules and regulations.

A critical FINRA tool available to fraud investigators is the agency's BrokerCheck® reports, which include a 10-year block of information about FINRA-registered or formerly registered brokers and brokerage firms. Box 11-2 compares individual vs. firm BrokerCheck® report elements.

Box 11-2: Individual vs. Firm BrokerCheck® Reports*

Individual BrokerCheck® Report Elements

- A summary, providing a brief overview of the broker and his or her credentials
- A broker qualifications section, which includes a listing of the broker's current registrations or licenses, if any, and industry exams he or she has passed.
- A registration and employment history section that consists of
  - a list of FINRA-registered securities firms where the broker currently is (or was) registered and
  - the broker's employment history (full and part-time work, self-employment, military service, unemployment, and full-time education) for the past 10 years—both inside and outside of the securities industry—as reported by the broker on his or her last Form U4 (which securities firms use to register brokers with self-regulatory organizations and states)
- A disclosure section that includes information about customer disputes, disciplinary events, and financial matters on the broker's record (FINRA lists each incident as reported by securities regulators, the individual broker, and any involved firms.)
- The broker's most recently submitted comment(s), if any

---

14   www.ncua.gov/about/Pages/default.aspx
15   Financial Industry Regulatory Authority (FINRA), "About the Financial Industry Regulatory Authority," accessed May 1, 2012, www.finra.org/AboutFINRA.

Box 11-2: Individual vs. Firm BrokerCheck® Reports* (continued)

Brokerage Firm A BrokerCheck® Report Elements

- A summary that provides a brief overview of the firm and its background
- A firm profile that describes where and when the firm was established and lists the people and organizations that own controlling shares or otherwise directly influence the firm's daily operations
- A firm history that details any mergers, acquisitions, or name changes
- A firm operations section that lists the firm's active licenses and registrations, the types of businesses it conducts, and other details pertaining to its operations
- A disclosure section that contains information about any arbitration awards, disciplinary events, and financial matters on the firm's record (FINRA lists each incident as reported by both securities regulators and the firm.)

* FINRA, "About BrokerCheck Reports," accessed May 1, 2012, www.finra.org/Investors/ToolsCalculators/BrokerCheck/P015175.

Publicly Available Information for Nonbanking Financial Institutions

Similar to publicly available information for banking and thrift entities, nonbanking financial institutions also maintain excellent sources of information free to the public.

Financial Institution Requirements to File Reports of Suspicious Activities

The Bank Secrecy Act of 1970 (BSA) requires U.S. financial institutions to assist federal government agencies with detecting and preventing money laundering. Specifically, the act requires financial institutions to record cash purchases of negotiable instruments, file reports of cash transactions exceeding $10,000 (daily aggregate amount), and report suspicious activity that might signal money laundering, tax evasion, or other criminal activities. The BSA is sometimes referred to as an "anti-money laundering" law. Since its passage by Congress in 1970, several other anti-money laundering acts, including provisions in Title III of the USA PATRIOT Act, have been enacted to strengthen prosecution of money laundering activities (see *Money and Finance, U.S. Code* 31, Section 5311–5330, and Title 31 U.S. *Code of Federal Regulations* [CFR] Chapter X [formerly 31 CFR Part 103]).[16]

---

[16] Financial Crimes Enforcement Network (FinCEN), "Bank Secrecy Act," accessed May 1, 2012, www.fincen.gov/statutes_regs/bsa.

As a part of the BSA's requirement to report suspicious activity, a broad range of financial institutions must file SARs. These institutions include

- depository institutions (such as banks, savings institutions, and credit unions),
- money services business (such as money transmitters and issuers, as well as sellers and redeemers of money orders or travelers checks),
- currency dealers,
- casinos, and
- securities and futures industries.[17]

In addition to money laundering, SARs are used to identify potential and actual illegal activity pertaining to terrorist financing or other financial fraud or abuse, detect and prevent the flow of illicit funds, and identify emerging threats through patterns and trends.[18]

Other than access by regulatory and law enforcement agencies, all SARs are confidential. The reports are filed directly with the Financial Crimes Enforcement Network, which allows various federal, state, and local law enforcement authorities to detect potentially fraudulent activities.

In order to comply with SAR filing requirements, many financial institutions employ staff responsible for testing, monitoring, and reporting suspicious activity. Outside forensic investigators may interact with such dedicated internal staff on investigations, the results of which often form the basis for an institution's SAR filing.

Other Financial Institution Regulations

In addition to SAR filing requirements, financial institutions must contend with a complex array of governing regulations. These regulations, generally in the form of laws passed by Congress, are enforced by various agencies that supervise banks. A notable exception is Regulation X, which is enforced by the Department of Housing and Urban Development (HUD). Regulation X covers required disclosures and sets limitations on real estate transactions.

Fraud investigators should have a solid understanding of the various regulations that govern financial institutions. Some of the more significant of these regulations are briefly described in Box 11-3.

---

[17] www.fincen.gov/forms/bsa_forms/

[18] www.fincen.gov/suspiciousactivityreport.ppt

Box 11-3: Common Financial Institution Regulation*

Regulation	Description
Regulation B	This regulation prohibits creditor practices that discriminate on the basis of race, color, religion, national origin, sex, marital status, or age (provided the applicant has the capacity to contract. The regulation also requires creditors to notify applicants of action taken on their applications, report credit history in the names of both spouses on an account, retain records of credit applications, collect information about the applicant's race and other personal characteristics in applications for certain dwelling-related loans, and provide applicants with copies of appraisal reports used in connection with credit transactions.
Regulation C	This regulation implements the Home Mortgage Disclosure Act, which is intended to provide the public with loan data that can be used to help determine whether financial institutions are serving the housing needs of their communities. In addition, Regulation C seeks to assist public officials in distributing public-sector investments to attract private investment to areas where it is needed and helps identify possible discriminatory lending patterns to aid enforcement of antidiscrimination statutes.
Regulation E	This regulation protects individual consumers engaging in electronic fund transfers (EFT) and carries out the purposes of the Electronic Fund Transfer Act, which establishes the basic rights, liabilities, and responsibilities of EFT consumers of financial institutions that offer these services.
Regulation J	This regulation governs the collection of checks, cash, and noncash items, as well as the handling of returned checks by the FRB. It also provides rules for collecting and returning items and settling balances.
Regulation M	This regulation implements the consumer leasing provisions of the Truth in Lending Act.
Regulation O	This regulation governs extensions of credit to insiders, which includes directors, executive officers, and principal shareholders of a bank and its affiliates. It includes special restrictions on loans to executive officers.
Regulation P	This regulation requires a financial institution to provide notice to customers about its privacy policies and practices, describe the conditions under which a financial institution may disclose nonpublic personal information about consumers to nonaffiliated third parties, and provide a method for consumers to prevent a financial institution from disclosing that information to most nonaffiliated third parties by "opting out" of that disclosure.
Regulation T	This regulation monitors extensions of credit by brokers and dealers. It imposes, among other obligations, initial margin requirements and payment rules on certain securities transactions.
Regulation U	This regulation imposes credit restrictions upon persons other than brokers or dealers who extend credit for the purpose of buying or carrying margin stock if the credit is secured directly or indirectly by margin stock.

Regulation	Description
HUD's Regulation X	This regulation implements the provisions of the Real Estate Settlement Procedures Act (RESPA). RESPA outlines real estate closing costs and settlement procedures, and it also requires that consumers receive disclosures at various times in a transaction and outlaws kickbacks that increase the cost of settlement services. RESPA is a consumer protection statute designed to help homebuyers be better shoppers, and it is specifically enforced by HUD.
Regulation Z	This regulation is designed to help consumers comparison shop for credit by requiring disclosures about its terms and costs. The regulation gives consumers the right to cancel certain credit transactions that involve a lien on a consumer's principal dwelling. It also regulates certain credit card practices and provides a means for fair and timely resolution of credit billing disputes. The regulation requires a maximum interest rate to be stated in variable-rate contracts secured by the consumer's dwelling. It also imposes limitations on certain home equity and mortgage agreements.
Regulation AA	This regulation establishes consumer complaint procedures and defines unfair or deceptive acts or practices of banks in connection with extensions of credit to consumers. It also prohibits certain practices, such as taking a nonpurchase money security interest in household goods.
Regulation BB	This regulation implements the CRA, which requires financial institutions to help meet the credit needs of local communities in which they are chartered. The act ensures that financial institutions do not discriminate by refusing to lend in certain local areas.
Regulation CC	This regulation contains rules outlining the duty of banks to make funds deposited into accounts available for withdrawal, including availability schedules, rules regarding exceptions to the schedules, disclosure of funds availability policies, payment of interest, and liability. It also contains rules to expedite the collection and return of checks by banks, including the direct return of checks, the manner in which the paying bank and returning banks must return checks to the depositary bank, notification of nonpayment by the paying bank, endorsement and presentment of checks, and same-day settlement for certain checks.
Regulation DD	This regulation implements the Truth in Savings Act, which helps consumers make informed decisions about deposit accounts. It requires depository institutions to provide disclosures so that consumers can make meaningful comparisons among those financial service providers.
Regulation II	This regulation implements the requirements of Section 920 of the Electronic Fund Transfer Act, in addition to Section 1075 of the Dodd–Frank Wall Street Reform and Consumer Protection Act, both of which limit debit card interchange fees, exclusivity arrangements, and routing requirements.

* The list is provided from www.bankersonline.com/abcsoup/abcsoup.html (accessed May 1, 2012).

Conclusion

Knowledge of the complexities related to financial institutions, including the unique structure, accounting, and regulatory environment will greatly aid the forensic investigator in performing a successful investigation, as evidenced by the following case studies.

Case Studies

Case Study No. 1

Background

An accounting firm's forensic accountants were retained by a publicly traded Midwestern bank in order to assist in the investigation of transactions performed by a certain bank branch manager due to a deposit customer alleging that unauthorized withdrawals had been made from four of her deposit accounts.

The investigative team worked with bank personnel to test branch transactions to determine if financial improprieties might exist. In addition to researching the specific transactions bank staff had already identified, the firm was also asked to determine if additional misappropriations might exist.

How the Fraud Was Committed

The bank branch manager had the ability to personally post transactions on customer accounts. He also had a teller drawer and the ability to access branch vault cash. This allowed this bank employee the unique ability to manipulate a customer account, post cash entries on the bank teller system, and physically withdraw cash from the vault and his cash drawer.

How the Fraud Was Investigated

The team traced the suspected transactions and noted the instances when the branch manager had posted transactions to the customer accounts in question. These transactions initially involved withdrawals from customer business accounts; however, the review of the transactions showed that the offsetting transactions always involved transactions on other nonrelated customer residential home construction and home equity loans. The investigators reviewed all instances when the branch manager had posted transactions to these loans and noticed that the transactions involved cash advances from the customer accounts, not check transactions, which would be consistent with advances for construction draws. Because the transactions were entered as being cash transactions, the branch cash transactions would cause the actual cash at the branch to be out of balance with the system cash totals unless the transactions actually involved cash.

The firm reviewed branch security video tapes and aligned the suspected transactions with the branch manager's locations at specific times. This also showed which terminal the branch manager used to post the transactions. At the time of each of the transactions, the branch manager was at a teller window and had access to his teller drawer. Each time the branch manager had just returned from the cash vault, where he had withdrawn funds. Each time he accessed the cash vault, he did so alone, in violation of branch internal controls, which required dual access to the vault. The review of the cash vault logs indicated that the branch manager had withdrawn large amounts from the cash vault immediately prior to posting the cash draws from the customer loans. Branch video surveillance also confirmed that there were no customers at the branch manager's teller window at the time of the transactions. After the withdrawal of funds from the customer loans, the branch manager was seen placing cash into an envelope and leaving the branch.

Based upon the work performed, the conclusion was reached that the employee's pattern of activities was consistent with an unauthorized misappropriation of cash from customer accounts.

Case Study No. 2

Background

A forensics team was engaged by a bank to investigate loans made by a senior bank lending officer. The accusation had come to light when an elderly bank customer's family had complained to the bank that unauthorized transactions had been made in the name of the family member without his consent.

How the Fraud Was Committed

The lending officer had created loans not authorized by the customers and had made advances on these loans. The loan officer had instructed bank tellers to issue large money orders payable in the name of other banks, but he had not named the recipients of those funds on the money orders or placed this information in the memo or remitter line of the checks. The banks named in these money orders were banks in which the loan officer maintained accounts under his control or in the name of entities that were not recognizably associated with him. The loan officer then instructed the other bank to deposit these funds in the accounts he controlled.

The lending officer attempted to hide his activities by engaging in kiting schemes.

How the Fraud Was Investigated

The investigation involved a detailed analysis of money orders authorized by the lending officer and a detailed review of the lending officer's loan files and transactions.

Case Study No. 3

Background

A forensics team was engaged by a bank to investigate the bank's secondary mortgage department. The results of the investigation confirmed that the bank's secondary market loan officer had misappropriated funds held in escrow for property repairs and applied unused bank checks payable to the U.S. Department of Agriculture (USDA) for guarantee fees for purposes not originally intended. The investigation showed that some funds were used to make payments on unrelated borrower loans or to cover instances when the loan officer had previously misappropriated funds.

The investigation showed that the bank had a very lax system of internal controls related to the secondary mortgage department which facilitated the misappropriating of funds. In addition, the bank's internal audit department limited its audits of the department and excluded important aspects of the department's functions.

Major issues existed with the bank's collection, distribution, and controls over borrower repair funds for property improvements on purchased homes. Large amounts of funds were collected at closing ostensibly for repair, but distributed immediately to the borrowers. In several cases, these funds were disbursed before the actual closing transaction date. An unusual number of these repair distribution checks were cashed immediately.

The forensics team found a pattern whereby the loan officer went to unusual lengths to facilitate the closing of mortgage loans including the following:

- Waiver of discount fees
- Use of premiums on Freddie Mac loan sales to cover borrower closing costs, borrower costs for repairs, and other purposes
- Payments of repairs funds made directly to the borrower which could be used to fund closing costs, down payments, or other expenses
- Closing of USDA loans despite not having received the USDA guarantee

12

Other Complexities

Sue Evelsizer, CPA
Eric Stephens

Introduction

In a world trending toward greater business and economic globalization and integration, the same rules that help global businesses and entities work together can be manipulated for fraudster gain. This chapter is designed to address several topics with regulatory implications that fall squarely in the realm of topics that cross over accounting systems, laws, political borders, and other investigative entities. Particularly, money laundering, Sharia Finance Law, and relationships with investigative partners are sometimes overlooked as a topic outside the scope of typical fraud investigative considerations. However, understanding the basics of money laundering schemes and anti-money laundering legislation can help the fraud investigator understand the scope of those schemes; in a global economy, fraud investigations can count on fraudsters manipulating Sharia Finance Law; and many investigations will include extra challenges, working with other investigative partners. The relevance of these topics to the work of those involved in investigating fraud will also be explained.

Money Laundering

Those involved in fraud investigations and other related types of investigations need to have a solid understanding of money laundering and anti-money laundering laws. The Financial Action Task Force observed the following:

> Money laundering is a threat to the good functioning of a financial system; however, it can be the Achilles heel of criminal activity. In law enforcement investigations into organised criminal activity, it is often the connections made through financial transactions records that allow hidden assets to be located and that establish the identity of the criminals and the criminal organisation responsible. When criminal funds are derived from robbery, extortion, embezzlement or fraud, a money laundering investigation is frequently the only way to locate the stolen funds and restore them to the victims.[1]

---

[1] Financial Action Task Force, "Money Laundering," accessed May 1, 2012, www.fatf-gafi.org/document/29/0,3746,en_32250379_32235720_33659613_1_1_1_1,00.html.

Money laundering is the process through which illicitly obtained funds are processed (or "washed") to disguise their illegal origins. Although money laundering was initially associated with organized crime or illegal drug activity, in more recent years, it has become a major tool to disguise terrorist funding activity. Thus, money laundering represents a substantial economic problem on a global scale.

Typically, money laundering involves three stages: placement, layering, and integration. These stages are described as follows:

1. *Placement.* Actual placement of cash obtained through illegal activity. This cash, usually in substantial amounts, may be deposited in a series of financial institutions. In fact, in the era of global business, it is becoming increasingly common for fraudsters to use off-shore financial institutions to house laundered cash.

2. *Layering.* Layering illicit funds in complex transactions. This step is taken in an effort to disguise and separate the funds from the original source. Layering may begin with a base of domestic or off-shore accounts, which are then used to purchase tangible goods, such as real estate, artwork, luxury goods, exotic collections, automobiles, precious metals, jewelry, or monetary instruments. Eventually, these items are sold, and the cash or proceeds derived from the sale are returned to the fraudster.

3. *Integration.* Injecting illicitly obtained funds back into the economy. This is often done by investing in regular businesses or other profit generating enterprises as "cover," because this gives an appearance of legitimacy. In some situations, investments are made through cross-border shell company structures (using multiple currencies), making it much harder for fraud investigators to trace illegitimate funds.

There have been a series of federal laws aimed at curbing money laundering. The earliest law is the Bank Secrecy Act (BSA), which was passed in 1970. The agency charged with administering this law is the Financial Crimes Enforcement Network (FinCEN), a bureau within the U.S. Department of the Treasury (the Treasury), which has as its mission "to enhance the integrity of financial systems by facilitating the detection and deterrence of financial crime." The BSA addresses record keeping and reporting requirements concerning cash transactions. The BSA has been amended through various federal acts in the years since its adoption. The laws are referred to as anti-money laundering (AML) or AML/counter-financing terrorism (CFT) laws. FinCEN has broad powers under AML/CFT laws, as explained on its website:

> The basic concept underlying FinCEN's core activities is "follow the money." The primary motive of criminals is financial gain, and they leave financial trails as they try to launder the proceeds of crimes or attempt to spend their ill-gotten profits. FinCEN partners with law enforcement at all levels of government and supports the nation's foreign policy and national security objectives. Law enforcement agencies successfully use similar techniques, including searching information collected by FinCEN from the financial industry, to investigate and hold accountable a broad range of criminals, including perpetrators of fraud, tax evaders, and narcotics

traffickers. More recently, the techniques used to follow money trails also have been applied to investigating and disrupting terrorist groups, which often depend on financial and other support networks.[2]

FinCEN provides rules and guidance related to a number of "financial institutions," a term that encompasses far more institutions than commonly thought. For example, casinos fall under this classification because of the wide array of financial services they offer. Those involved in the investigation of fraud and white collar crime should bookmark FinCEN's website, www.fincen.gov, and perhaps subscribe to its e-mail alerts (the service is offered without charge) to stay up to date.

Among the laws passed since the BSA, the Money Laundering Control Act, passed in 1986, is notable because it elevated money laundering to a federal crime. It also prohibited structuring transactions to evade BSA requirements. *Structuring* means breaking down a transaction that would otherwise be reportable under the BSA into smaller transactions for the sole purpose of evading reporting. This law also introduced civil and criminal forfeiture for BSA violations, and it directed banks to design procedures to ensure compliance with the BSA.

The USA PATRIOT Act[3] was signed into law following the terrorist attacks of September 2001. The act substantially enhanced the ability of law enforcement agencies to search various communications, financial records, and other domestic and foreign intelligence data within the United States. Additionally, the act expanded the Treasury's authority to regulate financial transactions, particularly those involving foreign individuals and entities. It also broadened the discretion of law enforcement and immigration authorities in detaining or deporting immigrants suspected of terrorism related acts. The act also expanded the definition of terrorism to include domestic terrorism.[4]

Today, many foreign governments support compliance with USA PATRIOT Act provisions surrounding the detection and prosecution of money laundering activities. Additional AML/CFT laws have been passed, and FinCEN's website is a good resource for obtaining further information on that topic.

Under pressure from the U.S. government, foreign countries are cooperating on a mass scale to address money laundering and minimize the flow of illicit money into the global economy. A key tool in that effort is the Foreign Corrupt Practices Act (FCPA), under which U.S. businesses and foreign government officials can face serious penalties if found guilty of illicit acts. While these violations occur throughout the world, violations have been increasing in regions such as South America, Asia, and the Middle East.

Although virtually all market sectors with global reach have had some FCPA-related violations, the telecommunications industry has been hit harder than most. As the global

---

[2] Financial Crimes Enforcement Network, "What We Do," accessed May 1, 2012, www.fincen.gov/about_fincen/wwd/.

[3] US Government Printing Office: Public Law 107-56 – Uniting and Strengthening America by Providing Appropriate Tools Required to Intercept and Obstruct Terrorism (USA PATRIOT Act) Act of 2001.

[4] *Id.*

economy changes and grows, many foreign governments have become increasingly willing to privatize their telecommunications sectors. To do so, these governments often allow the state-owned telecommunications firms to negotiate joint ventures with outside telecom providers. Due to complex licensing requirements established by many of these governments, it is not uncommon for officials working with outside telecom providers to demand payments (either directly or indirectly) in return for certain accommodations or permits.

For instance, one such situation involved numerous payments made from an outside telecom provider to a government official's spouse, who allegedly worked at the state-run telecommunications firm. A subsequent investigation determined the spouse was not—and never had been—an employee of that business. Under the FCPA, such payments are clearly illegal, because they are not made in the "normal" course of business operations.

Money Laundering and Terrorist Funding

In addition to money laundering connections with FCPA-related activity, another widening problem is how this scheme is being used to support funding for terrorist groups.

Unlike conventional money laundering, which is funded through illicit sources, terrorist funding usually starts with legitimate assets, such as private donations or funds from charitable organizations and businesses, and involves transfers of funds by way of financial support to terrorist organizations and activities. To cover their tracks, terror-sponsoring organizations take great effort to prevent disclosures of either funding sources or its role as a beneficiary of the cash.

With worldwide attention directed toward slowing the growth of terrorist groups, a major effort is underway to investigate, pursue, and cut-off all funding sources. Although this is a global endeavor, a critical focal point for this initiative is the Middle East. However, tracking terror-related funding in this region is quite challenging, given the limited state of political cooperation between the United States and these nations.

Compounding the political challenges, traditional Middle Eastern banking practices seldom allow for full disclosure of funding and investment sources. Culturally, these countries have endorsed generations of bank and financial secrecy (see the section "Sharia Finance Law" in this chapter for further discussion). From an economic perspective, these bank secrecy laws and a strong sense of anonymity have contributed to challenges in meeting global anti-money laundering initiatives. For example, a substantial number of transactions in the Middle East take place through "unofficial" financial institutions. Because most transactions through these institutions are not formally recorded, the detection of any money laundering or terrorist funding activity is hindered.

Despite these hurdles, progress is being made, as several Middle Eastern governments have taken a more active role in improving financial transparency. Regional AML initiatives, virtually nonexistent just a few years ago, are now being highlighted through organizations such as the Middle East and North Africa Financial Action Task Force, headquartered in Bahrain.

Money Laundering and Illegal Drug Activity

In addition to efforts to slow terrorist funding, the United States has also taken a strong stance on money laundering fueled by illicit drug traffic. This billion-dollar black market has attracted the attention of the Treasury, which has cracked down on tracking and prosecuting money transfer activities in targeted countries. The goal is to stem proceeds from the sale of illicit drugs, which are regularly funneled through major money exchanges and subsequently transferred through global financial institutions.

Regardless of whether money laundering activity occurred through illicit means or legitimate businesses, it can be detected through various tools. The most common tool is tracking illicit activity under AML reporting requirements, which are required of individuals, companies, and financial institutions. In addition, successful money laundering investigations often begin through audits by external firms and relevant tax authorities. The United States and other nations now have much better systems to gather and dissect intelligence data on terror groups, which makes it easier to track money laundering through examination and review of tangible evidence.

Convergence of AML and FCPA

Although risk mitigation and compliance with AML and FCPA have historically been viewed independent of one other, a new paradigm is emerging. Today, AML compliance requires a holistic view that includes risks related not only to FCPA, but also to fraud, tax evasion, and other criminal activity related to financial transactions. Because many large U.S. and European financial institutions have kept FCPA compliance separate from AML, this new imperative might eventually lead to convergence, which would provide for improved detection, enhanced investigations, and significant cost savings.[5]

Under this new paradigm, an AML compliance officer focuses on three specific risk areas:

1. The risk of providing services to persons whose funds may have originated from public corruption. Of the three risk categories, this may be the easiest to detect if AML protocols are robust. Virtually all financial institutions have (or should have) mechanisms for identifying risks related to politically exposed persons and other public officials in their screening systems.
2. The risk of facilitating corrupt payments to foreign officials by "legitimate" clients of the financial institution. Although such court cases historically have focused on corrupt officials, there is a trend toward prosecuting the financial institutions that accepted corrupt proceeds in transit or as deposits. This may involve personal liability, both civil and criminal, for officers and directors of a financial institution if they knew, should have known, or were willfully blind to such activity.
3. The risk that a financial institution is engaging in public corruption by making payments to gain business advantage. As financial institutions expand into global markets, there is a growing likelihood of the need to secure permits and licenses while seeking additional revenue from public sources (such as pension or sovereign funds). This activity

---

[5]   Law Journal Newsletters, *Business Crimes Bulletin*, 17 (February 2010).

raises the likelihood that lenders will conduct business with foreign public officials under the FCPA.

U.S. law enforcement officials and federal agencies view compliance with FCPA and AML rules as a national security imperative. As a result, increasing numbers of regulators across the globe are developing strict money laundering examination and compliance procedures. Failures to meet those standards have led to stiff fines and, in the case of the FCPA, a number of criminal convictions.

Sharia Finance Law

Sharia law deals with many aspects of the Muslim daily life such as economics, banking, and politics. It serves as the legal framework for the pblic and private aspects of Muslim life and is regulated for those living in a legal system based on Islamic principles of jurisprudence.

Sharia law is now the most widely used religious law and is one of the three most common legal systems of the world alongside common law and civil law and is gaining more momentum throughout the world. Once considered a fundamental legal framework in the middle east and Muslim countries, the introduction to Sharia law is now more prevalent and with a global footprint.

As of 2009, approximately 23% of the world population is Muslim.[6] Of these, approximately 62% live in Asia–Pacific,[7] 62% in the Middle East–North Africa,[8] 15% in Sub–Saharan Africa,[9] 3% in Europe[10] and 0.3% in the Americas.[11,12,13,14] The expansion of this geographic Muslim footprint has resulted in increased levels of demand and use of Sharia law (see figure 12-1.)

There has been a significant amount of interest to introduce the principles of Sharia law into the U.S. marketplace as a result of an increase in the U.S. Muslim population. Consequently, some U.S. financial institutions have implemented Sharia law compliant entities to cater to this market.

Often referred to as Islamic finance, Sharia law is derived primarily from fundamental Islamic tents found in the Koran. The standards of Sharia finance laws are summarized as a guide to the Muslim financial and investment community primarily by the Accounting and Auditing Organization for Islamic Financial Institutions (AAOIFI) and the Islamic Financial Services Board (IFSB).

---

6   "Executive Summary." The Future of the Global Muslim Population. Pew Research Center. 27 January 2011.
7   "Region: Asia-Pacific." The Future of the Global Muslim Population. Pew Research Center.
8   "Region: Middle East-North Africa." The Future of the Global Muslim Population. Pew Research Center.
9   "Region: Sub-Saharan Africa." The Future of the Global Muslim Population. Pew Research Center.
10 "Region: Europe." The Future of the Global Muslim Population. Pew Research Center.
11 "Region: Americas." The Future of the Global Muslim Population. Pew Research Center.
12 "Tom Kington (31 March 2008). "Number of Muslims ahead of Catholics, says Vatican." The Guardian
13 "Muslim Population." IslamicPopulation.com.
14 "Field Listing - Religions"

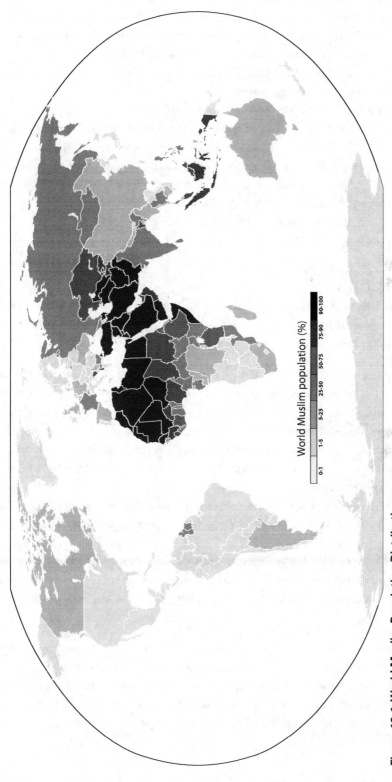

Figure 12-1: World Muslim Population Distribution

Fundamentally, Sharia finance law observes the overall framework of a market economy, supporting competition, supply and demand, and free enterprise. This form of finance operates primarily under the premise of a profit enterprise from the sale of tangible goods and provided services. Like U.S. and European banks, Islamic banks operate also under a profit basis, though revenues for Islamic banks are earned primarily through activities in trading, leasing, and profit and loss sharing contracts.[15]

Sharia finance law is gaining increased visibility, particularly in the Far East, Asia, and the United Kingdom, largely due to a broad spectrum of industries in those markets seeking new opportunities in the Middle East. That growth, coupled with increasing demands by regulatory bodies, investors, and Islamic financial institutions, has driven increased calls for adapting Sharia finance law in a more consistent financial reporting basis, such as International Financial Reporting Standards (IFRSs). The following sections will provide an overview of Sharia finance law, with an emphasis on its prohibitions, banking, challenges, and internal controls.

Prohibitions

Although there are numerous prohibitions central to Islamic finance, compliance with these restrictions from an IFRSs or GAAP perspective is not impossible. The main prohibitions include the following:

- *Riba*. Riba is a prohibition on paying interest. This term refers to the receipt and payment of interest or other usurious payments that are prohibited under Islamic finance law. More specifically, riba refers to any compensation for which consideration is not exchanged. This prohibition however, does not apply to a time value of money calculation. In order to accommodate certain Western financial products, such as mortgages, credit cards, and savings accounts, Sharia finance allows the use of certain programs and methods that meet its unique requirements.
- *Maisir*. Maisir generally refers to gambling or "games of chance," and it is prohibited under the tenets of Sharia finance. As such, any contracts and transactions based on gambling activity are strictly prohibited.
- *Gharar*. Gharar is used to describe speculative actions, especially those involving high risk or unknown variables. Gharar is prohibited under Sharia finance, and this restriction applies to transactions that include (among others) hedging or derivative contracts, short sales, forwards, and option contracts.

In addition to the restrictions noted previously, Sharia finance prohibits any investments in businesses that trade in non–Islamic values, including alcohol, gambling, pork, pornography, drugs, and tobacco. Sharia-compliant transactions must be ethically based; represent tangible assets, products, or services; and use clear, transparent, and fair practices. All Sharia–compliant transactions must be free from misrepresentation and fraud. For these reasons, financial

---

[15] Muhammad Ayub, *Understanding Islamic Finance* (West Sussex, England: Wiley, 2007), 129.

institutions with stellar reputations for honest, transparent practices have seen tremendous growth in Islamic finance assets.

Banking

Islamic banking principles are consistent with Sharia finance guidelines. Profits and losses, as overall risks, are shared in common with bank customers. Although these banks cannot charge interest, they can realize profit by executing formal investment contracts with customers to purchase real property. Additionally, a central theme of Islamic finance is that money itself has no value—it is simply a medium of exchange. Each monetary unit is 100 percent equal in value to another unit of the same denomination. For that reason, profit by way of exchanging cash with another person is disallowed.

The following are some key terms used in Islamic banking:

- *Sukuk*. Sukuk is an Islamic financial certificate, similar to a bond, that complies with Sharia finance. Because an interest-paying bond structure is not permissible, the issuer of a sukuk sells the certificate to an investor group, which then rents it back to the issuer for a predetermined fee. The issuer also makes a contractual promise to buy back the certificate at a future date at par value. If properly constructed, a sukuk certificate must link all financing returns and cash flows to the assets purchased, because trading in debt is prohibited under Sharia finance. Financing may only be raised for identifiable assets.[16] Sukuk are gaining popularity as an alternative source of funding, particularly for sovereigns and corporate bodies, and the growth of this financing tool has been fueled by strong global demand in capital markets for Sharia-compliant instruments.[17] Standard & Poor's has estimated the market for Islamic financial products (that is, banking, mortgages, equity funds, sukuk, project finance, and so on) at approximately $400 billion.[18]

- *Murabaha*. Murabaha is a term commonly used in Islamic mortgage transactions. In essence, murabaha takes place when a financial institution purchases real estate on a customer's behalf and then allows the customer to buy back the property from the financial institution on an installment basis. With murabaha, one contract is executed between the financial institution and the real estate seller, while another contract establishes the transfer or sale of the property between the financial institution and the buyer at a specified price (including profit margin). As collateral, the financial institution maintains its status as the registered owner of the real property until the terms of the purchase contract are fulfilled.

- *Musharaka*. This term refers to a partnership or joint venture in which participants agree to a methodology for distributing profits and losses. These distributions are usually made according to the basis of contributed capital.

---

[16] See www.Investopedia.com
[17] Muhammad Ayub, *Understanding Islamic Finance* (West Sussex, England: Wiley, 2007), 388.
[18] *The Economist*, December 9–15, 2006, 73.

- *Ijara.* Ijara commonly refers to a lease situation. Essentially, an Islamic customer wishing to engage in a lease transaction would ask a financial institution to initially purchase the asset. The customer would then "rent" the subject asset from the financial institution for a specified amount (inclusive of a profit margin). Depending on the agreement, installment payments would either emulate a true lease (in which the asset would not transfer to the customer) or would be applied toward eventual purchase of the asset.

Sharia Compliance and Standards

Islamic banks, as well as banking institutions that offer Islamic banking products and services, are required to establish a Sharia supervisory board (SSB). The SSB is tasked with ensuring that all banking operations and activities comply with Sharia finance principles. In the bigger picture, standard-setting bodies and global facilitators such as the AAOIFI, IFSB, International Islamic Financial Market, and the Liquidity Management Center are building recognition for Islamic finance and enhancing its credibility among both customers and regulators.[19]

Challenges and Trends

The Islamic finance sector faces a number of challenges. Despite growing demand, a substantial challenge is developing investment products and financing activities that are compliant with Sharia principles. To address this need, many major financial institutions have established lending offices that are either wholly operated as Islamic banking centers or split out as Islamic banking divisions within the company.

On the regulatory side, challenges facing the framework of Islamic finance parallel issues all banks face in the concurrent integration of IFRSs global accounting standards. With that in mind, commonalities between IFRSs standards and Islamic finance are being examined, and countries in which Islamic finance is dominant are either integrating or preparing to integrate IFRSs into their standard control framework. Long-term, this integration may result in an integrated concept that combines Islamic finance standards within an IFRSs framework or the development of global Islamic finance standards.

Investigative Partners

Fraud investigators often encounter law enforcement agents and prosecutors in the course of the investigation. These agents include the Federal Bureau of Investigation (FBI); state attorney's offices; and state, county, or local police. In many cases, the client or client's counsel will have already contacted one or more of these law enforcement agencies before an investigation begins. Federal and state prosecutors often hire forensic accountants, particularly in situations in which law enforcement does not have the internal resources to conduct a fraud investigation.

---

[19] Muhammad Ayub, *Understanding Islamic Finance* (West Sussex, England: Wiley, 2007), 15.

Because each fraud investigation is unique, the relationship and interactions with law enforcement personnel varies from case to case. However, a fraud investigator's report or initial findings are frequently used as persuasive tools to jump start criminal investigations of fraud. This evolving partnership between forensic accountants and law enforcement is well illustrated by the following case study.

Example

When Judy Wagner was employed as director of litigation and valuation services at Meyners + Company, LLC, she was appointed as receiver for a New Mexico company. Upon taking control, her duties included a review of financial operations, during which she became deeply concerned. Wagner went to the U.S. Attorney's office and the FBI with a 5-inch binder of financial summary schedules, checks, e-mails, contracts, and other documents, all of which showed connections between individuals she suspected were sharing in illegal proceeds from a municipal construction project. As a result of this possible public corruption activity involving millions of dollars, the FBI launched an investigation to identify, obtain, and analyze key bank documents. Wagner assisted the FBI in locating handwritten notes, checks, and financial documents, which showed criminal activity on other municipal construction projects. Ultimately, 8 individuals pleaded guilty in a $4.3 million scheme to defraud New Mexico taxpayers. For her efforts, Wagner received the 2009 Director's Community Leadership Award from the Albuquerque Division of the FBI.*

*   www.fbi.gov/about-us/partnerships_and_outreach/community_outreach/dcla/2009/albuquerque

---

Working With Investigative Partners

As noted in chapter 4, there is a distinction between the civil and criminal processes. While each may be done separately, these processes may be done simultaneously. In either case, criminal investigative partners are typically involved in some fashion in the criminal process.

The level of work with investigative partners may depend on the type or stage of fraud case. Consider the following three examples:

1. Investigating suspected fraud

   a. Law enforcement agencies may not have been contacted by a client if the presence of fraud is possible but not certain. The client, client's counsel, or both may not want to involve law enforcement investigators until circumstances and documentation are verified in such a way that a reasonable, prudent professional could believe a fraud has occurred.

   b. Criminal prosecution by a law enforcement agency can be somewhat complicated if the client is unsure who to call or how to present his or her case. Law enforcement agencies are more inclined to advance a criminal case when the client presents a complaint in an orderly, well detailed fashion. This usually includes a written report, physical and documentary evidence, and any additional information needed to substantiate the allegation. The fraud investigator can assist with this report and act as a liaison with law enforcement agencies.

c. Fraud investigators do not normally disclose an apparent fraud to law enforcement authorities, regulators, or potential victims of a scheme without the clear consent of a client or the client's legal representative.

2. Investigating assertions of fraud

a. Law enforcement is more likely to have been notified when there is a specific allegation of fraud. In some cases, law enforcement may participate in the investigative process, which makes it important for the fraud investigator to establish early and regular communication with these agencies and prosecutors. In some cases, law enforcement may also have forensic specialists perform similar investigative procedures.

b. As previously discussed, law enforcement will frequently use reports that support assertions of fraud. Any physical or documentary evidence contained in a report may be used by law enforcement agents to extract confessions or corroborate information obtained through witness or perpetrator interviews.

3. Developing fraud loss estimates

a. Quantifying fraud losses is sometimes necessary to determine what type of criminal charges may be filed. A fraud investigator's written report, physical and documentary evidence, and any additional information needed to substantiate the allegation often help determine the monetary amount involved in a fraud scheme.

b. In some cases, additional information needed to substantiate monetary loss may not be available to a fraud investigator, particularly if the loss is due to skimming. However, the overall report typically provides law enforcement with the underlying facts necessary to continue an investigation. This may include subpoenas of a perpetrator's personal or third-party records to substantiate the loss amount.

c. The fraud investigator may be asked to testify as an expert witness related to work performed during the engagement.

As a general rule, law enforcement can interview witnesses, run undercover operations, analyze financial records, map and manage crime scenes, develop informants, make arrests, conduct surveillance, and gather information and intelligence. This work typically involves use of forensic investigative techniques,[20] which private fraud investigators and other specialists also perform under more limited circumstances. (See box 12-1.) Although a forensic specialist may sometimes recommend physical or electronic surveillance in a

---

[20] AICPA Fraud Task Force of Forensic and Litigation Services Committee, *Forensic Procedures and Specialists: Useful Tools and Techniques* (New York: AICPA, 2006).

fraud case, these experts generally would not participate directly in an undercover operation of this kind.

Box 12-1: Seven Forensic Investigative Techniques

1. Public document reviews and background investigation
2. Interviews of knowledgeable persons
3. Confidential sources
4. Laboratory analysis of physical and electronic evidence
5. Physical and electronic surveillance
6. Undercover
7. Analysis of financial transactions

In many investigations, collection and preservation of electronic data is critical to success, which is why it is important for forensic accountants to confer with experienced electronic data collection professionals during this part of an investigation. For example, assume that an alleged fraudster's computer or hard drive is confiscated at the start of an investigation. The fraud investigator then uses a duplicate copy for the investigation (or the original if a hard drive image has been made and preserved by those skilled in the collection of such data). However, if that electronic data had been improperly collected, the evidence may become inadmissible in court.

Another area in which law enforcement agencies, prosecutors, or attorneys should be consulted concerns the gathering and use of third-party records. Third-party records are those held by others outside of a client's control, such as banks, vendors, suppliers, investors, competitors, employees, CPAs, or tax advisers. Sometimes, third parties have records that corroborate a client's files or statements, and they may provide those copies voluntarily or informally. On the other hand, many third-party documents cannot be obtained without a formal request from the client or a subpoena. For example, if a forensic accountant secures a suspect's personal bank account statements from a cooperative bank teller without proper authorization or consent, it could make the evidence inadmissible in court.

The bottom line is that fraud investigators' findings may be helpful to law enforcement and prosecutors, provided that these agencies do not view the work as counterproductive to their investigation.

A key objective of a fraud investigation is to gather sufficient relevant data to help the client or trier of fact reach a conclusion on the merits of the suspected or alleged fraud. The fraud investigator's report can be a persuasive tool in convincing law enforcement officers that a criminal investigation is appropriate. The report contains information needed by criminal investigators and helps them identify witnesses, obtain documentary support, and prepare record analysis. For that reason, law enforcement officers will ask for information and reports from the forensic investigation. The fraud investigator should be aware that communication with law enforcement is usually a one-way street. Law enforcement officers typically will not be at liberty to discuss the status of criminal investigations with the forensic accountant. Although these investigative partners may pursue additional information as suggested by the fraud investigator, the fraud investigator will likely not be provided access to that information and may, in fact, not be part of the investigation beyond his or her initial investigative report. Nonetheless, if the client or client's counsel has contacted law enforcement agencies or prosecutors, it is important for the fraud investigator to establish communication with those parties early and regularly. If no such contact has been made, it is important for the fraud investigator to obtain permission from his or her client or client's counsel before disclosing the investigative report to other investigative partners.

Investigative Partner: FBI

The FBI's Financial Crimes Section oversees the investigation of financial fraud via several dedicated subgroups, including the asset forfeiture or money laundering unit, economic crimes unit, healthcare fraud unit, forensic accountant unit, and national mortgage fraud team. In 2007, Joseph L. Ford, associate FBI director, addressed the AICPA National Conference on Fraud and Litigation Services. In his speech, he noted that FBI CPAs and private forensic accountants were both crucial to uncovering illicit activity at Columbia/HCA and Enron—two of the biggest fraud cases in modern history.

In his remarks, Ford described the FBI and private forensic accounting partnership as follows:

> Aside from Enron, the number of corporate fraud cases the FBI opened increased over 300 percent from 2001 to 2005. The FBI worked closely with partners in government and the private sector—including many CPA firms — to investigate these scandals and put the scammers behind bars. This approach has been highly successful. Our collaborative efforts have resulted in almost 1,100 indictments and over 850 convictions. But we still have over 500 open cases. Many of them involve shareholder losses of over $1 billion. We depend upon our financial investigators within the Bureau. And we also depend on our partners.[21]

Despite this strong internal endorsement, budgetary woes hinder the FBI from doing even more to fight fraud. A 2008 *New York Times* article[22] reported that the bureau slashed its criminal investigation workforce in favor of an expanded national security role after the 2001 terrorist attacks, shifting more than one-third of all agents in criminal programs to terrorism and intelligence duties. Current and former officials say the cutbacks have left the bureau seriously exposed in investigating areas such as white collar crime, which has taken on urgent importance due to the nation's economic woes. In fact, the FBI's

---

[21] Joseph L. Ford, Associate Debut Director, Federal Bureau of Investigation, "Address to the American Institute of Certified Public Accountants National Conference on Fraud and Litigation Services," September 27, 2007.

[22] Eric Lichtblau, David Johnston, and Ron Nixon "FBI Struggles to Handle Financial Fraud Cases," *New York Times,* October 18, 2008.

white collar investigative ranks are depleted enough that private sector executives say they have difficulty getting assistance on possible frauds involving millions of dollars. For that reason, the Department of Justice is relying more than ever on state and local joint task forces to pick up the slack. In some instances, private investigative and accounting firms are now collecting evidence, taking witness statements, and even testifying before grand juries in order to prepare courtroom-ready prosecutions that can be taken to the FBI or local authorities.

Investigative Partners: State Attorney's Office and Local Law Enforcement

A U.S. state attorney is, most commonly, an elected official who represents the state in criminal prosecutions. This person is often the chief law enforcement officer in a given judicial circuit, frequently acting as chief counsel for city, county, or state police within his or her jurisdiction. Accordingly, although local law enforcement may assist in a fraud investigation, such activity is frequently monitored or directed by the state's attorney's office.

Because most U.S. state's attorney and local law enforcement officers do not have in-house forensic accountants or budgets that allow the hiring of forensic accountants, most fraud investigators are hired by victimized entities or their legal counsel. Thus, fraud investigators should ask the client or client's counsel whether law enforcement has been contacted and determine what information the client wishes to voluntarily turn over to law enforcement officers or prosecutors. Once an investigation begins, fraud investigators should work closely with the prosecutor, ensuring that they always comply with legal requirements in the gathering and verification of evidence. Thus, if the client has already contacted authorities, a fraud investigator must still communicate with the local FBI, state attorney's office, or local law enforcement early in an investigation to ensure collaborative direction and instruction.

Conclusion

There is no shortage of complications when fraud investigations begin to expand in size and scope. In general, if a case that has the possibility of growing beyond investigating internal assets, the fraud investigator needs to adjust his or her layers of consideration to the possibility of external investigative partners. Working across national borders can sometimes result in investigations that include IFRSs considerations and specifically as they relate to Sharia Finance Law. Additionally, borders and layers of financial systems make it easy for money launderers to manipulate the rules guiding those systems.

Understanding how investigations can expand will help with decision-making processes discussed in the first section of this book, "Armed with Knowledge." As globalization continues to trend, there will be additional systems and considerations to make difficult fraud investigations even more complex. What is shared among the topics discussed in this chapter is the need for fraud investigators to have the ability to broaden the scope of their investigation appropriately, and when necessary.

Additional Resources

Business Valuation and Forensic & Litigation Services Section, *Practice Aid 07-1, Forensic Accounting-Fraud Investigations*, AICPA, 2007, New York, New York.

Business Valuation and Forensic & Litigation Services Section, *Special Report, Forensic Procedures and Specialists: Useful Tools and Techniques,* AICPA, 2006, New York, New York.

"Danger Ahead," A Guide to Conducting Successful Fraud Investigations, By Paul E. Zikmund, CFE, CFFA, CFD, *National Litigation Consultants' Review,* Volume 8, Issue 8, January 2009.

Modeling a Fraud Examination, *Fraud Magazine,* www.fraud-magazine.com.

FBI Struggles to handle Financial Fraud Cases, *New York Times,* October 19, 2008.

Joseph L. Ford, Associate Debut Director, Federal Bureau of Investigation. Address to the American Institute of Certified Public Accountants National Conference on Fraud and Litigation Services, September 27, 2007.

www.fbi.gov.

Various states' attorney's general websites.

Section IV

Advanced Concepts

Working the Case

Christyn Grommesh
Christopher J. Rice
Matthew Wolf
Randal A. Wolverton, CPA/CFF, CFE

> Legal Foundations of Fraud Investigations
>
> On- and Off-the-Books Fraud Schemes
>
> Civil Process and Criminal Procedure
>
> Jury Instructions
>
> Regulatory Complexities
>
> Working the Case
>
> Find It and Fix It

Introduction

Fraud schemes are as unique as they are pervasive, which is why there is no one recipe for a successful fraud investigation. The purpose of this chapter is to help fraud investigators understand the context of common fraud schemes and then effectively work the case, applying proven investigation methodologies in order to uncover the truth. The skill with which a case is conducted and presented can have a significant impact on the value of the work performed, particularly when the case becomes part of litigation. Working a case successfully involves both strong fundamental knowledge of fraudulent activity and skill in getting to the truth, as well as presenting convincing evidence to others.

The purpose of this chapter is to present strategies for effective case management. More specifically, this chapter will help a fraud investigator to

- apply the fraud theory approach,
- perform an initial case assessment,
- understand why individuals and groups commit fraud,
- understand the characteristics of the persons who commit occupational fraud,
- frame an asset search (for both known and hidden assets),
- understand the complexities of international fraud searches,
- perform effective interviews,
- use visual devices in an investigation,
- ensure proper handling of evidence, and
- understand the best evidence rule.

Using the Fraud Theory Approach

The fraud theory approach[1] has four basic steps:

1. Analyze available data
2. Create a hypothesis
3. Test the hypothesis
4. Refine and amend the hypothesis

In describing the fraud theory approach, the Association of Certified Fraud Examiners (ACFE) cautions fraud examiners to assume that every case will end in litigation. This is an important reason for ensuring that the examiner maintains a scientific approach. One must begin with an assumption based upon known data and postulate a theory, test it, and revise it as additional information becomes available.[2]

Fraud investigators should understand that the fraud theory approach has been well publicized in the profession and online, and it will be used by competent counsel. Fraud investigators who vary from these recognized procedures without adequate explanation can be vulnerable to intense cross examination. Therefore, familiarity with existing and well-recognized procedures becomes even more important to fraud investigators.

A case when the fraud theory approach was utilized was for a company that a firm was investigating due to a known, ongoing embezzlement. It is important to understand that steps of the fraud theory approach do not always fall into the sequential order that follows.

1. *Analyze available data.* In this case, the data available to the firm consisted of interviews of the key individuals within the company via telephone and policy documentation

---

[1]   Robertson, Jack. *Fraud Examination for Managers and Auditors.* Viesca Books, 2003.

[2]   Association of Certified Fraud Examiners (ACFE), *2011 Fraud Examiners Manual* (2011).

describing the revenue process for the company. Some key admissions had already been made concerning embezzlement of rebate checks. So, in this case, the investigative team had a lead on the nature of the embezzlement. The goal was to establish a hypothesis of how the embezzlement was committed, who else may have been involved, and how much money was embezzled. It was important at the outset of the case to assume that the admission made by the fraudster may have been nothing more than the tip of the iceberg.

2. *Create a hypothesis.* Based on the compiled information, the team formed a hypothesis regarding the actual process by which the fraudster was able embezzle funds, other potential ways monies could have been embezzled, and what steps would be necessary to provide the evidence of the fraud and establish the dollar loss. To formulate a working hypothesis, the team interviewed the accounting clerk to learn the processes and procedures surrounding the cash receipts and disbursement processes. Interviewing is a very important procedure that is performed in every case. By reviewing the policy documentation during the first step of the process, fraud examiners learn what *should* be happening within a certain process. However, by interviewing individuals that are "in the trenches" of performing specific duties, the examiners can learn what is *actually* occurring in these processes and more times than not learn that what should be happening does *not* mirror what is actually happening. Interviewing skills are addressed in depth later in this chapter.

Specific to the case example, the investigators learned that the fraudster was opening the mail, when processes dictated that a completely different individual should have been opening the mail. The initial hypothesis was that the fraudster was able to commit the embezzlement by skimming because she opened the mail prior to the checks being recorded in the books and records. Although the existing evidence suggested that rebate checks were clearly involved, based upon what was learned about the processes for handling incoming checks, there was a risk that other thefts could possibly be involved. Other comments regarding the processes led the investigators to question whether there were weaknesses in the cash disbursement process that allowed the company to be vulnerable to additional forms of fraud. At this stage, the team had a working idea of the procedures that would be helpful to test the hypothesis.

3. *Testing the hypothesis.* This stage of the investigation is the longest and most involved. In this case example, some specific investigative procedures included the following:

   a. The team created flowcharts to show the processes involved in handling cash receipts and disbursements. As will be discussed later in the chapter, such visual tools may be used both to guide the investigator and as a tool for demonstrating to juries how it was possible to commit a theft.

   b. The investigative team also exported cash disbursements and receipt reports from the accounting system.

   c. They then reviewed the supporting documentation of the transactions identified on the reports exported.

d. In addition to evaluating the support for the transactions listed, the team also performed data mining procedures on the electronic information obtained from the accounting records to look for trends and patterns in the data that might warrant further work.

4. *Refine and amend the hypothesis.* Through the combination of all of these procedures, the initial hypothesis was materially amended. Although the fraudster had admitted to taking rebate checks coming into the company and purportedly wanted to "make things right" by giving back the money, it turns out that this individual had stolen many incoming checks and her access to checks and accounting records made it possible for her to embezzle additional company funds through the disbursement process.

In testing and amending the hypothesis, it is very beneficial to review the gathered data more than one time. This is because the more times the data is reviewed, the better examiners can understand the story the data is telling. Consider for a moment watching a movie or reading a book. The first time through, one usually does not notice all of the intricacies of the plot line. However, during the second or third time of watching the movie or reading the book, one picks up on the details and meaning of the story becomes clearer and richer.

In working an investigation, examiners potentially have mountains of data to work through. Upon a first reading, the investigator notes certain information, but he or she is not aware of its relevance. Later, another document may shed light on the significance of information in the documents reviewed earlier. The pieces of the puzzle get a little clearer. As the data collection process plays out, the investigator begins to bring order and meaning to the combination of statements made by those interviewed, documents, and analytical data. The refinement of the hypothesis and its testing is an iterative and circular process.

Performing an Initial Case Assessment

Although taking a methodical, scientific approach that starts with analyzing available data is crucial, it is important when taking that first step to manage the information in an effective and efficient manner. When cases are first referred to forensic accountants, it is important for them to assess (or "triage") all available information. Without this quick initial review, the overall workload may increase, the chances of obtaining accurate information may be reduced, and the overall prospects for project success may be reduced or even eliminated.

Because the initial details about a case may be fluid, fraud investigators should carefully analyze the source (or sources), reliability, and timeliness of information, for example whether information coming from an anonymous rumor mill or from named persons. Thoughtful, appropriate questions at this stage may either refute the initial information (thus heading off a full scale investigation) or draw out enough detail to warrant further scrutiny.

After this initial vetting process, an investigator's next "triage" steps involve three key points:

1. *Gaining a clear understanding of the issues to resolve.* The scope of a case should be fully developed and understood as soon as possible. For example, does a fraud involve a violation of company policy, a human resource issue, a civil issue, or possibly criminal

violations? By clarifying this scope, clear investigative objectives can be formulated, allowing for proper allocation of resources. Bear in mind that any investigative plan can be evaluated and changed as new information is developed.

2. *Determining the status of financial losses.* Early in a case, forensic accountants will want to determine if potential fraud-related financial losses are complete or if further losses are a possibility unless the scheme is stopped immediately. If the latter is true, it is important to note that stopping the losses will notify the fraudsters of discovery, possibly resulting in the loss of valuable evidence that can make—or break—the overall case.

3. *Knowing who is aware of initial allegations.* If fraud allegations are not widely known, the investigator should assess what can be informally observed prior to interviews or formal evidence-gathering procedures. This soft investigative technique can yield valuable information that can be used in later interviews. Fresh evidence is preferable to dated information, because a fraudster may falsely claim lack of memory regarding older details.

Once these steps are taken, forensic accountants can then determine who should be interviewed. Under most circumstances, it is logical to start with persons having knowledge of processes and procedures under review, then progress to persons suspected of having knowledge about the alleged fraud. Generally, witnesses who are leaving (or have left) an organization should be interviewed first, because it is easier to secure interviews with current employees. Be aware that if witnesses are being intimidated or threatened with retaliation, those interviews may need to be expedited.

As mentioned earlier, the manner in which an investigation proceeds can affect how—and when—evidence is collected. For example, if no soft investigative techniques are in place before interviews begin, fraudsters may alter or destroy critical evidence and documents. For that reason, investigators should address timelines and techniques for evidence gathering as part of their initial assessment and action plan.

Understanding Why Individuals and Groups Commit Fraud

Donald Cressey's fraud triangle is the most prominent explanation for determining what elements lead to fraud. The theory states that the following elements are present when fraud is committed:

1. *Opportunity.* The fraudster must have the ability to commit the fraud. Typically, this involves a gap in the internal controls of the victim organization that enables the fraud to take place. This is something largely in the control of the organization, though no system of internal control can provide more than reasonable assurance. The value of

any control can be eliminated through collusion among employees or management override.

2. *Pressure or motivation.* This factor rests with the individual and may involve such things as greed, a desire for control, extreme financial needs, or dissatisfaction with wages or working conditions. Cressey's study of criminals showed that most committed fraud out of financial need. However, as the explanations and examples presented subsequently will show, there may be other complex reasons people get caught up in fraud.

3. *Rationalization.* In addition to having some type of pressure or motivation, the fraudster must somehow rationalize that his or her actions are not criminal and that they do not make him or her a "bad person." The rationalizations are highly personal to each potential fraudster. Some typical rationalizations might include that the fraudster was only trying to borrow money, not steal it. The fraudster may feel that he or she is not being properly compensated and that essentially the thefts represent wages in kind.

For those not facing challenges in meeting basic living expenses, the term "fraud based on desire" can be used to describe the pressure or motivation.

Fraud Based on Desire

Fraudsters will often scheme to finance personal hobbies, such as sailing or collecting classic cars. Thus, it is important for an investigator to seek out what a fraudster enjoyed doing in both personal and professional life. Evidence may be available that shows that the suspected fraudster was financing expensive collections, hobbies, or other activities and that the combination of these expenses on top of other living expenses exceeded the known and legitimate sources of income and accumulated wealth.

Fraud Based on Necessity

While some fraudsters use illicit money to fund extravagance, other fraudsters take the funds to stay one step ahead of creditors, and therefore their actions could be described as fraud committed out of economic necessity. Frauds based on necessity are committed to cover the following problems:

- *Debt:* Whether corporate or personal, high levels of debt can cause individuals to commit fraud. While many fraudsters know what they are doing is wrong, they often choose to commit illicit acts rather than file for bankruptcy or default on loans.

- *Other obligations:* Other obligations can include items such as spousal support (or alimony), property rental, or leases. Spousal support is a common motive because divorce as a result of a failed (or failing) business is common. In many cases, an alimony amount that one ex-spouse would have no trouble paying under normal circumstances can become a crushing burden if business goes bad. Under those circumstances, that ex-spouse may turn to fraud rather than admit that he or she is no longer able to make the payments.

- *Addictions:* Addictions take many shapes, including drugs, gambling, and shopping. Although addictions may seem to fit the first category of fraud motives (fraud based on desire), the person who commits fraud to support an addiction is not doing so for "the thrill of it." Instead, the addict operates out of need—often turning to non-sophisticated methods of fraud.

Example: Fraud Based on Desire

For more than a decade, Denny Hecker was a respected Minnesota businessman. At the peak of his material success, he owned 26 car dealerships, a leasing and fleet business, a mortgage brokerage business, Advantage Rent-a-Car, and several real estate and restaurant holdings.[1] In 2004, he led a group of investors that (unsuccessfully) attempted to purchase the Minnesota Vikings.[2]

In 2008, Hecker ran into trouble. As credit tightened during the financial downturn, he lost access to lines of credit he needed to keep his businesses operating. In November 2008, he even sued Chrysler Financial Services, alleging the company wrongfully suspended his lines of credit.[3] Shortly thereafter, he filed for personal bankruptcy by claiming $787 million in debt and $18.5 million in assets.[4] Still, he owned a 52-foot yacht and private jet, exquisite cars, and multimillion dollar homes. He traveled to luxurious destinations, visited Las Vegas casinos, and bought furs, jewelry, and other extravagant gifts for friends.[5]

With his businesses collapsing around him, Hecker turned to fraud, funneling money in complex schemes between his interrelated business enterprises. Ultimately, he was indicted on money laundering and wire fraud charges, the former of which was later dropped.[6] He was eventually sentenced in 2011 to 10 years in prison, the maximum allowable sentence under federal law for his crimes. In addition, a federal bankruptcy judge ordered Hecker to pay $31 million in restitution. Despite his personal bankruptcy filing, he also owes approximately $767 million to other creditors.[7]

Clearly, Hecker was addicted to living extravagantly. But when he turned to illegal acts to maintain his lifestyle, his own comments reveal a personality common to many fraudsters.

"I did it (committed fraud) because my ego was so big ... I thought I could conquer anything," Hecker said.[8]

---

[1]   Amy Forliti, "Ex-Minn. auto mogul gets 10 years for fraud," www.businessweek.com/ap/financialnews/D9LAO1IG0.htm.

[2]   *Id.*

[3]   Madeleine Baran, "Timeline: The Denny Hecker saga," http://minnesota.publicradio.org/display/web/2010/02/10/hecker-timeline/.

[4]   Martin Moylan, "Denny Hecker sentenced to 10 years for fraud," http://minnesota.publicradio.org/display/web/2011/02/11/hecker-sentenced/.

[5]   Amy Forliti, "Ex-Minn. auto mogul gets 10 years for fraud," www.businessweek.com/ap/financialnews/D9LAO1IG0.htm.

[6]   Madeleine Baran, "Timeline: The Denny Hecker saga," http://minnesota.publicradio.org/display/web/2010/02/10/hecker-timeline/.

[7]   *Id.*

[8]   Martin Moylan, "Denny Hecker sentenced to 10 years for fraud," http://minnesota.publicradio.org/display/web/2011/02/11/hecker-sentenced/.

Characteristics of Persons Who Commit Occupational Fraud

A fraudster does not necessarily stand out from the rest of the crowd and in fact could be someone who people would never suspect. Nevertheless, studies of numerous fraud cases show some patterns with regard to the characteristics of those who commit fraud. The ACFE conducts periodic surveys regarding fraud cases and publishes the findings of this work in its report to the nations which it makes available on its website, www.acfe.com. Its most recent version, *2010 Report to the Nations on Occupational Fraud and Abuse,* provides some interesting insights regarding statistics about perpetrators, some of which are noted subsequently. It is important to note that the 2010 report contains data from 106 countries, while the 2008 report contains data only from the United States. Readers who have a strong interest in regional breakdowns should consult the original report. General profile considerations include:

- *Position of perpetrator within the victim organization.* Approximately 42 percent of fraudsters were employees, 41 percent were managers, and only 17 percent fell into the category of owners or executives. This represents a shift toward more employee and manager involvement and less owner or executive involvement as compared to the 2008 study. However, median losses from the frauds perpetrated by owners and executives were substantially higher than those perpetrated by employees and managers. They also took much longer to detect.
- *Gender.* Nearly 67 percent of fraud cases were perpetrated by men, while approximately 33 percent were perpetrated by women. This represents a shift from the approximate 59/46 distribution found in the 2008 study. Median losses resulting from frauds perpetrated by men were substantially higher as well. The report speculates that the gender issue relates to the fact that men tend to occupy positions of higher authority within a company relative to women and thus their authority may contribute to the higher losses. However, even at the "employee level," the median losses associated with men are higher.
- *Age.* More than half of all cases involve people between the ages of 31 and 45; this shows a trend toward the involvement of younger people when compared to the 2008 study. The 2008 report found the highest levels of fraud occurred between the ages of 36 and 50.
- *Tenure.* More than 40 percent of fraudsters had between 1 and 5 years of tenure with the firm. About half had more than 5 years. Only a very small percentage had less than 1 year of experience. The probable explanation is that people tend to trust people who have been with the company longer. They are also likely to have higher authority and greater knowledge of how to evade control requirements. The median losses tended to be higher with the longer-tenured employees.
- *Education level.* 52 percent of perpetrators had a college degree or higher education.
- *Perpetrator's department.* The areas in which fraud was most likely to occur were accounting (22 percent), operations (18 percent), sales (13.5 percent), and executive or upper management (13.5 percent). The highest median losses were associated with those frauds committed by the executive or upper management group.

Framing an Asset Search
(Known and Hidden Assets)

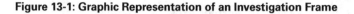

Fraud investigations often involve asset searches. It is important to build a frame (or context) for the asset search. A proper frame will create context for the investigation, isolate extraneous information, and control project scope. (See figure 13-1.)

Figure 13-1: Graphic Representation of an Investigation Frame

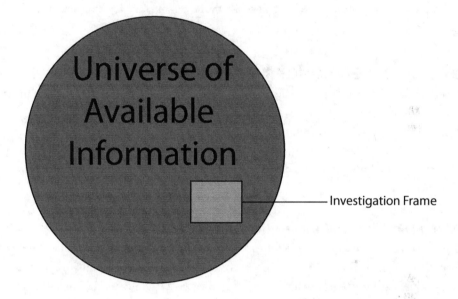

A proper frame benefits investigative clients in two primary ways: a well-framed asset search will increase the investigator's *effectiveness* during the assignment to uncover fraud and locate assets, and an investigator with a proper search frame will be more *efficient*, making better use of the client's time and resources. Because most clients will do a cost/benefit analysis to determine the value of a fraud investigation, the forensic accountant who can do more with less will always be considered more valuable.

A well-designed investigative frame should answer the following questions:

- Who committed the fraud?
- How did the perpetrator commit this fraud?

The answers to these questions will mostly be uncovered during a structured interview process and gathering of data and documents, as described in the section "Using the Fraud Theory Approach" in this chapter.

At a very basic level, the following table demonstrates a suggested search frame for the Denny Hecker example presented earlier in this chapter.

Question	Response
Who committed the fraud?	Denny Hecker. There do not appear to be any co-fraudsters at this time.
How did the perpetrator commit this fraud?	He moved money and other assets between his business entities in a complex way.

Within this frame, investigators were able to narrow the scope of whom to investigate and where to look. Although it is likely that important information will be discovered outside the frame as an investigation moves forward, the frame remains the guiding structure for the investigation.

Framing a Search for Known Assets

In a perfect world, a fraud investigator would have unrestricted access to all documents and data related to a fraudster's known assets. In the real world, investigators are typically constrained by imperfect or missing information. Holes in information will likely exist in every investigation, however, it is important to understand how to use available information to efficiently locate known assets. The following sections provide the steps for searching for known assets.

Starting With Public Information

Public information may include that information which a governmental agency is required to keep in order to perform the duties given to it under law. Public records are available to anyone for any legal purpose. Such records may be very valuable to a fraud investigator, not only in finding new information not otherwise known to the investigator but also in substantiating information provided by other people.

To make the search useful, it is important that the target be identified as narrowly and accurately as possible. Typical identifiers for purposes of performing searches would include the legal (or other commonly used) name, date of birth, Social Security number, and last known address.

Note that the following is not public information: banking records, tax returns, credit records (including information on credit accounts), and telephone records.

A serious fraud investigator should consider subscribing to an online database of public information[3] that compiles public and semi-public information, such as utility records, car titles, liens, and other records, in a way that facilitates searching and cross-referencing. For example, an investigator looking up a fraudster's previous addresses will also most likely find data on neighbors at those addresses, names of other people who have lived at that address,

---

[3] Many such databases exist and each investigator, private firm, and government will have to evaluate the various offerings to determine which database fits that investigator, private firm, or government's needs. The most important part of each database to evaluate is the source of each database's information. Different databases gather information from different sources, and it is of paramount importance to an investigator that those sources are reliable and auditable, to the extent possible.

and names of roommates the fraudster may have had. Although the database will likely offer some analytical tools to assist the investigator, it is still largely up to the human sitting in front of the computer screen to identify the useful nuggets from the mass of data. This process is outlined subsequently.

The first step to make sense of a database search is to look at the underlying source of the data the search returned. What is the source of, for example, "John Doe resided at 1337 Tarren Mill Way from June 2004 through August 2007"? Is it a cell phone bill or an electricity bill? A cell phone bill could be addressed to a fraudulent address, whereas a utility company would likely do its due diligence and ensure John Doe lived at the property before setting up service. Using databases such as these is analogous to doing research on Wikipedia. Yes, public information databases and Wikipedia both have useful information; however, because these resources are open-sourced, the information is unreliable unless someone (in this case, the fraud investigator) vets the source of that information. The information obtained via Internet searches is just a first step. It is important to take every reasonable step to verify the information against additional sources. Without such verification, the work is likely to lead to inaccurate assumptions and wasted effort. Once the information is verified, it is possible to use the information to discern relationships within the available data.

Various sources are available for tracking information related to a given individual or business and discerning possible relationships within the relevant information. Bear in mind that a number of limitations exist in using Internet-based information, including the frequency with which information is updated, the source of that information, and the extent of detail provided. Although an investigator can be very successful in identifying the existence of relevant information, in most cases, obtaining additional detail requires further work, and some information may require a visit to the department or agency responsible for maintaining records or that a request be made for a copy of the relevant record be mailed (a fee is generally involved with such requests).

Fine-line decisions need to be made about the likely relevance of the information to be obtained by examining the underlying information. As previously indicated, the universe of available information may be huge, but the body of relevant information may be quite small. Good organization skills and the discipline to systematically weigh and sort through information are crucial to performing an efficient investigation.

Personal Property

Information regarding personal property may be obtained from Uniform Commercial Code (UCC) filings if the personal property was financed. The bank, finance company, or other lender will create a record of the debt with the secretary of state's office or a county-level unit in order to record its interest in the underlying property. As such, UCC filings may be obtained directly from the secretary of state's (or similar) office. It is possible that registration to use the search feature will be required and fees may be incurred. Also, due to privacy concerns, the amount of information displayed on the website may be limited.

Some of the types of property for which UCC filings may have been made include household furniture, appliances, watercraft, automobiles, aircraft, and various types of equipment used in business. Some of the types of information available would include the

- name of debtor(s),
- current address of debtors,
- name of the lender,
- type of collateral pledged as security, and
- date of filings and continuations.

The information obtained in these filings can create valuable links in the context of an investigation, because there may be multiple debtors and their addresses may provide clues. The information may also disclose ownership of various businesses the subject of the search is involved with, and it may include information pertaining to parent companies, subsidiaries, or offices of a company. In addition to performing searches through the secretary of state's office, one may also use commercial services, such as Experian.[4]

To the extent personal property taxes may be collected by a governmental entity, the assessor's or collector's office of that jurisdiction may also have information on personal property.

Other State-level Offices

The secretary of state's office typically has a plethora of information regarding businesses and entities, such as corporations. Depending upon the organization of state-level functions, this office may or may not also have responsibility for issuing state business licenses. Fraud investigators may find useful information by consulting the taxation department for the state in question as well.

States often have responsibility for occupational licenses, and the records maintained by various licensing boards may contain a fair amount of information about a particular person, including employment information, addresses, and activity related to the license itself.

To sort through the organizational structure of state departments, start with a search of, for example, "State of Nevada" or "State of California." This search will help investigators locate the state's main website. From there, it is possible to find a list of state agencies and their contact information. A shortcut would be to enter in a browser's address bar nv.gov or ca.gov, for example. Even when a state uses its full name in its URL, searching via shortcut should quickly redirect to the state's main official website without further effort. Investigators should take a little time to read through the "business" section, as well as other general information on the main page, to help familiarize themselves with the state's organization. The state's website may also provide links to counties and cities within the state.

Real Property

Real property records typically are readily available on county websites. Current and previous owner information may be available, and information on the amount and status of any

---

[4]   ACFE, *2011 Fraud Examiner's Manual*.

tax payments may also be quickly located. The property may not be occupied by the person who owns it. The owner, not the occupant, is identified in real property records. One hint that the property is not occupied by its owner may be in the form of a separate mailing address for the owner. The existence of a separate mailing address may or may not be reliable in terms of making the determination about whether the owner occupies the premises, however. Details about real property transfers may be limited, and additional documents may need to be ordered or viewed at the county offices. Depending upon jurisdictional organization, some real property records may exist at the city level.

Court Cases, Including Civil and Family Law Issues

Records on such matters are most likely to be found within county court records. A large amount of information is available, but the trick is knowing what court in which to look for it. Just because a person lives in a particular county is no guarantee that any filings pertaining to him or her would necessarily be found within the records of that county. Moreover, different types of cases are handled by different types of courts. As such, the diligent investigator will not rely on a search of only one court in his or her quest for information. Some information may be available online, but accessing the court records will require the use of a case number. If an online search system is available, an investigator can find the case number by doing a search by party, that is, by using the name of the subject of the investigation.

Framing a Search for Hidden Assets

When framing a search for known assets, an investigator must often identify *where* an asset is located. However, in cases in which some (or all) assets may be out of plain sight, it is vitally important for a forensic accountant to identify both the location and disposition of hidden assets. Steps to accomplish this goal include the following.

Starting From a High Level

The starting point to frame a hidden asset investigation begins at a "big picture" level, comparing what evidence is available to what evidence the investigator would ideally like to have. The missing details identified in that comparison can then be used to inform a preliminary work plan, which outlines the investigative steps needed to fill in the gaps. However, excluding limited instances in which a forensic accountant has access to a subpoena, note that access to records stops at the fraudster's door. Even in cases in which the law clearly states that certain documents be released to the investigator, fraudsters will typically wait until the last minute to release required information, and even then, the information is often in a format that is hard to read or use. If the investigator clearly frames what information is (and is not) important at the start of a search for hidden assets, the pursuit of evidence becomes significantly less burdensome.

Following the Money

Once the investigator has gathered sufficient data, it is time to make sense of it all. This can be a challenging task, because the size, complexity, and format of information can range from vast electronic databases to carbon copies of invoices filled out by hand. To most efficiently navigate what can be a long and tedious process, investigators need to follow the money. This involves organizing data into a usable format (such as spreadsheets, databases, charts, or ledgers) with the goal of finding answers to the following questions:

- Where did the fraudster get the cash for this asset?
- Was the source of the cash legitimate or illegitimate?
- What is the fraudster's equity in this asset?
- Do the fraudster's cash disbursements relate to known assets?

By tracing the flow of money through the fraud, the investigator can begin to unravel the mystery surrounding the location and type of hidden assets.

Ignoring Materiality

Accountants are academically trained to be mindful of materiality (that is, determining whether accurately tracking and recording a piece of information is worth the cost involved). However, when fraud investigators are following the money in search of hidden assets, they cannot afford to overlook any transaction, regardless of size.

For example, as investigators worked on a large, multi-million dollar bankruptcy fraud case, they reviewed the primary operating company's check register and came across a $500 payment for landscaping services in Colorado. Although a typical audit firm would not consider $500 to be material to the operating company, fraud investigators saw it as a red flag, because the company's operations are limited to high-rise office buildings in Chicago and New York City. After reviewing more documents, investigators determined that a high-ranking fraudster was using a variety of company funds to pay for his condo in Aspen, Colorado. Because diligent investigators connected the dots on one questionable $500 invoice, they were able to frame a more extensive investigation that revealed several hundred thousand dollars of company funds siphoned off to pay for a hidden personal asset.

Understanding the Complexities of International Fraud Searches

As previously discussed in this chapter, hidden and known asset searches can be successfully pursued with the proper methods, at least in the United States. Once an asset search becomes international, the level of difficulty increases exponentially, primarily because information is harder to obtain. In addition, foreign asset searches typically require investigators to be physically present in a given country for a period of time, thus requiring more resources than a domestic investigation. To this end, an investigator should develop and maintain high quality contacts within a given country or networks of trusted contacts in order to access necessary information.

When considering a foreign asset investigation, it is important to think in relative (that is, cost/benefit), terms instead of absolute terms. Even if the foreign investigation is more expensive, with the proper frame and methodologies, it can be performed in an effective and efficient manner that delivers value to the client.

Performing Effective Interviews

In a forensic investigation, interviews are critical to uncovering the facts in a fraud case. But to accomplish that goal, practitioners need to develop a series of essential interviewing skills. This is especially useful when attempting to gain information from experienced fraudsters who understand the importance of proving fraudulent intent. In fact, it is not uncommon for experienced criminals to explain away illicit acts as unintentional conduct, accidental behavior, or simple mistakes. With that in mind, an effective interview must help establish a pattern of deceit, cheating, and possibly lying—all of which are vital to proving intent to defraud.

The primary purpose of most forensic interviews is to gather evidence through facts and other information supplied by witnesses. Interviewing is performed throughout an investigation. During each interview, the investigator should strive to obtain background information about witnesses, gather specifics about the alleged fraud, and identify potential suspects or additional witnesses. Although this chapter will discuss several interviewing techniques, all methods should strive to answer the same basic questions: who, what, where, when, how, and why.

It is important for forensic accountants to understand the distinction between interviews (as defined previously) and interrogations. An *interrogation* is generally viewed as questioning with force, a confrontational approach that often leads to a denial or a confession. In their interview work, forensic accountants must be prepared to avoid letting simple fact gathering sessions turn into interrogation, while still being ready to use stronger interview tactics with a difficult witness.

Accountants, whether performing attest or forensic consulting services, normally do not interrogate individuals to obtain admissions of guilt. However, forensic accountants may be present during an interrogation if retained by counsel to assist in a criminal investigation. Forensic accountants are fact finders who may quickly lose their objectivity if they assume the role of interrogators. Although fraud confessions may be elicited based on interview findings or other evidence produced by forensic accountants, remember that interrogations are normally reserved for experienced specialists, such as polygraph examiners or law enforcement officers.

Preparing for an Interview

The most successful forensic interviews require strategic planning, relevant questions, and an objective interviewer. Many interviews fail to gather enough information to address critical issues in a case, largely because of inadequate preparation or insufficient time allotted for the session. Thus, before any interviews actually take place, a forensic accountant should follow the following careful preparation steps.

1. *Determining when to involve legal counsel.* Forensic accountants should not initiate interviews without first considering the significant legal implications that may arise. Although most interviews will be straightforward fact-finding sessions, some may involve important legal considerations in which counsel can guide the forensic accountant's questions and activity. For example, interviews may be considered "privileged communication" if the forensic accountant has been retained by counsel. Privileged conversations are confidential and may be protected from further inquiry or disclosure. Without this protection, forensic accountants may be forced to disclose certain pieces of information, which could lead to negative legal ramifications.

   Forensic accountants should consult with legal counsel anytime sensitive interview issues are expected to arise. After interviews are concluded, it may be advisable to speak with counsel to determine what should happen with the original interview notes.

2. *Securing data, documents, and information.* Forensic accountants may wish to advise clients to secure data, documents, and information prior to beginning the interviews. Once people learn that an investigation is underway, delays in securing such evidence may result in willful alteration, destruction, or deletion. This task requires the use of proper chain of custody procedures, which will ensure the integrity of evidence, especially if documents and data are to be eventually relied upon in a legal proceeding.

3. *Segmenting types of evidence.* Depending on the allegations, evidence types that may be useful for interviewing purposes may include (but are certainly not limited to) whistleblower complaints, e-mails, corporate books and records, office contents, and any other information gleaned from relevant background research.

   Another type of useful (and often overlooked) evidence is the existence of previous statements by persons involved with an alleged fraud case. However, if such statements were made as "privileged communication" or under whistleblower protections, the use of such material may be restricted. For that reason, questions concerning the use of previous statements during interviews should be reviewed with counsel before moving forward.

4. *Avoiding spoliation.* Spoliation of evidence is defined as the "intentional or negligent withholding, hiding, alteration or destruction of evidence relevant to a legal proceeding." Forensic accountants should always consider the possibility that any investigative steps, including the use of evidence during interviews, can be part of a future legal proceeding, which is why it is critical for investigators to be familiar with acceptable forensic practices for gathering and handling evidence. Without that knowledge, something as simple as turning on a computer without the use of forensic imaging technology may result in spoliation of evidence.

5. *Making decisions on recorded interviews.* Recorded interviews create unique evidentiary and legal issues. For instance, if an interview is recorded, a transcription of the recording will likely be required. Accurate transcriptions can be difficult, because interview

participants may speak over one another or the recording may contain inaudible portions. Recorded interviews may also become inadmissible if the content is not properly authenticated.

If the decision is made to record interviews, reliable recording equipment is a must. All original recordings must be handled in a proper chain of custody, which ensures that the original recording has not been changed. Extreme care should be taken when making work copies of the original recording. If recorded statements are used in a later proceeding, note that those recordings will have to be authenticated and any transcriptions will have to be reviewed for accuracy.

When recording other persons, take time to review the specific consent laws in a given state (some states require the consent of one party, while others require the consent of all participants in the conversation) with counsel and any other pertinent individuals or authorities. The interviewer should also consider the possibility of an interviewee who may insist on making his or her own recording during a meeting. All of these contingencies should be reviewed with legal counsel in advance of interview sessions.

6. *Determining who should be interviewed.* Interviews should take place one at a time, usually beginning with neutral witnesses before moving on to corroborating witnesses. Actual suspects are normally interviewed toward the end of the interview process; however, other options may be considered depending on the nature of the case. In some circumstances, interviews with suspects may be done early in the investigation if it appears that evidence is at risk of destruction, the suspect is leaving the company, or threats to other witnesses are being made.

In most organizations, employees are willing to share information if they can remain anonymous (most often via employee hotlines and anonymous letters). Additionally, former employees may provide valuable information through letters of resignation and exit interviews. However, forensic accountants should note that confidential sources and former employees may have hidden motives for providing information that can discredit or embarrass a potential fraudster. For that reason, a savvy investigator should weigh the benefits of such interview (or noninterview) evidence against the risk of potential case damage if the information proves false. To the extent possible, information received from confidential sources should be corroborated through independent investigation.

7. *Developing an interview plan.* An interview plan and theme should be developed prior to the beginning of actual interviews. The plan should outline interview goals, who will be the lead interviewer, who will be taking notes, the role of the second interviewer, key subject areas, and potential safety considerations. Because this interview plan should complement the prosecution's larger investigative plan, forensic accountants should familiarize themselves with the nature of the case, list of potential witnesses, preliminary order of prosecution interviews, and other investigative work. In addition, investigators may wish to review their interview plan and preliminary questions with legal counsel.

8. *Understanding who will be in the room.* Just before the interview process is ready to commence, thought should be given to circumstances in which other participants may join a session. For example, depending on the specific interviewee and legal circumstances, an attorney representing the company may want to be present during an interview. Although an ideal interview has two investigators conducting the session (one at a time), note that there will be occasions in which only one interviewer will be present or the interviewee will be represented by an attorney or other company representative.

Conducting an Interview

The initial contact with an interviewee is the first, but not final, chance to set the interview's tone and establish rapport. Introductions should be polite and professional, avoiding forms of physical contact other than appropriate handshakes. Interviewers should clearly state the purpose of the interview in a manner that is logical and easy to understand, adding that the interview results may be disclosed to third parties. During the introductory phase of the session, interviewers should be nonthreatening in their demeanor, avoiding sensitive questions and emotive words.

In cases in which an attorney is present during the interview, forensic accountants should note that counsel may begin the session by giving the witness an *Upjohn* or similar warning. An *Upjohn* warning is a disclaimer issued by a company attorney to an employee witness, advising that person that the attorney is representing the company as a legal entity.[5] In cases in which forensic practitioners are conducting the interview without an attorney, the client's legal counsel should be consulted in advance to discuss how it prefers opening comments to be handled (especially if the witness is unaware that an active investigation is underway). Sometimes, counsel prefers that witnesses be given an introduction similar to an *Upjohn* warning, so that the employee understands the both the importance and confidential nature of the interview.

Once introductions and any disclaimer statements have been made, interviewers should begin by asking simple questions to put the witness at ease. This may include asking his or her name, address, phone number, title, or how long he or she has been in his or her position. Forensic accountants may also want to ask the witness if anyone has talked to him or her about the reason for the interview or about any public allegations that may exist in the case. After establishing a rapport, the interviewer can then start to probe for the names of other potential witnesses and the location of any documents supporting the witness's responses to questions. In some cases, the interviewer may also want to gather information about the target of the investigation, which may include work habits, personal lifestyle, usual activities, or any unusual behavior. This part of the interview must establish an interviewee's basis of knowledge for his or her statements.

---

[5]   Ivonne Mena King and Nicholas A. Fromherz, *Getting the Upjohn Warning Right In Internal Investigations,* March 2006.

By encouraging longer answers, interviewers can better assess an interviewee's verbal, non-verbal, and physical reactions to baseline questions. Challenges to information and statements at this point in the interview are not recommended.

When an interview reaches a sensitive stage, interviewers should broach such questions very carefully while continuing to observe verbal and nonverbal reactions. Interviewers should not express shock, disgust, or other emotions to any comments made by the witness, and they should remain nonjudgmental, fair, and objective throughout the session.

While interviewers should always be polite and professional, they also must retain firm control over the interview process. For that reason, all interview topics must be strictly controlled to stay within the designated subject matter. Investigators should be aware that some witnesses may attempt to wrest control of the interview by omitting key information, offering evasive answers, or engaging in direct deception.

When conducting interviews, forensic accountants can use a range of question types to elicit specific responses. Sample question types include the following:

- *Informational questions.* Informational type questions are unbiased, nonthreatening information gathering tools. As such, they serve as building blocks that should be asked to develop a chain of facts that eventually can support a case. For example, informational questions may include the following:

  — Where do you think the company is wasting assets or money?
  — Where you think the company is vulnerable to someone abusing his or her position?

  Interviewers should pose informational questions one at a time and allow sufficient time for the interviewee to respond. Interviewers should encourage interviewees to summarize the facts in their own words, which can reduce misunderstandings. To facilitate recall and responses, interviewers may consider showing the interviewee copies of data, documents, or other information. Questions can be repeated or rephrased for verification, and interviewers should make certain that they thoroughly understand all responses. In addition, interviewers should determine if a witness is providing information based on firsthand observation and knowledge or on second-hand information obtained from other persons.

- *Open questions.* Open questions encourage narrative-type responses, rather than yes or no answers. Examples of open questions are those that start with the words or phrases what, what about, how, could it be, and so on. By using open questions, interviewers can gather an orderly, detailed account of events or incidents. For that reason, interviewers should not interrupt the flow when an interviewee responds to an open question, because the response may yield vital clues in a case.

- *Closed questions.* Closed questions are designed to draw out a precise answer, usually yes or no. For instance, closed questions can be used to establish dollar amounts, dates, times, and locations. Closed questions should be avoided during the informational part of an interview when rapport building is important, but can be used extensively during the conclusion of the interview. Keep in mind that a series of closed questions may tip the interviewer's hand, because it will reveal considerable information about the subject matter. Thus, overuse of closed questions may not be desirable.

- *Leading questions.* In contrast, leading questions are often used to confirm facts that are already known, for example, "When you made the cell telephone call to your boss, what did he say to you?" By asking this question, the interviewer is prompting the witness to reaffirm his or her recollection to a specific situation. Although leading questions are generally not allowed in courtroom situations, they can be an effective technique during the interview process.

- *Double negative questions.* Double negative queries are confusing and often suggest an answer opposite to the correct answer. An example of a poorly worded double negative question would be "Since you did not have neither the address nor phone number, what did you do?" For obvious reasons, these questions should be avoided in the interview process.

- *Attitude questions.* This type of questioning can convey the attitude of the interviewer through the structure of the question, for example, "Can you explain why we have heard contradicting answers to the same question?" Based on the interviewer's tone of voice or body language, that question can be delivered with no emotion or with a considerable level of emotional emphasis.

Remember, skilled interviewers are those who can easily move between question types to advance the information gathering process. This serves to uncover necessary details while avoiding confrontational and emotive phraseology that may lead to a termination of the interview. Effective interviewers also are those who remain impartial and avoid polluting a session by injecting their own opinions or beliefs.

While it is appropriate to note issues that should be asked and resolved during an interview, the best interviewers do not use a question list, because that can interrupt the natural flow of the information exchange process.

The lead interviewer should focus on questioning and assessments of the interviewee's verbal and nonverbal responses, and the interview partner should take extensive notes and be prepared to ask additional questions. While taking notes, the interview partner should write down pertinent quotes and key facts. However, personal opinions of the interviewers should be omitted from notes and final reports.

Detecting Deception in an Interview

Open questions should be asked during the early part of a session, largely because they encourage dialogue and help the interviewer develop a behavioral baseline. During this important process, interviewers avoid calling attention to a person's behavior, but they should quietly observe the timing and consistency of behavior.

In this assessment of nonverbal activity, investigators must avoid misinterpretations of behavior, such as nervousness or stress present in a normal interview type situation. Interviewers should also be aware of cultural differences that may explain verbal and nonverbal reactions that they might otherwise find to be unusual. If a baseline of verbal and nonverbal behavior can be obtained, decisions can be made about whether certain physical reactions are signs of deception. For example, lying produces stress that often manifests itself in involuntary verbal, nonverbal, or physical reactions. In many instances, a person who decides to engage in deceptive answers will begin by omitting important information (or "lying by omission"). This deception produces less stress and is more difficult to identify though observation.

On the other hand, deliberate attempts to mislead interviewers by vagueness, insincere lack of memory, or intentional misdirection can generate physical cues of deception. These may include

- changes in speech patterns, such as speeding up or slowing down, talking louder or softer, or coughing or clearing the throat.
- involuntary physical actions, such as excessive hand motion or crossing of arms, picking lint off clothing, or playing with objects while attempting to answer questions.
- unusual facial movements, such as closing the mouth tightly, pursing lips, covering the mouth with a hand, biting the lips, excessive blinking, or chewing objects.
- postural movements, such as a fleeing position with the upper body facing the interviewers and feet and lower portions pointed towards the door.
- verbal cues, such as repeating questions or making off-topic comments or complaints regarding the interview.

When such cues appear, interviewers should first strive to identify the "triggering point" that pushed the interviewee toward deception. For example, it is possible that the interviewee heard a certain question that caused him or her to deceive to aid him or herself or protect someone else. Deception may also be the result of retaliation threats or an attempt to cover certain behaviors, such as an illicit affair. At this stage, interviewers are challenged to press for more information about the deception while still keeping the overall session on a positive note. That balance is important, because deceptive answers are often not discovered until much later in an investigation.

Bear in mind that experienced criminals may not exhibit some of the deceptive behaviors noted previously, largely because they are aware that interviewers will look for such indicators. In fact, some very skilled fraudsters can use their knowledge to completely disguise their activity or even manipulate the interview process.

Handling Experienced Fraudsters in an Interview

Forensic accountants, if possible, should become very familiar with a suspected fraudster's background prior to an interview. This may include a review of any previous interviews and oral, written, or audio representations made to victims. If the suspected fraudster is working for the victim organization, employment applications should be thoroughly reviewed because those records may often contain misrepresentations, which can now be used to create interview leverage. Other information sources to be checked include public databases, arrest records from local courts, and any negative reports with the Better Business Bureau.

If possible, the alleged fraudster's financial transactions should be thoroughly reviewed and investigated, because any trail showing how money was transferred from victims to the fraudster will give the interviewer an advantage.

By investigating and documenting previous crimes or questionable activity, interviewers can begin to establish a pattern of conduct. Armed with a demonstrated history of lies, false representations, and fraudulent documents, interviewers can be better prepared to address issues of criminal intent.

Note that many fraudsters will be confident in their abilities to deceive and will seek to engage in their own questioning of interviewers as a ruse to elicit information. In these situations, the interviewer must be very patient, understand the intent of the chatter, and allow the interviewee to speak without revealing any pertinent details about investigative evidence. In addition, the interview partner should thoroughly document the interviewee's representations in meeting notes.

Under certain circumstances, interviewers may wish to consider simultaneous interviews with witnesses and potential suspects, as opposed single interviews. This tactic can be useful in situations when investigators believe more than one fraudster may be involved, because it greatly reduces the possibility of post-interview chatter among conspirators to "get their stories straight."

When decisions are made to confront a suspect with information detrimental to his or her best interest, the interview should be planned and conducted with extreme care. For example, decisions must be made about whether the interview will be scheduled in advance or unannounced. An unannounced interview does not allow suspects to rehearse various responses, making it effective with inexperienced persons committing fraudulent acts. However, the approach may be less useful with experienced criminals who are often well-prepared for a confrontational interview. Additionally, safety considerations should be considered when choosing the best interview approach.

Interviewers planning a confrontational interview with a suspect should consult with legal counsel prior to the session to discuss potential legal issues. For example, if a suspect clearly asks for an attorney during the interview, all questioning must stop. The exact words used by the suspect to ask for counsel (and the time of the request) should be recorded in the interview notes.

When arranging the room for a confrontational interview, it is best to place tables and chairs in such a way that the entire body of the suspect is clearly visible. In addition, the suspect must have clear access to an exit, because any future judicial review of the session may rest on whether statements were made on a voluntary basis without threats or coercion.

Like a regular interview, a series of open and closed questions can be used to gather factual and narrative details from a suspect. However, interviewers in confrontational interviews may also use an admission seeking technique, which are direct accusation statements not expressed as a question. For example, an interviewer may say: "Our investigations have established that you…" The interviewer then observes the suspect's reaction to the statement, politely interrupting any alibis and denials offered by the interviewee.

During this process, interviewers should not argue with a suspect, but should take the opportunity to discuss any rationalizations or motives the interviewee may offer. It may be appropriate to leverage physical evidence or the statements of previous witnesses as part of the admission seeking technique, which may elicit additional explanations from the interviewee. After discussing the explanations, interviewers should explore how any identified acts of fraud were perpetrated. For instance, if money was stolen, the interviewer should press the suspect for details on how the money was distributed or what purchases might have been made with stolen funds. Again, all responses should be carefully recorded and time-logged in the interview notes.

If it appears that a confession is possible, interviewers may want to first focus on minor issues revealed during the session that all parties can agree about. When a suspect begins to confess, the interviewer must strive to elicit information that demonstrates the interviewee knew his or her conduct was wrong when an illicit act was committed. This is critical to establishing intent, which is a legal requirement in proving a fraud case. Proper questioning should establish when an offense was committed, when it ended, if other persons were involved and their identities, and what other physical evidence may be obtained. In addition, interviewers should also ask questions about the suspect's state of mind at the time offense(s) were committed, and document any information about medical conditions, alcohol or drug use, depression, threats, or coercion during this time.

If the interviewer successfully generates a *benchmark admission* (the first time a suspect admits to misconduct), that revelation should be recorded in the interview notes and later in the written report. Interviewers should also ask and carefully document that a confession was voluntary.

Bear in mind that although a witness may confess during a confrontational interview, in many instances the confession may not be complete or totally accurate. Remember, if someone has a history of being deceptive, a confession may not be completely truthful. Corroborating evidence and additional interviews may be required to substantiate the confession.

At the close of every interview, interviewers should leave the door open for additional contact. After any closing questions to elicit information about other witnesses or documents, the interviewee should be given one last opportunity to say whatever he or she desires. When closing the session, interviewers should provide a business card and contact information to the witness. This allows the person to contact the interviewers with any details and recollections they wish to share at a later date.

Written interview records should be completed as soon as possible following the conclusion of the interview. Interview reports should be written as third-person accounts, that is, the interviewer states his or her recollection of the events in narrative form. This report should also include the date, time, location, and persons present during the interview, in addition to an interview log that captures the time and description of significant events. All final written reports should be thoroughly reviewed and compared to original notes taken during the interview.

Legal Issues in an Interview

An interviewer should always assume that a fraud case will be brought to a testimony (or legal) forum, which may include everything from sworn depositions to a trial. With this in mind, the following issues, if not handled properly at the interview stage, could adversely the use of evidence in a testimony forum:

- *Relevant evidence.* Relevant evidence is any factual detail that adds value to a case. For that reason, an interviewer should not include personal opinions or judgments in a report, because that material would most likely be deemed legally inadmissible. Additionally, character evidence or mentions of other crimes, wrongs, or acts should also be excluded for the same reason.
- *Hearsay evidence.* Essentially, hearsay is a statement in which a person being interviewed (or testifying) repeats the words of another party. Hearsay is considered admissible evidence, as long as it is explained and presented. Evidence is not considered hearsay if the specific conversation or quoted material is recorded or if the interviewer has a signed statement from the party that made the statement.
- *Interview notes and written reports.* Keep in mind that written records and notes may be disclosed to opposing counsel, and that interviewers may be questioned about those materials. For example, if information is contained in the written report that is not in the original notes, an explanation may be required. Conversely, if information is contained in the original notes that is not in the written report, additional questions may be asked. Although it is generally not required that a written report be an exact match of the interview notes, interviewers should consult with counsel to determine if all original interview notes need to be retained.

There are a number of times during the investigative process when the investigators simply need to gather information from people who perform certain procedures within a company to study the relevant internal controls that may relate to occupational fraud. In those cases, the interviewer is gathering basic factual information and a more informal approach is appropriate. When gathering information about processes, the following tips may help ensure that the information obtained is both correct and useful to the investigation:

- *Interview the people who perform the relevant work themselves.* Do not ask the supervisor over their department. The supervisor knows what is supposed to be done; the employees in the department can demonstrate or explain what is being done.
- *Make sure the interview is an active process and should involve examining documents that the interviewee uses everyday in performing relevant tasks.* For example, if the company uses some type of log to record incoming mail payments, the investigator should ask the interviewee to show him or her the log so that he or she can ask additional questions based upon what the log contains. If the investigation leads the investigator to

use that log, he or she will be better prepared to use the information appropriately knowing who prepares the log, when it is prepared, and so on.

- *Because the interview is an active process, remain alert and listen attentively.* Sometimes the investigator will become aware of information that clearly shows an exception to established company policy. Such exceptions are often indicators of breakdowns in internal controls that could lead to fraud. Additional hints may surface that show a general laxity of controls that cause an investigator to realize that the fraud may be much broader than initially expected, as was demonstrated in the case used to illustrate the fraud theory approach at the beginning of this chapter.

- *Build rapport with the interviewees.* An investigator wants to put people at ease right from the beginning so that they do not withhold information out of fear or because they are flustered. Also, by remaining approachable, interviewees may volunteer information about things they have seen that "just didn't feel right" to them, but they did not know who to tell. As was mentioned in the preceding section, fraud investigators should always leave their contact information with interviewees so that the interviewees can follow up if they think of information they may have "forgotten" to share. Sometimes people do forget, but other times people have a change of heart and later decide to provide more information that could be relevant to the investigation. For example, the interviewee discussing cash receipts may realize that she forgot to tell you that there is another type of receipt that is handled in a different way than the others and simply wants to clarify the information previously given. On the other hand, the interviewee may have been cognizant of the difference in procedures at the time of the interview, but was uncomfortable sharing the information because she saw the difference in procedures as a problem with the control practices.

Using Visual Devices in an Investigation

Visual devices are graphic representations of facts and circumstances in a given case. These devices can take on many forms, such as timelines, Venn diagrams, or other, more complex illustrations, each of which can be useful in clarifying key information.

Visual devices are useful to fraud investigators in two ways. First, strong visual elements help an investigator to explain significant (and often complex) facts to key audiences, such as a company executive, attorney, judge, or jury. Without an easy-to-understand visual device or exhibit, an investigator will have a very difficult time explaining something such as money laundering to a jury, which may include members who have little knowledge of finance or accounting.

A second advantage to visual devices is how they help the investigator sort cumbersome financial information, dates, names, and other data in a cohesive way. In fact, visual devices can serve as an extension of framing the investigation, providing "at a glance" cues to remind the investigator what happened, who was involved, and what information is most important to pursue.

Example

All broadcast and online business reporting outlets share a common dilemma: how to report complex facts about economies and markets to a generally lay audience. So, when a business news source wants to tell viewers or readers how investment markets fared that day, the story will often be accompanied by a line graph of the specific index's value over a given time period. This easy-to-follow visual device summarizes the day's activity in a way that almost every viewer or reader will intuitively understand. The graph shows the passage of time from left to right and a line that is higher on the graph is better than a line that is lower on the graph. The news program producers have effectively communicated the intricate workings of our equity markets to the average viewer who may not know the difference between a stock and a bond.

Venn Diagrams

A Venn diagram can be used to show how two different subjects are different and how they are alike. (See figure 13-2.) In its simplest form, a Venn diagram has two circles. Information in the outer portion of the two circles would be things that differ between the two subjects. Where the two circles overlap, the information is the same with regard to both subjects. For example, take two fictional characters, Bob and Carol. The investigator wants a simple way to show how the two are "connected." In very few words, the investigator can show that Bob and Carol work the same shift at the same company and live in the same neighborhood. This simple diagram may also be a building block for demonstrating that not only is it possible that they knew each other socially in addition to professionally, but also that perhaps out of economic dependence related to raising four children as a single parent, Carol may have been subject to Bob's influence to participate in a fraudulent scheme.

Figure 13-2: Venn Diagram

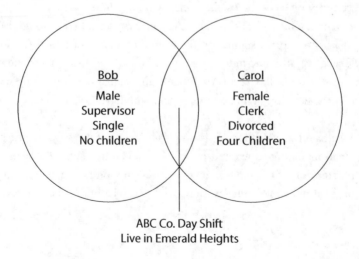

Bob
Male
Supervisor
Single
No children

Carol
Female
Clerk
Divorced
Four Children

ABC Co. Day Shift
Live in Emerald Heights

Timelines

Of all the visual devices used by fraud investigators, the timeline is often the most important. (See figure 13-3.) In most fraud investigations (especially those involving bankruptcy and divorce matters), the timing of events is critical. The investigator needs to understand what a *normal period* of time looks like for the subject organization or individual and then compare that period with a *dubious period* in which the fraudster may have hidden assets.

Figure 13-3: Sample Visual: Bankruptcy Fraud Investigation Timeline

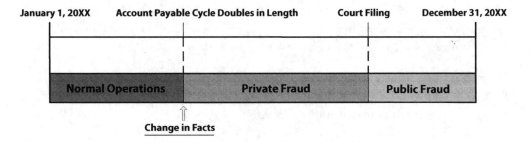

The careful investigator must understand that a bright line between normal and dubious periods does not always exist. For example, the transition may not be the day a company filed for bankruptcy or the day a finance department employee noticed an unauthorized draw from the capital account. Instead, the period of dubious behavior can often be traced to the time when a fraudster decided to begin hiding assets. Consider a perpetrator who decides she will file for bankruptcy in six months and begins to drain cash out of the organization before that date. If the investigator chooses to frame the analysis from the bankruptcy date forward, most (if not all) of the fraudulent activity will be missed.

When preparing visual devices, especially in divorce and bankruptcy fraud cases, it is important for investigators to address key points that show changes in a perpetrator's behavior patterns, facts, or actions.

Behavior or Fact Change—Divorce Fraud

- When did names begin to change?
- When did commercial bank accounts began to change (that is, money transferred from old accounts to new ones)?
- When were one or more bank accounts drained, especially if money was taken out as cash?

Behavior or Fact Change—Bankruptcy Fraud

- Was there a significant change in leverage (including draws from lines of credit, increased borrowing, or additional mortgages)?
- When did operations change? An increase in travel, meals, and entertainment expenses may indicate a change in overall behavior on the part of company executives. Additionally, an increase in accounts payable may be interpreted as intent with regard to repayment of debts.

Once the investigator has a visual timeline of important dates, the next step is to break down, analyze, and compare segments within the timeline. Typical segments will include the following:

- *Normal time period.* This is the period of time preceding the change in the fraudster's mindset.
- *Private fraud.* This is the period of time between the fraudster's change in mindset and the point when a fraud becomes public. For a bankruptcy or divorce fraud, the latter typically occurs when initial court documents are filed.
- *Public fraud.* This is the period of time after the public becomes aware something is not quite right. This can be when a couple files for divorce, an organization files for bankruptcy, or, in some cases, a story is leaked to the news media.

The first step in analyzing segments is to develop a control. Similar to a science experiment, the control is a dataset that represents a base case or operational standard. From these parameters, deviations can be identified and investigated.

Example: Analyzing Timeline Segments in a Divorce Investigation

A forensic accountant was retained to investigate a possible divorce fraud on behalf of the wife, who is the nonmonied spouse. The husband ran the couple's restaurant holding company, in which the wife was an equal partner. When digging into the case, the investigator worked with the wife to build out a timeline, tracing the change in the husband's mindset to approximately June 2010. The investigator then compared business operations before and after that date and noticed that travel and entertainment expenses had significantly increased. Additional digging uncovered the truth: The husband had been using company money to meet and entertain his many mistresses.

Month	Travel and Entertain-ment Expense	As a Percent of Revenue
May – 09	$4,167	0.4%
Jun – 09	$4,194	0.4%
Jul – 09	$4,222	0.4%
Aug – 09	$4,251	0.4%
Sep – 09	$5,135	0.5%
Oct – 09	$5,169	0.5%
Nov – 09	$5,203	0.5%
Dec – 09	$5,238	0.5%
Jan – 10	$5,273	0.5%
Feb – 10	$5,308	0.5%
Mar – 10	$5,344	0.5%
Apr – 10	$5,379	0.5%
May – 10	$5,917	0.5%

Figure 13-4: Principles as Graphics Example: The French Invasion of Russia

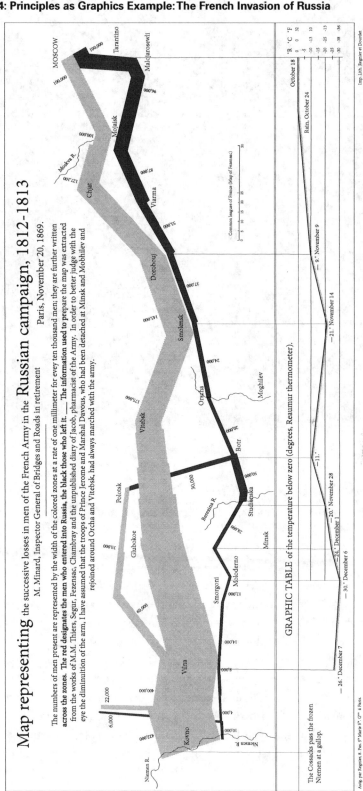

Example: Analyzing Timeline Segments in a Divorce Investigation (Continued)

Month	Travel and Entertain-ment Expense	As a Percent of Revenue
Jun – 10	$6,509	0.6%
Jul – 10	$7,160	0.7%
Aug – 10	$7,876	0.7%
Sep – 10	$8,506	0.8%
Oct – 10	$9,101	0.8%
Nov – 10	$9,738	0.9%
Dec – 10	$10,420	0.9%

Had the investigator simply looked at the big picture of operations activity, he may have simply assumed the increased travel and entertainment expenses had to do with rising airline prices or an increased need for the husband to be physically present at each of the couple's many restaurants. However, because the investigator spent time at the onset of the investigation to determine when the husband's mindset changed, he had a legitimate reason to question the increased expenses. Ultimately, this careful timeline segmentation—even though the expenses were small in absolute dollars—greatly enhanced the wife's divorce case. That effect was amplified by translating the timeline segments to compelling visual presentations.

Diagrams of Complex Activities

A famous visual device that portrays the importance of graphical representations is the *French Invasion of Russia*, illustrated by Charles Joseph Minard, which graphically represents Napoleon and the French army's invasion of Russia in 1812. (See figure 13-4.) It is a text-book example of a visual graphic that portrays so many different pieces of information and incorporates fundamental principles associated with visual devices.

The main subject of the illustration is the number of men who marched and were eventually lost by the French army. The *French Invasion of Russia* is important because it takes a very complex narrative and breaks it down into an easy to follow visual representation. The one graphic includes numerous elements such as a title that gives the design method and subject. It also gives the author's credentials and a paragraph that explains the color coding, the three scales of measurement, the methods used, and the five data sources that were utilized.

The figurative map itself is a map of Russia with lines representing the number of men and the path they marched through Russia. It also includes a table that represents the temperature (in three different measures), showing the freezing temperatures and dates for the French army's return march.

Summaries of Principles

Edward Tufte writes that "Minard's map exemplifies many of the fundamental principles of analytical design."[6] These principles include comparisons; causality, mechanism, structure, and explanation; multivariate analysis; integration of evidence; documentation; and content counts most of all. The following paragraphs explain the principles and illustrate them through Minard's *French Invasion of Russia*.

The first principle Tufte discusses is comparisons. When doing any evidence-based reasoning or performing statistical analysis, "the essential point is to make intelligent and appropriate comparisons…visual displays should show comparisons." In order for a visual representation to show comparisons, the information should be shown differently. This can be done with different colors, symbols, or line weights. Minard did this through the use of a thick tan line of 422,000 soldiers at the beginning of Napoleon's march and the stark contrast to the thin black line that shows the 10,000 soldiers left alive after the 6 month ordeal.

The second principle is causality, mechanism, structure, and explanation. One of the reasons to "examine evidence is to understand causality, mechanism, dynamics, process, or systematic structure." A visual representation should do more than merely show data. "Principles of design should attend to the fundamental intellectual tasks in the analysis of evidence." Minard's graph and map alone do not show the cause of deaths, only the remaining number of soldiers at a given point. With the inclusion of the temperature scale and dates, a thin causal analysis shows a -36 degrees temperature and loss of life on the Russian tundra. Minard gives a further explanation through the use of the five "historical sources that contain eye-witness accounts of the ghastly frozen soldiers."

The third principle is multivariate analysis. A multivariate analysis includes three or more variables. In order to understand most things, only looking at two dimensions will not suffice. Reasoning about evidence and causal relationships must be shown in a multivariate analysis. Minard did this through his use of six variables, "the *size* of the army, its *two-dimensional location* (latitude and longitude), the *direction* of the army's movement, and the *temperature* on various *dates* during the retreat from Moscow." If Minard only used the map with locations, or any other two variable combination, the analysis *French Invasion of Russia* would not have been nearly as in-depth as it needed to be. As Tufte writes, "to think multivariate, show multivariate."

The fourth principle is the integration of evidence. That is, visual representations should "completely integrate words, numbers, images, [and] diagrams." Tufte writes that this principle shows a "philosophy of inquiry: a broad, pluralistic, problem-directed view of what constitutes the scope of relevant evidence." Through the use of layering information and multiple modes of evidence, substantive analysis can be viewed as a whole rather than unintentionally narrowing and excluding data or findings. Minard showed this principle through the use of "a paragraph of words, a map with narrating flow-lines, and a statistical graphic" all in one place for the viewer to easily see. This gives a detailed, but not overwhelming, look at the situation without the reader needing to look up the data in an appendix or a supporting table.

---

[6] Edward Tufte, *Beautiful Evidence*, May 2010.

The fifth principle is documentation. Tufte explains that proper documentation serves to show the credibility, quality, and integrity of the author. The evidence can be properly documented if visual representations "provide a detailed title, indicate the authors and sponsors, document the data sources, show complete measurement scales, [and] point out relevant issues." By providing the author and related information, readers have a chance to see who is responsible for the work, can follow-up with the author, and see who paid for the research to make sure there is not a conflict of interest. Sources need to be cited to show where the information came from and if it can be trusted. Scales of measurement are important because they give the graphic context. All of these should be shown to the reader to show the credibility and lack of bias in the work. Minard listed most of the necessary documentation in a paragraph at the top of his map and three different scales of measurement.

The sixth principle is that the content counts most of all. Some graphics focus more on the report aesthetics rather than the actual content. Tufte asks, "What are the content-reasoning tasks that this display is supposed to help with?" This question focuses the graphic on what it is supposed to represent instead of it looking nice. Although the graphic needs to be useable, pleasing to the eye, and unobtrusive, these should be secondary to what the graphic represents. Minard does this in his *French Invasion of Russia* by never mentioning Napoleon. Even though this graphic is commonly called *Napoleon's* march, it does not mention his name. The graphic focuses on the content that is important to the author and readers; this content is the war and the loss of 412,000 lives, not the military campaign of the surviving 10,000 soldiers.

Minard's *French Invasion of Russia* is a visual masterpiece that embodies all six principles of analytical design. Through the use of these six principles, and Minard's work as a template, investigators can prepare visual evidence for statistical analysis of all kinds that is both effective and efficient.

Proper Handling of Evidence

Fraud investigators must be prepared to handle all types of evidence, including documents, books, records, and electronic information. Evidence is all means by which an alleged matter of fact is established or disproved.[7] A fraud investigator must keep in the forefront of his or her mind two aspects of evidence handling: the chain of custody and the best evidence rule.

As defined in *Black's Law Dictionary, chain of custody* is "the movement and location of real evidence, and the history of those persons who had it in their custody, from the time it is obtained to the time it is presented in court."

Fraud investigators will need to grasp the importance of maintaining a proper chain of custody over evidence if original documents are being used or if recordings are made during the interview process. Failure to recognize and adhere to legal requirements for a chain of custody may lead suppression of the evidence and dismissal of a case. Prior to initiating the investigation, fraud investigators should have established procedures for handling all types of evidence.

---

[7]   George A. Manning, Financial Investigation and Forensic Accounting (Taylor & Francis Group, 2005).

Best Evidence Rule

Fraud investigators must also be aware of the best evidence rule. The Legal Information Institute at Cornell University Law School states the following:

> The best evidence rule applies when a party wants to admit as evidence the contents of a document at trial, but the original document is not available. In this case, the party must provide an acceptable excuse for its absence. If the document itself is not available, and the court finds the excuse provided acceptable, then the party is allowed to use secondary evidence to prove the contents of the document and have it as admissible evidence. The best evidence rule only applies when a party seeks to prove the contents of the document sought to be admitted as evidence.[8]

Black's Law Dictionary defines the *best evidence rule* as follows:

> the evidentiary rule providing that, to prove the contents of a writing (or a recording or photograph) a party must produce the original writing (or a mechanical, electronic, or other familiar duplicate, such as a photocopy) unless it is unavailable, in which case a secondary evidence—the testimony of the drafter or a person who read the document—may be a admitted.

To ensure that the original evidence is not in any way defaced, investigators should make a photocopy of any documents they need to examine and work only with that photocopy, leaving the original document in pristine condition.

Conclusion

Effectively working the case involves knowledge of fraud schemes, many steps, and an open mind, as well as the appropriate knowledge of the rules, regulations, and other contractual influences in which the fraud investigator is navigating. Each case is unique in many aspects, however, the fraud investigator must break down the plethora of details into manageable units to investigate and present in a simple and concise manner. Thus, the fraud investigator must have deep technical knowledge and be an articulate and effective communicator. This book was designed to help the fraud investigator achieve these goals.

---

[8]   Legal Information Institute at Cornell University Law School, "Best evidence rule," accessed May 2, 2012, www.law.cornell.edu/wex/best_evidence_rule..

Find It and Fix It: Antifraud Tactics

Christyn Grommish
Brad Koranda, CPA/CFF, ABV
Scott Vanlandingham, CIA

Legal Foundations of Fraud Investigations

On- and Off-the-Books Fraud Schemes

Civil Process and Criminal Procedure

Jury Instructions

Regulatory Complexities

Working the Case

Find It and Fix It

Introduction

During many investigations, forensic accountants are discovering that the company in which the assets have been compromised and have lax internal controls.

Assets can be misappropriated through many different schemes. For example, an employee may send funds to his or her personal bank account, create fake invoices to bill the company for false items, or hack computers to obtain sensitive information. Or, employees may collude to create a nonexistent worker or write off assets to make it appear they were lost to damage or obsolescence. Forgery, skimming, larceny, misuse, and lapping are also schemes for misappropriating assets. These schemes are covered in detail in chapter 3, "On- and Off-the-Books Fraud Schemes," of this book.

The number one way to limit fraud is to implement strong internal controls, including those aimed at preventing fraudulent activity and those aimed at detecting it. Preventive controls will not completely protect a company from fraudsters. Thus, the key to limiting potential fraud losses is the early discovery of illicit activity. A cornerstone of early discovery is business leaders' understanding of the fraud triangle: pressure, rationalization, and opportunity.[1]

This chapter will explore (1) appropriate internal controls to help detect fraud, (2) developing sound organizational and process policies, and (3) fraud risk assessments and antifraud programs.

Internal Controls

Many organizations struggle with the cost/benefit relationship of internal controls. This struggle often centers on the need to have systems and methods in place that adequately safeguard assets versus the most efficient use of those assets. Small to midsized businesses are at a higher risk for fraud than their larger counterparts. This is often due to smaller businesses having less robust accounting, fewer antifraud controls, and a greater degree of reliability on a few key employees. Specific areas of concern for small enterprises are business segments which are staffed by a sole employee with little or no oversight by others. The inability of small businesses to segregate overlapping duties, such as the signing of checks and the reconciliation of bank accounts, also puts them at a higher risk for fraud activity. However, any organization that has ineffective management and internal controls for accounting and asset security is highly vulnerable to fraud. It is also important to recognize that it is impossible to completely eliminate fraud. It is important that in designing its internal controls, a company must determine how much risk it is willing to assume. It must then focus on identifying how fraud could occur in the organization and design controls around the risks, placing emphasis on those areas most subject to significant fraud risk. The creation of a strong antifraud program, including a fraud risk assessment, is covered later in this chapter.

Although internal controls will not necessarily prevent fraud within an organization, they can help ensure that illicit activity is discovered on a timely basis. A strong control system can help identify one or more fraudsters within an organization, and it can be a valuable defense against negligence if a loss claim is filed with an insurance carrier. Although strong internal controls are a good weapon in the fight against fraud, it is important to remember that internal controls can be overridden through collusive activity among employees.

Internal controls can be classified into three categories: access, accounting, and organizational or process.

---

[1]   Donald R. Cressey, *Other People's Money: A Study in Social Psychology of Embezzlement* (Montclair, N.J.: Patterson Smith, 1973).

Access Controls

These controls relate to safeguards around physical or virtual access to assets. This may include everything from the entry to the business and its facilities to safeguarding the company's computing systems. Typically, physical and logical access should only be provided to individuals who need it to perform job-related duties. This access should be monitored and assessed on an ongoing basis. Having the access controls in place and monitoring the access provides the added benefit that employees become more aware that the company is control-conscious.

Bear in mind that misappropriations are not always committed by employees. Companies can be attacked by outside hackers or thieves who find ways to penetrate inadequate physical or virtual security systems. To help minimize the risk of these threats, business leaders should consider the following actions:

- Installing cameras and enhancing security tools
- Keeping all sensitive files in locked cabinets
- Getting rid of excess or old information
- Strengthening user access controls (such as passwords)
- Encrypting data
- Safeguarding hard and soft data to mitigate unauthorized access to company information

Accounting Controls

As previously discussed in chapter 3, most fraud tends to be on-the-books, frauds that are recorded on the company's books. While accounting personnel should be trained to identify red flags and irregularities that may signal fraudulent activity for both on-the-books and off-the-books frauds, on-the-books frauds are typically easier to identify for accounting personnel. Below are some examples of accounting controls that the fraud investigator may note are not in place or not being adhered to that can potentially be recommended to the company:

- **Receipts and disbursements**. Because many frauds involve cash theft, one of the most effective tracking tools is a review of cash receipts and disbursements. This can be done by having someone outside the journal entry function perform monthly bank reconciliations for all accounts, which often reveal suspicious bank statement debits. For example, in small organizations with loose controls, fraudsters may simply transfer money from a corporate account into a personal account or use the funds to pay off personal credit card balances. In another scenario, cash thefts may involve employees issuing checks to themselves (or a shell company), then voiding the checks in the accounting system. To uncover this fraud, all cash transactions must be traced to supporting documentation that verify the transaction business purpose. Depending on the company's size, cancelled checks should also be reviewed (in their entirety or by sampling) to identify alterations, fraudulent endorsements, or unauthorized banks.

- **Account reconciliations.** In addition to cash accounts, all balance sheet accounts should be reconciled on the same date each month. Accounts receivable and payable should be reconciled to both the general ledger and subledger during these checks, and new customer and vendor additions throughout the month should also be reviewed (either completely or by sample, again based upon company size). Additionally, checks should be done to verify if the employees who added customers or vendors are authorized to do so. By providing a means in which errors and irregularities may be discovered, the frequent reconciliation of accounts sends a clear message: someone is paying attention, and management is interested in the accuracy of its financial records.

- **Payroll.** To protect against asset misappropriation in the payroll function, a company can protect itself by using checks that read "void" when photocopied, incorporate watermarks, and contain a high quality image or shiny chrome material. Authorized payroll employees must never print a check without verifying source documentation, and ensuring the proper disposal of voided checks. To prevent "ghost employees" in the payroll system, a company could require authorized personnel to seek positive identification before manually distributing the first payroll check issued to each employee, doing periodic electronic tests to determine if multiple employees have the same address, Social Security number, or other similar types of identifying information.

- **Expense schemes.** The most common means to control fraudulent expense activity is to carefully review reimbursement requests and require detailed expense reports from employees and full supporting documentation for any outside expenditures. If vendor-related expenditures seem out of line with normal patterns, auditors should investigate some basic clues. These might include vendors that are being paid more quickly than others (or receiving otherwise favorable treatment), the ordering of excess inventory, or payments made on nonfolded invoices (an invoice that is mailed to the company would ordinarily be folded. An unfolded invoice indicates a possible fraudulent invoice). Particular attention should be paid to personal service or consulting agreements to ensure that the work has been properly bid, approved, has measureable results, and a properly defined timeframe.

- **Tangible assets.** To help prevent fraud, proper authorization procedures must be in place for purchasing and receiving functions. All inventories should be guarded or locked, and unauthorized employees must never be allowed in inventory storage areas. Companies should also reconcile physical assets to the accounting records periodically. Additionally, no one person should authorize inventory purchases, disburse or receive inventory, or allow conversion of inventory to scrap.

- **Anomalies between time periods.** One review step that is often overlooked is vertical and horizontal account analysis. Because frauds often create bookkeeping anomalies, concealment over long periods often result in adjustments to offsetting accounts. For example, if cash is credited, some other account needs to be debited.

To do this, fraudsters will often look to accounts that are not closely monitored, such as miscellaneous expense, suspense, or fixed asset accounts. In order to detect fraud in a timely manner, managers who receive financial reports should begin with a horizontal variance analysis of profit and loss accounts, looking closely at budget to actual and current year to prior year data. Then, they should perform a vertical analysis of profit and loss accounts, with a focus on percentage of sales compared to current budget and historical patterns. Any identified discrepancies need to be researched immediately, because unchecked long-term fraud can effectively become "budgeted" in an organization's books. This detailed review will also build a perception among employees that strict controls are in place, helping to deter fraud before it occurs.

- **Regular and unscheduled audits.** Even if a company does not have a formal internal audit team, it should designate appropriate people within the organization to perform the internal control checks, which can greatly improve fraud detection. In addition, unscheduled audits of accounting records and general policy adherence should occasionally be performed throughout the organization. Unscheduled does not mean secret. In fact, once an unscheduled audit occurs, that fact should be communicated to employees, because it will reinforce the organization's commitment to strong internal controls.

- **Review and analysis of journal entries.** Write-offs of accounts receivables and inventory should be analyzed for any anomalies, as well as irregular entries to cash accounts.

- **Analysis of cash receipts and the recording process.** The company should have supporting documentation for all receipts. All information for transactions should be complete and verified. Companies should pay attention to complaints or inquiries of its customers. If they claim to have not received credit for a payment or the credit does not match their payment, then fraud may have occurred.

- **Comparisons returns and allowances to the actual physical flow of inventory.** Companies should analyze the occurrences of refunds and discounts given by each employee or department. A fraud scheme may be suspected if the relationship between returns and inventory levels get irregular, unless other legitimate reasons exist. Register tape destruction, checks for cash, reversing transactions, and sales to cash counts should be monitored for signs of fraud.

Organizational and Process Policies

Organizational and process policies can help deter fraud. The fraud investigator may note deficiencies in the following areas that may be helpful for a company to consider implementing.

- **Mandatory cross-training**. Cross-training essentially means having employees regularly learn and apply skills in a variety of business units. In addition to reducing fraud risk, a second benefit to employers is having multiple people trained on different systems throughout the organization. One way to accomplish this goal is to enforce a mandatory vacation policy and require that one or more workers are cross-trained and ready to fill in on those job duties while the regular employee is away.

- **Job rotation.** Although companies often believe that having the same employee cover the same duties for long periods of time is beneficial from an efficiency standpoint, this practice can also enable employees to devise fraud schemes and the means by which to conceal those schemes. Requiring both rotation of duties and regular vacations may help companies detect fraud.

- **Segregation of duties.** Segregation of duties is a key internal control for record keeping, physical access, and financial authorizations. For instance, a worker who opens the mail should not also have the ability to post journal entries. Fraud risk will be high for a company that has only one person collecting cash, depositing receipts, recording collection, and disbursing company funds. Even with other internal controls in place, this lack of segregation can enable fraudulent activity.

- **Specific job descriptions.** Defined job descriptions and duties for each employee are critical fraud prevention tools. If an employee is performing duties outside of the description (other than when cross-training), such acts may warrant a closer look. Well-defined job descriptions also provide the IT group with specific detail on employees who should—or should not—have access to IT systems.

- **Diligent use of pre-employment background checks.** Aside from having sound recruiting tools to locate and hire ethical individuals, it is also important to verify that information through background checks. This is an important step, because workers who have committed fraud at a previous employer have increased motivation to lie. As another layer of protection, a second background check could be performed after the employee was hired to identify any reporting gaps for the period immediately prior to hiring. Background checks should include verification of the applicant's education and work history, use of credit reports, reference checks, and criminal checks.

- **Implementation of a fraud hotline.** An anonymous fraud hotline that is advertised and available to vendors, customers, employees, and other stockholders can be a very valuable tool for companies in deterring and detecting fraud.

Fraud Risk Assessment and the Antifraud Program

As part of a robust antifraud program, companies will typically perform an annual fraud risk assessment wherein management identifies the areas within the company most susceptible to fraud. The fraud risk assessment should utilize a multidimensional approach to determine the most likely fraud scenarios. From the assessment, management can develop and implement priorities and mitigating factors. The dimensions of a fraud risk assessment should include discussions with and observations of personnel at all levels of the organization related to Cressey's fraud triangle (introduced in chapter 13):[2]

- Incentives and pressures
- Opportunity
- Rationalization

Incentives and pressures serve as motivating factors. Incentives may include large bonuses; access to business opportunities; personal loss avoidance; desire to develop or maintain an expensive lifestyle; and dissatisfaction with the company, management, or other personnel. Pressures generally refer to pressures placed on employees by higher level management. Pressure can include factors such as meeting business forecasts; zero tolerance for errors; and third-party pressures such as target stock prices, debt covenants, and capital calls.

Opportunity exists and is often greater in periods of significant change that drive uncertainty or headcount reductions (for example, mergers, divestitures, significant management changes, systems changes, relocations, and so on). Insufficient internal controls and management overrides are most common during these periods. Opportunity also exists when companies are in a "steady state." In this case, employees inclined to fraud are able to study the environment, systems, processes, personnel, and management oversight to identify and exploit weaknesses. Opportunity always exists when multiple parties are willing to engage in collusion. Companies can reduce the opportunity for collusion by rotating assignments or introducing other controlled variability into the system.

Rationalization is a normal mental technique humans utilize. For example, a manager might say a bad act is acceptable because it is in the best interest of the company. Likewise, a disgruntled worker may justify bad behavior by telling him or herself that he or she is doing it because the company deserves it. Two other common rationalizations are (1) "everyone else" does it and (2) that it must be done for family member health reasons.

Components of an Antifraud Program

Regardless of the fraud risk assessment findings, an effective antifraud program often includes five components that work together and build upon each other to discourage fraudulent activity within an overall company culture of risk awareness and respect for the importance of internal controls. (See figure 14-1.)

---

[2]   Donald R. Cressey, *Other People's Money: A Study in Social Psychology of Embezzlement* (Montclair, N.J.: Patterson Smith, 1973).

Figure 14-1: Antifraud Program Components

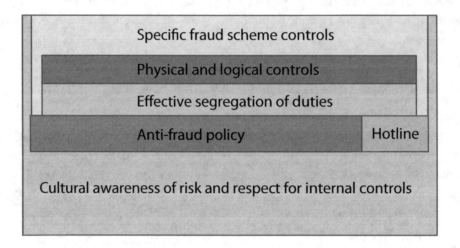

The first component is an antifraud policy. A policy in-and-of itself is a type of control. Overarching antifraud policies are part of "entity level" controls that help drive a culture of controls within a company. The antifraud policy typically states that when fraudulent activity is discovered, those involved will be fully prosecuted under the law. It should make clear that conflicts of interest are to be considered by all company employees before making any decisions and that all conflict are fully disclosed to all relevant decision makers. Conflicts of interest are often an issue for executive management and members of the purchasing department. Other components of the antifraud policy include general employee conduct, rules on gifts and entertainment, and penalties associated with unacceptable conduct.

The policy statement should also address the means by which questionable conduct can be reported. One common method for reporting is via a confidential ethics or fraud hotline which has been established by the company via a third-party hotline provider for employees, vendors, and other parties that do business with the company to report any concerning activities on an anonymous basis. This hotline is the second antifraud program component. Hotlines are discussed later in this chapter.

The third component is segregation of duties. Proper segregation of duties exists when no single employee is allowed to perform multiple components of a financial transaction. No segregation of duties is present when one employee performs all elements of a financial transaction from beginning to end, which would allow the employee to perpetrate and cover up a fraudulent transaction.

Physical and logical controls are the fourth antifraud program component. Some examples of physical controls include locks, gates, fencing, safes, security guards and cameras, control rooms, alarms, motion sensors, and entry/exit logs. Logical controls include IT system access controls such as logon names, passwords, user security profiles, sensitive data access logs, and other application controls.

The fifth component is a set of other preventive and detective controls designed to prevent and detect specific fraud schemes which are areas of inherent risk within the industry or the type of business enterprise. These controls are designed to protect known high-risk fraud areas within the company, which may include intellectual property protection, physical inventory protection, cash controls, and so on. These controls should be well known to all employees and serve as a deterrent for potential fraud perpetrators.

Whistleblower Hotline

A whistleblower hotline is arguably the easiest and least expensive means available to improve the reporting of corporate governance related issues. Although Section 301(4) of the Sarbanes Oxley Act of 2002 requires public companies to have a whistleblower system, it is important that all companies have a method in place to report issues. The following are some of the most important attributes of a sound whistleblower system:

1. The system should be operated by a third party, because employees or others who might want to submit a complaint may be more inclined to do so if they understand it is independently operated. However, if a company uses an inside system because it cannot afford a third-party resource, strong protections must be provided to ensure the caller anonymity. If this step is not taken, many employees will simply not risk making a complaint or reporting wrongdoing for fear of retaliation. For that reason, staff in the human resources or the legal departments are often designated by organizations to handle, document, follow-up, and resolve whistleblower complaints.

2. The system should have trained interviewers to handle complaints, instead of fully automated voicemail or Internet reporting systems.

3. The system should have a dedicated phone number that is accessible 24 hours a day, 7 days a week. Only 1 hotline number should be offered, which keeps phone reporting simple and avoids confusion for the employees. In addition, the whistleblower reporting system should also be able to accept complaints by fax, e-mail, or regular mail. The system should have multilingual capability, allowing it to receive complaints from people of multiple ethnic backgrounds or geographic locations. Complainants should also have the ability to receive a follow-up call or to otherwise provide responses to questions from investigators.

4. The system should have protocols for routing complaints to appropriate individuals within the company who are best able to address the specific issue. For example, complaints involving senior management are often automatically directed to a company's audit committee, which allows them to be reviewed without filtering by management or other internal personnel.

5. The whistleblower system's existence should be made known to employees, vendors, and other stakeholders via public documents, standard communications, and periodic reminder messages to each group. By making the hotline available to everyone, it is likely that the quantity and quality of reports will increase.

In addition to a hotline, employees should also be made aware of other reporting procedures. These procedures can be as simple as discussing a problem with an immediate supervisor or manager or notifying the employee hotline. Once again, confidentiality is paramount in the reporting process, because many employees will hesitate to accuse others of fraud, even when evidence supports the charge.

Conclusion

For an antifraud program to work effectively, policies must be consistently followed by employees at all organizational levels. The best internal controls and antifraud policies will mean nothing to rank-and-file employees if middle and senior managers are not visibly accountable to the same rules. Thus, management needs to set the right example by acting responsibly and creating an environment in which fraudulent activity is unacceptable—in policy and in practice.